MADELEINE BUNTING

Madeleine Bunting was born in North Yorkshire. After studying history at Corpus Christi College, Cambridge, she won a Knox postgraduate fellowship to study and teach history at Harvard University. She worked for an independent television production company before joining the *Guardian* as a reporter in 1989. After a period as a leader writer, she is now a columnist. She has won several awards for her journalism and is a regular broadcaster. She has three children and lives in London.

'I am full of admiration for this book. By careful research and sensitive use of light and shade, Ms Bunting holds the reader's attention through an uncomfortable passage in our history – and one which we have been most reluctant to inform ourselves'
Alan Clark, *Guardian*

'Excellently researched... This book...is an important historical document, if an uncomfortable one, in the understanding of our national character'
John Mortimer, *Sunday Times*

'The question is often asked: what would have happened if the Nazis had occupied Britain? Would most of us have acquiesced in collaboration, as, for instance, the French did? To a limited extent we know the answers, because the Channel Islands were occupied by the Nazis for almost 5 years. And any doubts on the matter have now been resolved by Madeleine Bunting's excellent book, which is thoroughly unflinching, fair-minded, humane and sensitive'
Paul Johnson, *Evening Standard*

'The chill which creeps over us while following this chronicle, a blend of smoothly accomplished narrative and pungent historical analysis, derives from Madeleine Bunting's unemotional clarity in weighing the evidence'
Jonathan Keates, *Observer*

'Scholarly and immensely readable'
Jack Higgins, *Mail on Sunday*

'A scrupulously fair account of life under occupation'
Kirsty Milne, *New Statesman*

MADELEINE BUNTING

The Model Occupation

The Channel Islands under
German Rule 1940–45

VINTAGE

19

Vintage
20 Vauxhall Bridge Road,
London SW1V 2SA

Vintage is part of the Penguin Random House group of companies
whose addresses can be found at global.penguinrandomhouse.com.

This edition reissued in Vintage in 2017
Published by Pimlico in 2004
First published in Great Britain by HarperCollins Publishers in 1995

penguin.co.uk/vintage

A CIP catalogue record for this book is
available from the British Library

ISBN 9781784707163

Printed and bound by Clays Ltd, Elcograf S.p.A.

Penguin Random House is committed to a sustainable future
for our business, our readers and our planet. This book is made
from Forest Stewardship Council® certified paper.

Contents

Illustrations

Guernseymen in St Peter Port in 1939, about to embark for the UK to volunteer for the Forces. (*Carel Toms Collection*)

Islanders gather at St Helier harbour to wave off reservists called up for the British Forces on 1 September 1939. (*Jersey Evening Post*)

The Bailiff of Jersey, Alexander Coutanche, and island officials greet Luftwaffe officers at Jersey airport on 1 July 1940. (*Carel Toms Collection*)

A Nazi propaganda film at the Gaumont Palace, Guernsey, in August 1941. (*Carel Toms Collection*)

A Guernsey policeman opens the car door for German staff officers in St Peter Port, 1940. (*Bundesarchiv*)

An islander nervously receives orders from a German officer in Gorey Harbour, Jersey, 1941. (*Bundesarchiv*)

Identity card of Raymond Falla, Guernsey's Minister of Agriculture and a member of the Controlling Committee. (*Carel Toms Collection*)

Tight rationing was introduced, and controls imposed on every aspect of food production. (*Carel Toms Collection*)

Initially at least, to the German soldiers a posting to the Channel Islands was more like a holiday than fighting a war. (*Johann Miesen; Eric Tostevin*)

German officer Hans Stumpf on Jersey. (*Hans Stumpf*)

Stumpf's best friend with Stumpf's girlfriend and her sister. (*Hans Stumpf*)

A young Jersey girl on the best of terms with three German officers. (*Hans Stumpf*)

Baron von Aufsess. (*Imperial War Museum*)

Island women found the attractions of the Germans difficult to resist. (*Bundesarchiv*)

Therese Steiner, photographed in Vienna before she fled the Nazis and sought refuge in England. (*Karl Steiner*)

Therese Steiner with the Potts family on Sark, summer 1939. (*Guernsey Evening Press*)

Marianne Grunfeld as a child in Berlin. (*Ernst Grunfeld*)

Sybil Hathaway, Dame of Sark, greets a German officer outside her home, the Seigneurie. (*Bundesarchiv*)

Ambrose Sherwill, with his wife May, at Buckingham Palace to receive his post-war honours. (*Rollo Sherwill*)

Alexander Coutanche and Victor Carey negotiate with Red Cross representatives in a conference chaired by Admiral Friedrich Hüffmeier. (*Imperial War Museum*)

Queuing for food supplies in St Peter Port. (*Carel Toms Collection*)

Old metal biscuit tins were made into saucepans, a meagre light came from a Brasso can, and a butter churn from a glass preserving jar. (*Jersey Museums Service*)

With islanders facing starvation, the British government finally agreed in November 1944 to allow the Red Cross to ship in parcels of food. (*Jersey Evening Post*)

By 1943 sixteen thousand foreign workers had arrived to work on the construction of the islands' fortifications. (*Bundesarchiv*)

Former prisoners Vasilly Marempolsky and Gasulla Sole, reunited at a post-war Liberation anniversary on Jersey. (*Vasilly Marempolsky*)

Georgi Kondakov and Kirill Nevrov in Orel, 1993. (*Madeleine Bunting*)

Georgi Kondakov's resistance membership certificate, retrieved from the KGB in the mid-eighties. (*Georgi Kondakov*)

Kirill Nevrov in Paris, 1944. (*Kirill Nevrov*)

Alexei Ikonnikov in 1944. (*Alexei Ikonnikov*)

Ivan Kalganov in 1993. (*Madeleine Bunting*)

Otto Spehr, believed to be the last surviving member of SS Baubrigade I, which came to Alderney in March 1943. (*Guardian/Reuters*)

Jersey boy Bernard Hassall tries on a German helmet in 1941. (*Bernard Hassall*)

Joe Miere in 1994. (*Roger Hutchings*)

A V for Victory sign in a St Helier street. (*Jersey Evening Post*)

The announcement of a £25 reward for information leading to the conviction of painters of 'V' signs. (*Carel Toms Collection*)

Stella Perkins in 1942. (*Stella Perkins*)

The Jersey resistance movement, with German deserter Paul Mülbach. (*Jersey Underground Museum*)

Jersey cinema projectionist Stanley Green smuggled a film and camera into Buchenwald, where he took the only photographs to be taken by an inmate. (*Stanley Green*)

Liberation. Troops arrive to a rapturous welcome, 9 May 1945. (*Hulton-Deutsch*)

German prisoners of war being loaded onto ships bound for England. (*Jersey Museums Service*)

Dolly and Willi Joanknecht on Jersey during the Occupation. (*Dolly and Willi Joanknecht*)

Dolly and her son Tony wave goodbye to Willi as he leaves for England in 1946. (*Dolly and Willi Joanknecht*)

Dolly and Willi marry in England in August 1947. (*Dolly and Willi Joanknecht*)

Russian slave workers' graves on Alderney (*The Royal Air Force Museum*)

British investigators with a false-bottomed coffin, which could be used for repeated burials. (*The Royal Air Force Museum*)

Maximilian List, SS commandant of Alderney. (*SS Document Centre, Berlin*)

Kurt Klebeck, List's deputy. (*SS Document Centre, Berlin*)

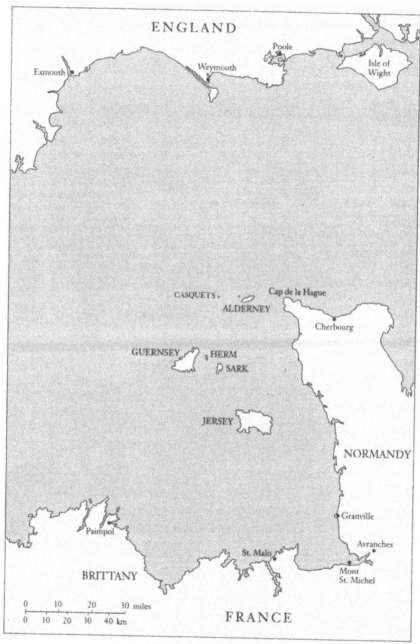

The Channel Islands

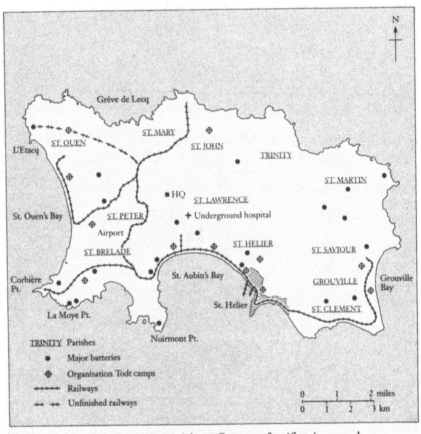

Jersey, showing parishes, German fortifications and
railways, and labour camps

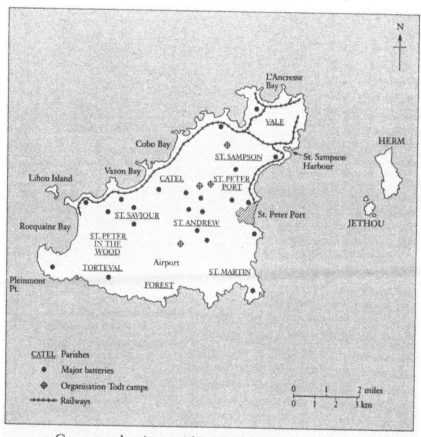

Guernsey, showing parishes, German fortifications and
railways, and labour camps

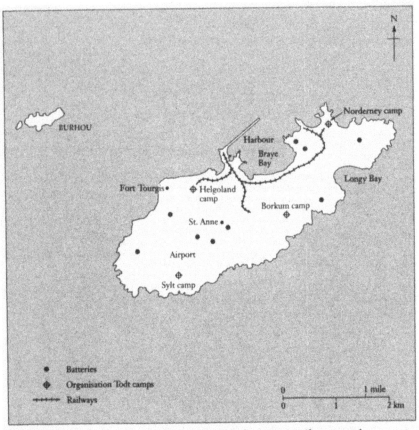

Alderney, showing German fortifications, railways and
Organisation Todt camps

Preface to the Paperback Edition

The writing of history is akin to a relay race: the baton is handed on to the next researcher who comes to the task with new energy and determination. Each researcher builds on the insights and material of predecessors, revising, adding and, in turn, bringing their own interpretation and understanding to events. To my great satisfaction, this book – first published in 1995 on the fiftieth anniversary of the liberation of the islands – proved a springboard for further research into this period of the islands' history.

One man in particular took on the challenges thrown down in my final chapter. Frederick Cohen, then president of Jersey's Jewish Congregation, began the painstaking research into the lives of all the Channel Island Jews during the Occupation which resulted in the publication of a monograph, *The Jews in the Channel Islands during the German Occupation.* After years of work, he has pieced together the circumstances of their lives and what happened to them.

One of the most extraordinary stories he unearthed was that of Albert Bedane. On Holocaust Memorial Day (27 January 2004), a small ceremony took place in the Occupation Tapestry Gallery of the Jersey Museum in St Helier. The Bailiff, the head of the Jersey government, unveiled a cabinet displaying the certificate and medal awarded to Albert Bedane, an islander, recognising him as a 'Righteous Among the Gentiles' by the Yad Vashem, the Holocaust Centre in Israel.

Albert Bedane makes a rather unlikely hero. As rumour has it, he was something of a 'ladies man', a physiotherapist and masseur to the island farmers. But for two-and-a-half years, he hid a Dutch Jewess, Mary Richardson, from the German authorities and Jersey police. He also offered refuge to escaped Russian forced labourers. If he had been caught, he would have been deported and would probably have died in a concentration camp (the fate of fellow islander, Louisa Gould). After the war, he was not one to blow his own trumpet and when he died in Jersey in 1980, few attended his funeral. By the time I began my research in the early nineties, no one mentioned Bedane's name to me – he merits only a footnote in my history. Now he is an island hero and his story is even featured in study packs produced by Britain's Holocaust Education Trust.

Nor was Bedane the only islander to shelter a Jew. Dorothea Weber hid Hedwig Bercu for over 18 months. The risks were enormous, and the difficulty of feeding such guests considerable. Bercu and Weber were helped by a German officer: an extraordinary story of friendship across enemy lines. Bercu subsequently married the officer and moved with him to Germany where they raised a family.

But while Bedane and Weber's bravery has given Jersey reason to be proud, the new material uncovered by other researchers such as Paul Sanders (*The Ultimate Sacrifice*) and David Fraser (*The Jews in the Channel Islands and the Rule of Law 1940-45*) has raised more difficult questions about the conduct of the islands' governments. Was there more they could have done to protect individual islanders, in particular the Jews? Why did they put such effort into protecting the Freemasons but not the Jews? Why did they agree to the German decision to make the possession of a wireless a criminal offence – an agreement that led the island authorities down the slippery slope towards collaboration? Their handing over to the Germans of islanders caught with wirelesses sometimes had tragic consequences.

The most egregious example was the case of Frederick Page, an English-born First World War veteran who was prosecuted for listening to an illegal wireless and, under a particularly harsh sentence, deported to Germany where he died of ill-treatment in 1945. More evidence has emerged in the last few years that some island officials were aware of the moral dilemmas they faced. They justified their actions on the grounds that they had to consider the greater good of the island populations, and that on a few occasions that required the sacrifice of individuals. The debate over the merits of this policy will continue; some historians will point to the decision of the Danish government to resign rather than implement the German order to deport the Jews; others will argue that the island authorities acted as a buffer, protecting islanders from the full force of direct German rule. Yet others will argue that this is a discredited position – one used in the sixties to defend the behaviour of the Vichy government in Occupied France but which has now been exposed as having little basis in contemporary records.

One of the most difficult aspects of the Occupation for the islanders to come to terms with was the close involvement of island officials in implementing the German orders against the tiny Jewish community. The new material shows that in Jersey at least, officials attempted to mitigate some of the anti-semitic measures: they refused to implement the wearing of gold stars; through an elaborate subterfuge, they Aryanised businesses by 'selling' them but returned them to their rightful Jewish owners after the war. But that is only one small part of the picture. Other documents give new detail of how island officials made no attempt to protect the few Jews on the islands. They quizzed frightened individuals about their Jewish ancestry, and imposed strict curfews on Jews – they were only allowed to shop between three and four o'clock in the afternoon. Jewish businesses were closed down and families struggled to survive without their livelihood.

The Jews were terrified. On Jersey, two committed suicide, one was admitted to a mental asylum where he died, the cause of death recorded as 'maniacal exhaustion, insanity'. A Guernsey Jew, Elisabet Duquemin remembered, 'every day for a year-and-a-half until I was deported to a German concentration camp, I lived in fear and terror. I was in trauma all the time. Every day I was frightened, and did not know if they would take me away, or my baby daughter, or my husband.' Elisabet, her eighteen-month-old daughter and her husband were all deported but mercifully survived.

What makes the documents so painful to read is the deference of these frightened individuals and their naive faith in the island authorities. Many of them made no attempt to hide their Jewish background and some attended the island government offices to volunteer information on their grandparents' ethnicity. One, Esther Lloyd, even did so erroneously and found herself deported to an internment camp where she fought to correct her mistake: 'never shall I be honest again. If I had not declared myself this wouldn't have happened' she wrote in a diary.

This is the kind of material which makes the Channel Islands' wartime history such a unique and vital part of Britain's Holocaust history. The level of petty detail pursued by island officials calls to mind Hannah Arendt's phrase, the 'banality of evil'. It was small actions on the part of thousands of local police and town officials all over Europe, unquestioningly obeying authority, which had terrible, evil consequences. What has always made the Channel Islands' record so important is that it punctures that British complacent assumption of a national immunity to this combination of amoral bureaucracy and anti-semitism.

For many countries occupied by Germany in the Second World War, facing up honestly to their wartime record has been a slow, piecemeal and painful process, because communities were so bitterly divided. What is evident since I published *The Model Occupation* in 1995 is how far Jersey has come. Key to that process has been the leadership of the Bailiff, Sir Phillip Bailhache. Born after the war, he has brought a new understanding of the imperative of accepting the 'warts and all' history of the Occupation as a way to shape his ideal of a 'socially inclusive identity' for Jersey in the twenty-first century. His innumerable speeches delivered at Holocaust Memorial Day services and other official occasions in recent years show clearly a man who has thought deeply about the issues. While he vigorously defends the island authorities, he also acknowledges openly the 'moral ambiguities' which confronted many islanders in the Occupation and which brought out both the 'worst and the best of human nature.'

Jersey now has a prominent memorial on the harbour quayside to the 22 islanders who died as a result of imprisonment in German prisons and concentration camps. In 1998, the first memorial service for all the islands' Occupation Jews was held in the Jersey synagogue; it was attended by the heads of the three island governments. A plaque has been put up on Jersey to their memory. A website, launched in 2003 and dedicated to the Occupation (www.occupationmemorial.org), carries information and photographs of each individual's story. Schoolchildren in Jersey are no longer just taught about the 'guns and tin-hats', but about the suffering of many islanders and of the thousands of forced labourers brought to build the huge concrete fortifications on the island – many of whom died from exhaustion and malnutrition.

While Jersey has done much to face up to its past, Guernsey has been more reluctant: a small plaque was finally put up in 2001 to the memory of the three Jews deported from the island who died in concentration camps. But at the 1998 memorial service for all the islands' Jews, the short speech of the Bailiff of Guernsey, Sir Graham Dorey, referred only to the fact that the Jews on Guernsey were foreign-born and their deportation was implemented by Germans without any reference to the role of the island authorities. There are other gaps due more to indifference and apathy than any active wish to forget. There is still no memorial on the site of the SS Sylt camp in Alderney. The concrete ruins which once housed many of the forced labourers – including many French Jews and German political prisoners who died there from ill-treatment – are barely visible under the bracken. As the Bailiff of Jersey himself said in his 1998 address, it was the carelessness and indifference of people which enabled the Holocaust to happen, and it is to combat those characteristics that the duty of remembrance lies so heavily on ensuing generations.

Madeleine Bunting
January 2004

Additional Bibliography

The Ultimate Sacrifice Paul Sanders. Jersey Museums Service 1998
The Jews in the Channel Islands during the German Occupation 1940-45 Frederick Cohen. Jersey Heritage Trust 2000
The Jews in the Channel Islands and the Rule of Law David Fraser, Sussex Academic Press 2000

Chronology

1940
15 June   War Cabinet decides to demilitarise the
                            Channel Islands.
16–20 June   All military equipment and personnel evacuated
                            from the islands.
19 June   Island governments informed of the decision to
                            demilitarise. Preparations for evacuation
                            begin.
21–23 June   Thirty thousand islanders evacuated to Britain.
28 June   Germans bomb St Peter Port, Guernsey and
                            St Helier, Jersey, killing forty-four people.
30 June   Germans land at Guernsey airport. The island
                            surrenders.
1 July   Jersey occupied.
2–3 July   Alderney and Sark occupied.
9–28 July   Philip Martel and Desmond Mulholland land
                            on Guernsey, but are forced to give themselves
                            up and are sent as prisoners of war to France.
1 August   Ambrose Sherwill, President of Guernsey's
                            Controlling Committee, broadcasts on Radio
                            Bremen.
4 September–21   Hubert Nicolle and James Symes hide on
October   Guernsey. On their surrender, fourteen
                            islanders who had helped them, including
                            Ambrose Sherwill, are imprisoned in
                            France.
27 September   Anti-Semitic laws are registered in the islands'
                            parliaments.
December   The islanders imprisoned for helping Nicolle
                            and Symes return from France.

1941
24 May   Bread rationing starts.
15 June   Hitler orders the fortification of the islands.

xvii

8 July	Victor Carey, Bailiff of Guernsey, offers a £25 reward for information leading to the arrest of anyone found guilty of painting 'V for Victory' signs.
November	Dr Fritz Todt, founder of the Organisation Todt, visits the islands as part of the planning for the fortification programme. The first OT workers arrive.

1942

January	Four camps – Helgoland, Norderney, Sylt and Borkum – are set up on Alderney for the OT workers. RAF bombing raids on St Peter Port harbour kill several islanders.
March	Eighteen Guernsey policemen are arrested for stealing from German and civilian stores and selling the goods on the black market.
21 April	Three Jewish women, Auguste Spitz, Therese Steiner and Marianne Grunfeld, are deported to France. All are to die in Auschwitz.
May	'Guernsey Underground News Service' starts publication.
June	All civilian radios banned.
16–27 September	Two thousand islanders deported to German internment camps for the duration of the war.
3–4 October	British raid on Sark. Two Germans killed, one captured.

1943

January	The *Xaver Dorsch* and the *Franka* run aground off Braye harbour, Alderney, leading to the loss of hundreds of slave workers' lives.
18 January	Teaching of German made compulsory in all island schools.
12–25 February	A second deportation of just over two hundred islanders.
March	SS Baubrigade I, commanded by Maximilian List and Kurt Klebeck, arrives on Alderney. Sylt camp passes to the control of the SS.
22 June	Louise Gould and Harold Le Druillenec sentenced for hiding a Russian slave worker. Le

Druillenec narrowly survives Belsen; Gould dies in Ravensbrück in February 1945.

23–24 October   HMS *Charybdis* and HMS *Limbourne* sink off the islands with the loss of 504 British lives.

17 November   Forty-one bodies washed up on Guernsey and Jersey are buried with full military honours.

1944

6 April   Members of the 'Guernsey Underground News Service' put on trial. Five are imprisoned in France, where two of them die.

6 June   D-Day. The Allied invasion of Normandy begins.

June–August   The Allied capture of Cherbourg, Granville and St Malo cuts the islands off from all supplies.

July   The remaining slave workers on Alderney are evacuated to France.

7 July   The *Minotaure*, carrying slave workers and French prostitutes, is sunk by British torpedoes with the loss of 250 lives.

9 September   Gas supply on Jersey comes to an end.

19 September   The German government informs the Swiss, as intermediary power, that civilian supplies on the islands 'are exhausted'.

7 November   Britain agrees to allow the Red Cross to provide food parcels for the islanders.

2 December   Suzanne Malherbe and Lucille Schwab are sentenced to death for spreading anti-German propaganda.

21 December   Gas supply on Guernsey comes to an end.

27–30 December   The *Vega* arrives with 750 tons of food and medical supplies for the islanders from the Red Cross.

1945

13 January   Milkless days introduced.

7–11 February   The *Vega* brings more supplies.

17 February–12 March   No bread available.

7 March   An unexplained explosion at the Palace Hotel, Jersey, kills nine Germans.

25 March	Admiral Hüffmeier, now Inselkommandant, declares that there will be no surrender of the islands.
8 May	VE Day. The Liberation Force holds talks off the islands with the Germans.
9 May	The Germans surrender the islands. Brigadier Alfred Snow sets up a military government.
14-15 May	Home Secretary Herbert Morrison visits the islands.
18 May	Major Haddock begins his investigation into the treatment of slave workers on Alderney.
7 June	King George VI and Queen Elizabeth visit islands.
25 June	The first evacuees return from Britain.
August	2190 deportees begin to return from Britain after being repatriated from Germany.
25 August	Brigadier Snow's military government hands over power to the island governments.
October	Captain Theodore Pantcheff completes his report on atrocities against slave workers on the islands. A copy is sent to the Soviet Union with a view to the prosecution of certain German officers. However, no further action is taken.
1946 November	Home Secretary James Chuter-Ede announces to the House of Commons that the Director of Public Prosecutions has decided that there will be no trials of collaborators as 'there are insufficient grounds to warrant the institution of criminal proceedings'.

Acknowledgements

The German Occupation is still a sensitive subject on the Channel Islands, and some islanders have been resistant towards what they perceived as my intrusive questioning of their personal histories. I hope my attempt to be balanced and charitable will repay the trust and generosity of the many islanders whose memories I have been privileged to draw on. I would particularly like to thank Dolly and Willi Joanknecht, Bob Le Sueur, Stella Perkins, Joe Miere and Bernard Hassall.

I am very grateful to Rollo and Jonathan Sherwill and their family for kind permission to read the private papers of Sir Ambrose Sherwill. Sir Peter Crill, the Bailiff of Jersey, agreed to allow me access to the Jersey Occupation Archives while they were being held by the Jersey police, and members of the force were extraordinarily helpful in accommodating my requests.

I owe much to the meticulous research of local historians who have generously shared their knowledge with me at different times over the last five years, including Michael Ginns, Brian Bonnard, Brother Andrew Marratt-Crosby, Richard and Margaret Heaume and Colin Partridge. M.R.D. Foot kindly helped to put the Channel Islands' Occupation within a wider context of occupation and resistance in Europe. I am grateful to my husband Patrick Wintour and to Adam Curtis for long, enlightening discussions in which the central ideas of this book were formulated. Thanks are also owed to Dr David Cesarani, Dr Anthony Glees, David Batty, Martin Doerry of *Der Spiegel*, Colin Izod, historian Peter King, David Millward and David Goodhart, all of whom helped the book's progress at key points. Despite the seemingly arcane interest of the Occupation for a newspaper, the *Guardian* has encouraged my enthusiasm and the editor, Peter Preston, generously gave me leave to complete the research for this book. Thanks also to my editor Richard Johnson and my agent Andrew Lownie for gently nudging me on, and my copy editor Robert Lacey, whose invaluable work has saved me from many heinous errors.

I have been lucky to have the help at different times of several able and enthusiastic researchers: Jamie Coomarasamy's Russian and Dorothea Slevogt's German were essential; Sharon Garfinkel gave up much time to plough through archives; Karen Haith and Euan Mahy kindly helped on Guernsey, where Odette Paul provided a warm welcome.

I am very grateful to the survivors of the slave labour camps. Norbert

Beermart, Otto Spehr and Ted Misiewicz all gave me a warm welcome to their homes in Belgium, Germany and London, and delved deep into painful memories to answer my questions. Mr Misiewicz's comments on drafts of Chapter Five were much appreciated. My greatest debt is to Galina Chernakova and Georgi Kondakov for their invaluable work in tracing survivors of the slave labour camps. The warm welcome in Russia and Ukraine which all the survivors and their families gave me will long remain my most powerful recollection of writing this book. It is to them – Georgi Kondakov, Albert Pothugine, Kirill Nevrov, Ivan Kalganov, Alexei Ikonnikov, Alexei Rodine, Ivor Dolgov and Vasilly Marempolsky, and to the memory of all those of every nationality who did not survive the islands' occupation – that this book is dedicated.

Note on Sources

This book is based on nearly a hundred interviews with islanders and labour camp survivors. This oral history is supported by a wealth of newly released archival material. In December 1992 the Home Office released twenty-eight files which were to have remained closed until the year 2045. Pressure in Parliament and newspapers persuaded the Heritage Secretary, William Waldegrave, to open the files to the public as part of Prime Minister John Major's 'open government' initiative. Their early release followed an agreement with the Channel Islands, and in January 1993 the Guernsey States Archives, with their unparalleled documentation of the Occupation government and the German military administration, were finally opened to the public. The Jersey archives were not opened until March 1994, the delay being largely due to the fact that in November 1991 the entire collection was stolen from an attic cupboard in the island's parliament building. The majority of the documents were recovered, and were held as police evidence for nearly two years, but by special permission of the Bailiff of Jersey, Sir Peter Crill, and the Jersey police headquarters, I was given full access to them.

I was the first researcher to see documents concerning Alderney in the Russian State Archives in Moscow, which had been declassified only a few weeks before my arrival in May 1993. This new material added to the large volume of documents, which had never been properly researched, in the Centre de Documentation Juive et Contemporaine in Paris, in the Imperial War Museum in London, and in the Public Record Office at Kew.

Many documents in Britain and on the Channel Islands have been destroyed, some probably as a matter of routine, but others possibly to prevent embarrassment.

I am very grateful to a number of islanders and historians who have provided new information or made suggestions following the publication of this book in hardback. I have incorporated a large number of their points in this paperback edition, which also includes a new appendix on 'The Jewish Question'.

THE MODEL
OCCUPATION

AN ISLAND PEOPLE

'Newspapers write about the Channel Islands' Occupation in the way they do because this was the only bit of the British Isles which was occupied, and we're supposed to have reacted like the British would. But we didn't behave as British people should. Since the war we have felt like a woman must feel in a rape trial. People accuse her of having led the rapist on. But just as a woman might co-operate for fear of not surviving, so did we.'

Guernseyman Rollo Sherwill,
a boy during the Occupation

What if Hitler had invaded Britain? Who would have plotted resistance? Who would have made a handsome profit selling guns and uniform cloth to the Germans and trading in black market whisky? How would the majority of the British people have muddled their way through? A German invasion so nearly came to pass that such questions have intrigued every generation since the war. The Channel Islands were as close as Hitler got; they were the one bit of British soil he conquered. That is why those blurred black-and-white photos of the Channel Islands' Occupation are so riveting: German soldiers marching past Lloyds Bank or flirting with island girls outside Boots the Chemists, or getting directions from a smiling British bobby. This is what life could have been like in Britain, with Germans on British streets and in British shops. What happened on the Channel Islands could have happened in the rest of Britain.

The Channel Islands' occupation, Hitler decided, was to be a model of Anglo–German co-operation. This was to be the testing ground for the occupation of Britain. For very different reasons, the islanders also wanted a model occupation. They wanted peace, a semblance of normal life, and the continuation of their own governments. It was an uneasy convergence of interests. But over the course of five years, the islanders were painfully to learn that there was no such thing as a model occupation under the Nazis.

In the scale of the history of the Second World War, the Channel Islands, with a total population of just under a hundred thousand, are little more than a footnote. But their fate warrants attention. Here, British communities lived under Nazi occupation, and their social fabric was stretched to breaking point. Since the war, that fabric has been darned and patched, and its unity has been reconstituted by the development of a collective memory which erases divisions, and formulates a past most can accept.

This book is a study of how small, tightly-knit communities cope with a traumatic event like occupation, and how such a divisive event is then defined in the communal memory. Islanders have sifted – and are still sifting – through the facts of the Occupation, and selected those which support their current understanding of it. Collective memory is not static, and this history is not finished. The islanders themselves have been the richest source of information for this book; as they spoke to me over the course of 1992 and 1993 they revealed both the memories they celebrated and the memories they had denied. Interviewing them was like an archaeological investigation into collective memory; digging down into the recesses of individual recollections, piecing fragments together with diaries and documents to build a history which had never been recorded before, and was in danger of going to the grave with the generation who had lived it.

There have been islanders who have resented my questions, such as the Jerseywoman who rounded on me in fury: 'I have two uncles who died fighting in the war, and their names are on the war monuments here. No one can dare say we didn't play our part in the war. The French and the Dutch tourists come and ask why we leave all the German bunkers lying around and why haven't we torn them down. Then they ask why there was no resistance here.'

One Guernseyman challenged me: 'How dare you English come over here, dictating and pontificating about things which you know nothing, absolutely nothing about. Would you English have done any different? Leave those who lived through it to write the history of the Occupation. You can't ever understand what it was like.'

I did not obey his advice, but I bore his words in mind. 'There but for the grace of God go I' was the motto of my research. The Occupation compromised almost everybody who lived through it; each individual faced moral choices, and only a few could claim a calm conscience by 1945. It is now a minefield of buried resentment and uneasy accommodation.

Much of the islanders' resentment appears to spring from two conflicting sources. On the one hand, they believe they have been misunderstood and misjudged. They feel they are criticised for having got on too well with the Germans, and for not having put up sufficient resistance. On the other hand, they feel guilty – they judge themselves. The man who demands 'Would you English have done any different?' exposes his belief that the islanders did indeed do something wrong.

Islanders prefer to mask the strength of these emotions behind an inscrutable, polite hospitality. As they press another cup of tea or biscuit on you, they blandly reply to your questions with, 'No, I'm sorry, I wouldn't know anything about that.' This is said with the relish of those who have made it their business not to know. Only a tiny handful of Channel Islanders admit to knowing anything about the Jews who were deported, or what happened in the slave labour camps on Alderney.

Love, hate, betrayal, defiance, resentment and tragedy spill from the cracks in the islanders' reminiscences, and pour across the pages of memoirs, diaries and government documents. Because many of this history's protagonists are still alive, telling their stories verges on intruding on their privacy. By changing or omitting certain names, I have tried to protect living individuals. I am very conscious that this history trespasses into some of the most painful, hidden parts of their lives.

There is another reason why the Channel Islands' Occupation deserves to be much more than a footnote to the history of World War II. The islanders' unique experience throws into question Britain's most basic assumptions about her own role in the war.

Fifty years after the war's end, the echo still reverberates in contemporary politics of Churchill's oratory that the British alone had fought – like David to Hitler's Goliath – an evil dictatorship from beginning to end. Only Britain had sought no compromise and had 'an unblemished record' in standing up to Nazism. The Channel Islands do not fit this history; islanders compromised, collaborated and fraternised just as people did throughout occupied Europe. Records documenting this were originally ordered by the British government to be closed for a hundred years, and some were destroyed. It is this history that the British people have been unable to assimilate; it directly challenges their belief that the Second World War proved that they were inherently different from the rest of Europe.

Over the last decade there has been a growing acceptance of the fact that some Channel Islanders collaborated with the Germans. The myth of the distinctiveness of the British character from that of Continental Europeans is slowly weakening its hold. The truth about the islands' war record should not be an opportunity for Britain to indulge in moral indignation, but a chance to gain an understanding of an experience shared with Continental Europe. The British can then begin to find room alongside their narrow, nationalistic understanding of the war for a recognition of the common European history of those tumultuous years.

In the 1930s, the Channel Islands held a place in the British popular imagination much as the Costa del Sol and Marbella were to do in the 1970s. They were holiday islands, famous for their beautiful beaches, semi-tropical climate and stunning cliff walks. They were seen as the ideal family holiday destination in the age before cheap Continental package holidays; they were accessible, and had a familiar culture, comprehensible language and no danger of political unrest.

There are parts of the islands which have changed little since that time. The back lanes are still sunk between banked hedgerows which teem with wildflowers. In parts of Guernsey, the fields are still divided into small strips by banks which are covered in wild daffodils in the spring. The typical granite Guernsey farmhouse, stolid and unpretentious, aptly expresses its builder's character. There is an extraordinary charm in these farmhouses: their plastered walls, the colour and appearance of melting ice cream; the short spiky palms beside the rarely-used front door; the camellia shedding its waxy pink petals on the front lawn. On Jersey the farmhouses are grander, and the granite a warmer pink.

All the islands are washed by brilliantly clear green-blue seas, glimpsed down narrow valleys or spread across the horizon in the big bays. There is an extraordinary variety of landscape packed into the forty-five square miles of Jersey, twenty-four square miles of Guernsey and mere thousand acres of Sark; wooded valleys, heaths covered with blazing-yellow gorse, cliffs and secret bays. Alderney is just under two thousand acres, and quite different from all the other islands; it has few trees, its bald, bracken-covered cliffs being more reminiscent of an isolated Scottish island.

Before the war, the islands were seen as quintessentially British. They were stubbornly independent, and proud of their history and ancient constitutions and their long tradition of democracy. They kept their distance from Europe, even though Alderney at its nearest point is only seven miles from Cap de la Hague on the Cotentin peninsula of northern France, and were very loyal to the British monarchy. They were considered hardworking, enterprising and pragmatic; both Guernsey and Jersey had healthy export industries, and had captured the British market in early potatoes, tomatoes, flowers and grapes. The financial acumen and discretion which was to make the islands major offshore banking centres later in the century had already begun to bear fruit.

The population had an island mentality not unlike that of the rest of Britain, with all its strengths and weaknesses; they were cautious and conservative about change, and distrustful of outsiders. Each island was proudly independent of the others. In particular, no love was lost between the two main islands; Guernseymen still call Jerseymen 'crapauds', and Jerseymen call Guernseymen 'donkeys'. Their rivalry dates back three hundred years, to the Civil War, when Guernsey declared for Cromwell and Jersey for the King. Now they are competitors in tourism, tomatoes and finance, and there is surprisingly little co-operation, either political or economic, between them. The writer John Fowles summarised island characteristics in his introduction to G.B. Edwards's masterful evocation of the Guernsey character, *The Book of Ebenezer Le Page*: 'All small islands conform their inhabitants in markedly similar ways, both socially and psychologically. On the credit side there is the fierce independence, the toughness of spirit, the patience and the courage, the ability to cope and make do; on the debit, the dourness, the incest, the backwardness, the suspicion of non-islanders.'

In 1939 the islands were still predominantly rural, and people did not move much outside their parish. The circumference of their whole lives might be only a few miles. Norman French, the original language of the islands, was still spoken, and an islander might not understand another from a parish only a few miles away, so thick were the accents, and so scanty the traffic between the communities. Most islanders left school at fourteen; going on to higher education was the privilege of a tiny minority whose parents could afford to send them to universities in England or France. Families intermarried. The entries for some surnames in the telephone directories run to pages and pages, although the blood connections may be so distant that people of the same name do not necessarily consider each other relations. In these isolated, tightly-knit rural parishes, incest was common. The pre-war Jersey police files list a remarkable number of convictions for incest; over the years the large mental hospital St Saviour's housed many of the products of these relationships.

In the first part of the twentieth century these old, rural island communities had been changing quickly, and were rapidly becoming Anglicised. English was being spoken more widely than Norman French. English 'incomers' were arriving to live in the bungalows and villas which were proliferating along the islands' picturesque coasts. Many were pensioners – retired army colonels and civil servants – taking advantage of the lower income taxes and warmer climate. There was another distinct element diluting the traditional island communities: seasonal labourers came from France and Ireland to work on the potato or tomato harvests.

Islanders had – as they still do – an ambivalent relationship towards the United Kingdom. They resent its power over island affairs, and are extremely critical of mainland Britain, which they see as riddled with social conflict, poverty and crime. But there are too many ties of history and culture for them to want to break away completely.

Few islanders will miss an opportunity of reminding you that they conquered England, and not the other way round. Since AD 933 the islands have belonged to the Duchy of Normandy (William the Conqueror stopped and recruited islanders before setting off to defeat King Harold at the Battle of Hastings in 1066), and this title has remained with the British monarchy to the Judge day. The Westminster Parliament has no jurisdiction over the islands, which are entirely self-governing, except in matters related to defence and foreign policy, for which the Privy Council is responsible.

Each island has an independent system of government, with its own parliament – known as the States – of elected Deputies. At the head of the government are the Bailiff, the Attorney General, and the Solicitor General on Guernsey and Jersey, the Judge on Alderney. Prominent islanders are appointed to these positions by the Crown. On Guernsey and Jersey, Lieutenant Governors are the official representatives of the British monarchy. Each island has its own civil service and system of local government based on the parishes into which the islands are divided.

Sark is a hereditary Seigneurie, which prides itself on having the last, working, feudal constitution. A Seigneur governs with the help of the island's parliament, the Chief Pleas. During the Occupation the Dame of Sark, Sybil Hathaway, ruled the island. She inherited the title from her father, the son of a Guernsey businessman who had bought out the bankrupt former Seigneur. Sybil Hathaway's strong character divided the island's population into two camps: admirers and fierce critics.

In the days immediately prior to the Occupation, Guernsey and Jersey streamlined their governments for quicker decision-making. On Guernsey, power was centralised in the hands of the eight-member Controlling Committee, appointed by the Attorney General, who was himself appointed its President by the States. Elections were abandoned for the duration of the Occupation and the States met only infrequently. On Jersey the eleven-member

Superior Council took over, appointed by the Bailiff. Democracy was put in abeyance and power was concentrated in this tiny group, which was to cause considerable resentment.

It was this cluster of beautiful islands, with their antiquated governments and their dogged independence, which was clearly visible through the binoculars of the German officers on the Normandy coast in June 1940.

CHAPTER ONE

DITCHED

'We were ditched by the UK government. We felt stripped naked. After demilitarisation, we had no means of defending ourselves. There's no resentment, we realised Britain had its back against the wall and we realised Britain had to stay in the war to get our liberty back. But the local politicians were amateur; and they were frightened.'

Jersey schoolteacher Harry Aubin

Every Channel Islander old enough to remember 1940 can still tell you what they were doing on the evening of 28 June of that year. The midsummer sun was still brilliant in the cloudless sky over the islands. On Jersey, children like Stella Perkins and her three brothers were playing on the beach; on Guernsey, Vivyan Mansell was milking the cows which had been put out to graze on the airstrip. Ambrose Sherwill, Guernsey's Attorney General, was on the telephone to the Home Office in London, running over official matters. There was little reason to take much notice of the small black machines which appeared high above in the sky. In the previous few months, planes overhead had become commonplace; British planes on their way to bomb Italy, and German planes bombing France. The little specks flying far above, to and from the war, seemed only to underline to islanders how remote they were from the convulsions Europe was undergoing. Belgium and Holland had already fallen to the German advance, and a week previously, France had accepted the most humiliating armistice in her history. As for the German reconnaissance planes seen over the islands in the previous couple of days, islanders were sure that their observations would have revealed how defenceless the islands were; there were no signs of anti-aircraft guns, naval ships anchored in the harbours, or army camps. In the few minutes it took to fly over the cluster of islands, they would have seen the rumpled green patchwork of fields dotted with granite farmhouses. They would have glimpsed rocky cliffs, brilliant white beaches and glasshouses blinking in the sun.

At 6.45 p.m. on 28 June, the planes came lower and nearer than ever before. They screamed over Sark, spraying bullets onto the roofs before heading towards Guernsey and Jersey. One hundred and eighty bombs were dropped onto the two main islands that evening in less than an hour, and countless rounds of machine-gun bullets were fired at the islanders as they tried to scurry to safety. The main towns of St Helier on Jersey and St Peter Port on Guernsey bore the brunt of the attack. St Peter Port's harbour had been teeming with activity only a few minutes before; it was the peak of the tomato season, and a long line of trucks were waiting to off-load the crop onto the ship for England. The mailboat was just leaving and, as usual, a crowd had gathered to see friends and relatives off.

The Methodist minister Douglas Ord noted down in his diary what he saw from his lawn overlooking St Peter Port: 'We saw six machines climb out of the east, turn, and run down with guns blazing and bombs falling on the defenceless town and harbour, the mailboat and the crowds. Against the perfect blue sky, the sticks of bombs could quite clearly be seen.' On Jersey, ten-year-old Stella Perkins watched with horrified fascination as the sunshine glinted on the bombs as they fell over St Helier. Edwin de Sainte Croix was working as a stevedore in St Helier harbour: 'There was no air raid warning. Nothing. There'd been lots of planes flying about taking photos over the previous few days, so we didn't take any notice of the low-flying planes until the bombs started dropping. There was panic. Some men dived under tarpaulin – but what shelter would that provide? We dived behind a tea-shack.' Jersey carpenter Sandy Whitley was living at the other end of the island from St Helier, but he could feel the bombing raid as the whole island vibrated under its impact.

On Guernsey, St Peter Port harbour was in chaos; the line of lorries burst into flames, incinerating drivers caught in their cabs or sheltering under them. Frank Falla, a journalist on the Guernsey newspaper *The Star*, described the scene in his memoirs: 'The blood of the wounded and the dying mingled with the juice of the tomatoes, and when I came on the scene just as the last Hun plane faded into the distance the sight was one I shall never forget; the flames, the bodies, the cries of the dying and the injured, and the straggling line of people emerging from their shelter under the pier.'

The air-raid warnings did not go off until ten minutes after the first bomb. There were no shelters. There was a shortage of men to help ferry the dead and wounded to hospital, because many had been evacuated to Britain or had joined up. Most of the St John's Ambulance men had gone to Alderney to clear up the island after it had been evacuated by all but eighteen of its residents; from there, several hours' sail away, they watched the raid helplessly. It took the fire brigade twenty-four hours to put out the fires. The final death toll was forty-four, with another thirty injured. The youngest person killed was fourteen, the oldest seventy-one years old.

In comparison with the bombing Britain was to experience the following autumn, the raid on the Channel Islands was small-scale; but the impact on the close-knit island communities was huge. Almost everybody knew someone who had been killed or injured. In an instant, the islanders' assumptions that this war would pass them by – as the last war had done – were shattered. As Jersey girl Kathleen Whitley said of the raid: 'We knew then it was serious; before that, it was so peaceful, we couldn't believe the war would really affect the islands.' Long after the German bombers had gone, six RAF planes appeared, painfully underlining the impotence of the country that had protected the islands for nearly a thousand years. When the *Courier*, laden with supplies evacuated from Alderney, docked in St Peter Port shortly after the raid, its master found the people very shaken: 'Many tales of "hate of England" came to my ears for leaving them unprotected.'

Even worse, this enemy seemed to recognise no moral law. Harold Hobbs, son of the coxwain of the Guernsey lifeboat, was killed when the Germans randomly strafed the boat as they flew back to France. Hobbs's death seemed a horrible intimation of the outrages against common decency which British propaganda had led the islanders to expect of the Germans. An enemy which attacked a defenceless, clearly-marked lifeboat could not be civilised.

The shattered tomato crates lying along St Peter Port's harbour spelled economic collapse. The islands produced little food for themselves; over the preceding century, their agriculture had been revolutionised, and by 1940 they primarily produced specialist crops for the British market. In return, Britain exported food, fuel and manufactured goods to the islands. At least Jersey's new potatoes and vegetables could be used to feed its inhabitants, but Guernsey was covered with glasshouses for tomatoes and flowers. June was the height of the tomato season, and two thousand tons were ripening every week; the disruption of the export trade threatened immediate bankruptcy for thousands of farmers. Since the possibility of invasion had scared off the tourists and frightened the English with their private incomes and pensions back to the Home Counties, the export trade was the last remaining pillar of the islands' economies. If trade links with Britain were cut, how could islanders feed themselves and keep warm? The future was suddenly full of frightening, unexpected possibilities – of invasion, atrocities, bankruptcy and starvation. Symbolically, the big clock on the Guernsey weighbridge by St Peter Port's harbour, a town landmark, had stopped during the bombing raid at two and half minutes to seven.

The bombing raid was a rude shock to the islanders, and the fact that it was a consequence of British government bungling would have been equally so. It was not until more than thirty years later, with the publication in 1975 of the islands' official history of the Occupation, that it became clear that a decision to demilitarise the islands had been reached in the War Cabinet thirteen days before the raid. A week before the German attack, all military machinery and men had been withdrawn from the islands. But unlike the French government, which had declared Paris an open city so as to avoid bombing raids, the British had omitted to inform the enemy of the demilitarisation.

Attorney General Ambrose Sherwill was on the telephone to the Home Office from his office in St Peter Port when the raid began. He held the receiver out of the window so that Charles Markbreiter, the Assistant Secretary at the Home Office concerned with Channel

Islands affairs, could hear the explosions. Sherwill tersely suggested that the British government should lose no time in letting the Germans know that the islands had been demilitarised.

Both the British and the Channel Islands authorities had assumed that the war would never reach the islands. The War Office told the Home Office in September 1939 that the possibility of an attack on the islands was 'somewhat remote'. In the same month Jersey had requested anti-aircraft and coastal guns, but was told by a hard-pressed Whitehall that the earliest date of delivery would be August 1940. Several government ministries considered the islands' position and complacently concluded that any interruption of food and fuel supplies would only be temporary. Encouraged by Whitehall's confidence, the island authorities promoted the islands as the 'ideal wartime holiday resort', safe from the bombing raids expected on London and the south coast, for the summer of 1940. Advertisements were placed in national newspapers extolling the islands' attractions.

Although the islands appeared to be under no direct threat, they rallied to the British cause as loyally as they had done in the previous war. Thousands of islandmen and women volunteered; in the course of the war ten thousand islanders served in the British forces, more than one in ten of the population – probably the highest proportion of any part of the Empire. Guernsey voted to double its rate of income tax so that it could give the British government £180,000 towards the cost of the island's defences. Jersey raised a loan of £100,000 as the first instalment of a gift to the British government – Jerseyman Lord Portsea pointed out in *The Times* that the proportionate sum in the UK would have been £118 million – and as late as 10 June 1940 Jersey was considering making arrangements for a loan of £1 million. War Savings Groups had been set up to collect voluntary funds, and the RAF Comforts Committee had got knitting; on 28 May 1940 they sent off a grand total of 235 balaclavas, 186 sleeveless pullovers and 167 pairs of oversocks to be distributed to those serving in the forces.

It was not until Hitler launched his Blitzkreig on the Low Countries in May 1940 that the possibility first dawned on the islanders that their role in this war might amount to more than knitting, saving their spare pennies and waiting for their loved ones to return. The extensive use of parachutists in the German attack on Holland had particularly alarmed the islanders. The letters columns of the *Jersey Evening Post* were filled with schemes for the islands' defences and panic about fifth columnists. Many of these letters have a taste of retired colonels brushing up their military skills over a whisky at the yacht club, but there were more serious voices. 'Jerseymen would do well to look at a map of France and do some hard thinking . . . Jersey may well be in a very unpleasant position indeed,' wrote 'Miles' on 21 May 1940. Two days later, Brussels fell and refugees flooded south to the French border. One Frank Johnson wrote presciently to the *Evening Post*:

> We are told that Jersey is the last place the Nazis would attack. It is of neither economic or strategic importance [but] so far from this being the case, I think – nay, I am sure – that the exact opposite is true, and that at the present juncture no part of the Empire is in greater peril. Just try to imagine the tremendous effect on the morale of his people, were Hitler able to tell them not only that he had commenced to attack England, but that the oldest part of the British Empire – Jersey – was in German hands. He would proudly point to it as the beginning of the end, the break-up of the Empire . . . And as I see the position at present, based on this fatal self complacency, it would be as easy as the proverbial 'falling off a log'.

On 28 May 1940 – the day on which the Belgian army capitulated – Major General James Harrison, the Lieutenant Governor of Jersey, pointed out to the War Office that he had only 150 members of the militia and fifty naval ratings, most of whom were mechanics, to defend the fifty thousand British subjects on the island. Islanders were demanding to know what arrangements had been made for their defence. The British Expeditionary Force had already begun its epic evacuation from Dunkirk, and Calais had surrendered. It was only a matter of time before France was defeated and the Germans reached the Normandy coast – a mere fourteen miles from Jersey.

Preoccupied with more pressing matters, the Chiefs of Staff Committee didn't find time to consider the defence of the Channel Islands until 5 June, when they were presented with a paper outlining the position. The paper reviewed in lordly manner the history of the islanders' fighting spirit since armed bands gathered in AD 578 to fight the Bretons, and concluded: 'If the enemy effected a landing on these islands, it would be essential to eject him as a matter of prestige.'

By 10 June the Germans were bombing Cherbourg, and the Channel Islanders could hear the rumble of the explosions. Windows vibrated in their frames, and from Alderney and Jersey smoke could be seen rising on the horizon where oil tanks were being blown up by the French to prevent them from falling into enemy hands. Still no one on the islands knew what was being planned for them, and Major General Harrison sent an irascible personal letter to the Home Office: 'One doesn't even know if the powers that be have considered at all what might happen to the Channel Islands and if so, what action they would like to take. If they have any views, I think we ought to be taken into their confidence. We are British Isles, though too far away for protection.' He and Alexander Coutanche, the Bailiff of Jersey, had already discussed the possibility of German occupation.

On 12 June, the War Cabinet considered the plight of the Channel Islands. Their first conclusion was to confirm the view which had held sway since 1928: that the islands had no strategic significance. The Chief of the Imperial General Staff, General Sir John Dill, said that two battalions had already been ordered to the islands to strengthen their defences; in the morning the War Cabinet approved this decision, but after lunch they changed their minds. With the French coast in enemy hands, the two battalions would be at risk of attack, and besides, the men might be needed to defend the British mainland. It was decided to withdraw the battalions. If the Germans landed, the Lieutenant Governors should surrender. These decisions were not conveyed to the authorities on the Channel Islands, and on 14 June Jersey officials phoned the Home Office to ask what was going to happen, and pointed out that if the islands were demilitarised – as was becoming increasingly likely – many islanders would wish to be evacuated. The following day the War Office telegraphed the Lieutenant Governors of Jersey and Guernsey that both islands' airfields should be defended, so that the RAF could support armies operating in north-western France. The telegraphs concluded: 'Thereafter the policy of demilitarisation will rule.'

At 5 a.m. on 16 June, the order came for the troops to evacuate Alderney. Frederick French, the Judge or chief administrator of Alderney, was bewildered, and could offer the anxious islanders no explanation. He suggested that perhaps the troops were being pulled back to Guernsey and Jersey. Meanwhile, all that separated Alderney from the approaching Germans was a meagre seven miles of water.

On the same day, the British government asked Jersey and Guernsey to help in the evacuation of British and French troops cornered in St Malo. Guernsey was too far away to get boats there in time, but eighteen yachts put out from Jersey to ferry soldiers from the beaches to waiting transports, in an operation akin to the evacuation of the British Expeditionary Force two weeks previously from Dunkirk. The troops stopped off on Jersey before going on to England, and Jersey boy Bernard Hassall remembers seeing French sailors pouring through the streets of St Helier. There was a strong smell of Gauloise cigarettes, and he stared at the blood seeping through their bandages. The war was encircling the islands.

Over the past ten months the islands had responded promptly and loyally to requests for help, but now Whitehall was proving more tardy. With no final decision forthcoming from the War Office, the Home Office had come to its own conclusion that the islands should be demilitarised, and called an urgent meeting with island representatives in London. The main subject under discussion was evacuation. It was decided that the priority was evacuating three thousand young men of military age and five hundred Irish labourers. Only after these had been evacuated could they deal with the thousands of islanders now becoming increasingly anxious to leave the islands.

On 19 June, Major General Harrison had still had no official word about demilitarisation from the War Office. He was addressing a session of the States of Jersey when he was interrupted and asked to take a phone call from the War Office: he was finally told that it had been decided that the islands were to be demilitarised. He returned to the chamber to tell the deputies. The islands' papers carried the news that evening. One reason for the delay in informing the islands of Britain's plans had been that the Prime Minister, Winston Churchill, was reluctant to give them up without a fight. On 14 June he had told the War Cabinet: 'It ought to be possible, by the use of our sea power, to prevent the invasion of the islands by the enemy and ... if there was a chance of offering successful resistance, we ought not to avoid giving him battle there. It [would be] repugnant now to abandon British territory which [has] been in possession of the Crown since the Norman Conquest.'

But the Vice-Chief of Naval Staff, Vice-Admiral Tom Phillips, pointed out that the anti-aircraft guns and fighter aircraft required for this purpose could not be supplied to the islands without denuding British defences; the islands were too far away from Britain, and too near Brest and Cherbourg, which it was clear would soon fall to the Germans, for a naval force to prevent invasion. Churchill was overruled, and he tetchily ordered that all food should be got off the islands to prevent it from falling into enemy hands – he didn't make it clear how he expected the islanders to feed themselves. It was left to the Home Secretary, Sir John Anderson, to urge the Cabinet that 'if the islands were not to be defended, the least we could do would be to provide the inhabitants with the opportunity of leaving'.

On 20 June, the last troops left the islands, and the submarine telephone cable – the last still linking Britain and France – was cut. The Lieutenant Governors left the next day, handing over their responsibilities to the Bailiffs. The Chiefs of Staff then informed the Foreign Office that demilitarisation had now been completed, and asked them to inform Germany of this through an intermediary government. The Home Office drafted a press statement to the same effect. But the Foreign Office did not arrange to have the Germans informed, and the Home Office's press release was held back. It was feared that letting the Germans know that the islands had been demilitarised would be tantamount to an invitation to walk in. The result was the worst of all possible worlds: the islands were in the dangerous position of being undefended, and yet were considered by the Germans as legitimate military targets.

The Bailiffs of Jersey and Guernsey received a message of sympathy from King George VI on 24 June: 'For strategic reasons it has been found necessary to withdraw the armed forces from the

Channel Islands. I deeply regret this necessity and I wish to assure my people in the Islands that in taking this decision my Government has not been unmindful of their position.' The royal message came with a covering note from the Home Secretary which contained the baffling request that the message should not attract too much publicity; the Home Office was anxious that German intelligence should not pick up the information that the islands had been demilitarised. The Bailiffs had no idea that the Germans had not been informed. The Chiefs of Staff pressed the Foreign Office on 26 June to inform the Germans of the Channel Islands' demilitarisation. They pointed out that the safety of the islands' populations depended on it, although they agreed that it would serve no military purpose to tell the Germans. The force of their argument was fatally undermined by their conclusion that 'it was almost certain that the Germans would have learned of the demilitarisation through intelligence channels and therefore they would be unlikely to waste their resources in bombarding the islands'. Two days later, on the fateful 28 June, in reply to a written parliamentary question, Sir John Anderson wrote: 'We have been at pains to prevent any publicity being given to the fact that a measure of evacuation from the Channel Islands has been carried out ... There are military reasons for this which I would rather not put in writing.' A few hours later, the islands were being bombed.

On the BBC radio news at nine o'clock that evening, two hours after the bombing, it was belatedly announced that the islands had been demilitarised, but it was not until the following morning that the bombing raid was reported. This sequence reinforced British propaganda that the Germans recognised no laws of war, and had bombed a demilitarised target. It was left to a member of Guernsey's Controlling Committee, in an emergency session the day after the bombing raid, to ask the awkward question which remained unanswered for over three decades: 'Had the British government informed the German government that Guernsey had been demilitarised?'

On 30 June the Foreign Office finally asked Joseph P. Kennedy, US Ambassador to Britain, to send the US Embassy in Berlin a message for the German government: 'The evacuation of all military personnel and equipment from the Channel Islands was completed some days ago. The Islands are therefore demilitarised and cannot be considered in any way as a legitimate target for bombardment. A public announcement to this effect was made on the evening of June 28.'

The Times accused the Germans of murdering civilians after the islands had been demilitarised, and stated that, morally speaking, the attack on the Channel Islands was worse than the German bombing of refugees fleeing the Lowlands; they at least were in an area of military operations, whereas the victims in the Channel Islands were not.

Confusion and misunderstanding between the islands and White-hall also characterised the evacuation of nearly thirty thousand islanders. For four days, from 19 to 22 June, there were scenes of complete panic in the islands. Almost half of Guernsey's population left (seventeen thousand out of forty-one thousand), while on Jersey only six and a half thousand out of fifty thousand decided to evacuate. On Alderney all but eighteen of the fourteen hundred residents left for Britain, but on Sark, of the six hundred-strong population, only 129 departed.

The documents revealing the chaotic, contradictory official decision-making in London, St Peter Port and St Helier were not opened to public scrutiny until 1992 – fifty-two years after the event, in response to parliamentary and public pressure. They were originally intended to be kept secret until 2045: one hundred years of quarantine was considered necessary to limit their potentially damaging impact on Britain's relations with the oldest possession of the Crown.

The first mention of evacuation was at a Chiefs of Staff meeting in London on 11 June, when it was decided that in the event of the islands' demilitarisation, 'it will be unnecessary and undesirable to evacuate women and children'. The prospect of having to set aside much-needed shipping for the purpose was unwelcome. But in case the position should change, the ever cost-conscious Home Office checked with the island governments that they would foot the bill for any evacuation judged necessary. As the days went by without any definite decision on either demilitarisation or evacuation, the islanders grew panicky, particularly on Alderney, the island closest to the French coast, where they could hear the bombing of the Normandy peninsula, and they could see German troops through binoculars. Even more frightening, a hundred starving and exhausted French women and children arrived on 13 June in overladen boats after having lost their way; they had been three weeks at sea, and two of their number had died. Alderney residents watched the last British troops depart, blowing up their vehicles and leaving behind quantities of stores in their haste, and yet still there was no word of evacuation.

It was not until 18 June that the Home Office decided to plan evacuation, on the presumption that the islands would be demilitarised, but nobody knew who should be evacuated. The first to go, the authorities agreed, would be men of military age, but after that it was unclear: should families be split up, and only children evacuated? What about mothers and fathers? The Home Secretary had said in the War Cabinet that any islanders who wished to go should have that opportunity, but his officials balked at the idea of ninety thousand islanders pouring through Weymouth in need of accommodation and economic support. Besides, there was certain to be a small number who refused to leave the islands, who would present the awkward choice between forcing them to go, or leaving them to starve.

A large portion of the blame for the panic has been laid at the door of the Channel Island governments. On Guernsey, officials gave no clear direction and contradictory advice. Some urged evacuation, others scorned such an option as cowardly. In Jersey the official line was more consistent, and many islanders who had registered for evacuation were persuaded to change their minds and stay. But the real blame lies with the Home Office, as the newly released papers show. In an internal Home Office memo reviewing the whole débâcle, dated 7 July 1940, Charles Markbreiter admitted to Sir Alexander Maxwell, the Permanent Under-Secretary: 'The general impression is that evacuation was bungled either by the Home Office or by the insular authorities or both. This was stimulated by the fact that the island governments (in fact at our request) did endeavour to stop any movement for mass evacuation . . . this resulted in many fewer people leaving Jersey than we had estimated for.' After the event, the Home Office acknowledged that there had been a muddle. But during the critical period in late June it had been adamant that total evacuation was not feasible. When Dr William Montague (a Guernseyman who was evacuated because his Jewish origins placed him in particular danger from the Nazis) went to the Home Office to request that all the islanders should be evacuated on the grounds that their health would be threatened if trade was cut with Britain, Markbreiter noted:

> Despite the possibility that the Islands may come under German Occupation, I think there are grave objections to any policy of inviting and encouraging the islanders to leave. Apart from the difficulty of absorbing them here, there is the consideration that we might have in the end to adopt some measure of compulsion, because those remaining would be too few to sustain a communal life. Tell Mr Sherwill that we think the present policy must be maintained of encouraging the population to stay.

A month later, after the Germans had occupied the islands, the subject came up in Parliament. The fact that British subjects had been abandoned to the enemy because of the 'difficulty of absorbing them' in Britain was not regarded as suitable for public consumption. The facts were skilfully reconstituted for the government's reply to the House of Commons:

> The information before the government indicated that substantial numbers of the inhabitants would be unwilling to leave their homes, and that any scheme for attempting by compulsion or inducement to transplant to this country the whole of the population of the islands including those who have been, for generations, settled on the land would be both impracticable and undesirable ... Evacuation was planned on the principle that women and children should be brought away but a sufficient part of the population should remain behind to enable the life of the islands to go on.

In fact, huge numbers of islanders were more than willing to leave their homes. On Guernsey they queued for hours following the publication of notices on 19 June which stated that all children of school age accompanied by teachers, mothers and small children, men of military age and 'all others' had to register for evacuation by that evening. On Jersey all women and children, and men aged from twenty to thirty-three, had until 10 a.m. the following day to register. On the same day a ship arrived at Alderney with strict instructions (no one knew from whom) that only schoolchildren and their teachers could board it for evacuation to Britain. Mothers waved their children goodbye in great distress.

By 10 a.m. on 20 June, 8800 Jerseymen and women had managed to register, and the queues still wound round St Helier. A young insurance clerk, Bob Le Sueur (whose father had decided not to evacuate as he had no intention of becoming a 'penniless refugee' at his age), got up early to register for evacuation at the Town Hall before going to his office:

> The queue was already six hundred yards long at 8.30 a.m. and I couldn't possibly be late for the office. When I got into work, there was only one typist and she was inundated by requests from people. There were huge queues outside our office. It took me two days to get through to our branch manager in Southampton. When I eventually explained the situation to him, he asked me if I had been drinking. Then he said that, 'If this cock and bull story is true and the Jersey manager turns up in Southampton, we'll send him back. Meanwhile you're to wait there until he does.' I waited five years.

Ultimately twenty-three thousand people registered on Jersey. In an attempt to calm the panicky crowds the Bailiff, Alexander Coutanche, addressed a huge public meeting, at which he said that he and his wife had no intention of leaving the island, and asked everyone to join him in singing the National Anthem. To the same end, Jurat Edgar Dorey gave an emotional speech in the States which was reported in detail in the *Jersey Evening Post* the next day: 'I have been filled with disgust ... I do not understand those of old Norman stock who should be rooted to the soil, pressing to leave. We, who were always a calm, steady people who have jogged along in our own way, loving our lands and our surroundings ... I would like the House to express its utter contempt at what these people were doing ... it is the worst characteristic of human nature

– cowardice – rabbits and rats.' The *Post* praised Dorey's stand: it was right to call those trying to leave rabbits and rats, its editorial pronounced. Those who had been proud to proclaim their devotion to their native island were now quick to desert it. The mother country had enough problems of her own without an influx of thousands of refugees.

Coutanche and Dorey's efforts had an impact; of the twenty-three thousand who had registered, more than two-thirds changed their minds, and only six and a half thousand finally left. By 21 June Jersey's evacuation was almost complete, and calm had largely been restored. It was a different story on Guernsey. Victor Carey, the Bailiff, was an old, weak man and Ambrose Sherwill, the Attorney General, genuinely didn't know what was the right thing to do. As he later wrote in his unpublished memoirs:

> The period of the evacuation was, I think, the most difficult and painful I have ever experienced. Waves of panic and indecision swept over people; official notices were misread, words of advice were completely misunderstood and the most grotesque rumours passed for truth. One official, at his own expense, had posters with 'Don't be Yellow' printed in black on a yellow ground, put up all over town. He then suddenly remembered that he ought to go and did so.

The doctors of Guernsey gave conflicting advice. John Leale, a Jurat, told the States that they had advised him that the population could survive on the milk and vegetables produced by the island, but two days later they changed their minds and told Sherwill that everyone should be evacuated. Sherwill wrote: 'One of them argued that total evacuation was necessary to avoid starvation ... I had never before, nor have I since, felt waves of panic emanating from a person near me. They were affecting my own judgement and, but for politeness' sake, I would have asked the source of them to go and sit at the other end of the room.'

But Sherwill recognised that even if the doctors were right, it was now too late to organise a total evacuation. In a follow-up phone-call to Dr William Montague's visit to the Home Office, both Sherwill and Leale repeated to Markbreiter that they would prefer total evacuation. But they were told that the British government would not countenance such a possibility, and to prevent a run on the boats the Guernsey authorities mounted a campaign to encourage people to stay. A member of the States broadcast on a public address system every evening in St Peter Port, and posters appeared on walls around the island: 'Why go mad? Compulsory evacuation A LIE! There's no place like home. CHEER UP!' The aggressive anti-evacuation campaign aroused the suspicions of the commander of HMS *Sabre* as he passed through the island, and he signalled to the Admiralty: 'Suggest this should be exposed as being of enemy origin and a vigorous counter-propaganda campaign instituted.'

On Alderney the Judge, Frederick French, was becoming increasingly exasperated by what he believed was the complete neglect of the island by Guernsey, the head of the bailiwick. French's repeated wires to the Guernsey authorities asking to know what arrangements were being made for Alderney received no reply, and islanders were resorting to hiring private yachts to take them to Guernsey. After several days of waiting for ships to evacuate the population, French took matters into his own hands and appealed directly to the Admiralty. On 22 June the *Vestal* came to collect lighthouse personnel; the captain offered to take 150 civilians, but French feared there would be a stampede for the ship, and turned down the offer. The following day, six ships arrived, and in the course of five hours took the entire remaining population of about 1100 off the island, barring eighteen who refused to leave. After his arrival in England, French was still seething with fury. In a memo to the Home Office he alleged that the panic on Guernsey was the result of the 'collapse of effective control in Guernsey civil government'. He accused the Guernsey authorities of:

> Complete failure to furnish help similar to that arranged for herself ... to give any information, any instructions ... giving the impression that the authorities were either panicking or incapable of dealing with the situation, or that they were deliberately seeing after themselves and their own people. I wish to lodge an official complaint against the Guernsey civil authorities. [They were] guilty of a gross failure to perform their duty ... their actions amount to criminal neglect.

Sark, also within the bailiwick of Guernsey, was governed by the imperious Dame of Sark, Sybil Hathaway, who was as unimpressed as French by the actions of the officials on Guernsey. She wrote in a letter on 24 June that the situation on Guernsey had been 'disgraceful, with no one taking the lead'. On 27 June she complained to the Home Office that Guernsey had 'officially forgotten us', and concluded, 'The responsibility of advising people to go or remain falls on me and I should be thankful for any assurance or hints from you. Personally I remain, unless ordered to leave, and all the Sarkese remain also.'

In Guernsey's defence, communication between the islands had become very difficult following the strict injunction against using radio telephones, which could be overheard by the enemy. And Sherwill had not found it easy to persuade ships to go to Alderney, which was by then within range of enemy guns. After French refused the offer of places for 150 civilians and the ship returned from the island virtually empty, Sherwill concluded that the Alderney people were, like the Sarkese, staying put. It should be pointed out that the Guernsey authorities were in the unenviable position of implementing a contradictory policy determined in London. Britain didn't want thousands more refugees; Coutanche, the Bailiff of Jersey, took the easiest option, and decided they wouldn't get them. On Guernsey the Bailiff was incapable of giving leadership, Sherwill didn't have the authority to do so, and to top it all the Lieutenant Governor, Major General John Minshull Ford, who could have offered much-needed advice in the days prior to his departure on 21 June, had only arrived for the first time on the island two weeks before.

It was a sorry débâcle, and every islander remembers it as such. Families had only a few hours in which to decide whether to stay together or be split up; parents were racked with indecision as to what was the best thing for their children – to send them alone to the uncertain safety of England, where they might fall victim to bombing raids, or to keep them on an island now facing starvation and occupation. Some islanders in 1940 spoke only Norman French; England was a foreign country with a foreign language. For some, the furthest they had ever travelled was the few miles to St Peter Port or St Helier; they had lived in country parishes all their lives, and had never left their island. Leaving for an unknown destination was a terrifying prospect. The few belongings evacuees were permitted had to be hastily packed; everything else had to be abandoned. The keys to homes full of antiques, paintings and books were handed over to neighbours who were staying behind. Valuables were buried in gardens, in a desperate bid to save something. Long queues formed at the banks and insurance offices, but withdrawals were limited to £20. Cars were given away for a few pounds at the harbour. Meals were left half-eaten on the tables in the scramble, and long queues formed at the vets' to have much-loved household pets slaughtered. On Jersey alone, 2200 dogs and 3000 cats were put down by the authorities.

Fifteen-year-old Dolly Joanknecht's experience was typical. On 19 June she was sent home early from her job as a nanny in St Peter Port, Guernsey. She found her great aunt's home, where she lived, in uproar:

> I had two cousins and they both wanted to be evacuated to England, but my uncle didn't. I sat on the stairs, saying again and again 'I want to go.' My cousin Jack wouldn't go because his girlfriend wasn't going, Aunty wouldn't go because Uncle wouldn't go, so they all decided I should stay. I tried to get in touch with my mother. I phoned her neighbours but they told me she had already gone with my brothers and sisters. I didn't know what to do; it was absolutely chaotic.
>
> The next morning, I got up early and packed my clothes in a brown paper parcel – my cousins had already taken the suitcases. It was 5.30 in the morning when I left the house, and as I walked through St Peter Port to the harbour I tried to imagine what it would be like when all the houses were empty and the Germans were here. At the harbour I sat on the coiled ropes, watching the buses going by to the ships full of schoolchildren. Their parents were carrying all their belongings in pillowslips – they had no suitcases. I stayed until 11.30 a.m. but I couldn't see my brothers and sisters. On my way home I met my cousins and they demanded to know where I'd been. I told them, then my parcel broke and all my clothes spilled onto the street. I was crying as I tried to gather them up. When I think about it now, I should have just gone, but you did what you were told then.
>
> My father sent a telegram from England to the Guernsey police asking them to put me on the next boat, but my aunty said no. I remember the boat going out.

Ten-year-old Guernsey boy Herbert Nichols was the eldest of six children. He was of school age, and therefore in one of the priority categories for evacuation. His family lived in Cobo on the west coast of Guernsey, only four miles from St Peter Port, but communications broke down: 'We were going to be evacuated. Two days in a row we waited all day at the school, but no buses ever arrived. At the end of the second day, they said to come back at 5 a.m., but we didn't believe them. Those that did were evacuated. The buses went away half-empty.'

Daphne Prins and her small son got as far as St Peter Port harbour. But when she saw the refugees being packed in like sardines, and noticed that the boats were unarmed, she turned back; she and her son remained on Guernsey for the Occupation.

Vivyan Mansell remembers that her family were half-packed and were waiting for her brothers to return from Alderney, where they had been sent by the Guernsey States to collect the cattle and pigs abandoned when the island had been evacuated a few days before. Both young men were of military age, and their mother was anxious that they should get to England, despite the States' injunction that farmers should stay to help feed the island. By the time the brothers returned from their salvage trip they no longer had any choice, as the last ship for England had gone. Vivyan helped the neighbours: 'I took three car-loads of kids down to St Peter Port to be evacuated. It was heart-rending. Mrs T. dressed all her children in their best clothes – nothing warm.'

On Jersey Bernard Hassall remembered:

> I got as far as the boats. A lot of people turned back at the last moment; it was hell. June 1940 was the most hair-raising and frightening month in the history of the islands. All one could hear was, 'What are you going to do?' People were crammed in those ships to be evacuated and the mind boggled at the idea of them crossing the Channel without escorts. On seeing those teeming pots of worms, my brother and I decided not to go.

The journey across the Channel, the chaotic reception in Weymouth, and the five homesick years in industrial towns such as Bradford and Glasgow led many islanders to regret their decision to leave the islands. Edward Hamel described in his memoirs *X-Isles* how, on the journey from Guernsey, the cabins were crammed full, and even the ship's decks were wedged with bodies and bundles. It poured with rain. When they docked in Weymouth, they weren't allowed to disembark. Finally the order came, only for it to be countermanded an hour later. After hours waiting on the ship they landed, but things didn't improve. The officials in Weymouth were swamped. Inevitably, children became lost. Nine-year-old Pat Nichols ended up in Glasgow despite the luggage label attached to her coat addressed to her grandmother in Kent. In Glasgow she was separated from her sister and four-year-old brother, and ended up in a children's home. Her mother crossed from Guernsey with her two youngest a few days after the older children, but it took her five months to find Pat and her siblings.

It was to be several months before many of the islanders had found homes, jobs and schools. They were assisted in their efforts to start a new life by a group of islanders based in London who set up the Channel Islands Refugee Committee.

Britain had failed in its responsibilities to the oldest and most loyal possession of the Crown. It had abandoned British islands without a shot being fired, and it had not even been able to provide safe haven to all those British subjects who wished to evacuate. But there were mitigating circumstances. By 4 June Britain had completed the evacuation of Dunkirk, one of the most ignominious defeats in its history. Its military strategy lay in tatters, and Britain itself for the first time in centuries faced the imminent danger of invasion. In the fiasco over the demilitarisation and evacuation of the Channel Islands, it is possible to trace characteristics of British government which disappeared forever in that summer of 1940: an arrogant and complacent confidence, and a faith in the invincibility of the Empire. These were to be smashed in the course of a few months. As late as 5 June, when Hitler's Panzer divisions had already redrawn the map of Europe and made redundant every British defence policy of the preceding century, the Chief of the Imperial General Staff, General Sir John Dill, felt it appropriate to waste the Chiefs of Staff Committee meeting on a review of the history

of the defence of the Channel Islands since the Dark Ages. When
he finally got round to the islands' current defence needs, it was
clear that he had failed to absorb the significance of what had
happened in Europe. If the Germans landed on the islands, he
asserted, it would be essential as 'a matter of prestige' to eject them.
He had not grasped that Britain was no longer fighting for its
prestige, but for its very survival.

This fact had escaped the most senior members of Britain's
defence establishment, but the island authorities clearly saw the
seriousness of what they were faced with: the safety and survival
of nearly a hundred thousand people lay in their hands. Officials
equivalent to county councillors were pitched into making decisions
of unbearable importance. The advice from Whitehall, usually so
readily forthcoming, and which for once the islands' rulers would
have welcomed – and which they had a right to expect – dried
up overnight. The little that trickled through was late and
contradictory.

To the Whitehall civil servants and the wider British public,
reading reports of the Channel Islands evacuation in the newspapers, it was utterly inconceivable that British soil could fall into
the hands of an enemy. Certainly not soil such as that of the Channel Islands. The islands triggered a host of powerful associations:
of delightful summer holidays; of delicious tomatoes; of the first
new potatoes and of sweet-smelling freesias and carnations. The
islands had been the personal property of the British monarchy
since 1066. The idea of a German occupation was simply too painful
and humiliating to contemplate.

The bungled demilitarisation and evacuation did not escape the
attention of two men, Lord Portsea and Charles Ammon MP. Over
the next five years they were regularly to raise the plight of the
Channel Islands in the Houses of Parliament, repeatedly pricking
the conscience of the government and securing at least a few column
inches in the press every time they did so. On 9 July, Lord Portsea,
a Jerseyman, rose in the House of Lords to speak on the subject
to which he was to return again and again, like a dog worrying a
bone. Why, he demanded, did these islands have to be abandoned?
Guernsey was further away from France than Dover; the islands
had generously donated men and money to the war effort, while

demilitarisation had broken ties more than eight hundred years old. Lord Mottistone followed up this passionate speech, saying that he was shocked that the British had abandoned the islands, on which the flag of Britain had flown for eight hundred years, without 'firing a shot': 'It is peculiarly cruel, because these people rightly say they are the oldest of us all. I spoke to an officer of the First World War and he said, "To think we sacrificed more than ten thousand men for one line of trenches and yet did not fire a shot to save these islands."'

In the House of Commons Charles Ammon, Labour Member of Parliament for Camberwell North, took up the subject in a written question to the Home Secretary, Sir John Anderson, on 11 July. He asked if it was true that a deputation from Guernsey had gone to the Home Office to ask for total evacuation, and were told that the matter was still under consideration on the very day the islands were bombed. Ammon was told that all those who wanted to evacuate had, and that there had even been boats which left the islands half-empty. The government's smug conclusion was: 'It is a matter for congratulations that so many people were brought away safely.' Ammon wasn't satisfied, and the following week he took up the cudgels again, armed with copious accounts which islanders had sent him. He started by accusing the government of suppressing news of the possibility that the Channel Islands were in danger of being occupied. Then he quoted from the letter of one islander who had evacuated:

So far from being 'voluntary' the evacuation was encouraged and ARP [Air-Raid Precautions] wardens went round (in my district at any rate) imploring the people to get out before they were blown out! We were told that the Jerries would be here in twenty-four hours and that the men would be taken to Germany to work as slaves in the munitions factories and as for our women – well, God help them!

The evacuation arrangements such as they were, were deplorable. I came over on the *Antwerp*, a troopship, licensed to carry and with lifebelts provided for seven hundred, and there were two thousand men, women and children aboard to be chased by a submarine half-way across. We reached Weymouth at 5 p.m. and we were left there without food or drink until 10 a.m. the next day when people started fainting in all directions and officialdom woke up at last.

Ammon quoted another evacuee who claimed that hundreds of people waited on the quayside on Guernsey all night in hope of transport. When one small boat arrived, several people were almost crushed in the hurry to board it. Ammon warned the government that the islands' food stocks were low, and that the islanders left behind because of the muddled evacuation were in a 'very parlous condition'. His efforts to raise these matters with the Home Office had been treated with indifference, he told the Commons. Meanwhile, two thousand refugee islanders in Britain had had to resort to seeking help from the Red Cross Society, because the meagre £20 allowance which they had been permitted to bring with them had quickly run out. Ammon concluded: 'The Department had failed to realise its responsibilities. To say nothing of the humiliation which every Britisher must feel because we have walked out for the first time in history without making any stand whatsoever against the invader.'

Other MPs followed, quoting letters from evacuees: invalids had been left in hospital waiting for a hospital ship which never arrived; people were still being evacuated from France after the government had decided it was no longer possible to evacuate anyone from the islands; ships bound for England had been laden with potatoes and tomatoes rather than with people wanting to be evacuated.

The government's response, through the Under-Secretary of State for the Home Office, Osbert Peake, was to ridicule Ammon and his colleagues, and to remain adamant that their conduct had been exemplary: 'I wish on all matters the government and the Home Office had as perfectly clear a conscience as they have on this question of the Channel Islands.' In fact, the Home Office had a far from clear conscience. There were embarrassing parallels to be drawn, which would not escape the notice of critics. The entire fifteen thousand-strong civilian population of Gibraltar had been successfully evacuated; the principle that British subjects were owed protection had held good there, so why not in the Channel Islands, so much closer to Britain and with even stronger ties of history? Charles Markbreiter at the Home Office drew up an anxious memo for Sir Alexander Maxwell, the Permanent Under-Secretary, in which he pointed out that the evacuation of the islands appeared in a very unfavourable light when compared with that of British subjects from the Riviera. But he added that most of the criticism could be dismissed because a 'number of influential people such as the Bishop of Winchester think we were right not to evacuate the islands to a greater extent'. The observation rang hollow.

On the islands, an uneasy calm had returned by 24 June after the last evacuation ship had left. Guernsey sent a working party to Alderney to try to persuade some of the eighteen individuals who had refused to be evacuated to England to come to Guernsey. They were only partially successful. Reginald Blanchford from Guernsey's St John's Ambulance was a member of the party:

> It was very traumatic. There were cows roaming the streets with udders bursting and an old gentleman was trying to chloroform them to kill them. Going into the houses, you'd find a sandwich with a bite taken out of it and half a cup of tea drunk. We heard a noise in one house, there was an old lady there dressed in curtains and she thought I was the SS because I was in my uniform. She was demented, she thought the Germans had arrived. We got her back to Guernsey.

On Guernsey, Jersey and Sark, there was a forced normality. People still went to work, cooked, cleaned, visited the beaches – and waited.

There was one particularly jarring note; some strange stories were doing the rounds. The *Jersey Evening Post* reported that at the time of the evacuation many cars had been stolen. People turned back from the overcrowded ships had returned to where they had parked their cars to find they had vanished. The *Post* alleged that one man had stolen five cars, with the intention of putting them aside until better days. One of the Guernsey rescue parties which went to Alderney came back with rather more than the authorities had expected: clothes, furniture and food were dumped in the empty public pool at La Vallette by St Peter Port for everyone to take their pick. One man returned to Guernsey with loot including seventy-six curtains and thirteen clocks. A subsequent police investigation led to the imprisonment of a number of men.

Jersey housewife Dorothy Blackwell remembered: 'There were

some people who, when they knew someone had gone, would go into their homes and take everything they could. One family I heard of went down to the boats, but they didn't go in the end and when they got back to their houses, there wasn't a thing left in it. Not even the lino on the floor. Unbelievable that people could do such a thing.'

According to Guernsey teenager Dolly Joanknecht: 'When I got back to my mother's house after the evacuation, it had already been vandalised. The doors were wide open and the windows were smashed. All the drawers were tipped upside down and the china smashed. They must have picked out what they wanted. That was before the Germans arrived; it wasn't touched all the five years of Occupation. Everything was exactly how it was left after being vandalised when my mother came back five years later.'

The islands had always been scrupulously law-abiding, and proud of the fact. Islanders had never needed to lock their homes or their cars before, and they were horrified by the thefts. Little did they realise that they were a foretaste of the way in which the moral fabric of these old communities was going to be tested and frayed over the next five years, in ways they could not have imagined.

Everyone was waiting, and as they waited their minds turned to what the Germans' arrival would bring. In his memoirs, Ambrose Sherwill remembered that he, like many islanders, had no idea of what to expect:

> Of the Germans I knew virtually nothing, I did not speak a word of German . . . My service in the Great War had certainly not endeared Germans to me. What I had read about their behaviour in occupied France and Belgium during the war made me gravely apprehensive of the treatment likely to be meted out to us when, flushed with victory and probably, drink, they arrived on Guernsey, as, to me, unlike those in Whitehall, it seemed certain they would.

Sherwill privately asked a British naval commander how he thought the Germans would behave. The reply horrified him: 'They would probably be brutal and he had heard of cases where soldiers on the march in France and Belgium had, with their bayonets as they passed along, hacked off the arms of children standing on the pavement.'

Dolly Joanknecht was warned never to walk in front of a German, because they could stab you with their bayonets: 'It suddenly came back to me how they used to talk in the First World War; they used to say that Germans ate babies and that they crucified girls on doors and raped them.'

It was a tense, eerie hiatus. Alderney housewife Daphne Pope was one of the few people left on the island; the memory of the abandoned dogs' howls echoing in the empty town of St Anne's haunts her still. Cows bellowed with pain as the milk filled their udders. On Guernsey and Jersey, streets which had once been busy were strangely quiet. Houses which had once teemed with children were silent. Sherwill noted that, as in the Bible, mothers whose children had been evacuated were 'mourning and would not be comforted'. The immaculately tended gardens began to look a little unkempt as the midsummer grass continued to grow.

CHAPTER TWO

CORRECT RELATIONS

'You couldn't stay enemies, living side by side for
five years.'

Jersey housewife Kathleen Whitley

On 27 June 1940, a letter was handed to the Guernsey police
station. It came from the Bailiff, Victor Carey, and was addressed
to the 'Officer Commanding German troops on Guernsey'. The
police were to deliver it; the ominous letter filled all who came to
hear of it with apprehension.

On 30 June, a sleepy Sunday morning, two days after the bombing raid, Guernsey police station received word that three German
aircraft had landed at the Guernsey airport. The chief of police,
Inspector William Sculpher, grabbed the letter and, accompanied
by police officer Albert Lamy, set off for the airport. They arrived
to find only the marks of landing wheels on the grass, and some
smashed windows where the Germans had broken into the terminal
building. The Germans had been scared off by the appearance of
three RAF planes. It had been a false alarm.

'It was a peculiar feeling at the airport – a place so usually full
of noise and bustle was then as quiet as a grave, with only sufficient
wind to rattle the hangar door, and these noises did not help our
peace of mind,' Lamy wrote later in his private memoirs.

On the evening of the same day, five German aircraft circled
Guernsey, and then came in to land. This time they had come to
stay. Sculpher returned to the airport to meet the aircrafts' occupants and to deliver the letter. He was commanded to escort
the Germans into town, where they commandeered a hotel for
their headquarters and asked to see representatives of the island's
government. Within a few hours, troop-carriers began to land.

This was the moment that Ambrose Sherwill, Guernsey's President of the Controlling Committee, had been dreading for nearly a month: 'As with my fellow islanders, I had awaited the coming of the Germans. I had ample time to reflect on the attitude I must adopt. God knows, my resources were slender enough. I must be courteous – it would be fatuous to be rude – I must try to appear to be honesty personified for they were bound to be suspicious,' he wrote in his memoirs.

Sherwill had watched the Germans land, and while Sculpher was on his way to the airport, he phoned the Home Office for the last time to tell them the news. Then he ate his dinner hurriedly.

'Soon the police car bearing a young German officer in flying kit arrived at my home. It was about 7.30 p.m. and my two children were sleeping in the hall for safety from bombing. I went out to meet him and asked him to come to the side door. He was instantly suspicious, but when I explained, he said he wouldn't dream of disturbing my children. He was charming and did his utmost to put me at my ease and not to make me feel the humiliating position I was in.'

Sherwill was taken to the Germans' headquarters, where he met Major Albrecht Lanz, the commander, and his aide Major-Doktor Maass. To Sherwill's relief, Dr Maass spoke impeccable English, having studied tropical medicine at Liverpool University. The three men sat down at the end of a long table covered with a white tablecloth. Sherwill noticed that Lanz seemed very tired. He described the occasion in his memoirs:

> I had put my decorations from the First World War [Sherwill had won the Military Cross] in my pocket and I now pulled them out and laid them on the table in front of Dr Maass, saying to him as I did so: 'Please tell Major Lanz that I, too, have been a soldier. I bitterly regret that I am one no longer. As there isn't a rifle in the island, I realise I must obey orders. As a former soldier, I know how to do this.'
>
> Lanz picked up my medals and at least went through the motions of examining them carefully and then gravely handed them back to me. He then proceeded to dictate his orders.

Sherwill drew up the orders as Lanz commanded, and they were published in a special edition of the island's papers the following day. The orders imposed a curfew, a ban on the sale of petrol and the use of boats or motor cars, the handing in of all weapons and the advance of all clocks one hour, in accordance with Central European Time. The papers published a signed statement from the Bailiff, Victor Carey, requesting that no resistance be made to the Germans and that their orders should be obeyed.

Jersey was occupied the next day, 1 July. Leaflets were dropped by German planes demanding that white flags be put out and white crosses painted in prominent places to indicate surrender. The order was promptly complied with, and a detachment of naval assault troops and an infantry company landed at the airport. In the afternoon troop-carriers arrived, also bearing German officials, and they were greeted with handshakes by Alexander Coutanche, the Bailiff, who headed an official deputation which included the Attorney General, Charles Duret Aubin. Similar orders of occupation to those Guernsey had had to promulgate were drawn up for publication, and Coutanche delegated a States official to find the Germans billets in local hotels. Afterwards, Coutanche returned home. As he recorded in his memoirs, he felt so depressed that he went into the garden to do some much-needed weeding.

Two days later Guernsey's lifeboat was used to carry Major Lanz and Dr Maass to Sark. Sybil Hathaway, the Dame of Sark, had planned their reception with a sense of the theatrical: the Seneschal (a senior island official) met the German officers at the harbour and accompanied them up to the Seigneurie, the Dame's house, where the Dame's maid announced them as if they were guests. After the Dame had undertaken to have the orders of occupation publicised, she invited them to lunch. They signed her visitors' book before leaving.

The Germans were delighted; the invasion had gone off without a hitch. Press releases were drawn up in Berlin celebrating another great victory for Hitler through the combined efforts of his navy, air force and army. In fact, the meticulous preparations drawn up by the German headquarters in France for a battle in the islands had proved unnecessary. Contrary to German expectations, the invaders had been greeted with polite deference by the conquered subjects of the proud nation. There seemed no greater possible proof of the invincibility of the Third Reich – the next stop would surely be Bournemouth. The Germans were flushed with their recent victories, and the charms of the Channel Islands seemed their just deserts.

Initially the Germans had only a small force on the islands, brought in by air to avoid the more vulnerable sea route. Men and equipment could be ill-spared from more pressing duties in France. After a few weeks, ships brought reinforcements from St Malo, and by December 1940 there were 1750 Germans on Jersey and a similar number on Guernsey.

Over the next five years, almost every German soldier arriving on the islands from France was struck by four things: the cleanliness, the flowers, the palm trees and the British policemen. The last reminded them of their school English textbooks. The first two made them feel at home, and the palm trees astonished them – they had thought they were on the Isle of Wight, but perhaps they were off the coast of Africa after all. Amused islanders put them right.

German soldier Werner Grosskopf was one of the first to arrive:

> I didn't know I was going to the islands. We got a top secret order and we wondered if we were going to invade England. We had been trained for weeks on the Normandy beaches. We weren't told where we were going until we were on the ships.
>
> It was a wonderful day when we sailed – a blue sky – and there was real enthusiasm on the ship. The harbour front of St Helier with the white villas and houses and the blue sky above and the blue sea below looked wonderful. When we landed I thought back to my time as an exchange pupil in England in 1929 when I learnt about English life. We were in a country where milk and honey were flowing day and night. We were all on top of the world at that moment. We felt like holiday-makers.

Another German soldier, Charlie Curth, was never to leave the islands, but stayed on in Alderney after the war. When he first landed, his unit was lined up in front of a bed of flowers and his Feldwebel (sergeant) barked at them: 'You can look at the flowers, you can smell the flowers, but in no circumstances are you to pick the flowers.'

This was to be a model occupation. The cordial relations between the German commander and the island authorities were to be matched by the polite helpfulness of the islanders and the law-abiding soldiers. It quickly became apparent that there was no need for the troops always to carry a pistol or to wear a steel helmet. After the fighting in Poland, the Low Countries and France, and the tense expectation of an imminent invasion of England, the Channel Islands seemed like a holiday camp to the Germans.

The sun was shining, the white beaches were unusually empty and as enticing as ever. There were empty hotels with the beds made up and the food sitting in the cupboards waiting to be eaten. It was easy for the Germans to forget that this was an occupation. They were enchanted by the islands' little coves, the steep cliffs covered with wildflowers and the bright blue sea. They responded with a touching romanticism, describing in detail the landscape and sunsets in their diaries, in poetry and in paintings.

There was an abundance of fruit just ripening: melons, figs, grapes and strawberries – not to mention tons of tomatoes. The shops were stocked with goods which had long been unobtainable back in Germany. The soldiers teemed through St Helier and St Peter Port buying stockings, shoes, make-up, lingerie, chocolates and souvenirs to send home to their loved ones. The islands' shop-keepers, glad of the custom, accepted the unfamiliar Reichsmarks happily enough.

The shops grew emptier in the course of the Occupation, but most of what the Germans discovered in their first few days on the islands was to remain true for the next five years. The soldiers who were posted there have the warmest memories of the islands, and frequently draw comparisons with the horrific suffering on the Eastern Front, where many of them also served. In Russia, thousands of their compatriots died in the inhospitable winters and fierce fighting. For much of the year the roads and the barracks were a morass of mud; there were few comforts, and constant fear of partisans. By contrast, the Channel Islands were among the safest places to spend the war: the RAF made only a few bombing raids, there was no fighting and no partisan activities. The billets were comfortable, with soft beds, clean linen and gleaming bathrooms. The officers were put up in the best houses and in the islands' many hotels. They drank out of crystal glasses and ate off china plates set on damask tablecloths. Such luxuries were unheard of on the Eastern Front.

Artillery officer Hans Stumpf was so impressed by the thick carpets and Persian rugs in the house where he was billeted that it inspired a post-war passion for collecting rugs. One German soldier spent much of his time buying George III silver from islanders to send home.

It was more like a holiday than a war, remembered nineteen-year-old naval rating Willi Reiman, who arrived on the islands in 1943:

> I remember there were a lot of palms on Guernsey. It was exciting to be in a foreign country and the climate was almost tropical. We all enjoyed the place without thinking about what we were doing there. I was fascinated by the light blue sea. We didn't take the war too seriously; we didn't think it was very important and we were very young. We enjoyed everything. On the Channel Islands, there was no war. We were playing at being at war.

The troops loved swimming in the sea, which they thought warm even in January. They played football on the beaches and were delighted to find a number of good tennis courts; their matches often drew a knot of islanders to watch.

Initially the islanders kept their distance, remembered Wemer Grosskopf: 'At first the inhabitants were, quite naturally, shocked. They were sad and surprised. They were speechless when the Germans came overnight. In the first few months, it was very difficult to make contact with the inhabitants because there were language difficulties. It was a period of probing. Everyone looked at everyone suspiciously, but later, that naturally changed. Human contacts were made.'

Even from the start, however, many Germans were surprised by the number of islanders who were prepared to be friendly. Kapitän Karl-Heinz Kassens described how the sports arranged for the soldiers helped to overcome the islanders' reserve:

In the beginning the atmosphere was really very good; we had a lot of fun. There was a lot of football – there were matches between batteries and companies – and once a year there was a big sports festival. We played handball as well and a lot of locals used to come to watch the games. You could easily meet civilians on Jersey and Guernsey. Even more easily in the summer when you met them on the beaches. Everyone looks the same in a bathing suit.

The Germans were surprised to find little trace of hostility or resentment. Hans Stumpf believes that the Germans behaved better on the Channel Islands than in France, where he was also posted. Leutnant Johannes Kegelman thinks there was an understanding between the British and the Germans which enabled them to live peacefully side by side:

We got on with the islanders because we had the same style of life and the same opinions. We both liked motor cars, radios and dancing and we had a lot of the same customs. I had learnt English at school and, as a young boy, we liked English things. Our parents and our history lessons told us that we were related to the British royal family. We couldn't understand why England was always fighting Germany.

The islanders were equally surprised by the character of their occupiers. British propaganda had portrayed these men as brutal, square-headed Nazis. Islanders were expecting the treatment they believed had been meted out in France and Belgium where, according to the newspapers, Germans had hacked off the arms of children with their bayonets as they marched past. Stories, dating from the First World War, had circulated around the islands that Germans raped girls and ate babies. Yet the German soldiers who occupied the Channel Islands were polite and friendly. The day after their arrival on Guernsey, they were buying girls and children ice creams at the harbour in St Peter Port. Guernsey farmer Tom Mansell recalled, 'The Germans didn't hate the British; they used to call out "Cousin, cousin!"'

Many islanders would have agreed with James Ryan, a cantankerous First World War veteran, when he admitted in his private memoirs how well-behaved the first Germans were: 'They got off pavements, admired our well laid-out gardens and they were wonderful with children ... It was a common sight to see them giving circus rides to small boys, playing ball games and nursing babies ... Surely, we all thought, men who loved children, flowers and animals must have a deal of good in them.'

All the islanders noticed the smartness of the Germans' uniforms; they wore real leather belts, and their boots and buttons were polished till they shone. Their discipline was impeccable – in the first few months there was only one allegation of rape, which provoked Dr Maass's fury and an immediate inquiry. The island girls' initial caution was soon worn thin by curiosity. A few weeks after the Germans' arrival, James Ryan was complaining in his diary that the girls had not hesitated for a moment, and that many of them were already flirting with Germans.

There were ample opportunities to meet the strangers. On 12 July 1940, the *Guernsey Evening Press* announced that a number of German officers had enjoyed a cricket match and 'joined players and their friends in the pavilion during the tea interval and they all appeared very much at home'. By 16 July – only two weeks after the start of the Occupation – the *Evening Press* was announcing that dances would be held every Thursday 'by kind permission of the German commandant', and the public was specifically notified that German officers and troops would attend. On 22 July, the paper reported a dance, well attended by Germans, which had pulsated to the rhythms of the tango and Viennese waltzes.

While the islands were adjusting to their new status as an occupied territory, the British government was devoting an extraordinary amount of time – given the threat of an imminent invasion of Britain itself – to planning their recapture. Prime Minister Winston Churchill had been reluctant to surrender the islands without a fight, and he lost no time in weighing up the chances of getting them back. Abandoning the Channel Islands had been a bitter blow to British prestige. Home Intelligence, which was monitoring British public opinion, reported 'the first real dismay' of the war at their loss, which may have brought home for the first time the very real possibility of the Germans landing in Britain. Churchill wanted a stunning military feat in order to restore wounded British pride. It was to take a string of costly and pointless military raids during the first few months of the Occupation to convince him that the Germans would be extremely difficult to dislodge.

On 2 July, the day after the German invasion, Churchill was ordering plans to be drawn up for raids on the islands: 'If it be true that a few hundred German troops have been landed on Jersey or Guernsey by troop carriers, plans should be studied to land secretly by night on the islands and kill or capture the invaders. This is exactly one of the exploits for which the Commandos would be suited . . . Pray let me have a plan.'

Four days later, Churchill had a plan – of sorts. Second Lieutenant Hubert Nicolle, a Guernseyman, equipped with a canoe, had left Devonport on the south coast in a submarine on a reconnaissance trip to Guernsey. It was the first leg of an ambitious operation codenamed Anger/Ambassador. The preparations had been rushed through to please Churchill. Nicolle had no navigation experience, and the canoe he had would not even fit through the submarine's hatch. After a few mishaps, he was eventually landed on Guernsey. Three days later, as the second leg of the operation, two other Guernseymen, Second Lieutenants Philip Martel and Desmond Mulholland, were landed on the island for further reconnaissance, and Nicolle was safely picked up.

On 14 July, the final and most ambitious leg of the operation began; 140 men were to land on Guernsey by launch, destroy the German planes at the airport, attack German billets and take prisoners, all within one hour and forty minutes. In the event, the raid was farcical. One launch headed off in completely the wrong direction, another sprang a leak, and the third successfully landed on the Jerbourg peninsula, only to find no Germans to attack. The expedition eventually made it back to Britain, but they had accomplished nothing, and had not even managed to pick up Martel and Mulholland. An inquiry was launched, and concluded that the commandos had shown a 'regrettable hesitation in entering deep water – even to avoid the risk of capture or death'.

The Germans were, however, unnerved by the failed raid, and ordered the island authorities to search for British agents. Ambrose Sherwill, President of the Guernsey Controlling Committee, told the island's police: 'I foresee all sorts of trouble if people land here clandestinely . . . however detestable the duty of reporting the presence in our midst of such strangers may be, in the present circumstances I can see no way of avoiding it.'

On 18 July, Sherwill wrote a letter to Charles Markbreiter at the Home Office which he hoped the Germans would help to deliver once they had read the contents. Sherwill was anxious to bring an end to the raids, which he believed were jeopardising good relations with the Germans: 'I do not know what the object of the landing was but to us it seems senseless . . . The Bailiff was amazed when he learned of the landing and in writing to you thus, I know I am expressing his view and that of prominent people here.'

The letter was never sent to the Home Office, but it reveals the extremely difficult position in which the Guernsey government found itself. Sherwill and his colleagues were at a delicate stage of launching the Model Occupation. They did not want British servicemen secretly landing on the island and confronting them with a difficult dilemma: it would be treason to hand them over to the Germans, but hiding them might end all hope of a peaceful Occupation. To further complicate matters, many senior members of the Guernsey government – including Sherwill – had sons serving in the British Forces, and they feared that if the British continued to use islanders for these dangerous raids, their sons could be on the next one.

Martel and Mulholland, tired of waiting for a boat to come and rescue them, gave themselves up with the help of Sherwill. Some militia uniforms had been found for them, and the Germans treated them as prisoners of war and sent them to camps in Germany, rather than as secret agents, which could have meant the death sentence.

Meanwhile, the pressure on the Germans was maintained. For three successive days in mid-August there were air raids on Guernsey aerodrome. An official German report said that on one of these, five English planes had killed one soldier and wounded four civilians. Periodic attacks by the RAF were to make islanders living or working near military installations extremely nervous, but the raids were restricted for fear of causing large civilian casualties.

Churchill still wanted more information about the occupied islands, and a few weeks later, at the beginning of September, Hubert Nicolle was sent back with Second Lieutenant James Symes, another Guernseyman. The two men were briefed to find out how well-off Guernsey was for supplies of food, fuel and medicines. They landed on the south coast of the island again, and as Nicolle had done on his previous visit, he made straight for the farm of his old schoolfriend Tom Mansell, who remembers: 'The first time Nicolle arrived at 5 a.m. and joined us for a big breakfast. He walked up from the shore. He knew I had a milk round and delivered milk to his parents, so I gave him a lift. I showed him gun emplacements near the farm. We didn't think of the danger.'*

The operation went according to plan, and Nicolle and Symes completed their research and were ready at the rendezvous point to be picked up at the arranged time. But bad weather and a series of moonlit nights prevented the boat from getting in to the shore. The two men were forced to hide with relatives and friends for more than six weeks, and became increasingly worried about the danger in which they were putting them. They decided to hand themselves in after the Germans, alerted to the presence of agents on the island, published a notice ordering all British soldiers who had not been evacuated to surrender, and promising to treat them as prisoners of war and to take no action against those who had helped them.† Uniforms were found for the secret agents, and Sherwill took on the unenviable job of persuading their reluctant parents that the Germans' word could be trusted.

This time, however, the Germans denounced Nicolle and Symes as spies. The two Guernseymen were imprisoned, court-martialled and sentenced to death. Thirteen of their relatives and friends who had helped them hide were also arrested. The Germans discovered that Sherwill had known of the agents' presence on the island, and he too was arrested. All civilian radios on the island were temporarily confiscated as a punishment for the entire population.

Tom Mansell was arrested for having helped Nicolle. His sister Vivyan recalls: 'The day the Germans came to arrest my brother was the worst of the Occupation. One of the soldiers who came to arrest him was a German Canadian who had been conscripted on

---

* Memories of these events vary among other participants.
† It is alleged that at this time the Germans threatened to shoot twenty leading islanders unless they could be satisfied that no one was harbouring members of the British armed forces.

a visit back to Germany to visit his mother – he told me this while
he watched me packing Tom's suitcase, and he urged me to put in
as many warm clothes as possible.'

The recently-arrived Befehlshaber (Fortress Kommandant, in
overall charge of the islands), Oberst Graf von Schmettow, intervened, halting the death sentence and referring the verdict on Nicolle and Symes to his superiors. The matter was taken all the way
to Berlin. At the end of December 1940, after the islanders and
agents had spent two months in Cherche-Midi prison in Paris, the
Feldkommandantur announced that it had been decided that Nicolle and Symes were guilty of espionage, and that those who had
helped them, Sherwill included, were guilty of high treason according to German law, but that they had decided to be merciful. No
one would be executed. The agents would be treated as prisoners
of war, and their relatives and friends would be released from their
French prisons. Sherwill would also be released, but he was banned
from holding public office.

Unfortunately the news came a few days too late for Louis Symes,
the father of James; he had been a prisoner of war in the First
World War, and faced with the prospect of another imprisonment
by the Germans, he slashed his wrists and was found dead in his
cell in Cherche-Midi.

The most persistent question in the minds of all those involved
was how the Germans had known that Nicolle and Symes were
spies. In Guernsey's German archives, it is recorded that one of
the 'friends' who helped hide the agents, and who was arrested
along with her parents, had given 'truthful evidence'. Opinion is
sharply divided as to this woman's role; Hubert Nicolle denies she
informed on them, but Tom Mansell is not so sure:

> I know she was keeping company with a German officer. I could
> never work out why her parents were interned too; they took it very
> badly. I wouldn't have anything to do with her. Collaborating with
> the enemy was about the lousiest thing you could do, no matter
> how nice they might be. If you inform the enemy of the where-
> abouts of a British soldier that is treasonable, surely? Nicolle and
> Symes were damned lucky to get away with it – they should have
> been shot. I don't know if I can forgive her after all this time. She

liked to be in the limelight. Her idea was that the Germans were going to win everything and she'd be fine going around with them.

We [Tom, Vivyan Mansell and Nicolle] have a tea party every 8 July – cucumber sandwiches and Guernsey gâche – it's the anniversary of Nicolle's first landing.

Ambrose Sherwill kept a diary of his three-month solitary confinement in Cherche-Midi prison; most of his daily entries consist of a terse 'Nothing.' He was very cold and very lonely. In his memoirs he wrote: 'I swung without evident reason from hilarity to deep depression and back again . . . I understood what it meant to talk of the balance of your mind being disturbed.' Sherwill spent his time working on the defence of the thirteen imprisoned islanders. He had been told their trial would take place in Paris, and he planned to argue that 'I had done my damnedest to run the civilian side in accordance with the laws of war, and that I had been completely frustrated by the, to me, utterly obnoxious action of the British government of sending in Guernsey boys for the purpose of espionage . . . either I was guilty of treason to Britain or of "treason felony" to the Germans. I was in an impossible position.'

The whole affair, and his own fall from power, was a tremendous personal crisis for Sherwill. He had been faced with a three-way conflict of duties: the interests of the islanders for a peaceful occupation; the safety of the individual agents and their families; and his oath of loyalty to the British Crown. In his memoirs he went over and over whether he could have acted differently. The only conclusion he appears to reach is fury with the British government for needlessly placing him in such an impossible position, and gratitude to the Germans for their mercy. He wrote: 'The Nicolle/Symes affair redounds greatly to the honour not only of the German High Command, but also of the more junior officers in command in both Jersey and Guernsey. Bandelow [one of the German officers on Guernsey] moved heaven and earth to get us released alive, and I thanked him in person.'*

---

* Sherwill felt such gratitude towards Major Bandelow that after the war he went to considerable lengths to help him when impoverished, defeated Germany had few jobs for middle-aged ex-majors. Sherwill arranged an anonymous donation of £100 through the Salvation Army for Bandelow and his family, and secured him a job as a caretaker with the Allied Forces in Germany.

By December 1941 the number of Germans on the islands had increased to 11,500, and by mid-1942 the total for all the islands had reached thirty-seven thousand, a higher concentration of armed forces per square mile than in Germany itself. The islands' population after the evacuation was just over sixty thousand, so there was more than one German to every two islanders. On Guernsey nearly half the population had been evacuated, and the ratio was almost 1:1. Such large numbers of Germans meant that all but a tiny handful of islanders on remote farms were forced into daily contact with the occupying forces. Many had soldiers billeted in their homes or as next-door neighbours.

One of the greatest dilemmas of the Occupation began on the second day, with those ice creams the Germans bought at St Peter Port harbour. Namely, how much social interaction with the enemy was compatible with patriotism? Every islander, from young children to the Bailiff, had to decide what kind of behaviour they were going to adopt towards the enemy. The simplest human exchanges became the subject of anguished moral searching. Did one shake a German's proffered hand? Did one reply to a cheery, guttural 'Good morning'? Did one give directions to a soldier bewildered by the islands' tiny back lanes? In his memoirs, Ambrose Sherwill minutely examined his conscience over the occasions on which he had accepted German hospitality. Had he been right to accept a glass of champagne? he asked himself, adding by way of partial exoneration that he loathed champagne.

There was no precedent in British history for this situation, and there had been no guidance from the British government prior to the Occupation. The island governments coined a phrase to indicate their policy on behaviour towards the Germans: 'correct relations'. Relationships were to be coldly polite: irreproachable but distant. At an official level this could perhaps be achieved, but in the day-to-day exchanges between islanders and Germans living cheek by jowl for several years, it was nigh impossible. While Sherwill might have satisfied himself that his behaviour met his criteria for 'correctness', his wife May was faced with far more complex problems when she had to learn to live with eighty soldiers billeted in her large house with her and her two small boys. Although her three older children were fighting in the war and her husband was

in internment, she wrote to him that the Germans were 'individu-
ally so nice, and the officer-in-charge is rather like our John [her
son, then serving in the Royal Navy]. He is most courteous and
considerate.' By the end of the war 'German John' and 'dear old
Fritz', who had smuggled in food for her younger children, were
firm friends.

There was no clear line between where 'correct relations' ended
and fraternisation began. What was perfectly acceptable to one
family was infamous fraternisation to another. Neighbours became
estranged over the issue; individuals within families disagreed. The
confusion generated accusations and counter accusations between
neighbours and relatives. There was ample room for misunder-
standings; a typically ludicrous example was when the mother of a
Jersey boy, Joe Miere, was told that her son had been seen out in
the town with two German soldiers; what the accuser had failed to
notice was that Miere was handcuffed to both of them, and under
arrest.

Dorothy Blackwell, a Jersey housewife, once walked into a neighbour's kitchen and, to her horror, found a German sitting there:
'To us, having anything to do with Germans was inexcusable; we
wouldn't have anything to do with them. It was quite difficult for
some people because the Germans – those who spoke English –
were quite friendly.'

To add a twist of bitterness to this vexed question of 'correct
relations', many families, like the Sherwills, had members serving
in the war; the friendly Hans who might appear on the doorstep
was this loved one's enemy. Tomorrow he might be firing the
torpedo which would kill your son or brother. Joe Miere refused
to shake a German soldier's hand because his brothers were serving
in the forces; this was a code of behaviour which the German
immediately understood and respected. But even the stiffest reserve
softened over the course of five years. Many Germans were clearly
lonely and homesick, and as Jerseyman Fred Woodall poignantly
noted in his diary, they 'would do anything to be invited to someone's house for a cup of tea'.

One of the main factors which led to the breaking down
of the barriers between the two peoples was the need for food.
The Germans would let islander neighbours come in to harvest

unwanted vegetables in the gardens of their billets, and there are many stories of Germans giving presents of bread or sausage. The Germans remember the 'common people' being the most friendly; perhaps they were in the most need. The stories of two islanders bear this out.

Herbert Nichols had reason to resent the Germans more than most, because his father was killed in action in North Africa in 1942. His mother would never have anything to do with the Germans, but thirteen-year-old Herbert was the eldest of six hungry children, and he keenly felt his responsibilities to obtain food. The beaches and headlands were heavily mined and fenced off, but Herbert climbed over the barbed wire in full view of the German sentry, and set his lobster pots off the rocks. No one else was trying to catch the spider crabs that were found there, and he got a good haul. After watching him several times, a German stopped Herbert on his return and asked what was in his sack. From then on the German would lift the pot before he arrived: 'I taught him how to bait it with limpets. I said I didn't mind him emptying the pot but he must bait it afterwards. After that he emptied the pot in the morning and I did in the afternoon and we'd compare our catches.'

Daphne Pope, one of the few civilians left on Alderney, had a growing family to feed – she had several children in the course of the Occupation. So when a German soldier whom she knew as Wilhelm offered her bread in return for doing his washing she readily agreed, as many island women did. It developed into a friendship which lasted the war:

Wilhelm was the sort of German who doesn't want to see or hear anything nasty. He kept his head down and he wanted a nice, quiet life in the army. I found out a little about Wilhelm, but ever so slowly. He was careful. He was a watch- and clock-maker and his mother sold them in a little shop. She wrote a letter to him which he brought to me: 'Thank the English family for looking after my dear boy. I know now there are kind people even among the English.' Her husband had been killed in the First World War. I asked him if he hated the English and he said, 'No. I hate war.' He was no Nazi.

Wilhelm was not unusual. It is striking how many of the German soldiers confided to the islanders their misgivings about Hitler and their reluctance to be fighting this war. In part, no doubt, they hoped thereby to win the islanders' sympathy and trust, but perhaps it was also a relief safely to give vent to their grievances.

Bernard Hassall, a Jersey boy, got to know many Germans while he worked in his father's photography shop in St Helier, and later when he was drafted to work in a German supply store:

> Most of the Germans that came into the islands weren't fighting men at all; they were family men. I had happier times during the Occupation than in all the years since. The Germans never talked about the war, I never heard them say, 'We've got the tommies!' They never threw snide remarks.
>
> After the war I used to write to Hans, who was a lovely chap. He was from the Austrian Tyrol; he was about fifty and a very quiet and unassuming man. Hans and I used to make out the progress of the war on the Eastern Front on a map. He would listen to German radio, and I had a crystal radio set [this was after all radio sets had been banned to civilians in June 1942] and we'd compare notes. He used to ask every morning, 'What news is there? What's up?'
>
> You couldn't be in the store room without them talking and they'd show you photos of their wives and kids. Once a man was sobbing his eyes out and he'd just had news that all his family had been blotted out in a bombing raid. I lit a cigarette for him and told him to put it in his mouth. People say, 'Well it was the enemy and damn good luck.' But they are still human beings.

Jersey clerk Norman Le Brocq also used to listen to the radio with a German after the ban. When he went to visit his grandparents in the country at weekends, a soldier known as Willi would come across the courtyard from his billet, bringing a radio, and they would listen to the news together.

Harry Aubin was a small boy when the back yard of his family's shop on Jersey was requisitioned as a bicycle park for the Germans' Soldatenheim (recreation centre) next door. Germans were in and out every day:

They were the enemy, but often we saw ordinary men who wanted to be at home with their family. One German once came in and he told us he had a six-year-old daughter whom he couldn't watch grow up. He added, 'Germany is quite big enough for me without this war.'

On another occasion, a German was talking with us about politics and my father said perhaps Hitler had done some good for the Germans with unemployment and welfare. The German replied, 'Hitler will be the undertaker of Germany and Britain must help us destroy the Nazis.'

Keeping a distance was particularly difficult when German soldiers and islanders shared a common religion. The soldiers attended the local churches on Guernsey and Jersey, and with the preacher telling his congregation to love their enemies, confusion in the minds of islanders must have been rife. Daphne Pope and Wilhelm on Alderney were both Catholics:

He did me a good turn by finding an empty building – it was a Methodist chapel – and going to the officer and asking to use it. The officer was very anti-religious, but Wilhelm persuaded him by saying there was a good organ which he wanted to play. Religion was no good, but music was fine with the Germans. The chapel was used by both the Catholic and the Evangelical padres throughout the war. I got my child christened by a German.

Vivyan Mansell, a Guernsey farmer's daughter, vividly recalled a poignant scene when an ethnic German Luxemburger serving in the Wehrmacht came to say goodbye after he had been ordered to the Eastern Front at short notice. Her mother had helped him when he was sick. The soldier spoke perfect English, having studied theology at a Jesuit college in London: 'He said he wanted to bless this house and he pulled out of his uniform a rosary and he blessed the house and each of us in Latin very solemnly. Then he shook each of us by the hand. It was very dramatic and rather sad. We told him to get in touch if he got through, but we never heard of him again. He said we should have both been fighting Russia together.'

There were many acts of kindness to the islanders on the part of the Germans. Maurice Green, the only diabetic to survive the

Occupation on Jersey, partly owed his life to the goodness of two
Germans:

> A German doctor took a liking to me; he used to come and do
> jigsaws with me. He was a really nice fellow. I discharged myself
> from hospital (I was only fourteen) because if I was going to die, I
> wanted to die at home.
>   One morning a German soldier appeared at the door. He said –
> in French – that he understood there was a diabetic boy in this
> house. The doctor had told him. The soldier had been looking all
> over Europe for insulin for his mother. 'Last week the RAF bombed
> Cologne and my mother is dead. You use the three bottles of insulin
> I found,' he said. I rationed it out at ten units a day and it kept me
> alive for several months.

Don Guilbert, who later became a Deputy in the Guernsey States,
recounts the story of a local musician who suffered from a skin
disease on his hands.

> A German gave him some ointment and to thank him the musician
> invited the German to his home. The musician's teenage daughter
> met the German and started going to concerts with him – but it was
> no more than that. Was that wrong? The German was a musician
> and the girl was something of a singer. The German went to the
> family to make music. What should the man have done? Not
> accepted the ointment? There are still a few who hold it against the
> musician.

If even simple friendships provoked controversy, it is easy to understand how, to this day, one of the most divisive issues of the Occupation has been the behaviour of the women who had affairs with
Germans. The subject has been shrouded in secrecy; the women
either left the islands, or they grew respectable with time, and their
German-fathered offspring were accepted as islanders.

What attracted the island women to the Germans? Did they feel
the tug of competing loyalties? How did other islanders treat them
at the time, and subsequently? What was their response to
the animosity they provoked? How many women were involved?

Piecing together the answers is like a detective story – without the criminals. The characters left no memoirs or diaries. Those women still alive have little wish to tell their stories; for many of them it is a chapter of great pain in their lives, and they see no point in reopening old wounds. The former German soldiers, however, are willing to tell the story, and they proudly show off the treasured, well-thumbed photos of their Guernsey or Jersey girlfriends. With the help of police records, newspaper articles, diaries and a handful of frank islanders, it is possible to sketch the outlines of an experience that hundreds of island women may have shared.

Islanders have always claimed that only a small number of girls went with German soldiers; the Germans disagree. Fifty years on, it is probably impossible to know the truth. What is certain is that during the Occupation the illegitimacy rate leapt dramatically on Jersey and Guernsey – particularly the latter. On Jersey it doubled to 11 per cent of all births, while on Guernsey it quadrupled to 21.8 per cent. These figures do not include the babies of married women whose husbands were away; on both islands, these babies would automatically be registered under the husband's name. The number of babies is not necessarily an indication of the number of affairs; not all pregnancies would have been brought to term, nor would all relationships have resulted in pregnancies.

Oberleutnant Randolf Kugler remembers that by the time he arrived on Jersey, in 1944, most of the young soldiers, and even some of the married ones, had girlfriends amongst the islanders: 'My impression was that it was like in a German port city.' Kugler came to Jersey shortly before all links with France were cut following the French liberation. Dances had been banned as a gesture of respect for those fighting on the Eastern Front, but none of these obstacles proved important; even at that stage of the war he quickly made friends with the many girls from St Helier whom he met in the cafés and bars. With one of them he was to fall in love.

Throughout the Occupation, there were plenty of opportunities for Germans and island women to meet. Werner Grosskopf remembers that it was easy to make dates with local girls because 'you could accost them when on guard duty in the country'. Swiss maids from the hotels became housekeepers in the German billets and introduced their friends to the young officers. A number of island girls took jobs as secretaries and interpreters for the Germans. Hans Stumpf met his girlfriend, 'Joyce', when she was working in an office with him. Some of these girls spoke German so well they could have been German, commented Kurt Spangersburg, a member of a machine-gun battalion on the islands from 1940 to 1945.

Several times, the German authorities issued bans against fraternisation, but they seem to have been completely disregarded. When Leutnant Johannes Kegelman arrived in 1944 he was told to impose such a ban among his men: 'Admiral Hüffmeier [the then Inselkommandant – Island Commandant] put out an order banning any relationships, but no one obeyed him. Men under my command had girlfriends. A lot of them had lived there for four years – you can't stop connections like that. I didn't stop them, I didn't try to implement Hüffmeier's orders.' Many other officers adopted Kegelman's policy.

The tolerance of the authorities is illustrated in a recollection of naval rating Willi Reiman: 'We weren't supposed to mix with islanders, but I remember one officer called Schmidt. He had a Guernsey girlfriend and she would come to Alderney to visit him and sometimes he would go to Guernsey. We knew because I was a telegraphist and we heard the messages telling him she was coming. She spoke very good German.'

In 1944 Baron von Aufsess, the Head of Civil Affairs in the Feldkommandantur, commented on the 'complete amity reigning on the beaches between German soldiers and local girls'. He added, presumably from his own experience: 'With a few exceptions, the girl will surrender to her partner readily enough, provided this can be effected in proper privacy. The Englishwoman is astoundingly simple, effortless and swift in her lovemaking. While the Frenchwoman involves herself totally in the game, which she likes to be conducted along intellectual lines, for the Englishwoman it is a surprisingly straightforward, physical matter.'

What attracted the island women to the enemy? Firstly, a large proportion of Channel Island men were away serving in the British forces. Many girlfriends and wives were left alone for five years, with little news of their men other than the short messages arranged by the Red Cross to be sent from England via neutral Switzerland, if they were lucky. Five years is a long time to wait for a loved one. A long time for girls in their teens coming to sexual maturity and surrounded by men, but of the wrong nationality. Some women didn't hesitate; they began flirting with Germans soon after their arrival, and enjoyed a string of liaisons. Others were more reluctant, and maintained a reserve which tantalised men such as Baron von Aufsess.

The Germans had powerful attractions. The most obvious was that among them were some strikingly handsome men. Island men tended to be dark, short and thick-set; many of the Germans were tall, blond and blue-eyed, and in their uniforms, gold braid and buttons, they were novel and very striking. Seventeen-year-old Jersey girl Mary McCarthy thought the soldiers looked bandy-legged from rickets, but 'the officers were magnificent in their uniforms. Jerseywomen had never seen such magnificent men; they were used to English tourists who were pale, skinny clerks from London.'

Nudity was part of the Nazi fetishisation of masculinity and athleticism, and the Germans flaunted their fit bodies on the beaches. The islanders were astonished by their craze for sun-bathing; all the more so when they heard that one German had died of sunstroke after covering himself in bacon fat and falling asleep in the sun. On all the beaches, that summer of 1940, the Germans stripped off to the barest minimum. Genteel old ladies were horrified by their lack of modesty, but their bronzed muscles caught the eye of some of the island girls. It was not easy to remember that these men were the enemy when they were wearing no uniforms, and were distinguishable from the island men only by their blond hair and impressive physiques. Such sensualism was beyond the experience of island life, bound by the strictures of church or chapel and the rigours of farm life.

Many women were won over by the chivalrous courtesy of the Germans, which was in sharp contrast to the way some of them were used to being treated. On Guernsey, Vivyan Mansell was astonished when a German soldier insisted on pushing her wheel-barrow of manure for her. Even the daughters of prosperous middle-class farmers were expected to milk the cows twice a day, before and after school, and in traditional Jersey families daughters, wives and sisters waited on the menfolk, said Mary McCarthy: 'Jerseymen were horrible to their women. Women had to do heavy work in the fields, milk the cows and look after the house and the children. There was also a lot of incest. Then along came the Germans; many of them had never known such kindness.'

German officer Hans Stumpf showed a meticulous concern for the proprieties of courtship when he fell in love with Joyce:

> She wanted to learn German and I agreed to practise with her. But I said we must get permission from her parents first. I went over to Guernsey [she was working on Jersey] to visit her parents and ask their permission. They had no objection.
>
> She was very kind to me; we liked each other but there were no bed stories. Nothing more than a kiss. I behaved properly – like a gentleman – we would never go arm in arm in the street. I didn't want her to get a bad name.
>
> I used to go to Normandy and bought perfume, soap and under-wear for Joyce and I bought presents for her mother and cigarettes for her father. I used to visit the family.

As the Occupation wore on, the Germans' attractions multiplied. They had more food than the islanders, and many Germans helped feed their girlfriends' families. Young mothers with hungry small children to feed and a husband away in the war were only too grateful for a loaf of bread or a piece of sausage. Randolf Kugler called some such women 'primitive': 'There were girls who expected "payment". They could speak German and they wanted food; they were basically selling themselves. Some women had husbands in the British Forces and they didn't stick to morals. They went very quickly with soldiers and they were like French women. But most of the Channel Island girls were not like that, they had more to offer as personalities.'

The Germans offered women the only release from the boredom and the constant scraping, scrimping and scrounging of life during the Occupation. Time-consuming tasks such as boiling sugar beet, looking after chickens and collecting twigs for fuel fell to women. Everything was shabby and the hard work was endless. Within a few months of the start of the Occupation, there were no new clothes to buy, and no fabric to make them with; it was patch and mend, borrow or barter. There were no cosmetics, perfumes or soap. Mary McCarthy wore the same tweed suit for most of the five years. Daphne Prins turned to her well-thumbed copies of *Vogue* to ease her craving for glamour. Dorothy Blackwell says she lived in wellington boots. The Germans came back from leave in Paris with precious luxuries like soap, lipstick and stockings for their girlfriends.

As the German officers had requisitioned many of the islands' most comfortable houses and hotels, they had access to their wine cellars, and they also brought wine and spirits back from the Continent. They held dinner parties and drinks parties at which it was almost possible to forget, with the music, fun and games, that there was a war going on. Even in the last year of the Occupation, Ober-leutnant Kugler organised parties in his billet, with dancing to his collection of jazz records which he had brought to Jersey. By then the Germans had been put on much-reduced rations, but girlfriends and fellow officers all tried to bring some food and drink. However, Kugler admitted that by the early months of 1945 he no longer had the energy to 'visit' his girlfriend, Colette.

Women who took up with German officers had the luxury of the use of their chauffeur-driven cars. A trip in a convertible, or a lift on a rainy day, were not small thrills when virtually all the private cars on the islands had been requisitioned. Most people counted themselves lucky if they still had the use of a rickety bicycle with hosepiping serving as tyres. Without transport, people couldn't move about the islands to visit friends, go to the cinema, or just have a change of scene.

A German boyfriend could act as a powerful insurance policy; if he was an officer, a woman could ask him to intervene if a friend or relative was in trouble. There were so many petty restrictions during the Occupation that it was almost impossible to avoid at some point being hauled in to the Feldkommandantur over some transgression, and the intercession of a German officer could make the difference between a modest fine and a prison sentence in France. For example, the curfew was strictly enforced by the Guernsey and Jersey police, and the list of those fined for breaking it was long. In summer it was particularly irksome, because the 9 o'clock curfew was before dark. Only girls accompanied by Germans appeared to be exempt. In 1943, Feldkommandant Knackfuss ordered that the Jersey police drop a curfew infraction case against a girl who had been out with a German soldier at the time.

Dancing, parties, picnics on the beach, rides in convertibles, favours from German officers; it was not in the interests of either the Germans or the islanders to talk about such goings-on after the war. They fitted ill with the myth propagated by both the British and the German governments that everyone suffered and 'did their bit' for the war effort. This is one reason why the diary of Cecil Bazeley, preserved in the Imperial War Museum, is so fascinating. It spans three and half years, from 1942 to 1945, and is the most graphic evidence of one story of the Occupation which no one – Germans or islanders – has ever wanted to tell: the privileged life of the top German officers on the island and their coterie of girlfriends. From the pages of cryptic entries in crabbed handwriting there emerges a gripping soap opera, interspersed with copious references to the workings of Bazeley's bowels (a common obsession during the Occupation) and the state of his vegetable patch.

Little is known of Bazeley himself, other than that he was forty-five in 1942 and died in 1988. During the Occupation he was living in one of the grandest houses on Jersey. 'Grey Gables' still stands at the top of the hill above the small town of St Aubins, a large granite mansion built at the turn of the century. Behind the wrought-iron gates a drive bordered with rhododendrons and azaleas sweeps up to the doorstep. It was an idyllic billet for 'Cappy', as Bazeley nicknamed Kapitän Bannach, and a Dr Muller, and it gave the grumpy Bazeley a ringside seat on the comings and goings of their fellow officers and girlfriends.

The most frequent visitors were Oberleutnant Zepernick, adjutant to the Inselkommandant (and, according to Bazeley, the head of the secret police, the Feldpolizei), whose nickname was Zep, and his girlfriend H., a Jerseywoman in her early twenties. Life was a continuous round of entertaining through most of 1942 and 1943. Dr Muller and his girlfriend A. from Norfolk held dinner parties, while Zep and H. enjoyed less sedate pyjama parties with a group of Jersey girls and German officers, at which they played cards and games like hide and seek. There was always plenty to drink, and the parties often didn't wind up until four in the morning. On one occasion there was a fancy-dress party for which H. dressed up as Pierrot and one of her friends as Harlequin. H.'s birthday was celebrated in great style, and Bazeley lists the drinks: champagne, chartreuse, cognac and red wine. In the summer the group of officers and their girlfriends played ping-pong, or took a bottle of wine down to the beach. Sometimes they just whiled away the time listening to records on the gramophone, eating chocolate or playing consequences.

Bazeley joined in the parties, and became a confidant of the German officers, many of whom spoke good English. He enjoyed lengthy conversations with Zep, who would come round for coffee without H. Although Bazeley resented the duties of a servant which Cappy forced on him, he still regularly consulted him over developments in the vegetable patch. But he commented on H.'s behaviour with savage contempt. In 1942 he wrote, ' "Jerrybag" little H carried on with one, or two, or more but she does get and get the things she craves for. They fall for her childish ways and put up with her moods . . . Zep lavished presents on her,' he added acidly. Another entry reads: 'H. gets Zep down – she wants shoes.'

A few months later, on New Year's Day 1943, he wrote that 'we pray the war ends this year, though some don't. They're having the time of their life and on Jersey of all places,' adding that H. is 'rumoured to have been engaged to a German officer – I think she wishes she were. She is desperate for a husband.'

Bazeley's diary charts Zep and H.'s increasingly stormy relationship:

> H. is all dressed up in a posh hat with long ribbons – she has been arguing with Zep. He says he has 180 boys with nothing to do who could follow her around to watch her. Zep has got her father and brother, J., jobs in the Organisation Todt [the German labour organisation] as drivers . . .
>
> Zep and H. are at loggerheads about Germans and British – it cannot last. She reckons she is 100 per cent British . . .
>
> H. puts roses in her hair and leans over the gate to flirt with an officer – Zep gets very fed up . . .

When Zep was away on leave, H. went out with a Jersey boy. More ominously, she also visited the Kommandant's chief of staff Oberst von Helldorf's 'hideout' (second home) at Brampton House where, Bazeley heard, 'they all got as tight as lords. Poor Zep's number is up – the little double crosser.' A few weeks later, Zep confessed to Bazeley that he was worried that H. would cause trouble between him and von Helldorf, 'in which case he will get sent to Russia'. Bazeley remarked that H. never slept with Zep because her mother was very strict, but that A. slept with Dr Muller while his car waited outside the house to take her home. Bazeley couldn't see what A. – unlike H. – got out of her relationship.

Zepernick could be invaluable in a crisis. Once, H. indiscreetly gossiped in town that her brother J. had a wireless after they had been banned, and islanders caught with one were being sent to prison on the Continent. Zepernick joined the family for a 'pow-wow' about how to avoid J. getting caught; the meeting went on for two hours, and Zepernick was much offended when someone suggested he should not be trusted.

H.'s flirtations were conducted very publicly. She enjoyed travelling with Zep in his convertible, and would arrive at 'Grey Gables' with her hair blown about after an exhilarating ride. Bazeley remarked that she went to an amateur opera performance in Cappy's car, arriving in full view of the islanders gathered outside the theatre entrance. H.'s lack of discretion reaped its reward; she and Zep began to receive anonymous letters, and Zepernick worried that others were being sent to his senior officers.

Not everyone was won over by Zepernick's charm. Bazeley's diary records a friend, Margaret, turning up at 'Grey Gables' unannounced and finding Zep there: 'she goes white and flees . . . We've been warned that Zep is the most dangerous man on the island – we know,' he wrote ominously.

Resentment built up against H. amongst the islanders, and it burst out at the funeral in June 1943 of some British airmen who had been shot down over Jersey. H. and a few friends had ostentatiously dressed in mourning, and were treated with bitter contempt by the large gathering of islanders. Bazeley noted the crowd's comments: 'One woman said "Look at that little bitch all dolled up!" Another said, "Wait until we get our hands on the German bags we know where they are."' He added that perhaps, in retrospect, H. wished she hadn't gone, or hadn't been so dressed up.

Many of the people mentioned in Bazeley's diary are remembered on Jersey. Bernard Hassall was a young man at the time, but he recalls Zepernick as 'very intelligent and good looking. He loved himself and his hat was always set on an angle. He dressed beautifully and his English was impeccable. He was not feared on the island – he went out of his way to make friends with islanders.' H. is remembered as a good-time girl, a bit saucy but not the kind of woman who informed on fellow islanders, as some of those who mixed with the Germans were wont to do. Joe Miere described H. as 'very good looking': 'She used to dance on the stage. She was a nice girl; she never told on anyone. Her father had fought in the First World War and her brother J. escaped from Jersey to liberated France. After the war, H.'s mother defended her daughter's behaviour, saying it was just "culture exchange".'

Bazeley's diary recorded the abrupt end to the partying and the intrigue. On 2 November 1943, Dr Muller told Bazeley that Zepernick had been killed in France when his train had been bombed as he was going home on leave. 'Poor Zep, he's had a beautiful existence for about three years, then this,' commented Bazeley. He stuck Zep's death notice in German from the *Jersey Evening Post* in his diary:

> His special duty was to oversee the moral welfare of the troops. Out of his deep human understanding, he applied his energy and working strength, often under the most difficult conditions to set up films and recreation activities for the troops ... We thank him for his inspiration and quite special love which he lavished upon the island choir and orchestra.

Zepernick had said he wanted to be buried on the island, and his body was brought back from France and buried in the cemetery of St Brelade's, which was used by the Germans. Bazeley noted: 'It's a "queer fate" that he has been brought back to be buried so near to where he spent so many hours of bliss.' Bazeley sent a wreath to the funeral, and the following year on the anniversary of Zepernick's death, when he laid flowers on the grave, he noticed there were already a few carnations there which he presumed were from H.

Zepernick had confided in Bazeley's wife Lucy that he would have liked to live on the island after the war, and Bazeley wrote: 'Everyone is talking of Zep in town. Z is a hero, H. anything but. Even H.'s mother is reported to have said that Zep had sent her some wonderful letters.'

Bazeley's diary continued to report the antics of H. who had now taken up with von Helldorf. Word had spread of her behaviour, and she was being ostracised by some islanders. The gossip was that a local club, the Green Room, had refused her entry, and in retaliation von Helldorf had ordered it to be closed down. H.'s mother looked a wreck, wrote Bazeley, while H. herself was going 'great guns on Helldorf – she tells someone she plans to have Grey Gables for the summer' (von Helldorf could have taken over 'Grey Gables' as his billet if he had wished). H. was rumoured to be engaged to Helldorf, who drove an SS Jaguar Coupe. There were still parties, but not at 'Grey Gables' – H. was reportedly too scared to come, remarked Bazeley. She grew much thinner, and when she performed in a cabaret in January 1944, most of the audience walked out. Finally, H. moved to Guernsey, and Bazeley turned his attentions back to his vegetable patch.

The sight of young girls wearing make-up, fancy hats and stockings was guaranteed to stir up intense resentment amongst some islanders. Friendships were broken over relationships with Germans, and families became bitterly divided. Having the run of requisitioned cars and the islands' grandest houses must have been a bitter pill for those with more principles, or less beauty. Jersey boy Maurice Green knew several girls who went out with Germans. His verdict is that 'they lived off the fat of the land. They had cigarettes, and extra rations.'

James Ryan, the First World War veteran living on Guernsey, vented his spleen in his memoirs:

Especially high was the percentage of young girls from fourteen to sixteen years. These brazen little beasts were proud to display their [pregnant] condition and the results to all and sundry. The usual shout was, 'Look out, here comes a platoon of German troop-carriers . . .' They aroused great indignation when the officials ordered that all women in a certain condition were to have first call on supplies and stores . . . Women waiting in queues were often pushed aside in favour of these girls . . . These illegitimate children were by . . . our enemies . . .

This behaviour was not confined to the lower classes [but also] most unexpected good girls from decent families. What was the inducement? The lure of uniform . . . One respectable couple's daughter came back in the early hours of the morning in a German officer's car . . . When her father threatened to lock her out, she responded by threatening to tell the officer.

Many of Mary McCarthy's friends and acquaintances had affairs with Germans:

I didn't mind about the poor women whose husbands were away fighting; they had children to feed and their husbands forgave them when they came back. But I begrudge people of my education like the two L—— girls whose father was a banker. They had been to school in England, and when you're more educated, you should represent your country. They would flaunt their bodies and cuddle and kiss Germans on the beach. When I went up to them once, they just told me to go away. One of them married an RAF officer after the war.

One girl I used to hate like poison. She got fatter and fatter and she would go by on horseback. She was very thick with the top Germans. She used to slip out at night to meet the Germans. She had always been boy mad and a bit of a nymphomaniac. She could have informed on us, you had to be very careful. We couldn't just cut her out of our gang so we just slowly cooled off.

The Germans called us 'ghosts' because we always looked straight ahead. If I'd gone with a German [my family] would have been better off, but I was never tempted. They had no sense of humour and my mother, being English, was very strict.

Mary remembered that the brother of one girl never spoke to his sister again after she had an affair with a German. Another Jerseyman's family were more forgiving. His brothers were away fighting in the war, and one day his mother bumped into her daughter-in-law in the street. She was holding her little son by one hand, and a German soldier was holding the child's other hand:

> My mother was furious but my sister-in-law just said, 'Shut up you old cow.' The German soldier turned round and said, 'That's no way to talk to the mother of your husband.'
>
> After the war no one said anything. Her husband came back and he'd only ever say anything about it when he'd had too much to drink. My mother forgave her and I did too – I liked my sister-in-law.

A few women, like H., appear to have enjoyed flaunting their new-found status. Many more avoided the animosity their relationships provoked amongst the other islanders by going to great lengths to keep them secret. This was often in the interests of the German lover as well. Baron von Aufsess discreetly visited a number of Jerseywomen. Since he was married he was prohibited from frat-ernising, and although his affairs were the subject of gossip amongst his fellow officers, they would have set a bad example to lower ranks if they had been more widely known. Keeping an affair secret could be done provided neither of two possible eventualities blew the discreet couple's cover. The first of these was pregnancy.

An unwanted pregnancy when food was so short could be disas-trous for a tight family budget. It also brought disgrace on the family in the conservative and strictly religious rural communities of the Channel Islands.

A brief note from one island father to Unteroffizier Duickmann at the German headquarters on Guernsey in April 1941 speaks volumes:

> Dear Sir,
>
> I expect you know why I am writing. It came as rather a shock to her mother and myself when we knew of her condition. So now that you have left I ask you as a gentleman for my daughter's sake and the expected child to write and come to some arrangement. Trusting we shall have an early reply.

The correspondence continued over several weeks, but finally the reply came back that it was not legally possible for a German and a Briton to marry while their countries were at war.

Girls went to desperate lengths to avoid the shame of a pregnancy. Abortion was illegal on all the islands, and during the Occupation there were a number of trials of abortionists, to which the local papers devoted pages of detailed reports. A sixty-year-old woman was convicted on Guernsey in 1941, and in 1943 the *Guernsey Evening Press* reported three trials, including one of a masseur who was accused of murder when a seventeen-year-old girl died while undergoing an abortion. The same person was also convicted of attempting to perform two abortions on Jersey. One of the other 1943 cases attracted a large crowd of young women in the public gallery, the *Post* reported. The abortionist, a Mr Brunt, told the court he had helped hundreds of islanders since arriving on the island just before the Occupation. A month later two more women were charged with performing abortions.

Eighteen-year-old Doreen, a domestic servant, resorted to an even more desperate ploy after a doctor had to be called in when her family discovered her in the middle of having a miscarriage. She claimed to have been raped, and gave a detailed statement of her ordeal to the police. Three days later she retracted her statement, admitting it was 'all lies'. She had been seeing a German soldier called Paul, she confessed, and they had had sex with her consent in a field.

A woman might be lucky (or careful) enough to avoid pregnancy, but there was another eventuality over which she had even less control, and which could destroy her reputation in a particularly humiliating fashion. The Third Reich ordered its men to look after their bodies as well as they looked after their weapons; this was a reference to venereal disease. Draconian methods were introduced to curb the spread of disease in occupied territories. Soldiers were inspected, and the Germans also considered it legitimate to inspect any women who came into contact with the troops. Prostitutes who had been brought from France for the brothels in St Peter Port, St Helier and St Anne's were examined. Some island women were snatched from cafés or the street and taken to hospital for inspection. Sometimes a German soldier had given the woman's name, sometimes the snatches were based only on hearsay or because the woman had been seen in the company of soldiers.

As early as October 1940, six maids at Old Government House

Hotel on Guernsey were ordered by the Germans to have a medical examination; not surprisingly, they refused. The Germans called in the local police. On another occasion Jersey policeman William Brown remembers having to collect 'two youngish women' and take them to hospital: 'They were wives of British men serving in the forces. They both had venereal disease and we were ordered to go and pick them up by the Germans – they had obviously given the Germans venereal disease.'

But as Betty Thurban, who was seventeen when she worked as a nurse on the venereal disease ward in Jersey's hospital, pointed out, some of the women rounded up had had nothing to do with Germans:

> You'd leave one evening with two or three patients on the ward and the next morning there would be twenty or so, because the Germans had raided all the cafés. If a German went to France and got infected he had to give the name of the girl who had infected him. He often didn't know the name of a French girl, so he gave the name of a local Jersey girl. They had to have daily swabs and only after three negative swabs and an examination by the German doctor were they allowed out.
>
> Some were ultimately jerrybags, some were very pleasant girls and weren't infected at all. The girls were very embarrassed and frequently in tears.

The Germans' attempts to control venereal disease verged on the farcical. In October 1942 an order was issued, signed by the Guernsey Health Services Officer, Dr Symons, and his German counterpart, that 'sexual relations either with German soldiers or with civilians are strictly forbidden for the next three months. In case of non-compliance with this order, severe punishment by the Occupying Authorities is to be expected even if no infection has taken place.' By 1943, punishment was indeed severe. According to Feldkommandantur records, girls (almost all of them teenagers) on Jersey were being transferred from the venereal disease ward to the prison or an institution 'where they will not have free access to the street' for a period of quarantine lasting up to six months. Five girls were rounded up from German billets with venereal disease in July 1944, according to a police report. The handful of Jersey and

Guernsey girls working on Alderney in 1944 were all found to have venereal disease and were brought back to their homes, presumably for treatment. On Guernsey a woman was fined £5 for having sexual relations with a German after she had been banned because she was infected. Dances were banned for a time in 1943 by the Kommandant in order to prevent the spread of disease.

For girls as young as seventeen, the experience of being rounded up by the police and then held in hospital, subjected to daily internal examinations with the threat of prison and quarantine, must have been deeply traumatic. And for some, after release from hospital there was the added humiliation of one's relationship now being public knowledge. Jersey clerk Bob Le Sueur recounted:

> I know one woman who married a Roman Catholic in 1939 and converted and became very devout. Her husband went off to fight in the war. In about 1943, the Germans came to where she worked in a quite important secretarial position. They took her away and everyone was aghast – what could have happened? She disappeared for two or three days and when she returned, she said nothing and everyone was very sympathetic.
>
> Later I heard that they had been rounding up all the women who were sleeping with the Germans because of the high incidence of venereal disease. How did I know? I had some friends who were fishermen, and they had a German guard with them who used to gossip about his boss. His boss had a Jersey mistress and he talked to his underlings about it. This boss enjoyed the piquancy of the situation: before getting into bed with him, his mistress would ask if he minded if she first prayed for her husband. It was this woman. Wild horses wouldn't drag her name from me.

Animosity, abortions, venereal disease: these are hardly the most propitious circumstances for love to grow. But it did, and the islanders appear to have differentiated between true love and mere flirtations. While the latter provoked hostility, islanders were supportive of the former. There were genuine attachments, but few survived the war; many soldiers were posted to the Eastern Front and lost touch, while the Germans who remained on the islands at the end of the war were rounded up and sent to prisoner of war camps in England. But there were a handful of marriages in the post-war years, and at least three couples stayed on in the Channel Islands. The German husbands became valued and respected members of the community, particularly Werner Rang on Sark, who was awarded the MBE for services to the island. A few island girls went to settle in Germany and married their lovers. All of them are reluctant to talk about the past.

One couple who now live in England, however, are proud of their extraordinary story. Their grandson, eleven-year-old Morgan Joanknecht, has written school essays about how his granddad is German and his granny is British, and how they met and fell in love in the midst of Britain's finest hour and Hitler's Third Reich. Morgan is the son of Tony Joanknecht, who was born a month after the liberation of the Channel Islands in 1945 to a Guernsey mother and a German father.

Dolly Joanknecht tells the story with candour and self-evident delight. She still has the girlish charm which first caught Willi's eye in 1943. Willi is more reticent, and motions questions away dismissively with his hand. 'Ah, what's the point?' he says, his accent still thick after more than forty-five years of living in Devon. But his face creases with happiness as Dolly recounts their courtship. Tony listens, as do his wife and Morgan; it's a familiar family tale, but it's as if they can never hear it too often.

Dolly and Willi first met on a boat from France to Guernsey when she was seventeen and he was twenty-one. Like many islanders during the Occupation, Dolly had been imprisoned in a French gaol, accused of petty black marketeering.

I was put down in the hold with all these Algerian and Moroccan forced labourers. I was terrified and then I saw these jackboots coming down the stairs. It was Willi and he took me up to the deck and gave me coffee and bread.

He already knew me. We'd never spoken, but he'd seen me and I'd seen him playing football near my house. He told me afterwards he had always liked me and had nicknamed me 'Blondie'.

[Willi interjected proudly: 'She was a pretty girl.']

Before I went to France, he used to salute me and I would put my tongue out.

On the boat I couldn't speak much German and he couldn't speak much English. All I could say to him was 'Football.' He told me he had a girl in Germany – I think it was to make me jealous. We didn't talk much.

Several days later I remember going for a walk in the park and Willi was out jogging and he saluted me. Then one day there was a knock on the door and there was this sailor and all he said was 'Washing?' Everyone did washing for the Germans because you got bread in return. I asked Aunty if she could do his washing. Aunty came to meet him and afterwards she said, 'Isn't he a nice boy?' That's how we started. He used to come up every day with a loaf of bread as a present.

We used to go out to the park; we couldn't go on the beaches because they were mined. He spoke pidgin German to me which I could understand. We used to go to the pictures. I loved the German films. The cinema was divided down the middle; one side for Germans and the other for civilians. I used to sit in the middle, in the last civilian seat, and Willi would go to the end of the German row so we could sit together.

I hated Willi's uniform. I used to look at him and wish he was a Guernsey boy. I'd look at his belt and see '*Gott mit Uns*' – 'God with us' – and that gave me some security. I used to think, well, if he's with God, he can't be bad – and he wasn't. He was very kind to me.

I liked Willi because he treated me well. In Guernsey the men are masters and my mother and my aunt were expected to do everything for the men. Us women were second class. The man ruled and what the man said, went. My aunt used to have to get up in the middle of the night to get my uncle something to eat sometimes.

Willi treated me as a person; he showed me love and he respected me. After the way I was treated the first two years, he was my saviour. I don't know what would have happened if I hadn't had Willi.

For Dolly, Willi's gentleness and kindness was a godsend. When Dolly was fifteen, shortly after the beginning of the Occupation, a distant cousin had made her drunk and had raped her. The sexual abuse continued for over a year. Dolly's mother was in England, and Dolly was too frightened to tell her aunt, whom she did not think would believe her. The years immediately prior to Willi's appearance in her life were a nightmare that haunts her still. She suffered from frequent periods of depression in her twenties, and even today the tears still flow uncontrollably at the painful memory.

The presence of Willi deterred any subsequent advances from her cousin.

> It was strange. We loved one another so much, but we were confused about what would happen after the war. Would we be able to stay on Guernsey or would we go to Germany? We married ourselves because we couldn't marry legally. A Quaker lady who was very kind to us said we could marry ourselves: all we had to do was stand in front of an altar, ask God and say 'We love one another, we are now man and wife.' So we went to a little chapel and married ourselves in August 1944. Willi gave me a curtain ring for my finger.
>
> I know by man-made laws, and if we were being patriotic, I should never have gone with Willi, and he should never have gone with me. By law we did wrong. Don't you think?

Willi interrupted: 'Why?'

'Because you fell in love with the enemy,' said Dolly.

'There's no law against it,' said Willi. 'Man-made law doesn't count at all.'

Dolly: 'But when there's war, it's illegal.'

Most islanders, recognising how much they loved each other, were sympathetic to Dolly and Willi. It was not until after the war that anybody ever called Dolly a jerrybag. But one girl with whom she was working at the town hospital was openly critical. Dolly's retort was swift: 'You're doing worse than what I'm doing. You're going round with a married man whose wife is in England. If you believe in the Bible, I'm loving my enemy, you're committing adultery.'

CHAPTER THREE

A MODEL OCCUPATION

'When I felt I had got the measure of the Germans, my ambitions soared. It now sounds ludicrous ... but what I hoped to do and, in fairness, sometimes succeeded in doing, although not for very long, was, to the fullest extent possible, to run their occupation for them.'

Ambrose Sherwill, President of the Guernsey Controlling Committee June–October 1940, in his unpublished post-war memoirs

The Channel Islands are intensely proud of their ancient system of government – they have some of the oldest legislatures in the world. In 1940, as the Germans bullied and humiliated the governments of each country in Europe they occupied, the islanders feared that the occupying forces would ride roughshod over the independence they had jealously guarded for centuries. But the Germans made it clear from the start that they wished the island governments to remain in place, with two conditions: all island laws required the approval of the German Kommandant, and all German orders had to be registered by the island governments as law. For administrative purposes the islands were amalgamated by the Germans into the Département de la Manche. Orders came from the German military government for occupied France, based in Paris. On the islands the military government, the Feldkommandantur, was set up on Jersey, with subordinate branches on Guernsey and Alderney. All civilian matters came within the scope of the Feldkommandantur. A parallel command structure headed by the Inselkommandant, the military commander of the islands, governed all military matters and was linked to the Oberbefehlshaber (West) – army headquarters – in Paris.

The island governments now found themselves reluctant dancing partners of the Third Reich. How were they to conduct themselves? There was no precedent for them to look to for guidance. Whitehall had as little idea as they did, and its advice immediately before the Occupation had been brief and vague: the Home Office had advised members of the governments to stay at their posts and to 'administer the government of the Island to the best of their abilities in the interests of the inhabitants, whether or not they are in a position to receive instructions from His Majesty's Government'. The islands were so ill-prepared that they did not even have to hand a copy of the Hague Convention – the international treaty of 1907 which outlined the responsibilities and rights of occupying powers. It took Guernsey twelve months to find a copy.

There was little time to consider what position to adopt. Within days of the first Germans arriving, the governments – still under their oaths of allegiance to the British Crown – found themselves surrounded by the reality of conquest. There were hundreds of German troops who demanded to be fed and housed; they needed water, fuel and electricity, cars, bicycles, buses, blankets, sheets and pillows. They required chauffeur-driven cars on twenty-four-hour standby; they demanded that the island police salute all German officers; they wanted German translations added to the signposts.

It was a bewildering and deeply frightening experience. The island rulers carried the heavy responsibility of the lives of thousands of islanders. They feared that one wrong step could result in disasters such as the islands had never known in their history. John Leale, Sherwill's successor as President of Guernsey's Controlling Committee, said in a speech after the war:

> Decisions, sometimes of a vital and far-reaching nature, had to be taken in a very short time and without a full knowledge of all the relevant facts ... If we had to live over those years again, there are, of course, a number of things we should do differently, [but] we were simply pitchforked into the task of adjusting the islands to a situation from which we, one and all, believed we were for all time safe.

Who were the men who were 'pitchforked' into the task of developing a policy of how, as subjects of the British Crown, they should deal with its enemy? How well equipped were they for their role?

Executive power had been concentrated in the hands of a few men through the creation of the Guernsey Controlling Committee and the Jersey Superior Council in the days leading up to the Occupation, and in the course of the summer of 1940, these men laid down the principles which were to determine the attitude towards the occupiers for the next five years. On Jersey the Bailiff, Alexander Coutanche, was an energetic, decisive and forceful man, who established his authority early on in the crisis. By contrast, the Bailiff of Guernsey, Victor Carey, was an elderly man on the point of retirement when war broke out, and the scale of his responsibilities seems to have terrified him. His leadership was weak and vacillating, and he went out of his way to help the Germans on a number of highly controversial occasions. Ambrose Sherwill, the first President of Guernsey's Controlling Committee, described the unfortunate Carey in his memoirs:

> No one suffered more greatly than did the Bailiff [Carey] from want of food and lack of heating . . . I was struck by his shrunken frame as he sat by his empty office grate huddled in a heavy rug and, at the end, his physical condition was pitiable. Month after month and year after year of the Occupation, he had no work to occupy his mind and nothing to do but worry, and he worried himself sick. Not about himself . . . but about Guernsey and its people.

The Germans increasingly bypassed Carey and turned to Sherwill and his successor, John Leale.

Sherwill, Leale and Coutanche had spent most of their lives on the islands. Leale, a Methodist minister and former Cambridge don, was an expert in finance and economics, and had inherited a profitable property business on Guernsey. Sherwill and Coutanche were barristers in island law. For most of their lives their talents had been applied to the islands' intricate politics and their anti-quated, feudal machinery of government.

Carey and Coutanche were – and still are – old island names, with a history of family influence in every aspect of island life. Sherwill was related to the Carey family by his marriage to May

Clabburn, a cousin of Victor. Sherwill and Coutanche were good friends, and Carey frequently sought Sherwill's advice during the Occupation. An elite of interconnected families was accustomed to ordering the affairs of the islands virtually unchallenged. This was even more marked on Sark, where Dame Sybil Hathaway effectively ran the island as a benevolent dictatorship. The island elite had guarded their independence from Whitehall and were as self-important as big fish in small ponds are wont to be, even though the business of government was largely occupied with street lighting, rubbish collection, planning permission and running the schools. It was the standard fare of local government, and a far cry from the huge tasks and moral challenges the island's leaders faced with the arrival of the Germans.

On 7 August 1940 Ambrose Sherwill delivered a speech at the first Occupation meeting of the Guernsey States, attended by the German Kommandant, Major Lanz, and his aide, Dr Maass. He laid out the position the island governments were to adopt towards their new German masters:

> May this occupation be a model to the world. On the one hand, toler-ance on the part of the military authority, and courtesy and correctness on the part of the occupying forces, and on the other, dignity and cour-tesy and exemplary behaviour on the part of the civilian population. I do not know how long the occupation will last ... when it is over, I hope that the occupying force and occupied population may each be able to say: of different nations, having differing outlooks, we lived together with tolerance and mutual respect.
>
> The German forces, fighting troops, flushed with success on the Continent, came to Guernsey and found the civilian population calm, dignified and well-behaved. Having us in their power, they behaved as good soldiers ... we, the civilian population, were sober, law-abiding, giving no cause for offence, courteous and polite ... we did not shed and were not asked to shed our loyalty to our King and country in one of the greatest tests which could befall us, we tried to justify the words of Victor Hugo when he called us 'ce noble, petit peuple de mer'.

There were three basic principles to Sherwill's concept of 'model occupation': scrupulous obedience to the occupied power; meek gratitude for the forbearance of the Germans; and a rejection of any form of resistance, in favour of what might be called 'passive patriotism' – loyalty to Britain which required no participation in its war effort. Alongside these principles, the island governments adopted a meticulous observance of the Hague Convention. According to its provisions, the Germans had a responsibility to ensure that the islanders had enough food, and to secure their safety and that of their property. In practice, the Germans ignored the Convention when it suited them. The islanders, in turn, had to supply the Germans with all the food, accommodation and transport they needed. The Germans had wide-ranging powers of requisitioning, but under the Convention they could not force islanders to work on projects of a military nature which could be used against Britain. As Leale said in a speech to the States immediately after the war, it had been 'our constant endeavour to make the Occupation, to use the words of the first President of the Controlling Committee, a model . . . Our policy was based on a realistic acceptance of a situation which we all deplored, but which we were powerless to prevent.'

The language which both Leale and Sherwill used – 'dignity', 'courtesy', 'loyalty to our King and country' – was the sugar coating which made the bitter pill palatable. In reality, the 'Model Occupation' was a deeply pragmatic policy: peace at any price. On very few occasions did the island governments oppose the Germans. There were protests, but they were timid. The islands' rulers were all too well aware that the Germans had force on their side. Their occupiers had chosen to show forbearance, and must therefore be conciliated and appeased at every turn.

The Model Occupation policy was for public consumption; it pleased the Germans, and guided the public. But Sherwill was more ambitious, and privately confessed his real aim in a startling passage in his memoirs: 'When I felt I had got the measure of the Germans, my ambitions soared. It now sounds ludicrous . . . but what I hoped to do and, in fairness, sometimes succeeded in doing, although not for very long, was, to the fullest extent possible, to run their occupation for them.'

What Sherwill's aim meant in practice was that if the Germans wanted to requisition a house, or a field, or a car, the island authorities would do it for them. If they needed plumbers or electricians, the island authorities would recruit them. Rather than expose the civilian population to the demands of the occupying authorities, the island government would act as an agency of the Germans – in the process, they hoped, softening their impact. On Jersey, Alexander Coutanche described the role of the government as a 'buffer' between the Germans and the civilian population.

It was a controversial policy, which led to allegations that the island authorities were collaborating with the Germans. The wrath of aggrieved islanders fell on the heads of the islands' rulers, rather than on the Germans, when unpopular measures were implemented. The 'buffer' role was a thankless task, and fuelled a thousand grievances – as when, for instance, one islander's house or bicycle, and not his neighbour's, was requisitioned, or when thirty soldiers were billeted on one islander and none on his neighbour.

The passage from Sherwill's memoirs reveals the nature of the compromise the island authorities made. The Channel Islands became heavily-armed fortresses in the course of the Occupation, supporting thirty-seven thousand troops by the end of the war. It became increasingly clear both to the governments and the German authorities that co-operation was crucial if the islands were to run smoothly. It was the island authorities who kept law and order, enforced German regulations such as those relating to curfew and blackout, organised the production of food for the troops, and provided and paid for their accommodation. The island governments had achieved Sherwill's ambition; they were running the Germans' occupation, and as a consequence they were contributing significantly to the fighting strength of the German forces.

Apologists claimed that the island governments succeeded in acting as a 'buffer' – to use Coutanche's word – and were able to ease the harshness of many German orders. Critics alleged that the authorities had effectively become service agencies of the occupying forces and accused them of aiding the enemy – a crime under British law. There was no authority to appeal to; the Home Office had told the islands' authorities to govern 'in the interests of the inhabitants', and this was how they understood those interests.

*   *   *

The Model Occupation would have been impossible without the co-operation of the Germans, and the occupation of the Channel Islands was quite unlike any other in Europe. It suited the Germans' interests. The men stationed on the islands wanted a quiet and easy life, and they realised that this was possible there, unlike most other parts of occupied Europe. With a little tact they could win the islanders' assistance rather than having to use coercion. They needed the islanders' help: the military government was severely understaffed and if the island authorities had refused to carry out many functions for them, they would have found it difficult to govern the islands.

The senior German officers usually made a point of being polite and respectful to the members of the island governments. John Leale said that they were never rude, and never shouted at him. The day-to-day conduct of government was accompanied by strict courtesies, and sometimes relations became warmer. Many of the German officers spoke excellent English, and the islands' officer corps – especially in the military administration – included a number of aristocratic and highly educated men. Oberstleutnant Friedrich Knackfuss, the islands' Feldkommandant, was the son of the court painter of Kaiser Wilhelm II. Baron Max von Aufsess, who was stationed on Jersey for much of the war, was a frequent visitor at the houses of prominent island families. Prince Eugen Oettingen-Wallerstein, Rittmeister on Guernsey, was friendly with the Dame of Sark, judging by their warm correspondence. Some of the officers posted to the Channel Islands' Feldkommandantur went on to hold prominent public positions in post-war West Germany: Dr Jacob Kratzer became the President of the Bavarian Supreme Court of Administration, and Dr Gottfried von Stein became Chancellor of the University of Bonn. A number of these men developed a genuine affection for the islands and concern for the welfare of the islanders; some even successfully moderated orders issuing from headquarters in France or Berlin.

Ambrose Sherwill admitted that he got on very well with Dr Maass, the aide to the first Kommandant: 'Although a German and an enemy, he was a man after my own heart. I can say no more and I owe it to him to say no less,' he wrote in private notes. Heiner Magsam, the Kommandant of Sark from 1943 to 1945, still has fond recollections of his weekly meetings with the Dame of Sark. He says they never disagreed about anything, and that their amicable discussions usually ended in tea and a game of bridge. The German authorities also made a point of maintaining good relations with the general population. Shortly after the Occupation began, the German Kommandant announced in the islands' press that he or one of his staff would be available between eleven and one o'clock every day at his headquarters if anyone wished to speak to him.

The politeness of individual Germans may have been genuine, but it was also an integral part of Berlin's policy towards its British possessions. This was spelled out in a report by Professor Karl Pfeffer, a German historian who visited the islands on behalf of the German government in 1941. His recommendations advocated the 'iron hand in a velvet glove' policy which became the hallmark of the Germans' administration in the islands.

Pfeffer's advice was that attempts should be made to drive a wedge between the English and the islanders. He advocated 'appealing very strongly to the Norman heritage, treating the islands like little Germanic states which only stood in personal union with England ... trying not to humble their pride but to turn it in our favour ... It is naturally difficult to promote a really independent consciousness towards England but not hopeless.' Allowing the islands to issue their own laws, he said, was part of this policy. This had resulted in no cases of sabotage, and the island farmers were 'contributing materially to the maintenance of fighting strength'. The success of this policy was dependent on German officers showing 'tact and self-confidence with severity when necessary'.

The Channel Islands Occupation was a trial run for 'meeting the English population', Pfeffer continued:

> conditions have been such that they have produced an important advance of German propaganda for the post-war period ... if, after victory, we intend to draw part of the British people over to our side the prevailing conduct of the German occupation troops can be abundantly employed as propaganda. Meanwhile the English-born serve as very useful hostages to be used as such if the Germans are badly treated by the British ...
>
> The inhabitants are co-operating very loyally with the Occupation

authorities ... in this way they can best endure the war, without thereby forfeiting any of their patriotism ... the inhabitants regard the Occupation as a temporary storm in which they almost commiserate with the individual German soldier on account of his unpleasant duty. One journalist told me, 'When I see your fine men in the streets here, my heart bleeds for this fratricidal war.'

The Germans cynically exploited independence aspirations all over Europe, from Croatia to the Ukraine. Respecting the Channel Islands' Norman heritage was a canny move, because the islands have always boasted of their political and cultural independence from England. But beneath the surface of politeness and respect was a harsh calculation, and an indifference to the interests of the islanders beyond those which coincided with the Germans'. From time to time the islands' rulers glimpsed the fact that they were a useful pawn which could be used to ensure the good behaviour of the British towards German citizens in any other part of the theatre of war. In September 1942 and February 1943 English-born islanders were used as hostages, just as Pfeffer had suggested, and the majority – 2200 of them – were deported to German internment camps until the end of the war. To those who remained on the islands, the point had been forcefully made: they were utterly dependent on the goodwill of their occupiers.

The propaganda value of the German-occupied British isles which Pfeffer identified was extensively exploited in the summer of 1940, when an invasion of Britain seemed imminent. The German public and armed forces were reassured that an attack on Britain would result in another swift victory, and a peaceful occupation akin to that prevailing at the time in Vichy France. There were articles in German newspapers and magazines, and clips on newsreels showing the conquest of the islands, and the Germans and British subjects living happily side by side as 'cousin' races.

Maurice Green, a schoolboy on Jersey at the time, remembers a big stand being put up in St Helier during the early days of the Occupation:

All the elementary schools were paraded down there. There were policemen in uniform on duty and signs for Player's, Quaker Oats and Bass, and in the background the British flag was flying alongside the Swastika above the town hall. A German officer in perfect English explained how the Germans were liberating Europe for a good cause because of the Communists. They were trying to save the world, he said. Then he said, 'Hands up all the children who would like to have a bar of German milk chocolate.' All the kids shot their hands up and the cameras panned round for the newsreels – it looked like the children were doing the Heil Hitler salute. I didn't put my hand up. I didn't want German chocolate. The front row did get some chocolate and cigarettes for their fathers. Kids trotted home and said how nice the Germans were.

The islands' Model Occupation was also used on German radio broadcasts to Britain in an attempt to persuade the British that they had nothing to fear from a German occupation. The American reporter Charles Swift was allowed by the German authorities to visit Jersey in August 1940, and he broadcast on German radio in English for a British audience:

Everywhere I went on the island I hear only praise in the highest terms of the German soldiers' conduct and a decidedly notice-able touch of bitterness and disappointment towards the London government at the way it has led the people by the nose. 'Why, the Germans are people just like we English.'* That was a remark I hear on Jersey dozens of times by men and women in every walk of life.

In the evening there was a big dance in the shore casino with the German military band supplying the music. It was amusing to see so many pretty English maids dancing with burly sunburnt German soldiers who evidently are on the best terms with the girls of St Helier . . .

I noticed later that whenever English policemen saluted German officers in the street it was done in such a matter of fact manner with both parties generally exchanging polite smiles that one would never have imagined that war was going on between them.

The broadcast was monitored by the BBC, and a transcript was sent to the Home Office. Probably it was dismissed as propaganda,

* In reality, no islander would ever describe him or herself as English.

but it was hard to be equally dismissive of another broadcast, also in August 1940, which horrified Whitehall. Ambrose Sherwill, the President of Guernsey's Controlling Committee, gave a talk on German overseas radio which could be heard all over Britain. He said that the island officials had been 'treated with every consideration and with the greatest courtesy by the German military authorities', he praised the 'exemplary' conduct of the troops, and declared:

> I am proud of the way my fellow-islanders have behaved and grateful for the correct and kindly attitude towards them of the German soldier. We have been and will remain intensely loyal subjects of His Majesty . . . this has been made clear to, and is respected by the German Kommandant and his staff. On that staff is an officer speaking perfect English, a man of wide experience . . . To him I express my grateful thanks for his courtesy and patience.

Coming from a British subject, such lavish praise of the Germans was bad enough, but what made it even worse was the introduction by a German presenter: 'The allusions he makes to the German troops are so favourable and fair that [Sherwill] himself seemed to deem it necessary to emphasise that no pistol was pointed at him while he was speaking.' The presenter went on to point out that this was the first occupation to be endured by the British since 1066, and that there had been doubts whether the islanders would 'cope' or that the Germans have the 'knowledge and tact' to carry out the Occupation successfully and peacefully. But, he added triumphantly, contrary to the allegations emanating from London that wherever the Germans went, the Gestapo followed, and 'starvation, persecution, unrest and dissatisfaction' resulted, a prominent islander from Guernsey would give 'his opinion of what British propaganda called "German persecution"'.

Sherwill's motive in making the broadcast was to reassure the islanders who had been evacuated to Britain that their relatives and friends left on the island were safe and well, but his good intentions went badly awry. Even those who heard the broadcast on the islands were critical, and Whitehall was furious; Sherwill's reassurance about the kindly, patient Germans was the last thing they wanted the British public to hear in August 1940, when every nerve on the Home Front was being steeled to resist German invasion. Only two months before, on 4 June, Prime Minister Winston Churchill had told the British people: 'We shall defend our island, whatever the cost may be, we shall fight on the beaches, we shall fight on the landing grounds, we shall fight in the fields and in the streets, we shall fight in the hills; we shall never surrender.' Sherwill had fallen into a trap. The news that the Channel Islanders were peacefully coming to terms with their German overlords was a masterful propaganda coup for Berlin.

The most urgent challenges facing the islands in July 1940 were how to feed everyone, and how to restore some semblance of economic life. The pressing nature of these tasks brought home to the island governments how much they depended on German goodwill. Formerly, the islands had relied on imports from Britain for all their needs. With this source now cut off, they had to turn to France for supplies of food, fuel, manufactured goods and animal feeds. Over the next few years the economies of the islands had to be completely restructured, and this led to a massive increase in the powers of the island governments. Over the space of a few months they had to reorganise the import/export trade on which the islands were so dependent, and to intervene extensively in the islands' agriculture to increase the production of food.

The Germans gave permission for a Purchasing Commission for the islands to be set up in Granville on the Normandy coast, staffed by islanders who were granted permits to travel all over France buying everything from buttons and medicines to seeds and oil. The German Feldkommandantur sometimes assisted in providing the necessary currency; for example, when all the islands' cars were requisitioned, compensation was paid into the islands' bank account in Granville. French banks also extended loans. The Germans provided ships, although due to Allied bombing and wartime exigencies the service was not always regular. The Purchasing Commission's task became increasingly difficult as the war dragged on, with goods becoming scarce and the French growing

increasingly reluctant to part with hundreds of tons of their flour
or butter for British islanders.

The difficulties of buying food in France made it all the more
important to increase agricultural output on the islands. As the
islands were expected to feed the rapidly growing German garrison,
the Germans also had an interest in increasing productivity. The
island governments were required to sell, or give, the Germans a
proportion of the crops. On Guernsey some of the glasshouses were
designated for growing vegetables for German consumption; it was
the Guernsey States who provided the seed and the labour. The
allocation of the harvest triggered some of the most bitter and
protracted disputes of the Occupation; there was never enough to
go round. The black market was a further source of aggravation;
some farmers came to arrangements with the Germans to sell them
produce – often at higher prices than the islanders could afford to
pay, thus inflating the cost of basic foodstuffs.

Agriculture on Jersey and Guernsey prior to the war had become
highly specialised for the export markets of tomatoes, grapes,
flowers and new potatoes. Now, grandfathers had to be brought
out of retirement to teach their sons and grandsons how to grow
cereal crops, and how to mill the wheat to make flour in the old
disused water mills. On Jersey the potato fields could be turned
over to wheat, oats and barley relatively simply. But on Guernsey
much of the agricultural land was covered in vast glasshouses for
tomatoes; vegetables could be grown in them, but despite many
experiments they did not succeed with cereal crops or potatoes. As
a result there was less food on Guernsey, while Jersey was able to
produce enough flour to fulfil its rations quota.

Agriculture was virtually 'nationalised' on the islands to speed
up the process of adaptation, engineer the most efficient use of
resources and redeploy the large numbers of unemployed. On
Jersey, the island's Department of Agriculture controlled the use
of agricultural land; the States provided seed and workers through
the Department of Labour. On Guernsey three control boards were
set up – Farm Produce, Potato and Glasshouse Utilisation. The
latter provoked furious resentment from farmers, and by the end
of 1941 the Glasshouse Utilisation Board had handed the
glasshouses back to their owners. But it continued to control

planting, and bought all the crops at set prices in an attempt to control inflation and ensure that there was enough for everyone.

One incident in November 1941, recorded in the minutes of the Guernsey Controlling Committee (GCC), reveals the kind of bargaining forced upon the islands' administrators by the occupying powers. The Germans pressed the GCC to sign a contract on food production; they wanted the Guernsey government and the private farmers Messrs Timmer Ltd (who have no connection with any company currently operating under a similar name) to produce between them thirty tons of vegetables per month for the Wehrmacht from December to March, and seventy tons from April to June. If the GCC signed, the Germans in return would endeavour to get potatoes from Jersey for Guernsey. As an added incentive, they were offering to pay above the retail price. If the GCC didn't sign, the Germans' demands would be increased by ten tons per month. Under the terms of the contract, the Germans' claim amounted to more than a quarter of the total island production, at a time when the German garrison strength was about eleven thousand and the island population twenty-four thousand. The Guernsey government had little choice but reluctantly to accept; too many hungry stomachs were in need of those Jersey potatoes. Only one member of the Controlling Committee, Sir Abraham Lainé, a distinguished retired Indian Civil Servant, voted against the measure. This was not the only occasion on which he found himself opposing a majority decision.

The Germans applied their customary bureaucratic thoroughness to the islands' agriculture, particularly after they discovered with horror that few of the Jersey farmers had attended agricultural school; food was too important to be left entirely to the island authorities. They demanded to know from each farmer every detail about his land, his livestock and his yields. They appointed 'agricultural commandos' to police the farms; they issued instructions about everything, such as when to harvest barley – 'when the ears have become an even yellow and are still standing upright' – and permits to take away manure from the Wehrmacht's horses.

The weight of regulations was just as heavy on the fishermen, provoked in part by the number of escapes from Guernsey during the summer of 1940, when a total of sixty people reached England.

Fishing boats were forbidden to go out in fog or rain, and if the weather turned bad they had to return to port immediately. Restrictions were placed on where they could land and where they could fish, and they had to hand over a proportion of their catch to the Germans. As a consequence the catches were small, and fish played a much smaller part in the islanders' diets during the Occupation than it might have done.

As the island governments scrambled to find food to keep the population and the garrison fed, they were faced by another serious challenge: unemployment. Hundreds of men and women on Jersey and Guernsey had been thrown out of work by the breakdown of trade with England. The islands' skeletal parish welfare programmes – which were only ever expected to deal with a tiny handful of applicants – threatened to collapse under the burden of need. Something had to be done quickly, and Departments of Labour were set up on both islands to tackle the problem in the summer of 1940. Ed Le Quesne, a colourful, stubborn administrator, was in charge on Jersey, and Richard Johns, a hard-working Methodist preacher, on Guernsey.

The first solution to the problem, which both Le Quesne and Johns adopted, was to set up public works programmes such as road-widening schemes, chopping wood for fuel, collecting carrageen moss (for food) and reconditioning old mills. The Guernsey Glasshouse Utilisation Board was heavily overmanned so as to prevent men being thrown onto parish relief. A factory making clothing and footwear was reopened on Jersey to provide work for 350 women.

Another potential solution was more problematic. Within a few weeks of their arrival, the Germans were asking the island authorities to supply them with labour. They needed electricians, plumbers, carpenters, truck drivers, cooks, cleaners and laundrywomen. The labour question provides a fascinating case study of how the Model Occupation worked: it could translate into subservience, or be cleverly used to conceal curmudgeonly awkwardness.

The demand for workers presented the island governments with a difficult decision; to recruit labour for the Germans would be a neat solution to the unemployment problem, but on the other hand it would mean islanders working for the enemy. The dilemma was

sharpened in August 1940, a month after the beginning of the Occupation, when the Germans asked the Guernsey Department of
Labour for men to repair and extend the airport. It was the height of
the Battle of Britain, and Guernsey airport was continually being
used by planes taking off to accompany German fighters. Under
Article 2a of the British Defence Regulations Act – which at that time
applied to the Channel Islands – working at the airport would have
been considered a crime, as 'aiding and abetting' the enemy. Furthermore, under the terms of the Hague Convention, the occupying
power did not have the right to force people to work on military
installations which could be used against their own country.

The Guernsey and Jersey governments were to adopt very different policies. John Leale drew the Germans' attention to the Hague
Convention's provision that the occupying power should not force
the civilian population to work on projects of a military nature, but
thereafter there is no indication in Guernsey's detailed government
records that they ever protested against German requests for labour.
By 10 August 1940, men were already at work at the airport, and
it had been agreed that they would be paid 'danger money' as an
added inducement because of British bombing raids. By 1 October,
ninety-three men were working at the airport. On 4 October the
Controlling Committee noted in its minutes that another thirty
carpenters had been requested by the Germans. The only note
of concern was that if the Germans requested any more men,
they would have to be drawn from private firms. The Committee
concluded by placing on record their 'keen appreciation of the
invaluable assistance afforded . . . by officers attached to the Feldkommandantur'.

On 5 November the Controlling Committee minutes recorded
that advertisements had been placed in the local press for people
to work for the Germans at wages a third above the local average.
Islanders were reluctant to work for the Germans, so incentives
were necessary. The Committee even considered as a further
inducement a proposal to cut welfare payments to those islanders
who refused to work for the Germans. It was quite clear that the
Guernsey government had set aside any scruples in order to solve
the unemployment problem. As the Germans requested more and
more workers, the Department of Labour acted as recruiting agent

and drew men from government employment. Their willingness to comply with German instructions is revealed in a note from the Glasshouse Utilisation Board in Castel parish to the German authorities, asking for a young man to be released from his job: 'In our haste to comply with instructions to send men from our district to work at the airport, we sent a lad who is only seventeen.'

By the end of November 1940, 235 men were working at the airport, but they were not happy with their employers, and the Committee were worried that the men insisted on doing only the job they were trained to do. Richard Johns suggested sending a note of reprimand to each employee; he feared that the Germans would lose 'respect for our labour.' The Committee agreed, with one notable exception – Sir Abraham Lainé. To keep the workers happy it was reluctantly agreed that 'danger money' would continue to be paid during the Christmas holidays. A considerable part of this wage bill was being picked up by the island.

By January 1941, the procedure had been formalised. The Guernsey government departments either did the work for the Germans themselves, acting as contractors, or they operated as agents and found private firms for the work. The Controlling Committee insisted that all German work contracts had to be channelled through the Department of Labour, and Johns bluntly told the Committee that 'all work for the German authorities was now given to the States who acted as contractors'. The States Electricity Department and the Water Supply Board were working almost entirely for the Germans. Nor did they balk at work of a military nature; in June 1941 the Electricity Department accepted a battery-charging contract for the airport. The Department of Labour passed an order for the building of two watchtowers to a local firm, and forwarded another order for the installation of perimeter lighting, floodlights and wiring in the hangars at the airport. Dr Reffler of the Feldkommandantur spelled the relationship out in one contract drawn up for the airport: 'The States of Guernsey will act, in relation to the Feldkommandantur, as contractors for the following work: fifteen hangars ... The States of Guernsey shall employ the required number of workmen [and] shall be responsible for the payment of workmen ... no orders shall be given direct to the men by the German command.'

This last was important, as workers were becoming increasingly resentful about taking orders directly from the Germans, who were furious at the slow pace of Guernsey workmen. John Leale, President of the Controlling Committee, tried to pacify the Feldkommandantur by writing to say that notices had been put up at the airport urging the men to 'increase their output and thus avoid unpleasant consequences'. This did not impress the workmen, and it did not satisfy the Germans.

The States Engineer, Ernest Lainé, was commissioned to investigate and produce a report on the men's workrate. He agreed with the Germans' criticism; the men, he said, worked slowly and with 'frequent and prolonged pauses'. They gave him three reasons for this: firstly, 'it is not right to compel men to erect hangars for housing planes which might be used to destroy their near relatives'; secondly, 'limited food rations'; and thirdly, 'the men consider that they are working for the Occupation Forces and that the States act as paymasters only and are unable to dispense with their services'.

Lainé conceded that there was 'some justification for the first two excuses', but he believed that the men were dragging the work out at the airport because they were getting such good wages. The copy of the report sent to the Germans omitted the first of the men's reasons altogether, and concluded: 'The men's ambition is to stay as long as possible in this delectable if dangerous area. Acts of generosity of the German soldiers in the distribution of tobacco coupons, bread etc. have no doubt contributed to the amenities of the airport.'

The disquiet felt by the workmen at Guernsey airport was shared by many islanders as they watched the planes taking off and assembling in the skies overhead before heading for England. Bernard Cochrane, who was working for the Germans, remembered how the 'German bombers would circle the islands before they all set off to bomb England. Escort planes would take off from Guernsey. The noise was terrible and our hearts would go out to England. They looked so sinister. We always thought, the RAF boys will be there to meet them.'

Ambrose Sherwill remembered one Sunday afternoon in the summer of 1940: 'Apparently Guernsey was the assembly point, for the entire sky – or so it seemed to me – was black with German bombers and, as I watched them, the fighters to escort them took off from our airport. I counted no less than sixty of these as they soared into the air above my head. My feeling of utter helplessness was terrible. If one could only have telephoned a warning . . . nothing to do except worry and grieve.'

In 1940 and 1941 qualms on Guernsey about working for the Germans may have been strong, but they were gradually eroded by the steep rise in the cost of food and the shortage of other jobs. The Germans continued to grumble about the lazy Guernsey workmen, but there was no shortage of volunteers. By April 1943 the Controlling Committee was concerned that there would not be enough workers for the island's glasshouses 'as a result of the drift from civilian employ brought about by the attractive rates of pay offered by the Occupying Authorities'.

After the hangars were completed, fifty men were kept on at the airport for general maintenance, and frequent building projects brought in many more workmen. In September 1943 Richard Johns could not find new men for the airport because most of the big private companies were already working there full-time.

On Jersey the situation was strikingly different. The Superior Council was more alert to the problem that most of the work for which the Germans wanted labourers was of a military nature. Initially the Council operated – like the Controlling Committee on Guernsey – as an agent, matching German orders with local private companies and government departments. But the co-operation became increasingly strained.

In August 1941 the Inselkommandant's chief of staff, Oberst von Helldorf, sent a memo to Jersey's Superior Council acknowledging that under the Hague Convention he could not force the civilian population to work on military projects, 'especially if these are against their own country. The enrolment of civilians for these purposes must be a voluntary arrangement.'

The Superior Council decided to inform all islanders working for the Germans that if there was any doubt as to whether work was of a military nature, the contractor could refer the case to the Department of Labour, which would clarify it with the Germans. The Department printed leaflets for the workmen with the relevant article of the Hague Convention.

In September 1941 the Department of Labour refused to recondition the avenue to a private house, Grainville Manor, because the building was being used as an ammunition dump, and they therefore considered it military work. Ed Le Quesne's responses to German requests for labour became increasingly curt: 'Unfortunately we cannot find either butchers, tailors or shoemakers. Skilled tradesmen being difficult to find in the present circumstances.'

When the Germans wanted workmen to go to Alderney in November 1942, Le Quesne said he could not help, and suggested advertising in the local paper. This produced little result, and the Germans turned to Le Quesne again. He asked them for a signed assurance that 'the work undertaken in Alderney will be of an entirely non-military nature. With this guarantee we feel there will be little difficulty in obtaining the men required.' The work consisted of repairing houses, assured the Germans. But few workers had volunteered by the end of February 1943, and an apoplectic Feldkommandant Knackfuss wrote, 'the States are hereby charged in virtue of Article 53 of the Hague Convention' to nominate the carpenters, electricians and masons required for Alderney by 6 March. Finally, on 12 May, twenty-two men and two women left Jersey for Alderney – more than six months after the Germans had first requested them.

The Germans became increasingly desperate for workers on Jersey, and finally resorted to forcing people to work for them. In March 1943 Knackfuss ordered the Bailiff, Alexander Coutanche, to draw up lists of workmen from which men would be drawn to work for the Germans. They were to be offered extra rations and higher wages. Two months later the Germans asked for some shops to be closed and for the names of the workers thus released to be passed on to them. Le Quesne replied nearly a month later: 'The [number of those] capable of undertaking other work in anything like an efficient manner would be out of all proportion to the domestic dislocation and human hardship involved.'

On 11 July 1943, Knackfuss again demanded a list of workmen, and two weeks later he demanded a pool of a hundred workers to be permanently on standby, and ordered the Jersey Department of Labour to recruit them from local businesses. The reply the following day from the Superior Council was: 'We are unanimously of the opinion that the Department of Labour could not make such a selection and that it must be left to the Field Command itself to requisition the services required.'

The Jersey Superior Council's lack of co-operation probably did not significantly reduce the numbers working for the Germans on the island. High wages and a shortage of jobs were as strong inducements there as they were on Guernsey. The officials' uncompromising attitude may even have led to some islanders being forced to work for the Germans, which did not happen on Guernsey.

Within a year of the Occupation's start, the entire economies of the islands orientated around the Germans; private companies were devoted to fulfilling their orders, and thousands of islanders worked for the Germans directly or indirectly. In 1944 Befehlshaber, General leutnant Graf von Schmettow calculated that three-quarters of the islands' populations were working, directly or indirectly, for the Germans.

One aspect of the labour question has remained buried in secrecy. When the Home Office released documents relating to the Occupation in December 1992, this aspect was still considered too damaging to be revealed, and the relevant papers were only released with some details censored in thick black felt-tip. What the Home Office did not want anybody to know was that islanders from both Guernsey and Jersey worked in the German forces – a few, it is alleged, in German uniform. From government and German records in the island archives, it is clear that islanders worked at gun batteries and in the German military administration. At one point, in 1943, there were fifteen Guernseymen working in the German forces, according to the records.

Islanders also worked for the Organisation Todt, the vast labour organisation of the Third Reich which employed hundreds of thousands of men and women throughout occupied Europe, either working voluntarily or taken as forced or slave labour from their homes. It was to play an infamous role in the appalling treatment of slave labour on the Channel Islands, in particular, on Alderney. The OT was a separate agency on the islands, administered from France by its own hierarchy. The Feldkommandantur had no authority over it. It was a Nazi institution, with all the paraphernalia of Heil Hitler salutes and Swastika armbands, and it operated its workforce along Nazi racialist policies. Poles and Russians were regarded as subhuman, but Channel Islanders were considered 'Germanic', and most of them were entitled to proper pay and conditions.

On 12 February 1941 the Guernsey States Labour Office wrote to the Feldkommandantur that 1400 men had been dismissed from the States-run Glasshouse Utilisation Board, and 'we will be in a position to send a large number of workmen to the Organisation Todt'. In subsequent correspondence, the Labour Office was even blunter: States labourers would be 'passed onto the OT when work was slack'. On 4 March 1942 Richard Johns sent the Feldkommandantur a list of 493 Guernsey men and women who were working for the OT; the OT firm Paulus alone was employing 339 at the airport. In the same year, one Jersey document indicates that thirty-nine men and ten women were working for the OT, and receiving full board in the Jersey labour camps; the real figure was as high as that on Guernsey. By January 1943 Johns reported that 1200 islanders on Guernsey were working either directly for the German authorities or for local companies under contract to the Germans. On Alderney, the number working either for the OT or for companies under contract to the OT was around fifty, drawn from both Guernsey and Jersey. No proof has ever been established that islanders were involved in the ill-treatment of OT slave labour, although there is anecdotal evidence. There are also stories that some OT workers were attracted by more than just the wages. One Jerseyman who worked on Alderney was said to have worn OT uniform and a swastika armband.

A crucial issue over which the island governments and the German authorities frequently squabbled was money. Under the Hague Convention, the Germans were entitled to expect the island governments to pay for the cost of the Occupation. But as the numbers of troops increased, the Feldkommandantur accepted that the full amount could not be borne by the island governments, and agreed that the Germans would take on some of the burden themselves. In 1942 three-quarters of the money already paid by Jersey and Guernsey was refunded.

The cost of a billet for one soldier was one shilling and sixpence per night, and by March 1944 Guernsey had paid 1,410,000 Reichsmarks and Jersey a million Reichsmarks in Occupation costs. In addition, the islands were paying for the supply of milk to the troops, for maids, charwomen and gardeners, as well as for lighting, heating and water, which added up to RM 2,500,000 on Guernsey and RM 2,000,000 on Jersey. The bills were well beyond the islands' means, and they paid them thanks only to credit from the French government and local banks. Vast debts were accumulated which would have to be tackled once the war was over.

The German Feldkommandantur rapidly extended its tentacles into every area of island life. Throughout Europe, Nazification policies were introduced to bring occupied countries into line with the authoritarian, repressive German Third Reich. On the Channel Islands, pounds, shillings and pence were gradually replaced by Reichsmarks and pfennigs; some places were given German names. All public organisations, from the Tiddlywinks Society to the Bowling Green Association, had to be registered with the Feldkommandantur, and permission was required for meetings. The iron grip over even the most petty details of islanders' lives tightened. The Salvation Army was banned as a paramilitary organisation, and in November 1941 the German military government insisted that all Freemasons' lodges be liquidated throughout the occupied territories. This was one issue over which the Guernsey government was prepared to protest. Bailiff Carey, in a rare exertion, sent a long memo to the Feldkommandantur pleading that the Masons on Guernsey be exempted because, unlike in France, they were 'apolitical and all political discussions are banned . . . If nevertheless the exigencies of War require the dissolution of the Guernsey Lodges and the disposal of their property, I suggest this should be effected by German Order rather than by local legislation . . . It would be asking a lot of those members of the legislature who are Freemasons to violate their undertakings by voting their associations out of existence.' The protests were in vain.

All publications were subjected to the scrutiny of a censor in the Feldkommandantur, who also instructed which items of German propaganda had to be printed in the islands' newspapers and where – usually on the front page. Frank Falla, a journalist on Guernsey for both the *Star* and the *Guernsey Evening Press*, felt he had 'no option' but to sign a declaration in September 1940 undertaking to submit all newspaper proofs to the censor. Like other island journalists, Falla took the pragmatic attitude that it was better to stay in one's job and try to slip in pieces of information which were genuinely useful to islanders than to confront the Guernsey censor, Sonderführer Kurt Goettman.

The journalists' compromise is clear in Occupation editions of the main Guernsey newspaper, the *Evening Press*. The paper greeted the Germans' first orders with a leader on 3 July 1940: 'I saw smiles light up faces which before had seemed a little anxious . . . remarks heard can be summarised as "very gentlemanly and wise" . . . Many Guernsey folk will wish that some of the wise rulings contained in the Commandant's orders may become permanent on our statute books.'

Two days later, the front page ran a story of how a German officer offered a 'cripple' a lift into St Peter Port, with the comment that 'it was one of those touches of nature which tend to make the world kin'. Within a week, the *Evening Press* was carrying German lessons. In a front-page article in November 1940 readers were told of the shame of the blockade of Germany in 1919 and instructed that 'to be true patriots was to admit proven crimes committed in England's name by the political thugs and hirelings that have brought our country to a useless war and unimaginable misery'.

By the end of 1940, the format of the *Guernsey Evening Press* which was to last the Occupation had emerged: the entire front page was given over to news of Germany's victories, Britain's imminent collapse, and the glories of National Socialism. Local news consisted of cookery tips, home hints and long columns of goods for barter or exchange. The German lessons continued, and the *Press* once even carried an editorial headed 'Why you should be learning German'. The writer quoted a story of how islanders had sung 'Silent Night' at a recent party, so that the 'guests would feel at home', and had then enjoyed a little informal German lesson. 'German is a great language . . . German has arrived for good whatever happens after this unhappy war.' The piece concluded that evening classes in German were now being run under the aegis of the Guernsey government. Most islanders ignored the reams of German propaganda and used the local papers mainly for the cookery hints and barter columns.

Frank Falla describes one battle with the German censor which indicates the lengths to which the Germans went to control the island press. The article in question could hardly have been more innocuous – it was a Christmas message written by a local vicar, the Reverend T. Hartley Jackson, and it concluded: 'The recognition that Christ was born into the world to save the world and bring peace on earth, is the need of the world.' The censor changed this to 'The recognition that Christ was born into the world to save the world and bring peace on earth, is the need of Britain and her Jewish and Bolshevik allies.'

Falla complained that his struggle with the censors was not made any easier by the attitude adopted by the Guernsey government: 'It often seemed to us that the civil authorities joined forces with the Germans in an attempt to stifle freedom of the Press. They would come down on the two newspapers [the *Evening Press* and the *Guernsey Star*] with "You had no right to do this" or "Such a thing was not in the public interest."'

The *Evening Press* staff helped the Germans to set up and publish a newspaper for the troops, the *Deutsche Guernsey Zeitung*, and it was printed on the *Evening Press* printing machines.

When Falla moved to the *Guernsey Star*, he found the situation even worse than on the *Evening Press*. 'One of the biggest Quislings Guernsey had was a senior employee of the *Guernsey Star* company . . . I just couldn't stomach this man and hated to see him fawning on the Germans and entertaining them as though they were long-lost brothers.'

Libraries were also censored after the Germans were outraged to find what they described as 'hate propaganda' in a book from a Guernsey lending library in December 1941. They demanded a list of all booksellers and lending libraries in the island from John Leale; he complied, and circulated the Germans' letter of complaint. The puzzled recipients were not entirely sure as to what might constitute 'hate propaganda', but by early January 1942 the libraries were falling over themselves to surrender offending books. *Hell Hounds*

of France and *Falcon of France* were amongst the four books sent in
by Argosy Library. The Home Circle Library sent in seven books,
adding that they had conducted their own search at the beginning
of the Occupation. One of the biggest libraries, the Guille Allès,
sent some books and anxiously enquired if the Germans could come
and examine their stock 'with a view to the removal of works which
in their judgement are of an offensive nature. As we feel hardly
competent to form an opinion in the matter.' All works by Winston
Churchill, Duff Cooper and H.G. Wells, among others, were
banned.

The islands' schools did not escape a dose of Germanisation.
The occupying authorities were anxious that everyone should learn
German as, if they were to be true citizens of Europe's Third Reich,
they would have to be able to speak its *lingua franca*. The Germans
ordered five hundred copies of *Deutsche Leben* ('German Lives')
from a local Guernsey printer early in 1941. By May of that year,
the Guernsey States Education Council told the Feldkommandantur that 71 out of 201 children over the age of twelve had volunteered to learn German. Adult evening classes were also set up, and
Leale told the Germans that 107 adults had signed and paid up for
thrice-weekly classes.

On Sark, the Dame wrote a handwritten note to Dr Reffler at
the Guernsey Nebenstelle saying that she had offered the use of
her own home for German classes on Saturday afternoons, because
there was no fuel for heat or light in the school. A month later she
wrote again begging for textbooks, because twenty-two children
were now attending the classes.

The Germans stiffened their policy in March 1942, when they
made German compulsory for all children over the age of ten, and
inspectors visited the schools to check on progress. In May 1943
they specified that four periods of forty minutes' duration should
be devoted to German per week, at a time when schools were
having to cut their hours because of fuel shortages. French teaching
was dropped in most schools to make time for German, which
assumed a disproportionate significance in the curriculum. The
islands' education departments made timid protests. Guernsey's
Education Council report in 1944 ventured: 'The order to teach
German to children [was] received with misgiving ... the Council

is not at all happy about the effect of a third language being taught to elementary school children.'

In 1944, when the school day was cut to four hours, and there was still a requirement to teach four forty-minute periods of German a week, the Jersey Education Department begged for a reduction to two periods, and promised that if their request was granted the children and teachers would work extra hard. The education authorities on Jersey and Guernsey pleaded with the Germans to let off children who were not up to learning a foreign language. Some children were also deliberately unreceptive. After the war, children who had remained on the islands throughout the Occupation were found to be considerably behind their contemporaries who had been evacuated to Britain; part of the reason was those precious hours squandered on teaching German to unwilling classes.

The Feldkommandantur occasionally sent an officer to attend ceremonies at which prizes were awarded for the children's progress in German. In August 1944, for example, Sonderführer Krefft accepted an invitation from Peter Girard, headmaster of the States Intermediate School, to a school concert where German poetry was recited. But the States Education Secretary, Archibald Winterflood, stood by his principles – much to Girard's annoyance – and refused to come to the concert.

One issue stands out over which the island governments failed to serve as the 'buffer' they claimed to be. In 1941 Guernsey and Jersey had been asked to draw up lists of the islands' residents, including their places of birth. The lists were compiled by the island authorities. They had little idea that the order had come from Hitler himself, who was considering how to retaliate to the British internment of five hundred German men in Iran in August 1941. All islanders who had been born in Britain were eligible for deportation, Hitler ordered. His first idea was to send the deported islanders to the Pripet Marshes in Poland, and to give their property to 'native-born' islanders. The move was in line with the policy advocated in Professor Pfeffer's report of setting the English and the native-born Channel Islanders against each other.

For a year nothing happened, but in September 1942, when Hitler discovered that the matter had been neglected, he demanded that it be put in hand immediately. The Feldkommandantur ordered that everyone on the islands be registered. All members of the population had to carry an identity card with them wherever they went, which bore the owner's photograph, occupation, date and place of birth. There were frequent prosecutions of those who failed to produce their card. A list of the names of all the residents of each house had to be nailed to the inside of every front door. The Germans wanted to be able to keep track of every islander. There would be no place to hide. The island governments complied with the request to draw up lists of those who fell into certain categories, such as having served in the British armed forces or having a criminal record.

In September 1942 and February 1943 a total of 2200 islanders were deported to German internment camps for the duration of the war. They were given only a few days – sometimes only a few hours – in which to pack their belongings and leave their homes. This was probably the grimmest moment of the Occupation for the islanders. There was no authority to whom they could appeal, and their governments did nothing but pass resolutions of protest, which the Germans ignored. There was no way of knowing what would happen to the men, women and children who boarded the ships for Germany.

On 15 September 1942, Bailiff Coutanche was summoned to the Feldkommandantur and was told by Oberstleutnant Knackfuss that all British subjects who did not have permanent residence on the Channel Islands, and all males aged between sixteen and seventy who had not been born in the islands, together with their families, were to be evacuated immediately. The first batch of 1200 would leave the following day, and the constables* would serve the evacuation notices and would be consulted as to who should go. Coutanche protested and threatened to resign. He insisted that constables could not select deportees, nor could they serve notices; Knackfuss agreed. In the end neither Coutanche nor any other

---

* The constables were the chief officials of the islands' parishes. They presided over the equivalent of the parish council.

member of the Superior Council resigned; they decided they could best help the deportees by staying in office. The first batch of deportees left the following day, and the operation was completed on Jersey by 22 September. The Superior Council submitted a resolution of protest pointing out to the Germans that on 1 July 1940 they had guaranteed the lives, property and liberty of islanders in the event of peaceful surrender.

Guernsey's Controlling Committee took a similar line. After initial protests, they drew up a list of British-born islanders as requested. They tried to help the deportees by providing clothes, transport to the harbour, a hot meal before boarding the ships and food for the journey. On 27 and 28 September 825 men, women and children left the island. Sark's quota of deportees was eleven, out of a total population of four hundred. Two of them failed to report – the husband was discovered dead, with his wrists slashed, and his wife was seriously wounded.

There were further deportations in February 1943, in retaliation for a British commando raid on Sark. The categories of those to be deported included islanders judged to be workshy or politically suspect, former army and navy officers, Jews and high-ranking Freemasons, as well as their families. Ambrose Sherwill and his family were on the list because Sherwill had been an officer in the First World War. Originally about a thousand people were intended to be evacuated, but this was subsequently reduced to around two hundred.

In the event, many of the greatest fears of the deported islanders proved groundless. Conditions in the camps of Laufen, Biberach and Würzach in southern Germany, where the islanders were imprisoned, were relatively good. Thanks to a regular supply of Red Cross parcels, the prisoners were even better fed than those who had been left behind. But the elderly, the infirm and small children did suffer, and for all of them it was a wrench from their familiar life. Prominent islanders such as Sherwill set up a highly structured, disciplined camp life complete with schools, a hospital, cleaning rotas, football leagues, drama clubs and craft sessions.

Many islanders found their governments' protests at the deportations feeble. They were baffled at how, under the pretext of being a 'buffer', island police and officials actually assisted the deportations. The operation could never have been carried out in so little time without the help of islanders: it was the island authorities who had drawn up the lists of those born outside the islands; it was the island police who guided the Germans to deliver the deportation orders; the buses which took the deportees to the port had been provided by the States – at least on Guernsey; and it was island policemen who assisted their embarkation. Whose side were the States on? At the end of the war, questions remained in islanders' minds. One C.B. Dunn wrote to the *Jersey Evening Post* on 30 May 1945: 'Who was responsible for drawing up the list of English residents deported to Germany? Was it necessary for local officials to co-operate so wholeheartedly with the enemy in this respect? ... The Germans would have been considerably hindered in the execution of their duty if this local help had not been forthcoming.'

Among the most poignant files in the Guernsey archives is one full of letters from islanders pleading with the German authorities to be exempted from deportation. They reveal a population full of fear of the arbitrary power of the Germans. Within this context, the sycophancy and special pleading are pitiably human.

One man successfully submitted that both his parents were Guernsey-born, and that he had only spent the first three years of his life in England. But another man in similar circumstances was refused. A.B. Barnet pointed out that he and his wife were caring for her elderly parents, and that as a hairdresser he believed he was doing useful service, because he was 'extensively patronised by the German forces'. His appeal was refused. Numerous other islanders wrote that they were working hard for the Germans but this was rarely sufficient to sway the decision. Francis de Norrisa tried another tack: 'For many years I have preached against war against Germany, both of the 1914 war and this war also, and have been ostracised for it. I have lived amongst German people in Canada, USA and Australia and formed the finest friendships among them.'

The Reverend Edwin Foley, Minister of Spurgeon Memorial Baptist Church on Guernsey, followed a similar line:

I am not saying this to curry favour, but to express my deep and long-cherished conviction. I have never had the opportunity of saying this yet to any German and should like to take this opportunity of saying it confidentially to you.

Though I am English-born, I am very, very sorry for all the wrong which I believe England has done to Germany. I was not in favour of England declaring war on Germany in 1914 and got into some trouble for saying so. I believe the Treaty of Versailles was iniquitous and did much wrong to Germany. I often said too that I thought the allied blockade of Germany during the long months of the so-called Peace conference in 1918 was very wicked and I was not in favour of England declaring war on Germany in 1939.

For nearly forty years, I have tried hard to foster friendly relations with Germany and a saner policy. I know that some English-speaking people on Guernsey and many in England think and feel as I do, but unfortunately we have been and at present are a minority – the propaganda forces have been too strong for us.

But I pray God the day may come when happier and friendlier relations may exist between these two countries who have so many words in common and are both loved by One Father in Heaven.

P.S. . . . sometimes good German Baptists come to our services and I always give them a warm welcome in the name of Our Common Lord. I try to say to them in my perhaps faulty and broken German 'Wie [sic] sind Brüder in Christ.' – we are all brothers in Christ.'

The Germans were impressed by Foley's eloquence, and he and his wife were allowed to remain. Three men working for Messrs Timmer Ltd were also exempted from deportation after the company intervened on their behalf, writing of one of them: 'Mr Camp is a very conscientious man, working from early morning until late at night including Sundays to see that the vegetables are ready for the troops each morning.'

The deportations provoked huge bitterness between islanders. Those who were particularly useful to the Germans – as mistresses, as informers, as contractors – were often exempted; one business-man was allowed to stay because the Geheime Feldpolizei, the secret military police, said he was 'used in various ways as an informer'. Cecil Bazeley noted in his diary that a girl asked Ober-leutnant Zepernick to get her father off the deportation list – which he did.

Many islanders believed prominent citizens used their connec-tions to get their names off the deportation lists. One man was exempted after he pleaded with the Germans that he was a Deputy of the States, Vice President of the Essential Commodities Committee and President of the States Electricity Board. Ambrose Sherwill begged Baron von Aufsess to exempt his wife and two small sons. He subsequently learned that von Aufsess had disobeyed the Kommandant's express command and saved his wife May and the boys from being deported.

There were no such exemptions for another category of deportees who, unlike the rest, did not return after the war. When they set up the islands' registration system, the Germans intended to establish the ethnic identity of each individual. The long shadow of anti-Semitism had reached the Channel Islands. The identity cards of Jews were ordered to be stamped in 'a conspicuous place with a capital J in red'.

The marking of the Jews' identity cards in March 1941 was one of a number of anti-Jewish measures ordered by the German military government in Paris. The first were registered in the local island courts in October 1940. This aspect of the Channel Islands' Nazification programme was to have tragic consequences, and is one of the most haunting stories of the Occupation.

Most of the islands' Jewish population had left in the evacuation. Both they and the island authorities had been aware of the special dangers to them of remaining. The Guernsey government, for example, urged the well-respected Dr William Montague to evacuate for 'racial reasons'. British Jews who lived in the Channel Islands had friends and relatives in Britain to go to, but there were a number of Jews who had only recently come to the islands. They were mostly single women fleeing persecution in Germany and Austria, who had managed to get work permits for the islands as domestic servants. The Rabbi on Jersey, Israel Cohen (who evacuated before the Occupation), helped four Austrian Jews who arrived in 1938. Several others arrived on Guernsey in the mid-thirties, and at least two married islanders and gained British nationality. After the war, many people on Jersey and Guernsey claimed to believe that there were no Jews left on the islands by the time the Germans arrived.

The first German anti-Jewish measures arrived on the desk of the President of the Controlling Committee, Ambrose Sherwill, in

mid-September 1940. Sherwill, troubled by the memory of his role
in the matter, went to considerable lengths to defend himself in
his post-war memoirs:

> I noted its provisions [from the German command in Paris] which
> included the required wearing by all Jews of the yellow star of David.
> It disgusted me and I visualised Jews being jeered at on Guernsey
> in the streets, pelted with filth and generally harassed, but I had no
> premonition of the appalling atrocities which were to be perpetrated
> on them by the Nazi regime.
>
> I made such enquiries as I could and learned, accurately as it
> turned out, that the few Jews who had settled on Guernsey had all
> evacuated. In these circumstances, I felt no purpose would be served
> in ... advising the Royal Court to refuse to register it. If I had,
> presumably the Germans would have threatened the Royal Court
> by marching in armed soldiers.
>
> Nevertheless, I still fell ashamed that I did not do something by
> way of protest to the Germans: a vital principle was at stake even if
> no human being on Guernsey was actually affected. The honour of
> refusing to concur in its registration fell to Sir Abraham Lainé who,
> when called on as a Jurat to vote on the matter, openly and categori-
> cally refused his assent and stated his grave objections to such a
> measure ... this courageous act of his should never be forgotten.
> As I sat listening to him, I realised how right he was.

Under the laws registered in the Royal Court on October 1940, a
Jew was defined as anybody with more than two Jewish grandparents; all such people had to present themselves for registration.
Jewish businesses had to be labelled as such in English, French and
German – there were three on Jersey and one on Guernsey, whose
owners had evacuated. More anti-Jewish laws followed in May 1941
which ruled that no Jews were allowed to enter public places, and
all Jewish businesses were confiscated without compensation.

Sherwill's belief that there were no Jews left on the islands turned
out to be incorrect; there were five living on Guernsey, and at least
twelve on Jersey. Dr Brosch and Dr Casper at the Feldkommandantur had been charged with drawing up a register of the Jews on the
islands, and they turned to the local police forces. The detailed
correspondence between the police, the Guernsey and Jersey

governments and the Germans survives, and makes grim reading. The island officials made no attempt to protest; on the contrary, they complied with every German request promptly and courteously, and with meticulous attention to detail.

In October 1940 the Germans asked for a list of the names and addresses of all foreigners living on Guernsey. The Inspector of Police, William Sculpher, sent the list to Sherwill, who then passed it on to the Germans. On it were two girls described as German – Therese Steiner and Auguste Spitz. All Germans, Italians and Austrians were ordered to attend German Headquarters.

In the course of his investigations, Sculpher had to interview people suspected of having Jewish blood. In November 1940 he wrote to Sherwill:

> I beg to report that I have seen Julia Brichta and Annie Wranowsky. [Julia] informs me her mother died when she was a baby and her father died soon after. She states she never knew anything of her grandparents. As far as she is aware her parents were not Jews and she is not related to Jews. [Annie] states that neither her parents nor her grandparents were Jews and that she can trace five generations in her family without encountering Jewish blood. Her passport issued in London in 1939 is stamped with a 'J'.

This report was passed on by Sherwill's successor, John Leale, to Dr Brosch at the Feldkommandantur: 'I have the honour to enclose herewith a report from the inspector of police on the subject.'

Violet Woolnough of Vauvert Manor, Guernsey, was interviewed, and admitted that her mother was Jewish but stated that she had been baptised and had married a gentile. The Germans ruled that she was not to be considered a Jew. By the end of November 1940, Sculpher had produced the names of five resident Jews. Two were British – Elizabeth Duquemin and Elda Brouard; two were German – Therese Steiner and Auguste Spitz; and one was Czech – Annie Wranowsky. Sculpher's report was sent to the Bailiff, Victor Carey, who passed it on to Leale, who gave it to the Germans.

On Jersey, the Chief Aliens Officer, Clifford Orange, similarly conducted interviews with Jersey residents to find out if they were

Jewish according to Nazi laws. Twelve individuals, ranging in age from twenty-one-year-old Romanian Hedwig Bercu to seventy-nine-year-old Therese Marks, were registered as Jewish by Orange. It is not known what happened to most of them, although according to several Jersey people Jews were hidden by sympathetic islanders. Hedwig Bercu was pursued by the German authorities after she disappeared in November 1943, and notices with her pretty photograph were printed in the *Jersey Evening Post*. In August 1944 her name crops up on a list of missing persons: the Germans threatened collective punishments on parishes unless the eighteen men and women presented themselves to the authorities. Hedwig Bercu was among them. It is not known what happened to her, although some islanders believe she was captured and sent to a European concentration camp.

The Jersey Bailiff Alexander Coutanche was vague on the subject of the island's Jews in his memoirs: 'The Jews were, I think, called upon to declare themselves. Some did, some didn't . . . Those who didn't, weren't discovered. I've never heard they suffered in any way.'

Jersey clerk Bob Le Sueur remembers more:

> I was horrified about the Jews having to register. I still feel it was bad but the Germans might have taken hostages if they had refused. There was a couple called Still and the wife was Jewish. When she was deported, her husband asked if he could accompany her. They were separated at St Malo and she never returned. John Max Finkelstein was also Jewish and he was sent to a camp. He was in a prison for the criminally insane I heard and the commandant once lined prisoners up against the wall and lunged at them with a bayonet. Finkelstein pretended he'd been hurt and collapsed, groaning. He was a very tough little man and he survived.

Three businesses belonging to Jews were auctioned off. In April 1941 Louis Feldman's dressmaking, millinery and furrier's business in St Helier's was sold for £150. The more substantial property of the Krichefski family, who had evacuated to England, went for £1050. On Guernsey a Mrs Middlewick's lingerie business was sold – she too had left for England before the Occupation.

The documents on Guernsey detailing the fate of the islands' Jews have survived. For the first few months of 1941 no more steps were taken. Annie Wranowsky began teaching children German in the Dame of Sark's home. In October 1941 John Leale wrote in reply to a letter from the Feldkommandantur that Therese Steiner, by virtue of her work as a nurse at the Câtel Hospital, was a 'key person', and therefore protected from being drafted to work for the Germans.

In January 1942 the Germans ordered the Guernsey authorities to investigate the financial affairs of the four Jewish women on the island. Louis Guillemette, Secretary to the President of the Controlling Committee, reported that the Guernsey police had established that Therese Steiner's income was £48 p.a. plus board and lodging, while Auguste Spitz was a housemaid earning fifteen shillings per week. Neither had any other assets. Elizabeth Duquemin had £83 in the Post Office Savings Bank, which she was saving for the education of her baby daughter, and Elda Brouard was paid ten shillings a week and had £250 in War Loans and £60 in Barclays Bank.

In April 1942 Leale wrote to the Germans asking them to grant the request of Edward Ogier for an interview: 'He is a well-known and respected Guernseyman who is doing useful work as a farmer in producing foodstuffs ... He wishes to discuss the possibility of retaining in his employment Miss M. Grunfeld.' This is the only surviving official reference in correspondence with the Germans to a Polish-Jewish woman, Marianne Grunfeld.

By the end of April 1942, three names were missing from a list of foreigners resident on Guernsey which Sculpher sent to the Germans: Steiner, Spitz and Grunfeld. They had left the islands. Only Annie Wranowsky remained; she is believed to have survived the war. The British Jews Elda Brouard and Elizabeth Duquemin, and her baby, also survived.

For the best part of forty years, little was known on Guernsey about the fate of Therese Steiner, Auguste Spitz and Marianne Grunfeld, and no one showed any inclination to find out more about this episode in the island's past. Over the last decade, however, much more information has emerged about Therese Steiner and Marianne Grunfeld, and their relatives have been traced. Of

Auguste Spitz, the forty-one-year-old hospital cleaner, almost nothing is known other than her name and the unhappy face which stares out from the one photograph of her which has survived.

Therese Steiner was twenty-six when she left Guernsey in 1942; she was deported to Drancy in the northern suburbs of Paris, the collecting point for railway transports from France to the concentration camps. On 20 July 1942, she and Auguste Spitz were in a convoy of 824 people who left Drancy and arrived in Auschwitz three days later. They are presumed to have died the same day. Only fourteen men from their convoy survived. One was Dr Andre Lettich, who described the conditions of the journey:

> We were loaded into cattle wagons, sixty-five to eighty people to a wagon, and the windows and doors were hermetically sealed. In the course of the journey, crammed against each other, we suffered terribly from thirst and we were forced to sacrifice the corner of the wagon for the necessities of nature. On 23 July at about 4 p.m., the train stopped and we experienced violent jerks and the unsealing of the wagons. With their usual cries, the SS made us understand that everyone should leave the wagon and unload the baggage. They ordered us to form up in five ranks. It was raining. We had mud up to our knees ... anyone who tried to put on his waterproof or hat to protect him from the rain learnt by blows to the head that this was forbidden. Finally we were directed to the camp. I can still see in the distance the women who went in a different direction.

Therese Steiner was born into a comfortable middle-class family in Vienna. Her brother Karl, a talented musician, taught her the piano, and they gave concerts together. Just prior to the *Anschluss* – when Germany invaded Austria in 1938 – Therese left Vienna and went to England to work, she believed, as a dental assistant for a dentist living in Kent. In fact, to her annoyance, she became the nanny to his family. Her brother Paul had also left Vienna because of the high unemployment, and had got a job in a factory in northern France. Only the musical brother, Karl, remained with his parents at home, because he had just been appointed director of a music school.

In the summer of 1939 the Kent dentist and his family took their annual holiday on Sark. War broke out while they were in the

Channel Islands and they returned to England, but Therese Steiner did not. All German and Austrian nationals were interned under instructions from the Home Office, and Therese was one of about thirty detained on Guernsey. After her release she found a job at the Câtel Hospital as a nurse, and made many friends in the three years she was on Guernsey. Work was hard, but on her days off she cycled around the island. Many of her nursing colleagues remember her playing the piano for her patients.

In 1939, it seemed that Therese and Paul were safe, and that it was Karl – imprisoned in Dachau after five thousand Jews were rounded up in Vienna on Kristallnacht, 9 November 1938 – who was in the most danger. In fact, Karl was the only member of the family to survive the Holocaust. He was released from Dachau and managed to get to France, and from there he fled to Shanghai; after the war he moved to Canada. Former neighbours in Vienna told him that in 1942 his mother had written a postcard to tell them that she had gone on a 'long journey'. Karl knew immediately that she had been deported to a concentration camp but had not dared to say so. There was no word of Paul or Therese.

For forty-eight years Karl filled in Red Cross Missing Persons application forms, fired by the hope that Therese and Paul might have survived. It was not until January 1993, as a frail octogenarian on holiday in Britain, that he heard what had happened to his sister. He was visiting friends when the television news came on. One of the items was the opening of the Guernsey Occupation archives; documents had been found relating to a Jewish woman, Therese Steiner, who had died in Auschwitz. Karl went to Guernsey, and was greeted at every turn by people willing to talk to him of his sister, unburdening a secret that had lain closed for nearly half a century. He found this overwhelming, in particular one telephone call; the caller said that he was a policeman who had collected Therese and handed her over to the Germans. Between incoherent sobs, he apologised again and again, telling Karl, 'If I'd known what was going to happen to her, I would have hidden her in my house. She was a lovely girl.'

The third Jewish woman, Marianne Grunfeld, was born in Poland to a prosperous German Jewish family. Her cousins moved to London in the mid 1930s, and a couple of years later she followed. She took a degree at Reading Agricultural College, and worked for a vet for a period; she loved the country and she loved animals. When word came early in 1940 of a job on Guernsey looking after cows on a large farm, she jumped at it. Her cousin Ernst, now living in Marlow, Buckinghamshire, remembers how Marianne came to his family home in London to say goodbye. His family tried to dissuade her from taking the job, but Marianne would not change her mind; she was a strong-willed young woman, Ernst remembers, and she wrote defiantly in her cousins' visitors' book, 'It doesn't always rain devils.' She arrived on Guernsey only a couple of months before the Germans. Later in the war Ernst's brother was to smuggle several members of the family out of occupied Poland, but Guernsey was to prove beyond their reach.

At first, Marianne's chances of going undetected appeared good. With her pale skin and red hair, she did not look particularly Jewish. Furthermore, Duveaux Farm seemed an ideal place to hide; the wonderful granite farmhouse still stands behind high stone walls surrounded by trees. Its owners, the Ogier family, liked Marianne. Their visitors' book is full of parties which she attended; one entry marks the celebration of 'dear Marianne's birthday', and the presents she gave Mrs Ogier for birthdays were affectionately recorded.

It is alleged that someone informed on Marianne, and told the Germans she was Jewish. However, Guernsey is a small place, and given the Germans' thoroughness – helped by the island authorities – in registering the entire population, it is possible there was no need for an informer. As John Leale's letter of April 1942 proves, the kindly Edward Ogier attempted to intervene to protect Marianne. He failed. A poignant, euphemistic entry in the Ogier visitors' book that month is the last which refers to Marianne: 'We celebrated dear Marianne's evacuation last night.'

Dr Wilhelm Casper, whose signature appears on so many of the Guernsey documents on behalf of the Feldkommandantur, is still alive, and lives in Bonn after a career as a civil servant. Questioned about the Channel Island Jews, his answer is a mixture of contradictions, evasion and euphemism:

The anti-Jewish measures were given to the military government on
the islands and they were discussed with the States. Almost all the
Jewish inhabitants had been evacuated. The military government
had decided on its own bat that it was not necessary to carry through
the order on the Star of David. At the same time came the order
for the deportations; the orders were not handed to the German
soldiers.

At this point, Dr Casper abruptly switched to describing how Jews
were saved in Denmark by being smuggled to Sweden. Then he
returned to the islands:

> Oettingen [the Rittmeister of Guernsey] told me that there were
> two Viennese Jewesses working in the hospital who decided to go
> back to Vienna and there was a Jewish wife of an islander. On Jersey
> there were no Jews left after the evacuation to Britain. In 1949 in
> Bonn, Oettingen when he was an MP in the Bundestag told me he
> had heard from Guernsey that the Jewish wife of the Guernseyman
> [Elizabeth Duquemin] returned.
>
> I had not permitted Hitler's persecution of the Jews in the islands;
> it contradicted the German Constitution and was not democratically
> legitimated.

The Jewish issue is one of the most sensitive aspects of the Occupation. In 1992, when official documents detailing the fate of Therese
Steiner, Auguste Spitz and Marianne Grunfeld were made public,
islanders defensively claimed that no one had had any idea of what
was happening to the Jews in Europe. They may not have known
of the horror of the Holocaust, but they did know that Jews were
in grave danger, as Sherwill's memoirs indicate. The truth is that
no official in either Guernsey or Jersey considered the welfare of
a handful of Jews sufficiently important to jeopardise good relations
with the Germans.

Officials could argue that the matter was nothing to do with
them; the three Jewish women who died in the gas chambers were
German and Austrian citizens. Island peoples are slow to accept
foreigners, and the Guernsey Jews had only arrived on the islands
a short while before the Germans, and had few friends to help them
hide. In addition, contemporary comments and jokes indicate the

sort of mild anti-Semitism which was common in Britain at the time. Archaic laws barring Jews from becoming representatives in the States had not been repealed. A mixture of ignorance, indifference and anti-Semitism all contributed to these British officials playing their tiny part in the tragedy of the Holocaust.

The island governments' aim of a Model Occupation, in which they served as a buffer, was inherently problematic, a delicate balancing act between expediency and principle. But the voices of principle, such as Sir Abraham Lainé on Guernsey, had little sway, and the balance tipped heavily in favour of expediency. The labour issue clearly shows how, step by step, Guernsey's government was drawn into a compromising position. The rewards for that expediency – peace, jobs and food – were considerable. By contrast, Jersey did invoke principles over the same issue, and its lack of co-operation does not appear to have significantly damaged relations with the German authorities. Jersey recognised the weakness of the skeletal German administration, and its own comparative strength, and exploited the situation; Guernsey remained intimidated.

But neither government was prepared to recognise that principles were at stake in the Jewish issue. Lainé did – and Sherwill later acknowledged that he was right. This was an instance in which, even by the standards they had set themselves, the island governments failed; they were not a buffer for the Jews, and Sherwill's aim of 'running' the Occupation for the Germans had led to the direct implementation of Nazi policies by island officials. This was the high price the island governments paid for their amicable relations with the German authorities. What is disturbing is how little protest they made at paying this price. The Jewish issue is the most clear-cut example of where the island governments' co-operation with the Germans tipped into outright collaboration.

CHAPTER FOUR

SURVIVAL

The largest part of islanders' reminiscences of the Occupation is devoted to the struggle and sheer grind of trying to keep healthy and cheerful. It is the memories of going to bed night after night with an empty stomach, and the long winter nights without light or heat, which are most vivid. This is the history which has been celebrated in personal memoirs, detailed in books and admiringly recreated in the island museums. Hardship, shortages, queues and drudgery were the islanders' war. The struggle of daily survival while keeping a sense of humour has been elevated into something heroic on the islands, just as in Britain the struggle of ordinary men and women in the Blitz has become one of the most powerful myths of the twentieth century.

But the islanders' struggle differed from that of relatives and friends across the Channel; their struggle was not only for their material well-being, but was also with their own consciences. Daily life in the Occupation was riddled with moral dilemmas which every islander, regardless of age or social status, had to confront. Every aspect of life – from jobs to shopping – was potentially loaded with the wounding accusation of collaboration.

It is difficult today to imagine the physical hardship and the moral anguish with which islanders lived. Even harder to understand is how bewildering the experience must have been to tightly-knit communities which had been stable, prosperous and law-abiding for generations. The Occupation was to strain, and in places shatter, the islanders' whole understanding of themselves and the nature of their communities as decent, conscientious and fair.

It is not surprising that this is a theme on which islanders prefer not to dwell. A few words often mask a wealth of confusion and uncertainty; the last fifty years, with all the judgements they have brought on islanders' heads, have only deepened the muddle of shame, humiliation and defiance, and drawn the repeated defence, 'We had no choice.'

Working for the Enemy

'My husband worked for the Germans – that's what they mean by collaboration, isn't it? But you must remember, he was only nineteen.'

Jersey housewife Kathleen Whitley

Thousands of islanders worked for the Germans. Did they feel uneasy about their work? If so, how did they square their consciences?

Edwin de Ste Croix was seventeen at the start of the Occupation, and was an apprentice with the Jersey Electricity Company, much of whose work was for the Germans. He describes how he came to terms with the problem:

All the orders for work came from the Germans straight to the Electricity Company. In theory all German work had to take precedence over the civilian work. Certain work of a military nature, you could refuse to do under the Hague Convention. The rest was things like fixing lighting in barracks, hospitals and offices.

If you refused to do the military work, you didn't always get away with it. You got an order from the Germans and the work wasn't always specified and when you arrived, the German would say that the gun bunker down there needs an alarm. You could refuse to do it in some cases. I'd point out to the German officer in charge that I didn't want to put alarms in gun bunkers to alert your fellows to shoot our fellows.

Sometimes they saw your point of view and they would say, 'Fine, we'll get a German electrician to complete it.' Others would tell you to get on with it or they'd arrest you. You didn't have much choice then.

Once you'd reached a point beyond which you were not personally prepared to go, you'd report it to the boss and the German would report it to his headquarters. My boss always supported me, but he was almost always overruled by the Germans.

You felt a bit uncomfortable and the only recourse was to drag the job out for as long as possible. I was frequently cuffed and beaten on the behind for speaking out of turn. I'd criticise Hitler or tell them that we'd win the war. You were as defiant as you could be. But what kind of resistance could you put up?

De Ste Croix recounts how in December 1944 fuel supplies were virtually exhausted, and the Germans ordered that electricity should be supplied only to the Germans, not the islanders. The Electricity Company staff refused to operate the grid under these instructions, and the Germans had to take over until the Liberation in May 1945. He proudly describes this as the only organised resistance of the Occupation.

Jersey carpenter Sandy Whitley volunteered to work for the Germans. He spoke openly about it, but his wife Kathleen was uneasy, and couldn't help interjecting her remarks in her husband's account:

SANDY: My brother was working for the Germans and he got me a job; he told me it was a cushy number. The Germans paid you £4.10 a week or even £5. Normal wages at that time were about £2 a week and I got German food rations.

KATHLEEN: Boys of that age – all they think about is food.

SANDY: If we hadn't volunteered, we'd have been forced – I was a carpenter. I worked for the Germans for four and a half years right up until two months before Liberation. I did the carpentry for the shuttering [the boarding] for the concrete. I started building sea walls when the Germans were building their own bunkers. Then the German workers were withdrawn and we were put on to building military bunkers and tunnels. I worked on one tunnel for twelve months with some Dutch workers; there were Russians working on the other side. The Germans were quite fair – they'd give you a cigarette – and the work wasn't hard. Everyone took it easy and pinched whatever they could; they'd come home with German bread and wood.

KATHLEEN: My husband worked for the Germans – that's what
they mean by collaboration, isn't it? But you must remember,
he was only nineteen.

SANDY: No one ever criticised me at the time for working for
the Germans, but after the war, tourists would come and stay
at the guest house we ran. They'd ask us about the
Occupation and they'd ask me why I'd worked for the enemy.

KATHLEEN: A lot of the people working for the Germans did
sabotage.

SANDY: I know now what we did was wrong. But you did try and
do little things like putting the iron bars in the concrete
anti-tank walls close to the edge, so they would rust through.
You never thought that would cause problems today for the
island [they are now used as sea walls] instead of the Germans.

On Alderney, George and Daphne Pope and their six children were
the only British family on the island; Daphne took in washing for
the Germans, and George worked as a pilot for the German navy,
guiding them out to the Casquets lighthouse. Islanders have always
accused them of collaboration, says Daphne, adding that they themselves were never bothered by 'such nonsense' for a moment. As
she points out, with no alternative employment on Alderney, their
only chance of keeping their large and growing family fed was to
work for the Germans: 'In exchange for bread I would do a German
called Wilhelm's washing. He was very generous, he would give
me a packet of cigarettes in return for my doing some darning. He
introduced me to a Czech who also brought me his washing and a
bit of meat at the end of the week. I know the old joke, did I
collaborate with him, or did he collaborate with me? – I don't care.
If you want to make me a collaborator out of that, you're welcome.'

Guernseyman Ron Hurford was equally untroubled at the time.
As a nineteen-year-old, he voluntarily went to work in the German
bakeries; he had been a confectioner in a cake shop but he lost his
job when the flour, yeast and sugar to make cakes ran out. He was
working as a porter in a vegetable market in 1941 when the Germans offered him twice the wages and the chance of stealing some
bread on the sly: 'I took three to four loaves a week for my two
brothers and my parents, and another two to three loaves for my

girlfriend's family. I don't like people saying we were all collaborators. In my view I was working for my family and friends, I wasn't
working for the Jerries.' Hurford was subsequently imprisoned for
five and half months after refusing to reveal the name of a fellow
Guernsey workman who had stolen some bread. The German
supervisor struck him, and he hit back.

Jersey teenager Bernard Hassall was working in his father's shop
when he was rounded up by the Germans for forced labour:

> This word 'collaboration' sticks in my craw. I was eighteen in 1943
> and I was working in my father's photographic shop. A staff car
> pulled up and a couple of Germans came in and told me to report
> to the Feldkommandantur. It was lies to say we volunteered.
>
> First I had to work shovelling pebbles up and down the beach. I
> pretended I had heart trouble and a doctor managed to get me
> transferred to another job at the German repair workshop. I worked
> in the spare parts supply store. I knew German. I used to steal
> weapons.
>
> You couldn't resist, but you could make life unbearable for the
> Germans by pretending that you didn't understand them and by
> playing stupid.

Some islanders, out of principle or envy of the high wages, were
very critical of those who worked for the Germans. Joe Miere was
a teenager on Jersey during the Occupation. Since the war his
judgement has mellowed:

> At first we looked down on those who volunteered to work for the
> Germans on the bunkers, but now, once you've had your own children
> and grandchildren, one looks at it differently. Some men refused to
> work for the Germans and some men worked for anybody. But in the
> end it didn't matter what you did, you worked for the Germans one
> way or another. Even in my barber shop I was working for the
> Germans – although perhaps the haircuts I gave them [he had had no
> training] would count as sabotage. They didn't half look a mess!

Miere was right: there were few islanders who were not working
for the Germans either directly or indirectly by the end, and even
fewer who could afford not to work for them. There is no doubt
that pressing need was a justification for many, and eased their

consciences. Others managed to feel a bit better by working slowly or shoddily, deliberately misunderstanding orders and generally trying to make life difficult for the Germans. Islanders tell numerous anecdotes of minor sabotage, although one suspects few were in fact as defiant towards their German masters as they have subsequently claimed to be.

The contrast with the thousands of Channel Island men – brothers, sons and fathers – who were serving in the British forces was painful. It was an uncomfortable position to be building the bunkers for guns which were to fire at British shipping. James Ryan, the Guernsey First World War veteran, took a very unsympathetic view, and in his private memoirs he bluntly castigated those working for the Germans:

> They were attracted by high wages, easy work and the goods they managed to thieve. It matters nought to them that they were aiding the Enemy, prolonging the agony of their countrymen. Their sons were serving overseas and dying for the cause of the British.
>
> Lorry drivers worked very hard – perhaps eighty-four to ninety-five hours a week, and got paid £6-18-9 compared to £2-8 before the war. What a contrast to the Guernsey boys who gallantly volunteered to face death and the unknown for the paltry pay of a soldier.

The local police forces were in a very difficult position; they were often the ones charged with carrying out unpopular German orders. Resentments still burn against certain policemen for having handed over islanders guilty of some misdemeanour to the Germans.

Guernseyman Eugene Le Lievre can proudly point to an appearance in the 1977 edition of the *Guinness Book of Records*, which features a photograph of him as a gawky young policeman pointing out directions to a German soldier during the Occupation. It was selected as a unique example of Anglo–German co-operation in the middle of the Second World War. Le Lievre was detailed to be a driver for the German Kommandant the night the Germans landed on Guernsey: 'I had to salute the German officers. I used to duck down side streets to avoid them, but you'd be reported if you didn't salute. You felt very uneasy because you were saluting the enemy which is not really the thing to do.'

William Brown was a policeman on Jersey: 'Conditions were chaotic, especially in the early part of the Occupation. There was no precedent for guidance. We had received verbal instructions not to interfere with the German armed forces, regardless of what we saw them doing.'

Francis Le Cocq, another Guernsey policeman, remembers:

When the Feldgendarmerie [German police] went to investigate civilians, we always accompanied them unless it was something really bad. The Germans respected us as policemen, if we behaved as strictly and as circumspectly as they expected us to. If you stood up to the Germans as a policeman, they respected the law and that was the end of the matter. They were odd that way.

We weren't directly under German control. People never accused me of collaborating with the Germans. I showed Germans where people lived. But I never came across hostility at the time – nor have I since – for having worked with the Germans.

A few of the Germans put themselves at risk to help islanders. Le Cocq was fortunate enough to work with an Austrian whom he describes as 'a gentleman':

He did his job as a policeman as little as possible. He spent his time here, he told me, buying King George III silver and sending it to addresses all over Europe. He said to me, 'Whichever way the war goes, I'll salvage some.' I got to know him as a friend. When we had to go and investigate a wireless set, he'd open the door and ask, 'You seen a wireless set?' 'No,' I'd say and he'd reply, 'No more have I.' He did as little as possible against the civilians.

Going Short

As food supplies became more scarce, the high German wages were much needed. Within months of the start of the Occupation, goods such as tea, sugar, coffee and chocolate were only available on the black market at exorbitant prices. Some islanders could dig deep into their savings to supplement their paltry rations, but the vast majority faced gruelling hardship for five long years. Families were deprived of things which for at least two generations they had taken for granted as the basics of life: heating, lighting, hot water, and bread and jam on the table for tea.

Rationing was introduced in July 1940 on staples such as meat, sugar, flour and butter. By summer 1941, the meat ration was down to four ounces a fortnight per person; cooking fat ran out early in 1944, and the salt ration fell to an ounce a week. Potato rationing began in December 1941 at ten pounds per person, and was halved in 1942, but by the end of 1944 there were none left. Bread was rationed at four pounds ten ounces per person in February 1941, and was cut by a pound for five months in 1943.

Bread was scarce, and as flour and yeast rations shrank, it became rough and brown. As for jam or tea, they were luxuries. There was no sugar to make jam. Precious reserves of tea were eked out teaspoon by teaspoon as a great delicacy; tea leaves were often dried and recycled. Substitutes such as dandelion coffee and blackberry-leaf tea were devised.

Food was one of the main topics of conversation; there was endless speculation and rumours about unexpected new supplies, or how some goods were suddenly available at a particular shop. While they lasted, potatoes were a staple, and every bit was cooked and eaten, including the peelings. Vegetables and fruit in season were invaluable. People braved the mined beaches to collect seafood such as mussels and crabs. Even limpets and ormers were gathered and minced, although, with the consistency of chewing gum, they were not a great success. Weeks could go by without any meat being available, although some families could resort to the black market for the odd chicken or bit of bacon. There were rations of milk for everyone, but before long it was always skimmed. The cheese and meat imported from France had often gone bad or had maggots by the time they arrived, after delays in shipping. Chocolate and sweets of any kind were a rare delicacy; children grew up not knowing what an orange or a banana was.

In an effort to vary the dull, limited diet of potatoes and swedes, islanders became extraordinarily resourceful and ingenious; they learned how to make a sweet syrup out of sugar beet as a substitute for sugar. They turned to the natural resources of the island such as carrageen moss (used as a setting agent in blancmanges), and used seawater for salt.

The only heating available by the end of the war was a small fire of twigs painstakingly collected from the roadsides, for a short period in the evening. Fuel was rationed, and the island authorities strictly controlled the felling of trees – wood was as precious as gold dust. Cooking stoves were useless without fuel, and the island governments organised communal kitchens to feed the people. Communal ovens were also set up; families would bring their food to be cooked and then carry it home. Hay boxes were used as slow cookers to save fuel; a dish would be heated up and then placed in a box full of hay for the night. By morning the dish would be cooked. As the Occupation wore on, the electricity worked for shorter periods every day, until it finally stopped altogether at Christmas 1944. Candles ran out, and smoky cooking oils in improvised tin cans, with bootlaces for wicks, were used as a substitute. The long winter evenings were particularly bleak, with virtually no light or heat.

The burden of finding food and trying to prepare palatable dishes fell to the women. Many tasks, such as making the syrup from sugar beet, or a coffee substitute out of parsnips or dandelions, or gleaning corn for flour, or hunting for kindling, were enormously time-consuming. On top of them came the task of scrubbing pots and pans, cleaning the house and washing clothes without the help of soaps or detergents. A grey bar of home-made Occupation soap is as heavy as a paperweight – it was mostly sand mixed with ash. If you were lucky you could make a better-quality soap of caustic soda and tallow. Toothpaste was made from soot mixed with chalk dust and peppermint essence.

The work of cooking, cleaning and mending for a family was never-ending. Guernsey housewife Daphne Prins remembers how it became instinctive to be constantly on the lookout for anything useful; she found herself still gathering twigs on the day of Liberation in May 1945 – until she remembered fuel supplies were at last on their way. Children were roped in to help with collecting fuel, fodder, seafood and gleaning. Guernsey boy Herbert Nichols, with five younger brothers and sisters, helped his mother by breeding rabbits, gathering fodder from the hedgerows, and catching seafood. The vegetable patch became the family's most precious asset; everybody was set to work digging and hoeing and planting the cabbages, potatoes and onions on which survival depended.

Jersey boy Joe Miere recalls even resorting to catching birds: 'We trapped seagulls on the top of houses but we couldn't eat them. We would eat sparrows which we caught in the hedgerows – they gave a bit of flavour. We had no salt so we had to boil salt water down and down to make salt. We made flour and alcohol out of potatoes.'

Daphne Prins was a comfortable, middle-class housewife; her husband was the Dutch consul on Guernsey (a number of Dutch workers remained on the island throughout the war), and she only had one son, but she too was forced to scrounge for food, and had to turn her coffee grinder to new purposes: 'I used to go into the fields to glean corn and grind it in a coffee grinder to make very heavy bread. We were always grateful for a few onions. We used carrageen moss for milk blancmanges with a bay leaf for flavouring. I missed things like marmalade, bread and butter.'

Guernseyman Ralph Durand published a history of the Occupation shortly after 1945. He drew up a week's menu typical of a family in May, the worst time of the year for food, in about 1943. Breakfast every weekday was 'grape-nuts' made from mangel-wurzel, moistened with milk; bramble-leaf tea and bread with a thin smear of a cocoa substitute mixed with sago, tapioca or ground macaroni. This spread could be flavoured with fruit later in the year. Lunch was boiled potatoes, green peas, swedes and cabbage with onion sauce followed by a pudding made of baked breadcrumbs and milk thickened with maize meal. Many weeks there was no meat, but if a family was lucky they might find a piece of fish. On Saturdays it was possible to cook lunch in the bakers' ovens, and the potatoes were baked rather than boiled. 'Tea' was two slices of bread with butter and two with 'cocoa' washed down with bramble-leaf tea. Supper was vegetable soup followed by stewed potatoes and peas. A big effort would be made for something special at Sunday lunch, with spider-crab, potatoes and peas and perhaps the family's last bottle of cider; there was no pudding. Sunday tea was a coffee substitute and a slice and a half of bread with jam.

The shortages did not affect everyone in the same way. Those who had access to land were in a much better position than those living in the towns. The size of one's garden and the quality of its soil became critically important. The best-off were the farmers, who could falsify their yields and keep some of their harvest back for their own use. They hid calves and pigs and secretly fattened them after the Germans instituted strict controls over the slaughter of livestock. Few farmers' families on either Jersey or Guernsey went hungry in the Occupation. But they did have to work, as Jersey farmer's daughter Dorothy Blackwell recalled:

> The shops were empty, you couldn't buy anything. If you went into town, everyone was talking about food. People did barter – a bit of butter for a few potatoes and that kind of thing.
>
> We did nothing but work on the farm. I've never worked so hard in my life. We mixed anthracite dust and tar to make fuel and we used to chop trees down. We made sugar beet syrup by boiling the beets. We made parsnip coffee which was very good and you could hardly tell the difference. You grated the parsnips, roasted them until they were black, and then made coffee. We couldn't make it after the fuel ran out.
>
> I bred rabbits; I started with two and reached two hundred. Finding the fodder for them was hard work; I used to search the hedgerows. We made a rabbit or a chicken last the whole week. We used to sell what we could spare to people who came from the town.
>
> The Germans would send a tester around to judge how much milk there was; we were supposed to hand it all over, except for our rations, but we'd trick them so that there would be enough left for our friends and we'd charge them sixpence.

After the war, Dr Angelo Symons, President of the Board of Health on Guernsey, drew up a report for the British government on the island's health. He said that the poor and the elderly, particularly in the towns, had suffered the worst. But almost everybody had suffered from deprivation:

> The effects of physical deterioration and mental strain became progressively more marked as the Occupation progressed. The physical effects were due to sub-nutrition and cold from lack of fuel, whilst the mental effects were due to depression, boredom, isolation and monotony ... In the case of the housewife, the mental strain was

increased by the anxiety and difficulty of obtaining sufficient food, and the lack of satisfactory means of cooking.

Dr Symons found that the death rate had risen considerably, with peaks during the winter months which could be attributed to the cold. After November 1944, when rations had fallen to three ounces of butter per week and sugar supplies had come to an end, Dr Symons commented that 'some cases of extreme emaciation have been admitted to the hospital from time to time and many of them died within a few days'.

Families who lived in the towns and whose main breadwinner was perhaps away serving in the British forces suffered very real hardship. Stella Perkins was the eldest child of a family of four; her father had gone to serve in the forces, leaving her mother and aunt with a bankrupt estate agency business to support them. Her mother, Augusta Metcalfe, showed remarkable prescience of what lay ahead when, in the midst of the confusion caused by the Germans' arrival, she went out and bought rolls of satin and rayon:

> She made cushion covers and nightdress covers which she decorated with oil paints. The estate agency downstairs was turned into a second-hand shop which my mother and my aunt ran and she sold these trinkets there. I used to make hats out of bits of material, and I made brooches out of beech nuts; I'd shave off the hair on the back, paint them with gold and coloured paints and put them on a pin. We also used to make calendars.
>
> Out of all these activities we just about survived. By the end of the war we had nothing left in the house but the barest minimum of furniture; everything else had been sold. It was horrendous. There were one or two financial crises when Mother had to go to the British Legion for help to feed her children – it was once thrown back at her in a public meeting after the war, as if it had been a crime to ask for help.
>
> We had no garden. My middle brother suffered in particular; I have a photo of him at the end of the war and his legs were like matchsticks. A medical examination years later revealed he'd had tuberculosis when he was about ten; he used to cough a lot but all we could give him was camphorated oil. Everybody did get terribly,

terribly thin. I got very anaemic and I needed lots of iron after the Occupation. One was very weak and the slightest effort could make you come out in awful sweats.

A Guernsey schoolteacher wrote in her diary in August 1943: 'For the first time since the fun began I saw myself in a dressmaker's full-length mirror and the sight was depressing. Every rib, every vertebra, every single bone in my body was shining through my skin.'

The last year of the Occupation was the worst, hitting even the most prosperous islanders, who until then had been able to cushion themselves against some of the hardship by resorting to the black market. All supplies from France were cut off after the D-Day landings of June 1944 and the liberation of France. In November of that year the Guernsey Bailiff, Victor Carey, wrote a short note to his counterpart on Jersey, Alexander Coutanche: 'The fact of starvation begins to stare us in the face and I can see no way out of it ... the small rations and the want of heat is really awful.' The islands were under siege, and a handful of people did die of malnutrition. Many more were so weak from lack of food that they succumbed to other diseases. People lost weight dramatically.

Finally, on 27 December 1944, the first ship bearing Red Cross food parcels from Britain arrived at Guernsey via Portugal. Guernsey policeman Francis Le Cocq says people were weeping to get the parcels. From then until the end of the war on the islands, five months later, the lives of the islanders depended on the arrival of the Red Cross ship, the *Vega*; once, the ship was delayed, and for six weeks the islands were without any flour to make bread. When at last the *Vega* arrived, in March 1945, there were great scenes of celebration. Seventeen-year-old Guernsey girl Dolly Joanknecht was working at the hospital at the time: 'I was the smallest nurse there, so when we made a big loaf, I was made to walk through the wards with this loaf on a big tray over my head. The patients were clapping and singing because of the loaf on my tray. It was a terrible thing to be hungry.'

The islanders' resourcefulness and ingenuity were applied to every area of life. Many cars had been requisitioned at the beginning of the Occupation, and fuel was in short supply, so islanders set their minds to inventing all manner of strange vehicles. There were no bicycle tyres, so hose-piping filled with sand was tied to the wheel frames, and old carts were brought back into service to provide a rudimentary form of public transport.

Clothes and shoes had to be mended, darned and patched because there were few new supplies coming in from France. Shops which had no more new stock to sell set up as second-hand shops to exchange goods, and the barter columns of the newspapers were invaluable. Resourceful dressmakers turned to the curtains and bedspreads to make dresses and shirts. Jersey girl Mary McCarthy remembers blankets being used to make coats and handkerchiefs being turned into bras. Shoes were made out of bits of leather, wood and rubber. Many children went barefoot through most of the summer.

There were terrible shortages of medicines and supplies in the hospitals. Surgery was restricted to emergency operations because of the shortage of anaesthetics. Diabetics presented one of the greatest problems after the insulin ran out; they lost a lot of weight because there were no carbohydrates in their diet, and they became vulnerable to liver and kidney infections and pneumonia. Thirty-two of them died on Jersey, twenty-six on Guernsey and one on Sark. The survival of Jersey boy Maurice Green was something of a miracle, and after the war he became the subject of medical research. For sixteen months he had no insulin; he discharged himself from hospital and devised his own treatment: 'Every day I dug up the garden which made me burn up energy. I didn't eat any carbohydrate or starch. I took a morning job for which I was paid in eggs and the odd piece of pork. I ate dandelions and roots and lost a lot of weight.'

The hospitals ran short of most medicines, and many islanders turned to grandmothers for old herbal remedies. One of the most common problems was constipation, because of the starchy diet, and contemporary diaries make frequent references to bowel movements. Sub-nutrition made people more vulnerable to infections such as 'flu and colds, and pharmacists were hard-pressed to devise alternative treatments. Fifteen-year-old Betty Thurban began working in Jersey Hospital as a nurse at the start of the Occupation:

'All the malt and cod liver oil which was destined for the cattle was requisitioned and given to the children for vitamins A and D. The hospital pharmacist steamed fish livers for oil for a vitamin supplement. He also made tincture of foxglove as a remedy for heart conditions.'

Among the most common complaints the hospital had to deal with were skin conditions such as scabies and impetigo, caused by vitamin deficiencies. Children were particularly prone. The improvised treatment was rough and ready, remembers Betty Thurban: 'The infections quickly became secondary between the fingers and toes. The cure was daily baths for five days followed by scrubbing from head to toe and then covering the body with ointment which contained sulphur and smelt terrible. The children used to scream and scream.'

Hardships and deprivation provoked a remarkable sense of camaraderie which broke through the islanders' deeply-entrenched class consciousness. A measure of comfort – at times it was a matter of survival – depended on a revival of self-sufficient craft folklore, and exchange of this knowledge was vital. People swapped tips on cooking, cleaning, gardening and health remedies, and they exchanged surplus food and clothing. There was a clear *quid pro quo*; if you showed your neighbour generosity, he was more likely to show it to you. Islanders fondly recall this co-operation, and grow nostalgic describing the sense of communal solidarity and unity. Rollo Sherwill, the son of Ambrose, was only a boy on Guernsey, but he remembers: 'If you wanted to know how to make anything, you only had to ask a neighbour. Everybody helped everybody. If people had food they shared it because there was always a pay-off – if I help you, you'll help me. There was the most extraordinary spirit of co-operation which died of course after the war.'

This comradeship was only part of the truth. Co-existing alongside it were bitter communal divisions and resentments which were to strain the fabric of the island communities in ways no one had envisaged.

The Black Market

27 April 1943: It was a meatless weekend and on
Sunday, the rector climbed into the pulpit and
announced as his text, 'I have meat that ye know
not of.'

'Black market' thundered a voice in the congregation.

'Occupational Observations by One Occupied',
unpublished diary of a Guernsey schoolteacher

Wherever goods are in short supply and prices are controlled, a
black market develops – and so it did on the Channel Islands during
the Occupation.

The islands' black market had three main sources of supply;
farmers kept some of their produce back to sell privately to friends
and relatives, or to traders at above the official prices; traders set
up supply lines on ships to and from France, and imported goods for
the black market; and some of the goods intended for the German
garrisons found their way onto the black market, either via islanders
working for the Germans, or corrupt German quartermasters out
to make a few Reichsmarks.

The quantity of food stolen from German supply ships at the
island ports indicates a well-organised operation. In May 1943, the
Feldkommandantur was investigating the theft of foodstuffs worth
10,549 Reichsmarks. They listed 300 kilos of flour, 838 kilos of
wheat and 40 kilos of chocolate as having been stolen. The previous
month 200 kilos of flour had been stolen, as well as 40 kilos of
margarine, 101 kilos of chocolate, 780 pairs of silk stockings, 50
kilos of soap and 269 boxes of camembert.

There was no shortage of customers for black market goods.
Hundreds of French, Belgian, Spanish and Dutch workers had been
brought to the islands by the Germans to work on construction
projects, and they looked to the black market to supplement their
dull, small rations. Everything on the official market was reserved
for islanders with their ration cards. Germans were keen customers
on the black market, as were wealthy islanders.

The prices on the black market rose steadily during the Occupation, and after D-Day they became astronomical. A pound of tea, which would have cost 2s.8d in 1940, rose to £25 in 1944; a tin of fruit cost a shilling in 1940, and £1.10s. in 1944; a pound of butter cost 1s.6d in 1940, and £1.5s. in 1944. A bar of soap cost £6.14s.7d, a bottle of whisky £10, and a tin of Bird's Custard £4.2s.6d in 1944. Average wages in that year were about £2 a week.

There are – obviously – few documents to indicate the scale of the black market, but it would be a fair assumption that the majority of islanders who could afford black market prices did at times resort to buying goods on it. There was much resentment towards the black market's regular customers, and even more to its regular suppliers, who made considerable profits. Police records reveal a constant stream of fines and prosecutions for infractions against price regulations.

Some of the more sensational cases reached the newspapers. In 1943 the *Guernsey Evening Press* reported the case of seventy-year-old Pierre Mahy, of Figtree Farm, who was charged with having sold sugar without a licence and in excess of the fixed price, and for having sold beans and onions illegally. Denounced by the Bailiff for 'underhand, underground' black marketeering, Mahy was fined £105 (a farm worker's annual wage at the time was £90). The Bailiff complained that many others like Mahy had no conscience, and were undermining efforts to keep food prices down. Mahy pleaded in his defence that the French and Spanish workers who bought the food were desperate, and he told the court: 'These men are so insistent. To them the price is nothing. These men have plenty of money, but they can't buy anything. They offer so much at times that you have to refuse the money – you have to. They know they are offering a great deal more than they should pay. I've done my best in other respects to get as much food for the civilian population as possible. I've done much more manual labour in the last two years than in the previous forty-five years.'

Jersey boy Bernard Hassall says: 'Everybody was up to their necks in the black market. You couldn't have survived without it. The market was mainly organised between the farms and the shops and there was a clique of about forty people on Jersey who ran it with someone at the top of it all. They also took in food which came from France. Butter was imported in 20-kilogram wooden cases from France. Brandy was imported and watered down, as well as sweets and dragées [sugar-coated almonds]. People didn't worry about being informed on, because everyone was in it.'

Mary McCarthy claimed that prior to the Occupation, many of the farmers who were the main beneficiaries of the black market had been in a parlous financial position: 'The Occupation and the black market was the saving of them. Many managed to pay off their mortgages and they moved up the ladder socially. There were some people who used their profits to buy up properties – they're the kind who would have been strung up in France after the liberation. But what would we have done without the black marketeers? We'd have had no sugar if it hadn't been stolen from the Germans.'

Some of the islanders' resentment was directed at people who were making a lot of money out of the black market, some at people who had plenty while others were going hungry. Jersey policeman William Brown had a wife and three small children to support. Because of his job, he felt he could not buy food on the black market:

> I let the children have anything extra that was going. I suffered terribly from hunger. I remember going to bed and the pains of hunger stopped me sleeping; I dropped from fifteen stone to ten stone. We put boiled, minced limpets on bread – the bread was made from oatmeal and potato.
>
> We were invited at this time to the house of a shopkeeper for supper; we stocked up on boiled swedes before going round to their house because it was polite as guests not to eat too much. But they had nearly everything you could imagine – brandy, whisky, jelly; our stomachs just couldn't cope. They were full of swedes anyway, but we couldn't face that rich food.

Late in the Occupation, Jersey police raided the home of an islander and found a vast quantity of food hoarded there; the haul (lavishly reported in the newspaper) was displayed in a shop window in town, to the amazement of islanders. The pile of tinned food, wine, tea, and spirits made their mouths water at the distant memory of food they had almost forgotten about. The German Feldgendarmerie also conducted house-to-house searches, and on one occasion they found a man who had hoarded 363 tins of soup, vegetables and fish.

Jersey boy Maurice Green ran an errand to the home of a member of the Jersey government one evening during the bleakest days of war shortages: 'I saw so much food, my eyes popped out. Some people on the islands never starved. They always got hold of milk and, unbelievably, sugar and real coffee. The rich had a different war. Those in government were rewarded for helping, or rather co-operating with, the Germans. They got hold of food and favours were given. The fact that they got rich really annoyed people, I think, more than the fact that they had been collaborators. The farmers did very well out of it.'

The black market covered all sorts of goods. People desperate for food sold family heirlooms such as furniture, silver and jewellery. Jerseyman Fred Woodall complained in his diary that one neighbour was buying radios and selling them to the Germans. 'This occupation has made me lose more faith in humanity than anything else in my life,' he wrote.

Woodall complained of a couple who frequently entertained Germans in their home. He noted down a conversation with the husband, who was a trader: 'He was talking his usual rot. He is a typical Jerseyman, avaricious, grasping, narrow, self-centred. He said it wouldn't make much difference whose rule we lived under. He said if the Germans won, he wouldn't clear out; he would find some way of getting on with them. He is just a Jersey quisling, which is about the lowest of species.'

Making money – and there was a lot to be made – was often at the expense of islanders and to the advantage of the Germans. Many shopkeepers kept food under the counter to sell to Germans at higher prices than the islanders could afford. Dorothy Blackwell said: 'A next-door neighbour used to sell all the best vegetables to the Germans, and sell the worst to the locals. The Germans could pay more and he got goods like tobacco in return.'

Within a few months of the start of the Occupation the Guernsey Controlling Committee was investigating the farmers Messrs Timmer Ltd, who had established themselves as the major supplier of vegetables to the occupying forces, after repeated allegations that they were charging high prices to the Germans. The Committee decided that the prices were justified because of the fact that the vegetables were washed and chopped, but resentment did not abate, and after the war the company had to go to great lengths to clear its name. Perhaps Timmers was envied because of its lucrative arrangements with the Germans; letters have survived from other farmers who wrote to the Germans offering to grow food for them.

During the siege conditions of 1944–45, the German soldiers became desperate for food as their rations shrank, and they were forced to buy on the black market at ludicrous prices. Both the German and the island authorities attempted to stamp out this illegal trade, and there was a steady flow of traders coming before the island courts. On 20 September 1944, a leader in the *Guernsey Evening Press* chastised the black marketeers who postured as patriots: 'The profiteers considered it their duty to mulct the civilian public for as much as they can, but, in the long run, they have found the soldier represents a 2–300 per cent profit; the civilian a meagre 150 per cent ... They sell to the soldier using one hand to grasp the money and reserving the other fist to shake at the retreating uniformed back.'

UnChristian Lives

3 April 1942: Crime is growing enormously. Everyone pinches or does a bit of quiet black market; no one is honest, not even the clergy, one of whom remarked ingenuously, 'It will be nice when the war is over, then we shall be able to lead Christian lives again.'

'Occupational Observations by One Occupied'

The black market was one illustration of the way in which the islands' traditional law-abiding values had been subverted by the Occupation. It turned the *status quo* upside down; those who might have been prosperous before the war found themselves bankrupt and hungry, while others perceived unprecedented opportunities for making money. It was a topsy-turvy world, in which everything was up for grabs. Some families which had been looked down on as 'common' were now among the best fed and best dressed. The unequal distribution of food and goods triggered envy and bitterness. It eroded the trust which islanders had shared for generations, and led to an exponential rise in petty crime. Jersey policeman William Brown commented sadly:

> The morals of the local population fell considerably; the veneer of civilisation seemed to depart. I think it applied to nearly everyone. For the sake of obtaining food, they were prepared to break most of the regulations. These people were not criminals, but they broke small regulations and committed small offences. People would walk around in the blackout with a load of wood which they had ripped out of an unoccupied house. You wondered how far you should go to stop it.
>
> There was one man, quite a decent fellow, who was in charge of a store which had some grain left in it. During the blackout one day, I saw the doors of the store open. There were two men inside – they were stealing grain. Both were sentenced and one man was imprisoned. He came out a broken man and died shortly after. He felt disgraced. He would never have behaved like that in normal circumstances. I felt sympathy for them.

The collapse of morals affected sections of the population which had previously been considered beyond reproach. One of the most extraordinary cases, on Guernsey in 1942, was covered in minute detail in the local papers. Over a period of several months, a number of thefts from shops had gone unsolved by the police, so the German Feldpolizei stepped in to investigate. Suspicion had fallen on the police themselves, as they were the only people who had complete freedom of movement after the curfew. At the time, discipline in the police force was at a low ebb. Men on night duty spent much of their time at a colleague's flat, drinking and playing cards. The Germans finally caught two policemen breaking into an Organisation Todt store. Eighteen of the thirty-strong Guernsey police force were tried by a German military court for pilfering from German stores. They were also tried in the Guernsey courts on charges of having stolen foodstuffs including tomato preserve, French beans, butter and cooking oil from island shops. They had also stolen a large quantity of liquor: one police constable had forty bottles of spirits and wine, while another had eighty-six bottles of port and twenty-eight of spirits. Stephen Duquemin, the seventy-year-old landlord of the Victoria Hotel, was accused of buying stolen goods.

The policemen were given prison sentences of between four weeks and four years in France. The Bailiff, Victor Carey, said in his summing up, 'I am filled with shame. It is revolting to think how you have abused your position. I cannot imagine what all the foreigners in the island ... think of you.' The police corruption case was extremely embarrassing for the Guernsey government, and weakened its hand with the German authorities. It also lowered morale in the population; it was widely believed that the convicted men were not the only ones abusing positions of power to enrich themselves.

Most of the islanders considered stealing from the Germans legitimate, and if the policemen had restricted themselves to that, they might have won sympathy, but they had also stolen from civilians. After the war several of the police appealed against their dismissal from the force; they argued that they had been motivated by patriotism, and inspired by the BBC broadcasts of 'Colonel Britton' (Douglas Ritchie), who issued stirring appeals to occupied Europe to resist the Germans. They claimed that they had intended to hand out the much-needed food to hungry islanders, and that the thefts were 'part of a campaign of opposition to the Germans which included, inter alia, cutting telephone wires, painting anti-German slogans and otherwise attempting to hamper and obstruct the enemy'. One of those found guilty in 1942 says the thefts were sabotage, and all he ever got from them was thirty pounds of oats.

Police claims that their theft of wine and spirits was in fact 'sabotage' look thin, but the dividing line was not always clear. Many people felt that pilfering goods from the Germans was in some way 'patriotic'. The case of the Guernsey police shows how lawlessness could not be kept within bounds; stealing from the Germans spilled into stealing from islanders. Furthermore, if people in positions of authority were stealing, why shouldn't everyone else? Allegations were levelled at States officials. An entry in Baron von Aufsess's diary in 1944 notes: 'I fear that many [Jersey]

States officials do not, in their position, set the example they should. Current rumour credits them, with the exception of Duret Aubin [the Attorney General], of generally dabbling in the black market and taking advantage of their privileged position.'

Some islanders persuaded themselves that stealing from houses abandoned by those who had been evacuated to England was legitimate; they argued that if they didn't take the goods, they would fall into the hands of the Germans. Alderney, with hundreds of abandoned homes, was particularly tempting. French refugees fleeing the Cotentin peninsula in 1940 were alleged to be the first to ransack abandoned shops before they continued their journey to Brittany. Then the Guernseymen sent in 1940 to collect the harvest and the cattle on the island took a share. Ten Guernseymen were tried in 1941 for pilfering on Alderney, including Charles Hutcheson, who had been appointed by the Guernsey government as the Civil Commandant of the island.

Many of the eighteen British residents living on Alderney felt that goods and foodstuffs remaining on the island were theirs for the taking. One man, James Rutter, took it upon himself to clear the homes of his former neighbours. By the time the Germans caught up with him and put him on trial, the list of his stolen goods ran like the contents of a department store: ninety-six curtains, seventy-five pillowcases, fifty blankets, five wirelesses, twenty-five carpets and more than a hundred pieces of silver. More useful for surviving the Occupation were the sixty-two kilograms of flour, hundred kilograms of sugar and eighty-two jars of jam he had stolen. Rutter claimed he had bought everything legitimately, but the German police report pointed out that there was hardly room to move in his tiny flat for the piles of goods heaped in baskets and crates, while the carpets were 'stored in such quantities that they are laid one on top of the other in two or three layers'. Daphne Pope commented on the case:

Mr Rutter was a very stupid and greedy man, and he didn't do what we advised, which was to take what you need, not what you fancy, and then it will look right. Then, when the Germans came into your house and looked round, they wouldn't notice.

One farmer, who was a neighbour of ours, could get from one

farm to another and he could grab anything out of these houses without being seen. As he said, 'What fits on one farm, fits on the next.' If you went along these lines, you were sensible, but this Mr Rutter took everything. He could get from his garden to the next without setting foot on the road, so he wasn't seen, or perhaps the Germans shut their eyes.

When the police discovered him, he had enough food to feed my family and yet he used to come to us for food. The farmer said he would have liked to shoot him because he had made trouble for us all. Life got very tricky and the Germans came to search us but we managed by simply taking things that looked right.

Stealing was easier on Alderney, where there were no civil authorities or police, but thefts from abandoned houses were also common on the other islands. Store cupboards and wine cellars in evacuated houses were quickly emptied. The island authorities stepped in and gathered all the furniture from the deserted homes into warehouses to preserve it for its owners' return after the war – German requisitioning orders were often met out of these stores. But not even wooden banisters, skirting boards and doors were safe from the depredations of hungry, cold islanders; they were ripped out and burnt for fuel.

Children learnt to steal, and if they took things from the Germans, they were unlikely to be punished by their parents. Rollo Sherwill recalls: 'We stole potatoes from German stores. Children learnt very quickly how to make skeleton keys and we could open any door, or any padlock. That kind of information got around very quickly. I never used that skill after the war. The Germans were a legitimate target, but it was absolutely taboo to steal from a neighbour.'

Sherwill remembers that when the children who had been evacuated to Britain during the war returned, those who had stayed on the islands were, in comparison, 'a bit wild': 'We gave people in authority hell. We did anything to buck authority because during the war we had learnt it was legitimate to do that, because authority had been the Germans.'

The taboo of not stealing from neighbours did not always hold. It was hard for those with hungry stomachs to live beside a farmer whose family had more than enough, and who was supplying the

Germans at a huge profit. Farmers found it difficult to guard their
farms and livestock. Herbert Nichols was a well-brought-up Guernsey boy, but the needs of his five brothers and sisters and harassed
mother were such that scruples were laid aside: 'I'd go to the milk
depot to steal the cream; I dropped through a skylight and once
we nearly got caught by a joint patrol of Guernsey and German
police. We also used to milk the cows in the summer at night when
they were sleeping outside. I'd crawl along in the grass because it
was after curfew; I used to go fairly regularly with some friends.
My mother didn't say anything, but she was scared. Sometimes I'd
bring home a chicken I'd stolen. Once we stole 5–6 hundredweight
of potatoes from the greenhouse.'

Islanders complained bitterly of how bicycles they had left for
a minute disappeared, of how clothing vanished from the line
and apples from the trees before they were ripe. Some of the
culprits were foreign labourers, and in the last year of the war
German soldiers, desperate for food, turned into armed burglars
for precious potatoes and carrots. It was a far cry from the pre-
war days, when islanders never had to worry about locking their
doors.

One of the hardest memories of the Occupation for islanders to
come to terms with was the fact that many of their neighbours
turned informers. It was a deep shock to realise that people could
betray their own kind. This transgressed every notion of decency
and good neighbourliness which the islanders had believed were
respected – if not always followed – on their islands. The trust
between neighbours broke down, and islanders quickly learnt to be
careful of who they spoke to and what they said to them. No one
was sure who could be trusted. A Guernsey schoolteacher wrote in
her diary:

> *4 August 1942*: I blush for my fellow islanders, they are giving one
> another away right and left about black market dealings. How they
> find each other out is remarkable but the way they do betray their
> friends is hateful (worthy of the Hun himself!)

Informing was a way of getting back at a neighbour who had refused to lend some sugar or flour, or at a shopkeeper who was charging high prices. It was also a way of settling old scores. Informers were paid handsomely on occasions, with rewards of several pounds for betraying someone with an illegal wireless. Island post office workers claimed that they managed to stop hundreds of letters addressed to the Feldkommandantur from islanders informing on neighbours for having illegal radios or secret supplies of food. Albert Lamy, the head of Guernsey police, said the police ignored the informers' letters they received, as they realised that they were often unreliable, and inspired by malice. Even the Germans sometimes found these betrayals beneath their dignity, although they did rely on paid informers, and granted them favours in return.

Some of the letters have survived:

'Why is Jack Cornu, 4 Boyne Terrace, Great Union Road, allowed to have received one ton of anthracite coal when other people have none at all. Also call and see his stock of food in bedroom cupboards and billiard room and see what you make of it,' wrote a Jersey informer in 1944.

'Please search Brampton Villa, Great Union Road for at least two wirelesses hidden under floorboards, loft and cellars. It is a lodging house,' wrote another.

In 1943 'a stranger' wrote to ask the Germans to search Frank Powers, 'who sells black market cognac, sugar, butter at terrible prices. The cognac is German property and he dilutes it. One more point, he is believed to have a wireless set hidden in one of the house walls. Anyhow I hope you will do something. Best of luck.'

Some of the women who slept with Germans were accused of being informers. One of the most infamous was a woman on Jersey called Mme Baudains who was nicknamed 'Mimi the spy'. Joe Miere said, 'She would listen to you on the streets and in the cafés and she would phone the Germans and they would be around immediately.' Bernard Hassall was equally wary of her: 'She used to wear black with a fox fur around her neck with a silver end to the tail. You'd see her going around town but you didn't dare look at her. We kept well out of her way – she was lethal.'

Hassall says that both he and his brother Peter were informed on by women. He ended up in Jersey prison, while Peter was sent to the Continent, after an escape attempt to England failed: 'The woman who put me inside is living in London. A friend of mine got friendly with her, and tried to impress her by telling her that I had some weapons hidden in my bedroom. I should never have told him. She was also friendly with the Geheime Feldpolizei [the secret military police] down at Havre des Pas. There were more women than men who informed; they did it in return for favours such as stockings, food. Informing is as low as you can go; it's shocking.'

Some of the women Mary McCarthy knew to be dating the Germans became informers. When Mary called one girl a 'dirty jerrybag' the girl retorted, 'Shut up, and if you don't, there are ways of making you shut up.'

Sometimes informing had tragic consequences. In one case two women, a mother and daughter, alleged that a young Guernsey boy, John Ingrouille, had a gun, and was planning armed resistance against the Germans. No gun was ever found, but John's denials, backed by his parents, were ignored at his trial on Jersey, and he was sentenced to five years for treason and espionage. John was a much-loved only child, and his father's diary vividly records his anguish:

2 January 1941: Two German officers of the Military police came and searched my house . . . taking with them a knife which they said my boy had stolen. However, they came on several occasions and carried on their work of searching my house and turning everything upside down . . . But the climax came when one day these same officers brought with them a woman . . . That same woman told one under-officer that my boy had two hundred men ready to revolt in the island of Guernsey . . . I can clearly state that it was a lie.

John Ingrouille was sent to prison in Caen, Normandy, and he wrote regular, affectionate letters to his parents. In one he wrote, 'I'm keeping my spirit up as much as I can. It will be everybody's birthday when I come back home, and I hope it will be soon.'

It was not. With an uncharacteristic scrupulousness for legal niceties, the German authorities decided a retrial was necessary in Germany. The two informers were taken to Germany to give evidence, and again John was found guilty. Victor Carey, the Bailiff, attempted to intervene with the German authorities,

pointing out that the boy was considered by his employers to be
below average intelligence and that 'his parents are simple and
industrious peasants and he is their only child'.

On 6 August 1942, John's father received a letter from the Berlin
Army Justice Inspector saying that his son's sentence had been
revoked. But he was not released until the following year. It was
too late; he had contracted tuberculosis, and died in Brussels on
his way home.

A female informer is alleged to have revealed to the Germans
that two British agents had secretly landed on Guernsey in September 1940. The agents subsequently handed themselves in, and
the informer's act led to the arrest of fifteen people, who were
imprisoned in France.

There was one other category of collaborators, a tiny handful who
went further than informing, and actually volunteered to work for
the Germans in Germany. At least one was working alongside William Joyce – better known as Lord Haw-Haw – in broadcasting
German propaganda to Britain. Judging by their surnames, most
were originally Irish and could not therefore technically be accused
of treason, but a few were British. In May 1942, the Jersey Bailiff
Alexander Coutanche wrote to the Feldkommandantur with the
names of five men working in Germany who wished their wages
to be paid into their island bank accounts. A letter in the Guernsey
archives enquires whether wages owing to those working in Germany could be deposited with the Westminster Bank in Paris; it
mentions no names.

One of the men who worked in Germany, James Lingshaw, was
originally among those deported in 1942 and 1943, when 2200
islanders were sent to German internment camps. Ambrose Sherwill met him at Laufen internment camp, and after the war he
drew up a statement for the investigating British authorities on his
recollections of the man:

> He had a room to himself which he had been given a key for and
> he had a pass which enabled him to leave the camp ... there was
> considerable resentment against Lingshaw for these privileges.

On 16 August 1943, Lingshaw told me that he was going to Berlin
to coach fifteen girls in English and I gathered these girls were connec-
ted to the German radio propaganda service. I explained to Lingshaw
that such work was incompatible with his duty as a British subject . . .
and that I should be compelled to regard him as a renegade Englishman and that he should consider the matter carefully . . . There was
something lacking in his mental make-up. [He was] almost obsequious
and what I said was passing over his head. He sought to shake hands.
I refused but he was still most polite. His attitude was rather that of a
schoolboy about to embark on a pleasant vacation.

Lingshaw was put on trial after the war, and was imprisoned for
five years. In court it was pointed out that he was not being tried
for any crimes he might have committed while in the Channel
Islands.

In 1946 James Gilbert, who had briefly lived on Jersey and was
perhaps the 'Gibson' mentioned in Bailiff Coutanche's letter to the
Feldkommandantur in 1942, was tried in the Old Bailey, London,
and sentenced to nine months' imprisonment for working at a German radio station and 'aiding' the enemy. After the trial his sister
unsuccessfully appealed to King George VI, stating that her brother
had had no choice but to help the Germans, after he was beaten
and threatened with death in a concentration camp. She said that
James was a pacifist, who had arrived on Jersey in 1940 in search
of work; he was 'extremely gullible', and was 'tricked, trapped,
tortured and now, worst of all, branded as a traitor'.

Living in Fear

It was almost impossible to abide by every German and island
regulation and still make a living and have enough food on the
table. Thousands of islanders broke the curfew, did a bit of trading
on the black market, had a banned radio, stole food from the Germans or chopped some wood down illegally. No one had a spotless
record, and everyone lived in fear of the heavy boot-tread, the knock
on the door and the house search. The islanders were completely
powerless in the face of the German authorities, who were

accountable to no one, and thousands of civilians found themselves up before the courts in the course of the Occupation.

Most black market or theft charges were dealt with in the local courts, but the more serious cases were tried in German courts. The lucky ones got a fine or a sentence in an island prison. All the islands' gaols were full by the middle of the Occupation, and many of those convicted had long waits before they could serve their sentences. Dozens of others had to be sent to prisons in France, where the conditions were bearable and sometimes the food was more plentiful than on the islands, but it was lonely to be in a foreign country, with no one speaking one's own language. Most French people found the islanders' Norman French virtually incomprehensible.

Seventeen-year-old Dolly Joanknecht had never been abroad when she was sent to prison in France in 1943. The only other time she had left Guernsey was to go to Southend for a holiday. She was accused of handling stolen goods at her uncle's shop where she had been working. The German police came one day to take her name, and two months later she received a form telling her to go to the German headquarters.

A German said to me, 'You are a German undesirable. You have received stolen food from the German forces. You are going to prison for four months.' Bang, he stamped my form. I didn't know what he was talking about. Later, I learnt my uncle had been a black marketeer and was also sent to prison.

I was very proud that I was going to prison; I thought it made me something of a resistance heroine. I expected to go to the Guernsey prison, but some time later I got a letter saying I was going to prison on the Continent. A car came to collect me; I wasn't scared, I was excited. I was handed over to a German gendarme who looked after me very well.

When we arrived in St Malo he took me for breakfast and then we walked all over the town, sightseeing – our train wasn't until the evening. We had a lovely dinner in a café and the gendarme got drunk on beer and I had to help him out of the café and I sat him on a seat on the wall around St Malo to sober up. I could have run away but I didn't know where to go so I just sat there and waited for him.

Dolly served her sentence in Lille women's prison, where she was nicknamed 'La Petite Tommy'. She learnt some French and made some good friends. She received French Red Cross parcels with delicious food, and she managed to survive a number of scrapes and adventures, including falling seriously ill. On the boat back to Guernsey she met Willi, her future husband, as we have seen.

Imprisonment could be highly arbitrary. Stella Perkins's mother and aunt were arrested around the time of the D-Day landings simply because they were of Russian birth. Fourteen-year-old Stella was left to look after her three younger brothers for several weeks.

In such a situation there was no island official to turn to for help. Only in the very gravest cases did the island governments intervene to plead an islander's case with the German authorities.

John Leale, President of Guernsey's Controlling Committee, pleaded unsuccessfully for the release of John Ingrouille. Early in 1945, Jersey Bailiff Alexander Coutanche intervened in the tragic case of 'Alice', an eighteen-year-old girl who had fallen in love with a German soldier. With the end of the war in sight the soldier had decided to desert. Alice hid him, but he was found, and they were both sentenced to death. Coutanche appealed to the German authorities: 'I have seen the father of this young woman and he had told me that for some four or five months a great friendship had arisen between his daughter and the German soldier . . . Alice was, it would appear, passionately in love. A young woman in love does not always weigh the consequences of her acts, when they are dictated by what she believes, however wrongly, to be for the welfare of her lover . . . I appeal for mercy.'

To everyone's relief, Alice's sentence was transmuted to ten years' imprisonment. Joe Miere was in the next cell to her, and from his window he glimpsed her German boyfriend wave goodbye to her on his way to the place of execution, where he was shot.

Coutanche also successfully pleaded for a stay of execution on two middle-aged ladies, Suzanne Malherbe and Lucille Schwab, sentenced to death for resistance activities. He cleverly couched the plea in terms designed to appeal to the Germans: 'The sentence is causing anxiety and distress amongst the population, not because of any particular acquaintance with, or sympathy for the condemned persons, but because of a feeling of repugnance against the carrying

out of a sentence of death on women ... in view of the great
difficulties which are facing the civil population in the future and
of my desire to avoid anything calculated to arouse passion ... I
appeal for mercy.'

Senior members of the government usually managed to get off
more lightly. When Ed Le Quesne, the head of the Jersey Department of Labour and a member of the island's Superior Council,
was sentenced to prison for having an illegal radio, he served only
two weeks of his sentence before being released. Von Aufsess wrote
in his diary that he was furious with his colleagues for ever allowing
the case to come to court.

A prison sentence in France was not too great a hardship, but
the terrible fear was that one could get ensnared in the system and
end up in a concentration camp, where unknown horrors were
being perpetrated. Between twenty and thirty islanders were sent
to concentration camps, and about half of them died there. Some
of their offences were relatively trivial: Canon Cohu of St Saviour's,
Jersey, died in Spergau, to which he was sent after an anonymous
informer reported that he had a radio. Stanley Green, the Jersey
cinema projectionist, survived a terrible ordeal in Buchenwald, also
for possessing a radio. Informers caused the arrests of Louisa Gould,
her brother Harold Le Druillenec and her sister Ivy Forster. Louisa
died in Ravensbruck. Her brother and sister survived, but Harold
suffered appallingly in Belsen.

The islanders learned to live with constant fear. At any time they
could be reminded of their vulnerability, their isolation from the
rest of the world and from their traditional protector, Britain, and
the overwhelming strength of the Germans. William Brown, the
Jersey policeman, remembered: 'At night, you sometimes heard five
hundred of them on a route march at one or two o'clock in the
morning, and they'd be singing victory songs. You'd be the only
local person out, and they'd come up the town, roaring at the top
of their voices every time, as if they wanted to waken everyone up
to German supremacy.'

It is not surprising that many islanders who lived through the Occupation wanted to forget about it as quickly as possible after 1945.

It had been morally confusing, and had made people bitter and cynical; it was hard work, and dreary; it was frightening; it was boring and monotonous. As the medical report to the British government immediately after the war commented, depression was one of the biggest health problems on the islands. Cut off from the outside world, the islanders had little to talk about. Rumours and gossip festered on the smallest scraps of information, fuelling unjustified and justified resentments alike: 'Some high official is being accused of shady dealings. It is all quite exciting and relieves the monotony of our dreary existence, for we are all feeling bored,' wrote one diarist.

Amateur dramatics and entertainments were a great morale booster to some; religion or reading to others. Because keeping cheerful was so difficult, it became a much admired quality. Those who kept their sense of humour – as many did, judging by the ribald Occupation jokes – were nothing short of heroic, as they eased the burden of woes for everyone.

CHAPTER FIVE

LES ROCHERS MAUDITS

In its early days, the occupation of the Channel Islands bore little resemblance to what was happening in the rest of Nazi-occupied Europe. Life was comparatively safe and peaceful, and there was none of the systematic brutality which was terrorising communities on the Continent. This was not to last.

Between 1941 and 1944, about sixteen thousand foreign workers were brought to the islands to build their defences. Many of them were harshly treated, and islanders witnessed cruelty towards their fellow human beings on a scale the islands had never experienced. The islands, like the rest of occupied Europe, were drawn into the web of institutionalised viciousness which characterised every corner of Hitler's empire.

The presence of thousands of emaciated foreign workers was painful evidence of Nazi brutality. It drove home the islanders' awareness of their own vulnerability and the fact that their well-being depended on the fragile goodwill of the Germans. It also presented them with the most uncomfortable moral challenge of the Occupation: should they avert their eyes and thank God that the Nazis had other victims on which to vent their fury? Or should they do something to help these benighted workers?

At first the islanders did not know where these foreign workers had come from, or what they were doing among them. They were forbidden to talk to the worst-treated, from Eastern Europe, and gleaned only scraps of information from brief glimpses of the camps, or as they marched to and from their worksites. Those memories have haunted many islanders, and left them uneasy all their lives.

In the autumn of 1943 Maurice Green and his younger sister had gone out blackberry-picking near the vast German fortification

works on Jersey, where tunnels were being excavated out of solid
rock:

> We were in an area where we weren't supposed to be because there
> were a lot of Organisation Todt working on the tunnels there. I saw
> a German beating a French worker. He knocked him down and then
> kicked him and beat him with his rifle; I think he must have killed
> him. Then he sat down to have a smoke. He glanced up, and saw
> me and my sister. We were terrified. He shouted to us, 'Come over
> here.'
>
> He patted my sister; she was a little blonde girl and three years
> younger than me. Then he opened his haversack and took out his
> lunch and he broke his bread and cheese into three pieces, and gave
> me and my sister a piece each at a time when rations were very
> short. The worker was still lying there, behind him, with his head
> smashed open. He couldn't have survived being beaten around the
> head with that rifle.

A Jersey policeman remembers passing one of the makeshift camps
which housed the slave workers: 'One of those Russian workers
was hanging by his feet and he was still wriggling a bit. I made it
my business to pass along the road the next day, and he was still
hanging from that tree, but there was no movement in him. I didn't
mention it to anyone. I didn't find it over-necessary to speak
about it.'

Mike Le Cornu, a teenager, lived at L'Etacq, in the remote
north-west corner of Jersey: 'There was a quarry nearby. They used
to bring slaves in lorries to unload huge machines for the quarry.
Once one of these machines fell on a slave worker's legs. They got
two other slave workers to pick him up and throw him in the lorry
and he was just left there all day. He must have died there. It was
a very hot summer day. We could see this from our house.' Every
year, on the anniversary of the Liberation, Le Cornu returns to a
particular field where there used to be a camp. For him it is a
private moment of remembrance for the suffering he witnessed as
a boy:

> I've never forgotten the sound that came out of the huts there. I
> still get emotional. When people are starving, the pitch of their

voices rises. The sound was like lots of birds in an aviary. As children, we used to go close to the camp fence and watch. Sometimes we pushed nuts and apples through the wire. The OT had big whips and would put yokes on the little children to fetch water. There was one Russian who stood out so clearly; he used to pat the children on the head as they went past. He must have been the only light of hope in that camp.

While I was watching, there was a Jersey farmer beside me and he saw this cruelty as well and he said [of the foreign workers], 'They're just savages from the mountains.'

A Jersey policeman recalls one particular Russian prisoner being brought into the police station. The police considered the Russians as something of a menace both to themselves and to the local population when, as he puts it, they were 'running wild around the island', and they regarded it as their duty to send them back to 'where they belonged'. The policeman was deputed to return the prisoner to his camp. In a gesture of kindness, rather than march him up to the front entrance, he took him round to the back of the camp, where the Russian began to scramble under the rolls of barbed wire. Unfortunately he became trapped in the wire, and was soon spotted by a senior Organisation Todt officer. The officer rushed up and began savagely kicking the prisoner, who in his desperate efforts to escape became even more entangled. The kicking continued until the prisoner was motionless, presumably unconscious. By this time the OT officer had drawn his revolver. The policeman vividly remembers his feelings of powerlessness. There was nothing he could have achieved by attempting to intervene, and he remembers being very much aware that, if anything happened to him, his wife and two young children would be left unprovided for on the island. In the event, there was nothing he could do but walk away.

Some islanders distanced themselves from the tragedy they were witnessing. They belittled the suffering of these foreigners, dismissing them, like the Jersey farmer, as 'savages'. They regarded these unwashed, unshaven creatures as scarcely human, and complained that they spread diseases. They were also exasperated by the foreigners' continuous plundering of food stores, livestock and crops in the fields. Many farmers saw them as a nuisance, rather than recognising that their thieving was born of desperation. Some still say today that the wartime foreign workers were all criminals and homosexuals the Nazis had plucked from Soviet jails. A significant number of islanders, however, risked imprisonment – and in some cases even their lives – in order to show compassion and offer help to the prisoners (see Chapter 6).

The sad story of the foreign workers takes us deep into the organisation of the Third Reich's war effort, where millions of people were transported from one end of Europe to the other to fulfil the Nazis' need for labour. The experiences of the workers on the Channel Islands explodes the myth of the Model Occupation.

Adolf Hitler was immensely proud of his British conquest, and after the series of ineffectual British military raids on the Channel Islands in 1940–41, he became alarmed that they might be recaptured. On the eve of Operation Barbarossa – the invasion of the Soviet Union – in June 1941, Hitler was worried that his empire could be vulnerable to attacks on the Atlantic coast. He believed that battered British public opinion would demand some bold military achievement, and that nothing would suit that purpose better than a daring recapture of the British Crown's possession.

Hitler became obsessed with ensuring that this tiny part of the Reich should not be lost. He argued that it had a strategic value, and was his 'laboratory' for Anglo–German relations. After the war was over, he postulated, and France was independent, the islands would remain German, a valuable U-boat base for the western Channel and a perfect place for good Nazi families to holiday in a 'Strength Through Joy' camp.

In the midst of feverish planning for the biggest invasion ever launched in human history, Hitler found time to study the defence plans for the Channel Islands. He was not satisfied, and ordered a host of new measures. The Organisation Todt was to provide the labour. Hitler demanded twice-weekly progress reports and the drawing-up of long-term fortification plans. He was determined that the islands' defences should be impregnable, and should be built to last into the next millennium.

Over the following eighteen months the islands became a vast building site, as a crash building programme was implemented to fulfil Hitler's ambitions. The sleepy holiday islands were transformed into the most strongly defended possession of the Reich. Hitler's alarmed commanders whispered about the Führer's 'Inselwahn' – island madness – and worried that the resources devoted to the Channel Islands would weaken defences on the much more important northern French coast.

More than 484,000 cubic metres of reinforced concrete were poured into the Channel Islands, and 244,000 cubic metres of rock were excavated. Anti-tank walls three metres high and two metres thick were built along the beaches. Gun emplacements were constructed on the cliffs and headlands. The biggest gun, the Mirus battery on Guernsey, took eighteen months to build and had a range of fifty kilometres; 45,000 cubic metres of concrete were needed to build its base. An adjacent underground barracks was excavated, with the capacity to house four hundred men.

Roads had to be built or widened to transport materials to building sites, and on Jersey, Guernsey and Alderney, railways were specially constructed. Mines were laid along all the islands' coasts. In June 1942, eighteen thousand mines had been laid, which was judged sufficient by the German experts. By April 1944, this figure had swollen to a fantastic 114,000 on all the islands, and the final figure for Jersey alone was sixty-seven thousand.

According to German records, at the peak of the construction work in May 1943 the OT had brought sixteen thousand foreign labourers to the Channel Islands; 6700 on Guernsey, 5300 on Jersey and 4000 on Alderney. This was a tiny part of the vast labour army of occupied Europe – by 1944 it had swollen to 1,360,000 people – which the OT was using to build roads, bridges, fortifications and factories to support the Nazi war machine.

The workers on the Channel Islands had come into the OT by four routes.

Firstly, the OT contracted out work to private companies. Dutch, French, German and Belgian building firms and civil construction companies worked on the islands' fortifications, and recruited their own workforce. Channel Island companies also worked under contract to the OT. These foreign workers, who made up about ten per cent of the total, were usually skilled and relatively well-treated; they received pay, adequate food and holidays.

Secondly, when there were insufficient volunteers, compulsion was used, and forced labourers supplemented the workforce. Labour quotas were imposed in countries such as Holland and France. Eighteen-year-old Dutchman Gilbert van Grieken officially 'volunteered' to join the OT to work on Guernsey. In reality, he was told he would have no ration cards if he refused to comply with his local employment office's instructions. He worked as a builder on Guernsey; he was paid, and was free in the evenings to come and go as he wished. Skilled OT workmen like van Grieken, from 'Germanic' nations like Belgium and Holland, lived in requisitioned private houses in St Peter Port and St Helier, or in camps closer to their place of work. They may have got a few kicks up the backside and some verbal abuse, but they lived to return home after the war. Between twenty and twenty-five per cent of the islands' OT workforce could be included in this category.

Thirdly, the bulk of the OT workers on the islands, about forty per cent, came from the occupied territories of the Eastern front, where they had been rounded up behind German lines. They included prisoners of war, and boys too young and men too old to have been conscripted. They were mostly from Russia, Ukraine and Poland. According to Nazi racial theories, Slavs were '*Untermenschen*' – sub-human – and were consequently used as slave labour; they were not paid, and had little freedom or time off. They were seldom deliberately killed, but the inadequate food, arbitrary beatings, utter disregard for their safety at worksites and lack of medical care exacted a heavy price in lives.

The remaining quarter of the workforce was something of a ragbag of different nationalities. Each had their own story. Several thousand Spanish Republicans arrived in the islands; they had fled to France after Franco's victory in 1939, and were handed over to the Germans to help fill France's labour quotas. Similarly, the French rounded up North African dockworkers from Algeria and Morocco and a few Chinese in ports such as Marseilles. French Jews also appeared on Alderney, as did a thousand-strong SS building brigade which included German, Czech, Dutch and French political prisoners.

The concrete bunkers are now overgrown with brambles, and the anti-tank barriers serve as seawalls. It is hard to imagine the suffering their construction entailed now, especially on a sunny summer's day, when families picnic on their concrete bulk and the beaches are dotted with the brightly coloured towels of holidaymakers. Even the dank, dark tunnels of Guernsey, Jersey and Alderney, used for fuel and ammunition depots and underground hospitals, have almost lost their power to disturb. Having survived the depredations of generations of inquisitive children and memorabilia hunters, several have been converted into highly successful museums, bustling with coachloads of tourists snapping up souvenirs and scones.

A few scraps of graffiti, such as a star of David, or initials scraped into the setting concrete, hint at the hundreds of men and boys who lost their lives building these vast monuments to Hitler's grandiose ambitions. For the last fifty years, most of the individual workers have remained nameless and faceless. Little was known about where they had come from, how many of them were brought to the islands, the conditions of their lives there, how many died or what happened to those who survived the war.

There were survivors living in London, Paris, Belgium and Cologne, but few people were sufficiently interested to listen to their stories. Hundreds more disappeared behind the Iron Curtain in 1945, and returned to their homes in Russia, Ukraine and Poland. Most have now died, but since the collapse of the Soviet Union, sixty-four of the last Channel Islands survivors have been traced there. Many of those I met were astonished that anyone was interested in the memories they had buried in their hearts for half a century, and which some of them were telling for the first time. It has finally become possible to put names and faces to these victims of the Channel Islands' war.

VASILLY MAREMPOLSKY

Vasilly Marempolsky was fifteen when he arrived on Jersey in August 1942:

My sister had been selected to go and work for the Germans in Germany, but she ran away, so the Germans took me. I was put in a cattle truck and travelled through Poland and Czechoslovakia to Germany, and then on to Paris and finally St Malo. We were beaten with sticks as we were loaded onto the ships; it was the first time I had seen the sea.

After we landed on Jersey, I was taken to Lager Himmelman on the west coast near St Ouen's. The camp consisted of only six huts and was surrounded by two rows of barbed wire. In the huts there were three wooden platforms, one on top of the other, which served as beds; there was a bit of straw on them, but no blankets. There were about five to six hundred people in the camp, and we were organised into working units of fifty men. We nicknamed the guard who was in charge of our unit 'Cherni' – 'the Black' – because he had black hair.

We got up at five o'clock and had dirty black water called coffee. After breakfast, we heard the whistle and we had to stand to attention for the Germans; those who were slow were beaten.

We were building a railway and we had to level the ground. Sometimes we had to crush rocks. Between one and two o'clock we had a lunch break and we were given turnip 'soup'; it was water with a tiny lump of turnip in it. We usually worked for twelve or fourteen hours a day. The Germans watched us from behind, and as soon as anyone paused to straighten their back, they would beat him. We had to stay bent over and pretend to work all the time. Then the Germans got wise to that and watched to see if we were working hard enough. If they decided we weren't, the Germans would beat us.

At the end of the day, we all received tiny cards with 'supper' printed on them. This entitled us to half a litre of soup and 200 grams of 'bread' which had bits of wood in it. Every second Sunday we had a day off and then we didn't get any food because we weren't working.

Sometimes as we marched back to camp, we would steal a turnip or a beetroot. Sometimes an islander would put out some bread or

proper soup for us. I never knew the islanders' names but we knew
they had a lot of sympathy for us. Within a few months of arriving,
my jacket had disintegrated. As we marched past a farm I saw some
people waiting by a gate. One of them was an island girl and she
had a big jacket and she threw it over my shoulders. It was very
useful.

Lice were a great problem because there was no disinfectant.
People began to catch illnesses like typhus and dysentery and many
people died of exhaustion. By the end of October I couldn't walk, I
was so weak from exhaustion and dysentery, but my friends helped
me. One day I had stayed behind when the others went to work and
I went to the camp medicine post. A Spanish doctor and nurse at
this post took me to a hospital the Spanish had set up for the foreign
workers. A Spaniard took pity on me and nursed me back to life;
his name was Gasulla Sole. A Jerseywoman also came to the hospital
to give me bread.

When I was better I had to go back to Lager Himmelman. The
men had begun work on the underground hospital.* We thought it
might be some kind of mine but it had no coal. We had to march
from the camp to the underground hospital every day. About a
quarter of our brigade died, and they were replenished by men from
another camp on Jersey.

It was barely light when we began the march to the underground
hospital. We were very young boys, we were thin, exhausted, dressed
in torn clothes and blue with cold. The worksite was a huge labyrinth
of tunnels. I was terrified. The roof was supported by wooden props
in some places and we could hear running water and smell damp. It
felt like a grave. The walls were rough-hewn and there was mud
underfoot. Everywhere there were people working like ants. It was
hard to believe all these tunnels had been dug out by the weakening
hands and legs of these slaves. People were so frail, they could barely
lift a spade. The future for everyone was the same – death.

During the night shifts, they blew up the rock with dynamite and
slaves had to crush the stones into small pieces and then load the
trucks with the debris which was taken out and emptied. We were
making a tunnel through virgin rock and thousands of tons of rock
were excavated. For twelve hours a day we were underground. Many
people died, especially during the dynamite explosions, when they

* This vast complex of tunnels has been restored and is now used as an Occupation
museum.

were wounded by falling pieces of rock. Those who were seriously wounded were taken out by SS guards* and were never seen again. I remember one morning three prisoners had been killed in the next-door tunnel where there had been a rockfall. A week later eighteen people were killed when some wooden props collapsed and the roof fell in.

I think about five hundred Russians and Ukrainians died on Jersey. The same lorry which brought the soup took the corpses away from the worksite. 'Cherni' killed more than one person by beating them with a wooden stick or a rubber hose filled with sand.

Most of the prisoners on Jersey were either Spanish or Russian. Some of the Spanish were doctors, and they helped the Russians because they remembered how the Soviet Union had helped them in the Spanish Civil War.

Vasilly Marempolsky is now a Professor of Ukrainian Literature in the industrial city of Zaporozhye in eastern Ukraine. He was fortunate enough to be able to resume his studies after the war, and was chosen to visit Jersey as part of Soviet delegations in 1975 and 1985, to mark the thirtieth and fortieth anniversaries of the Liberation.

Gasulla Sole, the Spaniard who saved Marempolsky's life, stayed on Jersey after the war and married a local girl. Before he died in 1980, he told his life story to the Imperial War Museum's sound archivist:

I was born in 1919 in Barcelona into a Republican family. When the Civil War ended in Spain, I escaped to France where I was put into one camp after another; the conditions were terrible. When the war was declared the Spaniards were forced to work for the French and I worked on the Maginot Line. After the French had been defeated, the Germans asked for volunteers to work for them. About a thousand Spanish were swapped by the French government for French prisoners of war captured by the Germans. We had no choice

---

* Marempolsky was told the guards were from the SS, but there is no documentary evidence that there were any SS on Jersey. They may have come from Ukrainian units recruited by the SS and the Wehrmacht, whose uniforms were very similar to those of the SS.

about it; all we could think was that every day we were alive was a bonus.

I worked on the submarine base in La Rochelle before I was sent with another three hundred men to Jersey. We had to build a camp at St John's [a village in the north of the island]. Jersey was painful, but it was not like Belsen; we were lucky. I worked as a nurse in the Spanish hospital. Twice, patients we couldn't cure were taken off Jersey in Belgian boats which had been used for transporting cement.

Rations consisted of a tiny piece of what was called cheese, a few carrots and vegetables and some bread. There was no meat. People ate worms, there was so little food. We did some petty sabotage such as derailing trains and breaking cement mixers.

As Marempolsky and Sole's accounts indicate, there were small ways in which islanders on Jersey helped the foreign workers to survive. The jacket flung around Marempolsky's shoulders and the bread brought to him in the hospital may have saved his life. Many slave workers also managed to steal the odd bit of food from the farms and villages. The Spaniards set up a hospital in one of the camps, in which they treated the slave workers with the help of islanders concerned at the danger of infectious diseases spreading.

On Alderney, these forms of help were not available. The few Britons living or working on the remote island were vastly out-numbered by the thousands brought to it to build fortifications. This was one of the factors which made Alderney a hell on earth for the workers who lived and died there between 1942 and 1944.

There were four camps on Alderney, each named after a German island in the North Sea: Borkum was largely for skilled (and paid) 'Germanic' workers from Belgium, Holland and Germany. Helgo-land, Norderney and Sylt were for the slave workers. The last two were the worst.

It was not the OT's job to run death camps, but the combination of their haste to achieve construction targets on Alderney, the cor-ruption which flourished on this outpost of the Reich, and their disregard for the safety of the slave workers ensured a terrible cost in human life. There is evidence that the higher reaches of the OT

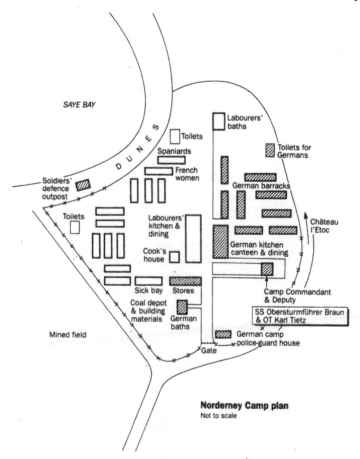

SAYE BAY

DUNES

Soldiers' defence outpost

Toilets

Labourers' baths

Toilets

Spaniards

French women

German barracks

Toilets for Germans

Château l'Etoc

Labourers' kitchen & dining

Cook's house

German kitchen canteen & dining

Sick bay

Stores

Coal depot & building materials

German baths

Camp Commandant & Deputy

SS Obersturmführer Braun & OT Karl Tietz

German camp police-guard house

Mined field

Gate

Norderney Camp plan
Not to scale

Norderney, based on a plan by slave camp survivor Ted Misiewicz

attempted to check the loss of life and instituted inquiries on the island, and complaints were allegedly made by the military authorities on Alderney. But Alderney was too distant for the writ of German rule to run effectively; black marketeering was rampant, and only a fraction of the rations calculated as necessary in Berlin reached the bowls of the Alderney workers. The German authorities on Guernsey and Jersey heard disturbing rumours of what was happening on the island, and islanders returned to Jersey and

Guernsey after their stints working on Alderney shocked by what they had seen. The island was referred to in hushed voices – a horrible and embarrassing secret.

Alderney's Untermenschen

About twenty Alderney survivors live near the city of Orel, four hundred miles south of Moscow. They form the remnants of a contingent collected from villages in the district in June 1942, when it was deep behind German lines.

The region around Orel is a land of undulating fields which stretch to the horizon under vast skies. The scale is continental; forests cover huge patches of the map. The roads are wide and the verges even wider. Space is abundant, and the land provides no obstacles such as mountains, ravines or even boulders.

A few of the run-down wooden houses where the Alderney slave workers would have been born remain, shabbily painted in bright colours and with carved shutters. The gardens are carefully tended, the orchards full of twisted old apple trees and surrounded by rickety wooden fences. The winters here are harsh, but they give way to sweet summers when the gardens are full of the much-loved dill and coriander, and the forest floor is carpeted with rich, fleshy mushrooms.

The landscape of the tiny island of Alderney must have been as alien as the moon to the slave workers from this country. They had never seen the sea, and had little conception of what an island was. On Alderney the great body of water, the Atlantic, is visible from every point, pressing in, pounding at the cliffs and rolling over the sandy beaches. Alderney is tiny; there are few fields and virtually no trees behind which to shelter from the gales which sculpt the bushes and hedges.

The Russians remember being terrified of the sea and its strange sounds. They hated the island's wetness, its frequent rain and mists heavy with water. They were stunned to see houses made of stone with little walled gardens, and the narrow, paved streets of St Anne's, Alderney's small town. Perhaps it is because this environ-

ment was so strange and unfamiliar that Alderney has remained
stamped on the memories of the survivors with an extraordinary
clarity and detail.

GEORGI KONDAKOV

Georgi Kondakov, one of the survivors of Alderney, has doggedly
traced sixty-three other survivors over the last ten years. He lives
in Orel in a tiny two-bedroom flat, bulging with family and books.
He had puzzled over his recollections of that strange, wet island
for twenty-five years before he managed to find out where Alderney
was; a British businessman at a trade fair was finally able to tell him.
At first, the other survivors Kondakov contacted were suspicious of
him, and feared he might have links with the KGB, but they were
won over by his remarkable charisma, his wide smile, handsome
face and self-evident integrity.

Kondakov tells his story with slow deliberation, as if it requires
a great effort to put words around these memories. At one point,
his voice grew husky and his eyes were wet.

I was eighteen, and was working in a shell factory when the Germans
arrived in Orel in October 1941. All the munitions factories were
being blown up to comply with Stalin's orders of 'scorched earth'.*
They didn't usually bother to tell the workers when they were going
to blow them up. Besides, the factories were guarded, so there was
no way out. Many were killed in this way. It was chaos, with the
NKVD† ordering one thing, and others ordering the opposite. I
escaped from the factory and saw the German tanks in Orel. There
were women screaming in the streets and fires burning everywhere.

I ran back home to my village and stayed there until 20 June
1942. The crops hadn't been harvested because the men were at the
front, so food was very short. We collected grain left over from the
silos which had been burnt by the Russians to prevent them falling
into German hands. The grain had been doused in petrol and we
had stomach-aches after eating it. We even dug the snow to find

---

* Stalin had ordered that all installations and crops of potential use to the Germans
be destroyed.
† The Soviet secret police, precursor of the KGB.

left-over potatoes. That winter of 1941–42 was little different from life in Alderney, and I think surviving these conditions helped me to survive later.

The Germans imposed labour quotas on each village, and the *skood* [the village assembly] had decided that the fairest way to fill the quota was to take children from the largest families. I was selected to go and work for the Germans. My family were very shocked, my grandfather burst into tears and my mother fell ill.

We were loaded onto trains by the Germans. When the doors were first closed in the cargo trucks, people kept silent, and some were crying. Then the pain calmed down and we began talking to our neighbours. There I met the boy who was to become my friend, Kirill Nevrov. We mostly talked about one subject: where were we going, and what did the future hold for us?

We arrived at a huge sorting centre at Wuppertal in Germany. They decided where you should go according to your appearance. The older and weaker were led outside, and we never saw them again. Men were separated from women. People had to declare their professions, and they were led off in different directions. The young and healthy were designated for hard labour in the mines or on construction projects. I saw a hut full of people who had come back from the mines in Belgium. They were so exhausted they looked like walking skeletons, and they cried out for food. I was completely overwhelmed.

Kondakov was sent to St Malo, where he was loaded onto a ship to be taken to Alderney. The boat journey took several days, and the German guards poured water into the packed hold for the thirsty prisoners, who had to open their mouths and cup their hands as best they could to catch the precious drops. On arriving at Alderney, the slave workers were divided between Helgoland, Sylt and Norderney camps. Kondakov was sent to Helgoland.

About four hundred people died in Helgoland while I was there; many died at the beginning of January 1943, when it was cold. One of the most common signs of the approach of death was that people started to swell. When we were woken in the morning, there were corpses in the beds beside us. Those who had been allowed off work because they were sick had the job of collecting the bodies, which were then thrown from the breakwater into the harbour. When I was building a road in the harbour, I saw special lorries come to the breakwater and tip bodies into the sea two or three times. Each lorry contained at least eight corpses. Human psychology is a strange thing; one gets used to even the most terrible experiences. Nature created human beings to adapt quickly to any situation.

All our conversations on Alderney were about food or the death of someone we knew. On our one day off a month we discussed home and the progress of the war. If my brain was not too exhausted I would always dream of home.

At first I had the trousers which I had been wearing when I was taken from home, but the fabric disintegrated. I found a blanket and cut holes in it for my arms and head. For a belt I used some wire. The blanket covered my knees like a poncho and I attached sleeves to it with wire; the sleeves were different colours initially, but they both became cement-coloured. I wrapped my feet in cement bags and wore sabots, but my legs were open to the wind. I suffered from the cold and wet. I had blisters and boils on my hands which eventually got infected.

Many times when I was on Alderney I thought death was close. Most of my worst memories come to me now as nightmares; in the daytime I can suppress those thoughts in my subconscious, but against the nightmares I am powerless. One nightmare I had on Alderney came to me at the end of October 1942. I was completely exhausted at that time, my hands and legs had started to swell and I thought I was dying. I dreamt we were building a road, and we dug a hole and suddenly a staircase opened up, going down to a huge long hall with a vaulted ceiling. Sitting at long tables eating were rows of naked people. I was also naked and very hungry, but there was no room at the table, so I slipped under the table and gathered breadcrumbs. One of the people sitting at the table kicked me and told me to go and bow to Death. I was frightened, but they motioned to me that she was next door. I followed their instructions and was greeted by a skeleton in a red robe. When I fell on my knees and kissed her feet, the skeleton said to me, 'Go back, go back.' I woke up, and found myself lying on my bunk. My heart did not seem to be beating and I was covered with sweat; I didn't know whether I was dead or alive. I still don't know whether it was a dream or whether I nearly died, but death had not wanted me, and after that dream my life improved.

We had a guard who let us go off to steal food. I often stole food at night. The Germans started shooting prisoners who were stealing potatoes out of the fields, but the desire for food was much stronger than the fear of death. The will to live is instinctive in each living creature. We were also determined to defy the will of the Germans, who had told us that no one would leave the island alive.

The prisoners worked in pairs; one would steal and one would protect him from being robbed by other prisoners. The Russians never stole anyone's bread ration, that was sacred because someone's survival was at stake, but anything they might have managed to steal could be taken; it was an unwritten law.

I was imprisoned and beaten for stealing food three times. Once I was selected to go to Sylt camp,* but I escaped by hiding in a sewage ditch. I almost died there because my arms and legs went numb with cold and I couldn't move them.

But Kondakov survived, and in October 1943 he was taken to northern France to work on construction projects; the work was easier and food more plentiful, and his health improved.

KIRILL NEVROV

The friendship between Kondakov and Kirill Nevrov, who met on the train journey from Orel to St Malo, has lasted fifty years. It has been punctuated by astonishing coincidences, which both delight in recounting.

On arriving at Alderney, to their bitter disappointment, they were separated, and Nevrov was sent to Norderney camp. It was not until two years later that they bumped into each other in Paris, during the jubilant celebrations following the city's liberation in August 1944. They travelled home to Orel together in 1945, and then lost contact for several years, until by pure chance they were allocated flats almost next door to each other and Kondakov was offered a job at the plant where Nevrov worked.

Nevrov has an air of faded refinement, which he attributes to the year he spent in hiding with Russian émigrés in occupied Paris. He made a point of using his rusty old-fashioned French as he kissed my hand and offered hospitality with the ceremony appropriate to Paris in the 1940s.

---

* Sylt camp was taken over by the SS in March 1943 and used as a punishment camp.

Nevrov was seventeen, and living in a village about twenty-five kilometres from Orel when the Germans invaded. His family had been relatively well off, and his father was the accountant with the local collective farm.

Our homes were taken for the German soldiers and we were forced out into hastily constructed shelters for the harsh winter. When spring came, the Germans started to round up young people, and I was unlucky. My father was very sorry for me, but there was nothing he could do.

We were transported in cargo trucks; they packed us in so tightly it was as if we were cattle. But even cattle are treated better. There were only tiny windows for fresh air and we were given food only twice on a journey which lasted several days. [People had to urinate and defecate in the trucks.]

In St Malo, I was very frightened by the sea. When we got onto the ship I felt we were floating in the air and the horizon was just a line of water. I was so relieved to see Alderney because it was land in the middle of this ocean, and I wanted to get off the water, which seemed like hell. I did not know that the island would turn into a hell. I still remember the sound of the sea roaring all day and all night.

We worked sometimes for as long as sixteen hours a day, building concrete walls around the island. Often we worked for twenty-four hours at a stretch, and we were then given half a day's rest before resuming work. My only wish was to rest; it was completely exhausting. I didn't even have the strength to move my hand. On one occasion we were working with the huge concrete-mixing machines and one man was so exhausted he lost his balance and slipped into the concrete. We told the German supervisor that someone had fallen in, but he said it was too complicated to stop the machine. It carried on pouring concrete over him. Many people died at the construction sites.

After two or three months people started to die at the rate of about twelve men a day. There was a yard in the centre of the camp where people were shot for stealing cigarettes. In the morning many people were found dead in their beds, and the naked corpses were loaded into trucks. A truck would tip the corpses at low tide into pits dug in the beach fifty to a hundred metres off the shore. There would be about twelve people in each pit. You could never find the grave after the tide had been in and out because sand had been washed over it. I saw the bodies being buried with my own eyes, because I was working about fifty metres away on a concrete wall.

Kondakov and I have discussed many times why the corpses were naked. Perhaps it was because people came from work in clothes which were soaking wet, and they would take them off to sleep naked and then die in the night. We also took off our clothes to get some relief from the parasites at night. People stole blankets, but they wouldn't have bothered to steal clothes, because they were no more than rags.

I was nothing but skin and bones, and I had only the clothes I was wearing when they rounded me up in Russia the previous summer, which quickly fell apart. We made replacements out of old cement sacks; we cut off the corners to make holes for the arms and I used a rope as a belt. We used cement sacks for everything: blankets, leggings and even hats. We slept in cement powder because it was softer than our beds. We were covered in cement day and night and our hair got cemented. There was nowhere to wash it off, but it did give us some protection against parasites. My trousers went so stiff with cement that when I took them off they remained standing. I used to be able to jump from my bunk into my standing trousers.

Our huts were about thirty metres long, with men sleeping on either side on two levels of planks. At first it was one blanket per person, but after people began to die they gave us more blankets. When you lay down you fell asleep immediately; there was no time to feel cold. It was the sleep of a dead man.

There was a passageway about one and half metres wide down the middle. At either end there were doors. There was a rail along the ceiling which the guards would beat with a hammer to wake everyone up. The last to leave the hut was beaten by the guards. We went to the canteen for breakfast, which was only a cup of herb tea that tasted of copper. There was about thirty minutes for lunch, which was cabbage soup; it only took a few minutes to drink it. Supper was more soup and bread. There was a one-kilogram loaf to share between seven people.* The flour had been mixed with bone-meal and sawdust, so it wasn't like proper bread, and it was as hard as a brick. Occasionally we got 10–15 grams of margarine. Going to the toilet during work was a farce; a German guard would hold out the spade for me to do it on.

One of my happiest memories was when a German supervisor

---

* The equivalent of two thin slices of bread per person.

with a pair of binoculars was standing near to where we were working. He was looking in the direction of England. You can't imagine
how strong my desire was to see England through those binoculars.
The German saw me looking at him with shining eyes, so he offered
me the binoculars and showed me how to adjust the focus. I was
very happy to see England – it was as if the Holy Spirit had come
down upon me!*

The worst times were when the weather was bad and the sea was
roaring. Then I could have committed suicide. Alderney left a mark
on the lives of all of us. Each time I go to bed or have a spare
minute, I remember the things that happened on Alderney. I want
people to know what it was like and to remember what happened.
It was my sacred duty to come and talk to you.

I thank Our Lord for my survival, I never thought I would live
to sixty-eight – not that I believe in God. None of us old people
who have suffered so much in our lives believes in God. How can
a superhuman being like God allow atrocities to happen to innocent
people?

Ivan Kalganov, Alexei Ikonnikov, Alexei Rodine, Ivan Sholomitsky
and Ivan Dolgov have less detailed memories. Their rough faces
are worn by hard work and vodka. Talking of Alderney broke these
tough men, and they tried to brush away the tears which spilled
over their gnarled hands.

IVAN KALGANOV

Kalganov is a simple man with a sheepish, boyish smile. He was so
nervous about talking of his experiences on Alderney to a British
journalist that his plump, red-cheeked, grown-up son Vladimir had
accompanied him. Vladimir listened closely; it was the first time
he had heard his father's story.

Kalganov was working at the same munitions factory in Orel as
Georgi Kondakov in 1941 when the Germans arrived, and he too
fled to his village.

---

* Nevrov must have been looking at the French coast – you cannot see England from
Alderney.

No one in our village had been able to evacuate east because we had been encircled by the German advance. We were trapped behind their lines. Everyone knew what occupation would mean, and we were all talking about atrocities before the Germans even arrived. It was a terrifying feeling, waiting for them to come. It took them a few months to reach us because the road from Orel was very bad. I remember the Germans arriving in my village. They had machine guns and they shot all the birds; they just sprayed bullets at the geese, chickens and hens. Whatever moved, they shot. Then they demanded sheep and all the cattle. They killed some with their machine guns to feed themselves. They only stayed a week at our village before moving on.

In the spring, the Germans divided the *kolkhoz* [collective farm] land up and distributed it amongst individual farmers. My father was a Communist, so my family got no land, although I had seven brothers and sisters. The only job I could get was tending other people's cows.

In the summer of 1942 I was selected to work for the Germans. It was a complete surprise. A Russian policeman and a German came to where I was looking after the cows and told me. I was allowed home to say goodbye to my family, and I remember vividly my three-year-old brother running after me, waving goodbye. They put me in a cart along with about fifteen others from my village and took us to the railway station.

I saw the sea for the first time in St Malo, and I liked it; it was night and the water was calm, and the stars were reflected in the water. It was very beautiful.

Alderney was covered with barbed wire and signs saying 'Beware of the mines'. I was sent to Sylt camp where I stayed until March 1943, when the SS arrived and I was moved to Helgoland. Sylt was terrible, terrible. If they caught you at the rubbish heap, you would be beaten. Dogs were used against us in Sylt.

Kalganov stumbled to a halt. He was crying. He insisted he would go on, but asked for a few moments to collect himself. Georgi Kondakov provided a glass of vodka, and Vladimir took him aside. Then he continued:

Sylt was much worse than Helgoland, because it was in a very exposed position on top of the hill and open to the winds. How

Guernseymen in St Peter Port in 1939, about to embark for the UK to volunteer for the Forces.

Islanders gather at St Helier harbour to wave off reservists called up for the British Forces on 1 September 1939.

The Germans have arrived. The Bailiff of Jersey, Alexander Coutanche (second from left), and island officials greet Luftwaffe officers at Jersey airport on 1 July 1940.

Sieg im Westen - 'Victory in the West' – a Nazi propaganda film, is shown at the Gaumont Palace, Guernsey, in August 1941.

Islanders adjust to German Occupation

Above: A Guernsey policeman opens the car door for German staff officers attending the military administration's headquarters in St Peter Port, 1940.

Right: An islander nervously receives orders from a German officer in Gorey Harbour, Jersey, in 1941.

Nazi bureaucracy bears down on the islanders

Every islander had to have an identity card. This one belonged to Raymond Falla, Guernsey's Minister of Agriculture and a member of the Controlling Committee.

Tight rationing was introduced, and controls imposed on every aspect of food production.

Initially, at least, to the German soldiers a posting to the Channel Islands was more like a holiday than fighting a war. The islanders were peaceful and food was plentiful.

German officer Hans Stumpf (photographed on Jersey, above) has happy memories to this day of the friends he made during the Occupation.

Stumpf's best friend with Stumpf's girlfriend and her sister.

A young Jersey girl on the best of terms with three German officers.

Baron von Aufsess, a senior member of the German administration on Jersey, who enjoyed a string of affairs and flirtations with island women, while also establishing friendships with many members of the islands' governments.

Island women found the
attractions of the Germans
difficult to resist.

The Jewish women of Guernsey

Therese Steiner, photographed in Vienna before she fled the Nazis and sought refuge in England. This picture was cherished by Therese's brother Karl during his fifty-year wait for news of her. She was deported from Guernsey in 1942 and died in Auschwitz.

Therese Steiner enjoying a beach holiday with the Potts family on Sark in the summer of 1939. She was trapped on Guernsey when, as an Austrian citizen, she was refused permission to accompany the family back to England after the outbreak of war.

Marianne Grunfeld (front right) with her cousins as a child in Berlin, already showing the stubborn determination which was to prove her downfall. In May 1940 she defied the advice of her relatives, including her cousin Ernst (back left), who had sought refuge in London, and took a job on a Guernsey farm. She was deported in 1942 and died in Auschwitz.

The burden of island government

Above: Sybil Hathaway, Dame of Sark, and her husband greet a German officer outside their home, the Seigneurie.

Right: Ambrose Sherwill and his wife May, reunited after his imprisonment and internment, at Buckingham Palace to receive his post-war honours.

The negotiations on which the islanders' well-being depended: the Bailiff of Jersey, Alexander Coutanche (centre), and the Bailiff of Guernsey, Victor Carey, negotiate with Red Cross representatives in a conference chaired by Admiral Friedrich Hüffmeier in December 1944.

Queues formed quickly when food supplies arrived from France, as here in St Peter Port.

Old metal biscuit tins were made into saucepans, a meagre light came from a Brasso can, and a butter churn from a glass preserving jar.

With islanders facing starvation, the British government finally agreed in November 1944 to allow the Red Cross to ship in parcels of food.

Above: Hitler ordered a crash building programme to make the islands' fortifications an impregnable part of the Atlantic Wall defences. By 1943 sixteen thousand foreign workers had arrived to work on their construction.

Left: Ukrainian Vasilly Marempolsky (right) arrived on Jersey in 1942, aged fifteen. He believes he owes his life to Gasulla Sole (left), a Spanish Republican prisoner who nursed him back to life after discovering him weak from exhaustion and dysentery. The two were reunited at a post-war Liberation anniversary on Jersey.

Survivors of Alderney's slave-labour force Georgi Kondakov (left) and Kirill Nevrov (right) in Orel in 1993. Their friendship dates back to the train journey they shared from southern Russia to Alderney in 1942.

After being transferred to labour camps in France from Alderney, both Kondakov and Nevrov managed to escape. Kondakov joined the French resistance. He retrieved his resistance membership certificate (below) from the KGB in the mid-eighties. Nevrov (right) was hidden by a Russian émigré couple in Paris.

Ivan Kalganov in 1993.

Alexei Ikonnikov in 1944.

Otto Spehr, a German socialist imprisoned by the Nazis and believed to be the last surviving member of SS Baubrigade I, which came to Alderney in March 1943.

Joe Miere in the Jersey Underground Museum, 1994. Both he and Bernard Hassall were arrested and imprisoned by the Germans.

Resistance

Jersey boy Bernard Hassall tries on a German helmet in 1941.

A V for Victory sign in a St Helier street, inspired by the BBC campaign for occupied Europe.

Right: Under pressure from the Germans, the Bailiff of Guernsey offered a £25 reward for information leading to the conviction of painters of 'V' signs. Islanders at the time, and the British authorities after the war, were shocked by his action.

EVENING PRI

" La Gazette Officielle "

REWARD OF £25

A REWARD OF £25 WILL BE GIVEN TO THE PERSON WHO FIRST GIVES TO THE INSPECTOR OF POLICE INFORMATION LEADING TO THE CONVICTION OF ANYONE (NOT ALREADY DISCOVERED) FOR THE OFFENCE OF MARKING ON ANY GATE WALL OR OTHER PLACE WHATSOEVER VISIBLE TO THE PUBLIC THE LETTER "V" OR ANY OTHER SIGN OR ANY WORD OR WORDS CALCULATED TO OFFEND THE GERMAN AUTHORITIES OR SOLDIERS.

THIS 8th DAY OF JULY, 1941.

VICTOR G. CAREY,
Bailiff.

Stella Perkins in 1942. Her home in St Helier, Jersey, was a refuge for a string of escaped Russian prisoners.

The Jersey resistance movement: Norman Le Brocq (standing, second from right), Rosalie Le Brocq (front right) and Les Huelin (standing, far left), with German deserter Paul Mülbach (standing, third from left). They printed illegal leaflets throughout the war, and plotted a German mutiny.

The only photographs to be taken inside Buchenwald by an inmate. Jersey cinema projectionist Stanley Green was sent to Buchenwald for possessing an illegal radio. He survived, and returned with the film and camera he had smuggled into the camp.

Liberation. Troops
arrive to a rapturous
welcome on 9 May 1945.

German prisoners of
war being loaded onto
ships bound for
England, where they
faced at least three
years in camps before
returning home.

A wartime romance

Dolly and Willi Joanknecht courting during the Occupation on Guernsey.

Dolly and her son Tony wave goodbye to Willi as he leaves for England in 1946.

WAR ROMANCE SEQUEL

Dolly and Willi are finally married in England in August 1947. Willi, still a prisoner of war in a camp in Devon, has no shirt or tie to wear at his wedding, which was covered in the local press.

Graves of Russian slave workers on Alderney.

Below: British investigators examining reports of atrocities committed by the Germans on Alderney discover a false-bottomed coffin, which could be used for repeated burials.

Maximilian List, SS commandant of Alderney.

Kurt Klebeck, List's deputy. Both were listed as wanted by British officials investigating war crimes on Alderney; neither was ever tried for them.

many died each day varied. Sometimes it was six, sometimes a dozen. People died of dysentery, hunger or bad food. More Ukrainians and Poles than Russians died because the Russians were used to living in bad conditions. There were about five hundred men in Sylt camp, and at least three hundred died while I was there. I don't know how I survived. I had boils, I was always wet from the rain and I was exhausted from the work. I nearly died on the ship back to France, but my friends helped me.

I hardly remember those friends now. If I had something to eat I shared it with them, and they with me; that was all our friendship consisted of. If we had any spare time we were too tired to talk, we just fell asleep.

We were marching from the camp to work once and I saw a man who couldn't walk any longer. He was shot down right there by the Germans. I saw one man crucified for stealing; he was hung by his hands in the hut where the corpses were piled up. I think he was still alive when I saw him.

When I got up in the morning I saw dead bodies in the neighbouring bunks. Sometimes I saw that their lips, nose and ears had been eaten by rats. Rats ran over our bodies while we were sleeping, looking for the dead. There was a special hut in Sylt where the dead corpses were piled in the morning. Later they were taken away, and I saw corpses being loaded onto trucks. Other prisoners told me that they were dumped in the sea.

The food was just water with a few bits of turnip floating in it. Life was a constant struggle to find food. I found a good rubbish heap near to the construction site where I worked. It must have been near where German officers lived because there were different kinds of vegetable peelings and even cabbage leaves. I would fill a bag I had with this rubbish. Once someone from the kitchen saw me and set a dog on me. The dog tore all my clothing; I was very weak at the time. Again and again the dog attacked me. When the dog let go and I got back to work I was beaten with a stick by a German.

I didn't know how many hours we worked or slept. Everything was a blur. All I know is that we went to bed when it got dark. I was working on the Westbatterie, the largest gun emplacement on Alderney, and sometimes we worked all night, especially when we were concreting the base of the guns.

I didn't wash myself once the whole time I was there. My clothes were those I had brought from home, and they were crawling with lice. I could have scooped a handful of lice out from under my armpit. When we came back to the hut after work, we would shake out our clothes over a stove to burn the lice.

I still suffer from the memories; sometimes I can't get rid of the thoughts. When I go to bed, it all comes back to my mind, and in my dreams I revisit all those places.

ALEXEI IKONNIKOV

Ikonnikov's face is raddled by drink. As he talks of Alderney, his eyes are wild:

On Alderney, people were treated like cattle; there was no hope of surviving. I was called number 146, no one ever used my name. A Dutchman in the Strabag Firm* used to say that after the roads had been built on the island, we would be killed. We would either be destroyed or worked to death. People who stayed in the hut because they were sick wouldn't be there in the evening. A man was killed for stealing bread in our camp. We came back from work, had supper and immediately fell asleep, and we never considered the question of how many people had died, or how they had died, or where they were buried. When a man is exhausted, he doesn't talk.

I wouldn't have survived if another prisoner hadn't pointed out that the Germans kept pigs and grew potatoes in a place near the camp. He kept watch while I crawled under the fence to get potatoes. When one of the prisoners found something to steal, he shared it with the others. Once we broke the lock on the kitchen door and put all the rubbish in bags to take back to the camp. Two of my friends were caught by German guards and I hid amongst the pigs, but one of my legs was sticking out and they found me. We were put in a lorry, and we heard the Germans discussing what to do with us: the younger one said they should shoot us, but the older one disagreed, and said that we were dying of hunger and that when he had been a prisoner of war of the Russians in the First World War he hadn't been shot. So we were sentenced to twenty-five blows with a stick. We were lucky – the commandant was a Polish German, and only the first few blows were on my body, then he ordered me to continue screaming while he beat the wall.

* One of the firms contracted to the Organisation Todt.

Once I found some cow leather which we boiled and ate. People were so desperate for food they went down to the beaches to get seafood. We gathered oysters, mussels and fish. But you had to be careful. Half a dozen people, maybe more, were blown up by mines on the shore. The area around the bakery was also mined. Some Russians tried to get bread by squeezing through the bars of the window. One of them was blown up and the German commandant ordered that a special coffin be made, and asked to see the corpse of a man brave enough to risk death for bread.

Not all the Germans were bad; some shared their food with us and some secretly helped us, but I don't think the SS should ever be pardoned. To make Germany a human nation will take another fifty years. Some of the SS prisoners cried out to us that they had been in concentration camps since 1933, and told us we were only beginners compared with them.

I often think about Alderney, and I still have nightmares. Once I dreamt I was being eaten by a German, and I was so desperate to escape that I put out my arms as wings to fly, and then I saw the sea beneath me and found I was too weak to fly; I was terrified of falling into the sea.

One Sunday after the battle of Stalingrad* we were allowed to bathe in the sea; I was frightened of it at first, but I came to like it. It was transparent and I could see the fish. The island was very beautiful when the weather was fine. I liked the air – it was very soft and salty and had a strong smell of grass. I liked the stone houses around the harbour and the little gardens they each had. I liked seeing the other islands in the distance. I always had this idea that Alderney was a place where people before the war were happy and free, and when the war was over, they would be so again. We dreamt about escaping to England, but it was impossible to swim there.

ALBERT POTHUGINE

Like Vasilly Marempolsky, Albert Pothugine lives in Zaporozhye in the eastern Ukraine, a huge steel- and iron-making centre where a forest of metal chimneys blaze brilliant flames and endlessly puff

---

* The Russians believed they were better treated after the German defeat at Stalingrad in January 1943.

thick smoke into a polluted sky. Pothugine worked in these plants until he retired on invalidity benefit. The combination of his time on Alderney, a lifetime of smoking and Zaporozhye's pollution has left his health in a parlous state.

Pothugine told his story with a fierce intensity; at times he staggered to his feet and flung his arms about in wild gesticulations, and at the points of greatest horror he fixed me with a penetrating glare. His diminutive wife Anna watched anxiously, for fear that the emotion the memories aroused would give him a heart attack.

Albert was born in 1928 in Belorussia, and when he was only four his father was killed in a peasant uprising against collectivisation. When the Germans invaded in 1941, his mother was drafted to dig anti-tank ditches around Bryansk, about a hundred miles from Orel, and was forced to leave twelve-year-old Albert and his ten-year-old brother to fend for themselves. They survived by collecting wild berries and exchanging them for milk. Their mother eventually returned, and in occupied Belorussia the family scraped a living for a few months, trading old clothes in remote villages for food to bring back to the town. On returning from one of these long journeys by foot, Albert found his home had been bombed and his mother murdered. He believes the culprits were 'partisans' – who, he claimed, were no more than bandits. He and his brother were forced to forage for food in the ruins of bombed buildings until the Russian police arrested them and handed them over to the Germans as 'partisans'. They were separated, and it was not until 1953, eleven years later, that the brothers saw each other again.

Albert ended up in a forced labour transport which took him across Europe to Alderney; he was fourteen years old when he arrived in Helgoland camp. He never knew where the island was or what it was called; he only knew it as 'Adolf'.

I worked at the stone crusher where I was given a thirty-two-kilo hammer to crush the stones, but I was too young and weak to do that work, so they made me load sand into trolleys and take it to the shore, and when I was there I slipped off to hunt for mussels.

I avoided all the Germans, but there was one who picked on me. Every time I went past he beat me, and once he beat me so hard he broke my ribs. Later, I heard that his son had been killed in Russia, so he was taking out his anger on me.

I'm still angry with the Germans. It wasn't just the fascists who beat us but the civilians [OT personnel] as well. When I saw the English planes coming over I wanted them to bomb Alderney with all my heart. Not a single British plane was shot down over Alderney while we were there because we prayed to God to look after them. All our hopes were with Britain to liberate us.

We suffered from fleas and sometimes my blanket was white with their eggs. They were so bad I don't know how I slept. Between ten and fifteen people died every day, especially in the winter of 1942/43, when there was terrible dysentery. A loaf of bread was a matter of life and death, but I would still exchange my share of bread for tobacco, I needed cigarettes so much.

They used dynamite at the quarry to blow the rock out. On one occasion we were told to take shelter from the explosion, but the force of it came from exactly the opposite direction and I received the full blast. My ankle was hit by a rock and to this day I am lame. I couldn't walk back to the camp, and an old Russian sailor hid me in sacking at the quarry for three days. He brought me water, but the only food he could give me was wild blackberries. I had to start work again to get my food rations. People helped me by loading the trolley and pushing it to the beach. First my foot started to swell, then the other leg started to swell and then my face. I would have recovered if the wound had been cleaned but there was no medical care. The Lagerführer's method of curing people was to beat them. People were either dead or working; you couldn't be ill.

Early in 1943, between six and seven hundred of the weakest people, including myself, were loaded onto the *Xaver Dorsch*, and more on another ship, the *Franka*. The plan was to take us to Cherbourg in one day, so they had packed the ships with as many people as possible. A severe storm shipwrecked both ships and they were pushed onto Alderney's rocks by the waves. For fourteen days we were kept inside the wrecks with no bread and no water. Each day six barrels of soya flour mixed with water were distributed amongst the prisoners. The Germans didn't go into the hold and they appointed the Russians to distribute the 'soup'. The Russian 'police' always took one barrel for themselves, which meant that a lot of prisoners got no food at all. The prisoners crowded around the barrels, knowing that there might not be enough for the last in the queue. In the rush, about six people were crushed to death every day.

The Russian police then found a big long stick and stood on the ladder which led up to the deck and beat those who were near the front of the queue on their heads. These prisoners lost consciousness and fell, and the people behind them would rush forward and trample them to death. After the stick was introduced, the number who died went up to ten or more a day.

The most dreadful thing on this wrecked ship was the toilet. There was only one barrel for more than six hundred prisoners, and it was emptied only once a day. Because of the rough seas, the boat was moving all the time, and the excrement slopped over. In fourteen days at least four barrels were poured over the floor. No one was allowed out on the deck, and the air was so thick that if you had lit a match there would have been an explosion. I was sitting near the staircase leading to the deck. Everyone was wet with excrement and the lice multiplied so quickly you could collect handfuls under your armpits, but there was nowhere to drop them other than on your neighbour. There was no room to lie or stretch your legs. We were covered with wounds and our skin was eaten up with lice and sores.

The dead people were taken out of the hold by a rope around the neck, but the rope broke sometimes, so they changed the technique and passed the rope round the body. Then the Germans decided the bodies had to be buried with a priest. There was no Russian priest, so a Russian policeman who wanted to ingratiate himself with the Germans selected one of the slave labourers. This man had been a poet and a writer before the war, but he had been beaten by the Germans for stealing potatoes and he had gone mad. The Russian policeman told him to pray, and ordered all the other Russians to copy the madman. Fifteen corpses had been taken out of the hold and were laid out on the deck. For the first time we were allowed up onto the deck; we were wet with excrement. The Germans watched the 'funeral' and we knelt in circles around the corpses. The 'priest' started crossing himself and singing – not prayers, but a Ukrainian folk song. It was a farce. The Germans rewarded the 'priest' with bread. Then the corpses were thrown in the sea and we were sent back into the hold.

The next day we were taken off the ship. We were told to take all our clothes off and to leave them behind in the ship. We were each given a blanket smelling of horses, otherwise we were naked. I cut a hole in the blanket and put it over my head. Two or three days later, after the ship had been repaired, we were finally taken to Cherbourg.

Pothugine's suffering didn't end with his departure from Alderney. In Cherbourg he was beaten by one of the Russian policemen from

Alderney with a metal rod and lost all his teeth. For the rest of the war, he could only eat wet bread and mashed cabbage.*

Another Alderney survivor who lives in Zaporozhye, Ivan Sholo-mitsky, was trapped in the other wrecked ship, the *Franka*. He still works at one of the steel plants, and in his lunch hour he came to Pothugine's flat and gave his account. He thought that there were about three hundred prisoners trapped with him for ten days amongst drowned bodies in a half-submerged ship.

TED MISIEWICZ

Ted Misiewicz has lived in London since the war. He was born in 1926 in a village in eastern Poland, from where he was taken for slave labour in 1942 and sent to Alderney. He never returned to Poland after the war, but came to England from France. After a period in the British army, he trained to be an architect.

My village of Niemilla was about twenty-eight kilometres from the Russian border. It was at the conflux of two rivers and had very poor, sandy soil, and there was only subsistence agriculture. Life was never easy. The rivers regularly flooded and then we were cut off on both sides. We lived a very introverted life, but we were never bored because there was just too much to do; everyone worked from sunrise to sunset. There was no electricity in the village but we did have a radio and in the evenings everyone would come and gather round it to listen.

We would spend all year preparing, pickling and storing food for the long winter months. February was usually the worst month – sometimes we only had boiled salty potatoes to eat for a whole week at a time. At these times it was very tense in the house. There was a cold wind that was so sharp that any exposed skin would dry and crack up.

The first sign of spring was the appearance of the sorrel, and my mother would send me and my sister to gather it for soup. The next sign was the new potatoes; only then did you start living again.

---

* See Chapter 8 for the post-war experiences of Pothugine and other Russian survivors mentioned in this chapter.

Misiewicz's village heard on the radio that Germany had invaded
Poland in September 1939, but they believed the war would pass
them by, much as the First World War had done. They saw the
Russians cross the border (Poland was partitioned by the Molotov–
Ribbentrop pact in August 1939), but the soldiers didn't come to the
village. Then came the German invasion of the Soviet Union in 1941:
'We knew about the German invasion from the Russian newspapers.
For days we could hear distant guns rumbling. We saw a lot of Russians withdrawing; they marched barefoot with their boots hanging
around their necks. Then the Germans attacked and the Russians
were thrown back; there were tanks and abandoned armaments
everywhere. Many of the defeated soldiers slept in the forest.'

The war moved on, leaving the village in German-occupied
Poland. The Germans intervened in village life only for work duty
and requisitioning foodstuffs. In spring 1942 the Germans gave
the village a labour quota, and the sixteen-year-old Misiewicz was
selected: 'Only three of us went from our village, and each of us
took a small bundle of food. We were made to sign papers which
said we had volunteered to work for the Germans, and we were
then loaded into cattle trucks with the Russians. On the journey
we were given no water, and some of the Russians even drank their
urine. I think the journey lasted ten days.'

After stopping briefly at a camp in Kestelbach in Germany,
Misiewicz was put on a train for St Malo. He reached Alderney by
boat in June 1942, in a transport of 1500 prisoners. He was among
the first to arrive at Norderney camp.

I was taken to start work in the quarry. At first I was working as an
interpreter, because nobody could speak a word of German in our
group. But I quickly found out that it was a privileged position which
also obliged me to beat people, and I resigned.

There were eight Russian and Ukrainian police chosen from
among the slave workers. One of them was a tiny fellow called Boris
who was only seventeen, but he was a real little animal. Of course
you could never fight back if you were being beaten by one of them.
All you could do was fall down, curl up and hope they would only
kick you a couple of times. If you fought back you were dead. I
suppose they had to beat people, it was their job.

A lot of the workers were very heavy smokers, and they would often trade the little pats of margarine we occasionally got for cigarettes. The old men told me that these boys were sentencing themselves to death, that they were committing suicide by giving away their food. They were right – after a few weeks they looked like living skeletons. The wind blew them down and they didn't get up.

There was no money, so prisoners bartered. There were fights, and gangs who bullied other prisoners. There were some beatings in the barracks, and some murders as well. The Germans didn't give a damn. The body would be thrown outside the barracks, and in the morning the Germans would collect it. Different nationalities kept together; we Poles were a small minority.

Misiewicz fell ill. His body began to swell, and the camp commander's interpreter, Jean Soltisiak, who was a Pole, took pity on him because he was one of the youngest in the camp. Soltisiak saved Misiewicz's life several times over the next few years. He managed to get him small jobs in the camp, thus sparing him the hard construction work and giving him more time to hunt for food scraps. One of these jobs was cleaning the home of the camp commandant, Karl Tietz. Misiewicz had been almost beaten to death by Tietz once, and now his job included cleaning up the blood after other prisoners were beaten. He also had the task of clearing the tables: 'So started my slow recovery. The Germans would always leave food on their plates and they always had more bread than they needed. I never ate it all at once, but put little pieces of food away in a small suitcase.'

Then Soltisiak got Misiewicz an even better job, in charge of the baths.

During the winter I made a small bed next to the hot-water boiler with some roofing felt and nailed it round my bed to make it very cosy and warm. I finally began to live again. I was quite comfortable and for once I even had enough food. In return for food, I used to let the cooks use my machine room for meetings with their French girlfriends.* Even the Germans liked me, because there was a small spyhole in the machine room and I would let them watch the French girls bathing.

* These meetings were for sex. The Germans brought French prostitutes and kitchen workers to the islands. Some had sex with foreign workers, who either gave them food or with whom they had relationships. Cooks, with their access to food, were in a position of great power and influence in the camps.

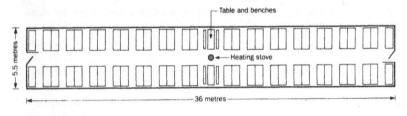

Typical barrack
Capacity 120
Assumed width of bed 800mm
Passage between beds 700mm

A typical Norderney barrack, based on a drawing by Ted Misiewicz

We had big political discussions, and sometimes we had parties. One night the hospital staff supplied some ether which we made into 'punch'. Luckily I was late and there was very little left to drink. The next day several people who had drunk the punch found they had gone blind. One of the cooks whom everyone, including the Germans, liked never regained his sight; the Germans injected him with something in the sick bay and he died. They told me to write to his relatives to say he had died defending his country.

In July 1943 a Spaniard who acted as postman came running up to me shouting my name; I was one of the lucky few to have received a letter, and he thought I would be pleased. He was not to know what it contained. It was from a cousin who had fled to Austria. He wrote to tell me that our village had been destroyed and everyone had been killed by the Ukrainians. It hit me very hard. My brother, my mother and my sister had all been killed. My sister's breasts had been cut off before she was burnt. My cousin had survived by hiding underwater in the roots of a tree.

In October 1943, Misiewicz was transferred to Sylt camp without explanation. 'That was very bad news. To be honest, in Norderney or Helgoland we could live. It was hard, but we could survive. In Sylt, you died. We were made to work very hard on the Westbatterie, pouring concrete and bending the steel reinforcements. One time we worked non-stop for a day, a night and another day. They brought us soup from time to time. It was raining. By the time we eventually returned to the camp, ten people had died.'

Misiewicz is the only slave labourer known to have escaped from Alderney during the Occupation.

> I honestly don't remember why I decided to escape, because it was an enormous risk; escapees were always recaptured, and they did not just kill them, they tortured them.
>
> One evening at sunset when the dogs were being fed and all the SS were in the outer compound, I decided to go. Other slave labourers posted a lookout and spread two blankets over the first wire. I climbed up over the second wire and jumped down into a field of beetroot. I crawled on my stomach along the furrows for a hundred yards until I found the road.

Misiewicz went to Norderney camp to find Soltisiak, but as luck would have it, his friend had just left Alderney for the Continent. Other friends told him that another transport for the Continent was due to leave in about three weeks. For three days and nights he hid in an old fort above the camp. One night, the German anti-aircraft guns used the fort for target practice, terrifying Misiewicz. He then spent two weeks hidden in the roof of one of the barracks in Helgoland camp while the Germans searched the island for him.* Friends brought him food. 'Eventually my friends came and told me the transport was in the harbour. They told me a Belgian would meet me at 7 p.m. This Belgian told me I should wait until a particular Russian name was called, and then I should board the ship. I was so nervous I completely forgot the name, and it had to be called out three times before I got my wits together. I reached Cherbourg safely.'

NORBERT BEERMART

Norbert Beermart insisted that before he talked of his experiences on Alderney, we should first visit the tiny Chapel of Our Lady of the Old Mountain, which sits on a small hill overlooking the old

---

* The security around the camps on Alderney was quite lax – there were few places on the island for escapees to hide. One ex-inmate's account refers to Ukrainian guards who could be bribed or who sometimes struck up relationships with prisoners and allowed them in and out of the camp.

Flemish market town of Geraardsbergen in Belgium where Beermart was born and to which he has retired. It is crowded with
the paraphernalia of devotion, and the walls are lined with marble
plaques commemorating a prayer answered, or a loved one lost.
When sixteen-year-old Beermart disappeared from his home in
1940, his mother put up a plaque asking for the safe return of her
son. In 1944, when she had lost hope, he arrived in the town in an
American Jeep. It was a miracle, she believed, a gift from Our Lady
of the Old Mountain.

Beermart's miraculous survival is a continuing source of boyish
delight to him, and he regales any willing listener with his wartime
stories in the bars of Geraardsbergen. He has revisited Alderney
frequently, and he recounted his story wearing a baseball cap embla-
zoned with the logo of Alderney Channel Islands Yacht Club. 'For
me,' he says, 'the war is never over. Some people don't like to talk
about it, but I talk about it all the time. I was a little hero in this
town when I returned.'

Beermart was born into a family of six children, and was appren-
ticed to his uncle, a butcher. The skill was to stand him in good
stead in the camps. On 18 May 1940, he and his older brother,
along with thousands of other men of military age, were told to
leave their homes and join the Belgian army in France. They walked
to the border, but in the chaos of German bombing, Beermart was
separated from his brother. A French soldier took the boy under
his wing, and together they travelled south through France, away
from the advancing German army. When the Frenchman rejoined
his regiment, Beermart was forced to steal to eat, and before long
he was caught and imprisoned in a camp full of Spanish, Belgian
and Russian refugees who had fled across the Pyrenees after fighting
in the International Brigade in the Spanish Civil War. A few months
later the French handed the camp inmates over to the Germans,
to fulfil demands for labour. Beermart found himself amongst a
contingent of twenty-four prisoners boarding a ship in Cherbourg
in December 1940.

> We sailed to Alderney and disembarked with no food, no German
> guards and no shelter. It was very cold. We could have been in
> Africa for all we knew. Before 1940, the furthest I'd ever been from

Geraardsbergen in my life had been a few miles with my friends on our bikes.

The next day it was lovely weather and we began to look around. All the windows in the houses had been shattered and the doors were broken off their hinges. Books were scattered everywhere. There was no sight of any Germans.

The first man to die on Alderney was an American called Williams; he was born in 1915 in Boston, Massachusetts. I know because I made his cross. He'd fought in the International Brigade. There was a motorbike lying on its side by the road. It was a booby trap, but he didn't know and he went over to pick it up and it blew him up.

After several days without any food or water, about twenty Germans arrived with some horses and we started to build Norderney camp. One of the horses stepped on a mine and was killed, and I volunteered to cut it up. That's how I started working in the kitchen.

My best friends were Polish. They've been an unlucky nation but they have a lot of character. On Alderney they believed that they had to survive, and they never doubted that sooner or later they were going to get their own back on the Germans. I learnt to speak Polish and Russian on Alderney. Janek Novak was Polish and he worked in the kitchen with me; he was one of my best friends.* I took Janek's shoes off his feet before he was dead because I had no shoes. I arrived on Alderney a small boy. I was growing and I had to steal clothes and shoes. Now it seems terrible, but you stole anything. Many times I feel guilty about the things we did.

Those of us working in the kitchen were a strong gang of friends, and we all had the same tattoo done. I designed it and the Poles used three needles and made colours from the ashes. Some prisoners died from the tattoos going septic. The Germans wouldn't let you do tattoos but we did it to prove we were stronger than the Germans.

There were about 150 women on Alderney who were brought over from France in batches of about thirty at a time. They were either French or Portuguese workers. They had been hand-picked by the Germans in France; they were all under twenty-five and beautiful. It was like a cattle market the morning after they arrived when the German officers looked them over. If they 'stayed' with an officer all they had to do was clean his room, make his bed and sleep in it. If they refused to do that, they ended up working in the camp kitchen, peeling potatoes. I know of only one woman,

* Novak was the popular cook who went blind referred to by Misiewicz.

a Belgian, who held out against the Germans, and she eventually committed suicide.

A lot of us used to go and use a peephole in the washing room to look at the girls bathing. We used to pay the head of the washroom in cigarettes, which were the currency of Norderney. There was one very beautiful Polish girl, and I think she knew we watched her. All the men with good jobs such as the Ukrainian guards, the barbers and the kitchen staff used to go and look at the women.

The Germans had plenty of parties on Alderney. If a prisoner was good at dancing or singing or playing the guitar, they'd be called in to entertain the Germans. Even the gypsies danced for them. Anyone who had a special skill survived. I remember one night the gypsies danced for us around the bonfire. It was beautiful. The Russians were good at dancing and singing. We even played football with prisoners from Sylt. We weren't allowed to talk to them. The Russians played football in bare feet but they were very good.

The big boss was Adler, who was drunk from morning to night, and all the time he played with his gun. Heinrich Evers, the deputy camp commandant in Norderney, was a small man and a sadist; I saw him beat people to death many times. I was forgotten on Alderney as if I was just a dog hanging about in the kitchen; nobody could remember what I was doing there.

There were a lot of suicides. Once, a former jockey went into a minefield. The Germans offered to help him get out by going to fetch a map of the mine positions, but he refused and danced on the mines until he was blown up. It took him twenty-five minutes.

Every day you saw perhaps as many as five people die. At the beginning of 1943, ten people were dying in Norderney daily. I saw several people being buried in one grave. Other prisoners took the clothing off the corpses so there was no means of identifying them or their nationality. Three men worked full time as gravediggers, and four men in a truck used to go round picking up the dead bodies from the fields or from where they had fallen.

Beermart eventually managed to get transferred to Cherbourg. Once there, he slipped through the German net and joined the French resistance.

THE JEWS

It was the French Jews who christened Alderney '*le rocher maudit*' – the accursed rock. Eight hundred of them were brought to Alderney to work for the OT after they had been rounded up in the '*rafles*' (raids) organised by the Vichy government. They were all married to 'Aryan' Frenchwomen, and were thus designated 'half-Jews' by the Germans. Instead of being sent to the gas chambers, they were detailed to work as slave labourers. They counted themselves the lucky ones; a few food parcels managed to get through to them from their families, and few of them died.

Albert Eblagon, now a frail nonagenarian, was lucky enough to be sent to Alderney because he was married to an Aryan; his unmarried brother died in Auschwitz. Most of the French Jews sent to Alderney were older than the Russian slave workers. Many of them were middle-aged or even elderly, highly educated, and had held prominent positions in pre-war France; they included a large number of doctors, the former head of the Pasteur Institut, a parliamentary deputy, First World War veterans, civil servants, writers and lawyers. Eblagon had been a publisher's travelling salesman; he says modestly that everyone else was much more high-powered than himself. The Jews' consignment also contained a handful of Chinese, Arabs, Spaniards, Italians and Greeks who had been included in the *rafle* of Marseilles to augment the numbers.

The first transport of French Jews arrived on Alderney in July 1943. They were put in Norderney camp, in a separate section from the Russians. Accounts vary as to their working conditions. Some of the Russian survivors claim that the Jews were better treated, and Albert Eblagon says that less than a dozen French Jews died, although the low death toll may have been due to the fact that they were only on the islands a few months, at a time when most of the hard construction work had already been completed. But according to statements made to French war crimes investigators in 1944 by two doctors who had been among those transported, Henri Uzan and J.M. Bloch, the treatment of French Jews was as cruel as that meted out to the rest of Alderney's slave workforce.

In August 1943 [Uzan's report reads], we were loaded onto boats with kicks and shouts. The Germans spat on us from the bridge above us. We stayed like that for twenty-four hours. It was a very rough crossing for everyone. A German, Heinrich Evers, greeted us with slaps, kicks and threats of his revolver. I was carrying two suitcases, and a soldier grabbed them from my hands. We had to march to the other end of the island. There were among us many who were more than sixty years old and who were ill. We were put to sleep in barracks without straw or blankets – only some dried leaves to sleep on. In the morning we discovered that we were covered with lice.

All our luggage was taken except one blanket, one shirt, one pair of trousers and shoes. Then a very watery soup before we began work at 5 a.m. the following day. We had to be inspected by a German doctor; we waited naked for four hours. The German doctor came for twenty-five minutes to inspect four hundred men; he picked out the unfit. There was a quick interrogation by the German company to which I had been assigned. They asked if I had any skills. I said I was a doctor, and the German just dictated to the secretary that I was a 'labourer, unskilled'. I was assigned to carry fifty kilos of cement. It was the same for a deputy, a famous lawyer, a pianist of world reputation, a lieutenant colonel.

Dr Uzan mentions the use of one particularly 'cruel and sophisticated' technique. The Germans would order a prisoner to beat a fellow inmate – even his best friend. If they didn't beat hard enough, another friend would be chosen.

Dr Bloch told the investigators how some work teams had to work sixty hours at a stretch, with only twelve hours' rest.

An Armenian who was already very weak and on the list of 'unfit' fell from the scaffolding from a height of two metres. His comrades were forbidden to go to him; he was left without cover in the open air. At about 11 p.m. a German officer went to him and said that he was not yet dead. He died at about two o'clock in the morning from cold. We never knew where he was buried.

One deportee was blinded by kicks in the eye, another's arm was paralysed after he was hung for two days by his arms. Another had his ear ripped off. I think about eighty per cent of deportees were this badly treated.

THE BRITISH

Two British men, both from Jersey, were imprisoned in Norderney camp. Both Gordon Prigent and Walter Gallichan survived the war, although Gallichan never recovered his sanity. It was not until the end of his life that Prigent could bring himself to talk about his experiences on Alderney.

The eighteen-year-old Prigent was branded a troublemaker after a dispute with the Germans over a job at the airport on Jersey, and sent to Alderney. At first he thought little of it; some Jersey lads had been to Alderney the previous year for six months with a labour gang, and they said you got double pay and extra rations.

He began working in the kitchens at the Soldatenheim. Sometimes he and Gallichan would sneak into the German officer's office to listen secretly to the radio. They were caught, and sent as a punishment to Norderney camp:

The guards made sure you did your work. They were always nervous of being caught being lenient because they might be shipped to the Russian front. We slept on straw and bare wood. I got very hungry; some chaps died of starvation. Once you'd been there nine months, the Germans thought you were so starved you weren't fit to be on the islands any more, and they would ship you back to Germany to a camp which had gas chambers.

I was lucky, I was only eighteen and I had stamina, but the ones over forty died. There were burials several days a week. They used to bury them on Longy Common. Us English didn't get sick.

Norderney was like the concentration camps in Germany without the gas ovens. There was a tunnel and one end was sealed. At the other end there was a machine gun. If there had been an invasion, we had two minutes to get in the tunnel and they'd have shot us all.

If you dragged your feet – and we did, because we were exhausted and starved – they would whip you. If you were working too slowly they would beat you. One night they came in every hour to do a roll call; I was a bit slow getting out of bed one time and they hit me and knocked my teeth out. Chaps would just disappear. I saw people being hit, kicked at roll call, and then they'd disappear.

Prigent saw his friend Gallichan hit so hard over the head with a spade that the spade broke. After D-Day they were transported to Cherbourg for evacuation to Germany, but communications were breaking down in France and they were moved back to Guernsey and then Jersey. They were released in July 1944 and allowed home.

'THE STRIPED'

Perhaps the most mysterious part of the Alderney story was the appearance in March 1943 of an SS brigade on the island. There they set up the only SS camp on British soil in the Second World War. Many questions surround this camp, and there are few references to it in the SS archives in Germany. It was uncharacteristic of the SS to site a camp in such an exposed front-line position. Russian survivors remember being baffled at the arrival of the 'striped' (as they called the SS prisoners because of their striped pyjama-suit uniform) because it seemed to them that by March 1943 the pace of work had slackened; some of the fortification constructions had been completed, and the Germans did not need any additional labour.

The SS brigade prisoners had come from Sachsenhausen, the first concentration camp set up by the SS and the headquarters of the SS camp administration system near Berlin. About half of the thousand-strong Baubrigade I were Russian prisoners of war or partisans. Two hundred were Germans who had been designated 'workshy'; they included conscientious objectors, criminals and political prisoners. The remaining three hundred were mainly political prisoners from Czechoslovakia, France, Holland and Poland. The brigade was formed in September 1942, and until the transfer to Alderney in March 1943 half of it was stationed in Duisburg and half in Düsseldorf. The SS staff who accompanied them were drawn from the SS Totenkopf unit at the SS Neuengamme concentration camp outside Hamburg. SS Kapitän Maximilian List was in charge of the Duisburg unit, and he took over command of the whole brigade with two deputies, Kurt Klebeck and Georg Braun. A surviving letter signed by Heinrich Himmler, the head of the SS, to List orders that in the event of an attack on Alderney, all the prisoners were to be shot; they could not be allowed to fall into enemy hands.

SS Baubrigade I was one of about twenty 'aussenkommando' – outside – units under the authority of Neuengamme camp which were assigned to construction projects and bomb disposal duties in the Lowlands and France. Alderney was the furthest outpost; deaths on the island had to be registered in Neuengamme's books, and some sick prisoners from Alderney were transported to Neuengamme – where they were probably killed. About half of the 110,000 prisoners who entered Neuengamme are believed to have died . A similar fate was expected to befall a large proportion of SS Baubrigade I.

No communication was allowed between the Russians working for the OT and the SS prisoners, so the Russians could only speculate as to who these prisoners were. They were intrigued that many of them were German, and that these men were relatively well-treated; some claim they saw SS guards giving these men cigarettes, and allowing them to sit down during working hours to smoke them. Perhaps SS Baubrigade included former Nazis who had fallen from favour and had been banished to the isolation of Alderney. No SS archival records provide evidence for this theory, but such an operation would have been conducted with the utmost secrecy.

Otto Spehr is the only known living survivor of SS Baubrigade I. He now lives in a small town amongst pretty wooded hills outside Cologne. He is in his late eighties, but his mind is clear and he willingly recounts what he remembers of Alderney. He spent nine years in Nazi concentration camps, and the experience permanently damaged his health. He has been on an invalidity pension since the mid-fifties, but he has a remarkably buoyant sense of humour and displays a touchingly warm friendliness to those who ask him about his past.

I was a police officer at the German border with Lithuania, close to Tilsit, in 1934. I was accused of helping enemies of the state to escape across the border and leafletting. One of my friends had informed on me and I was sentenced to prison. I was judged an enemy of the state because I was a socialist. I was twenty-four years old and I spent the next nine years, nine months, eight days in Nazi concentration camps.

I was a member of a Himmelfahrtskommando unit – which means in English 'a free trip to heaven' – so called because the work of clearing the bombs off the streets of Düsseldorf and Duisburg was suicidally dangerous. I spent some time in Sachsenhausen, and then one of the SS guards realised I had a better chance of surviving if I went to Alderney, so he told me to volunteer for it. I did, but someone removed my name from the list; the sympathetic SS guard put it back on.

When I first arrived, there weren't enough huts so I and some others had to sleep outside for the first week while we built the huts. All I had to keep warm and dry was a cotton drill suit and a couple of blankets. We kept warm by sleeping as close as possible and holding onto each other. After the huts were built people with dysentery still had to sleep outside.

In general, the political prisoners were treated worse than the Russians. The 'politicals' came from a special punishment unit in Sachsenhausen. We had to work harder and we got less soup and we were beaten more often. People were beaten with rubber truncheons and sticks. I was whipped with an ox-whip but I was never tortured. Maybe that was because there was a Nazi general called Spehr, so people treated me carefully. The worst thing was the hunger.

A friend of mine was hanged. We had been in the same hut in Dusseldorf and Alderney. I believe he was hanged on the orders of Kurt Klebeck, the SS deputy commandant in spring 1944. I don't know why. There was a rumour that he had been a Gestapo spy.

Twenty to thirty prisoners fell ill with tuberculosis and they couldn't work. In the eyes of the SS, if you couldn't work, that meant you were a useless eater. Sometimes they couldn't send them back to Neuengamme because it was so far, so the Lagerführer, Puhr, gave the order to shoot them. But they needed a reason; they cut down the fence of the camp and pushed them outside the camp perimeter, and the moment they stepped over the fence, they were shot down for 'escaping'. These deaths are listed in the Neuengamme book on different days.

Klebeck told the guards that anybody who stepped out of the line when marching must be shot at once. It was to be seen as an attempt to escape. On Alderney quite a lot of people were 'shot while escaping'. But where can you escape to on Alderney?

Once a kapo told me that on Klebeck's order they had hanged the prisoners' cook the previous night. I thought probably the cook knew too much about the SS who were involved in black marketeering. The SS Kommandant of Sylt, Maximilian List, and Klebeck were court-martialled in an SS court for black marketeering. List went on leave from Alderney once and he had six big pieces of baggage. The military police insisted he open the bags and they found sugar, meat and cheese. All the SS staff were involved in black marketeering of the prisoner's rations. One SS guard was good to the prisoners. He was Romanian and he gave us food; he used to say the food rightfully belonged to us anyway.

When we were evacuated in June 1944 there were only 650 left out of the thousand who had arrived. The boat journey from Alderney to St Malo took a week, due to bombing raids. We were packed so tightly into the cargo hold that there wasn't enough air, and many prisoners died from suffocation.

After SS Baubrigade I left Sylt, the camp was largely destroyed. The prisoners were loaded onto trains in France, and joined other convoys heading to the German concentration camps. Several times, prisoners attempted to escape from the overcrowded trucks. On 26 July an attempted break-out at Breuvannes, near Nancy, led to the massacre of eighteen prisoners by SS guards with machine-guns. According to statements given to post-war investigators from the UN War Crimes Commission and to Dutch and French war crimes inquiries, the corpses were buried by the side of the railway track. Further on in the journey, at Toul, up to ten more corpses were unloaded – they had died of wounds inflicted at Breuvannes – and buried alongside the platform. Jan Woitas, a Polish prisoner in SS Baubrigade I, said that forty prisoners were killed during the journey across France, and that all the SS guards on the train were from Alderney; they included Maximilian List and Kurt Klebeck. Woitas described the punishment he saw arbitrarily dealt out to the Russian prisoners after an escape attempt at Rennes:

Several Russians were bound hand and foot and were beaten so hard that by the evening they were dying. Wolf [a guard] returned in the evening and hit three boys with the butt of his rifle until they fainted. Then he pumped them with bullets. They stayed twenty-four hours in the truck with us. They were examined by a German doctor who was not interested in the manner of their death.

In Kortemark, Belgium, Woitas and several others who later served as witnesses at the war crimes inquiry succeeded in escaping. Otto Spehr also escaped in Belgium and, in an extraordinary feat, managed to steal a plane and fly to Britain. After extensive questioning by military intelligence about his experiences and his remarkable solo flight, he worked for the BBC's German service for the last few months of the war.

Hundreds of slave workers were not as fortunate as Otto Spehr, or Georgi Kondakov, or Vasilly Marempolsky. They remained on the islands. The Russians' stories are full of references to friends and neighbours who never returned. Georgi Kondakov has recently bought a plot of land outside Orel on which to grow food for his family; next door is the tumbledown ruin of an abandoned thatched wooden house. An Alderney slave worker was born there, but he never came home.

CHAPTER SIX

RESISTANCE?
WHAT RESISTANCE?

'I always felt we'd done our little bit. We didn't do it out of patriotism, but out of defiance. There wasn't much you could do here in the war by way of resistance. We knew the Germans shouldn't have been here, but they were good and very gentlemanly.'

Jerseywoman Kathleen Whitley, imprisoned
for painting 'V for Victory' signs

'Every occupied country in the Second World War had its resistance movement,' said the French historian Henri Michel. Resistance fighters became the stuff of national legends, and their heroes and heroines became national icons. They were honoured with medals and pensions. Their actions spawned an industry of films and books. The importance of resistance was not in terms of military strategy; on only a few occasions, as historians now acknowledge, did it make a significant impact on the progress of the war in Europe. The resistance's importance lay in terms of a more intangible quantity: a nation's honour. The fact that people made huge sacrifices and gave their lives to resist German aggression is a consolation for the national humiliation of defeat. There was no famous resistance movement on the Channel Islands, and there are no heroes or heroines about whom films have been made and books written. Resistance is a sensitive subject, and islanders are defensive. They quickly provide explanations for the absence of a resistance movement by pointing to facts such as the high ratio of Germans to islanders, the lack of escape routes and the strategic irrelevance of the islands. Attempts to resist would have achieved nothing for the British war effort, and would have provoked terrible retaliation on the part of the Germans, they add, and demand of their questioner: 'What would have been the point?' Furthermore, islanders argue, ten thousand men and women from the Channel Islands served in the British Forces in the Second World War; they would have been the section of the population most likely to form the backbone of a resistance movement if they had remained on the islands. The resistance in France and the Low Countries was fuelled by young men forced underground to avoid labour drafts. The islands contributed one of the highest proportions of their population in the whole Empire to the war effort. The islands' honour lay in their achievements, islanders claim. These young men and women were fighting the Nazis, and the role of those left at home was to endure and survive, not to indulge in ineffective and costly gestures of resistance.

It is an argument which has almost convinced islanders, but they are uneasy. They are quick to point to resistance activities, however petty, that they may have been involved in. They are anxious to demonstrate their defiance and bravado towards the Germans. Their defensiveness stems from a feeling that in a war which has passed into the popular imagination as one of extraordinary feats of heroism, their stock of brave exploits is meagre.

There is a further twist in the history of Channel Islands resistance. Most islanders are reluctant to mention that there were instances of significant resistance. They did not constitute a movement. They did not kill German soldiers. Unlike the European resistance movements they received no encouragement, support or supplies from Britain. They had little or no effect on the Germans' fighting strength. But in disobeying or frustrating German orders, they saved some lives, and they were evidence of a bravely defiant spirit. The names of the Channel Islands resistance heroes and heroines have passed into local folklore, but they never received official national or island recognition for their bravery. There are no plaques or statues to the memory of women such as Louisa Gould and Marie Ozanne, who both paid for their compassion with their lives, nor men such as Canon Cohu and Harold Le Druillenec. No honours were handed out by the British or island governments at the end of the war to those who had printed illegal news leaflets or harboured escaped slave workers.

The history of the islands' resistance has been neglected for two reasons. Firstly, the story of those men and women who sacrificed their lives is an embarrassment to the many islanders who could not match their courage. Secondly, many islanders who did make gestures of defiance paid dearly for them, and could not look to their government, for protection. Their stories show up the relationship the island governments had formed with the Germans, an integral part of which was that resistance would not be tolerated.

The island governments had to impress on islanders very quickly that the beginning of the Occupation marked a dramatic break between the sentiments of defiance and resistance towards the Germans peddled prior to July 1940, and the compliance and co-operation now demanded by the presence of the Germans on the islands. They had no time to lose if they were not going to endanger the smooth development of relations with the Feldkommandantur and the policy of Model Occupation.

In the first month of Occupation there were two cases in the island courts – one on Jersey, one on Guernsey – which made it very clear to islanders that resistance of any kind would incur not just the judgement of the German military courts, but also the full force of island law. Both cases were reported in detail by the newspapers.

Two days after the Germans arrived on Jersey, an Irishman who had served in the Guards entered a café in St Helier where some German officers were sitting at a table. One of the Germans knocked the Irishman's hat off, saying he should take it off in front of a German officer. The Irishman responded by knocking him out. The next day, islanders were shocked to see the Irishman up in front of the Jersey – not German – courts, where he was given a sentence of six months' imprisonment. The judge admonished him for jeopardising good relations with the Germans. Joe Miere was only a boy at the time, but he still remembers the case: 'The Germans in the café were with two Englishmen who had collaborated pretty quickly. People didn't like the Irish, and the authorities were trying to appease the Germans, so he got a prison sentence.'

The Guernsey case was even more telling. An assistant at the Le

Riches store in St Peter Port was half-German, and would abandon any customer he was serving the minute a German soldier came into the shop, to act as interpreter. The manager considered this bad manners and forbade him from doing it. The assistant reported him to the Germans, and the manager was arrested and accused of spreading anti-German propaganda. Ambrose Sherwill, the President of the Controlling Committee, protested that the manager was much respected and in ill-health. The Feldkommandantur offered to let Guernsey's local court try him instead of the German military court. Sherwill left a detailed account of the case in his memoirs: 'I feared a stiffer sentence if the Germans tried him – so I hurried a law through the Royal Court, the effect of which would be to "make an offence any behaviour by a civilian likely to cause a deterioration in the relations between the occupying forces and the civilian population", and this with retrospective effect back to the date of the German occupation. I drafted the ordinance and got Victor Carey's agreement to it.'

Sherwill's move was a remarkable piece of pragmatism. Retrospective legislation is anathema to the islands' (and Britain's) legal tradition. Furthermore, this ordinance ensured that it was now the Guernsey authorities' responsibility to ensure that no civilians disrupted relations with the Germans.

This was an extraordinary turnaround, from the defiant, patriotic island governments of May 1940 to the frightened compliance of July 1940. It was eased by the development of a concept which could be described as 'passive patriotism', which both island officials and the Germans recognised would be a vital safety valve for frustrated nationalism

On the evening of the Germans' arrival in July 1940, the first Kommandant, Dr Lanz, dictated the orders to Sir Ambrose Sherwill which were to be published in the *Guernsey Evening Press* the next day. Sherwill recalls in his memoirs that he suggested it be incorporated into the orders that prayers for the British Royal Family and the Empire could be said in church, and that islanders could listen to the National Anthem on the radio. Dr Lanz agreed. This was a shrewd move, because it reassured islanders that they could maintain this vital part of their identity – there are no stronger monarchists than Guernseymen and women. Dr Lanz had immediately recognised that loyalty to the British monarchy did not present any threat to the German supremacy on the islands. By tolerating the islanders' allegiance to the Crown, one of the few issues which could have served as a rallying point for resistance was defused. Passive patriotism presented no threat to the Germans' war effort, and it did a power of good for the morale of the islanders: cocking a snook at the Germans eased their sense of humiliation at being occupied.

There were two main expressions of passive patriotism. Firstly there was a myriad of tiny, individual actions which had little or no impact on the Germans. Secondly, there were a few public demonstrations of patriotism during the Occupation; they were spontaneous displays of emotion, not calculated to humiliate or defy the Germans.

In retrospect the individual secret gestures of defiance can sometimes seem slightly ludicrous. For example, shortly after the Germans landed, Jersey teenager Audrey Anquetil watched her father strip a sheet of wallpaper from a wooden partition in the hall of the family home, nail a Union Jack up, then paper it over again. The flag remained unnoticed until Liberation on 9 May 1945. The Miere family on Jersey had a Union Jack hanging openly in their sitting room for the entire duration of the war, and no German ever commented. It was a cause of great delight to the Mansell family on Guernsey that they supplied the German soldiers billeted on them with red, white and blue tomato papers for toilet paper.

Guernsey teenager Dolly Joanknecht was typical of girls of her age in her range of 'patriotic' pranks, which included spitting in the Germans' soup and stealing their clothes: 'When the soldiers went swimming on the beach, we used to take their clothes and boots and put them in the water. I used to sew up the arms and legs of the underclothes they gave my aunt to wash, so that when there was an alarm, and they had to get out of bed quickly, they couldn't get into their clothes.' Dolly once even stitched up the underwear of Willi, the German soldier who was to become her boyfriend.

Jersey nurse Betty Thurban used to play 'The White Cliffs of Dover' on the piano. She said, 'It was my little bit of fighting the war.' The Jerseyman who designed the island's postage stamps put a minute letter 'A' in each corner, which he claimed stood for 'Ad Avernum Adolfe Atrox' – 'To Hell with you, Atrocious Adolf'.

Most of this kind of resistance probably went completely unnoticed by the Germans. If they did notice, most of them realised they could safely ignore it. The second form of passive patriotism was potentially more serious. There were at least three occasions on which islanders gathered in sufficient numbers to warrant the description of a demonstration.

In June 1943 the bodies of two RAF men were washed ashore on Jersey, and a funeral was organised by Oberleutnant Zepernick, Adjutant to the Inselkommandant. Thousands of islanders attended, and they laid more than two hundred wreaths. H. and her friends in their mourning finery were jeered at and scorned as jerrybags by other mourners. Journalist Leslie Sinel commented in his diary: 'A couple of ugly incidents were narrowly averted outside the cemetery during the day when some young men gave expression to their feelings to some women there who were known to be friendly with the enemy.' According to the diarist Cecil Bazeley, Zepernick felt his arrangements had been hijacked by hostile elements and the event had turned into a demonstration. He vowed that in future such funerals would be held after curfew, so islanders could not attend.

In October 1943 a British light cruiser, HMS *Charybdis*, sank after being attacked not far from the Channel Islands, and the bodies of twenty-one Royal Navy sailors were washed up on the shores of Guernsey, twenty-nine on Jersey and over a hundred in France. It was a gruesome reminder of the thousands of Allied lives being lost in a war which had largely passed the islands by. Feelings were running high, so the Germans arranged the funeral themselves, rather than leave it in the hands of the island government. On 17 November the sailors in their Union Jack-draped coffins were buried with full naval honours – performed by the Germans. German marines formed the escort, Germans fired the salute, and the Inselkommandant, Graf von Schmettow, gave the funeral oration: 'In the death which follows and results from duty done, the heart knows no frontier lines, and mourning becomes international.'

The Inselkommandant then laid a wreath on behalf of the German authorities. The Guernsey Bailiff followed suit on behalf of the island government. Four thousand islanders who came to pay their respects witnessed this German display of 'international mourning', and themselves laid over nine hundred wreaths, in the biggest floral tribute ever seen on the island. The event went off peacefully, but the scale of the crowds and the intensity of their emotion alarmed the Germans, and made them decide that the funerals of Allied servicemen should be conducted more quietly in future. Guernseyman Frank Falla commented in his memoirs: 'The Germans were completely taken by surprise . . . they were almost lost in this great mass of passive demonstrators who were determined that they should be left in no doubt where our sympathies and true feelings lay.'

There was one other occasion which turned into a demonstration of defiance during the five years of occupation. When British-born islanders were deported to the German internment camps in September 1942, islanders gathered at the quaysides to see them off. Apart from a scuffle on the St Helier quayside in which fourteen teenage boys were arrested (they subsequently received short prison sentences) and a German soldier's helmet was knocked off, the crowds were orderly. Jersey clerk Bob Le Sueur was there:

> I don't want to sound over-emotional, but perhaps for the first time in my life I felt rather proud to be British. Whatever scenes there had been at home, such as breaking down and tears, by the time they got to the quayside the stiff upper-lip was showing. It was almost as if it was a Bank Holiday, and the people who looked the glummest were the Germans. Everyone had put on their best, warmest clothes, and some were being deported in fur coats. There was an air of gaiety born of bravado – a 'We'll show them' attitude. The crowd sang 'Rule Britannia' and the National Anthem as the deportees boarded the ships. It was a deeply emotional moment for many islanders as they watched them setting off on a difficult journey, with a very uncertain end.

Jersey clerk Arthur Kent remembered a similarly emotional scene as those who had served in the British Forces were deported:

The day the first batch left to go to Germany they had to pass my office, which was near the harbour. It was a sight to see. Many of the men were veterans of the First World War. They came wearing their war ribbons and red, white and blue rosettes. Many people had come in from the countryside in horse-drawn wagons to which they had attached ribbons and rosettes. It was a pity there was no camera to capture that. It was as if they were going to a great picnic. They were singing war songs. It was a splendid example of patriotism.

Islanders wanted 'to do their bit' – the very words were disparaging. They felt useless; they knew that across the Channel a massive effort was being made to defeat the Nazis, and it was frustrating to keep silent and hope that others would win the war. Passive patriotism shaded into defiance; what one German soldier might tolerate, even chuckle over, would lead to immediate arrest with another. It only needed one German officer who was particularly sensitive about his dignity, and an islander could find him or herself in front of a court. Some Germans enjoyed the small measure of power they had, and were quick to use it if challenged.

The Guernsey Feldkommandantur records reveal a long list of islanders given sentences for trivial offences. The most famous case was that of Winifrid Green, a hotel waitress, who when told to say 'Heil Hitler' when she received her rice pudding, said, 'To hell with Hitler for a rice pudding – and one made of skim milk too!' She was accused of spreading 'anti-German information' and imprisoned in Caen prison for six months, where she embroidered Churchill's name on a handkerchief. She became a folk heroine.

A month after the start of the Occupation Ruby Langlois, a cook, was sentenced to fourteen days' imprisonment for having, according to the German charge sheet, 'publicly and repeatedly abused the German Reich and the German forces and maliciously, and with intent making them an object of contempt [by saying] "The Germans are all blackguards; they have occupied the islands; they fill their bellies and the islanders must starve. The Germans should leave the island."' She had also used the expression 'shit-house' of the Germans. She was denounced and admitted her guilt. Housemaid Mabel Gill and eighteen-year-old nurserymaid Leona Le Blond were each sentenced to seven months for treason; the records don't reveal what kind of 'treason' the pair were concocting.

Occupation licensed childish mischievousness and teenage delinquency and awarded it the grand accolade of 'patriotic resistance'. While many adults had children and elderly parents to consider, the children themselves had little to lose, and a lot of fun to gain at the Germans' expense. It was a temptation many could not resist. Their 'resistance' ranged from stealing German bicycles – which had to be dismantled and incorporated into island bone-shakers if they were to be concealed – and food from German stores, to defusing mines, cutting wires and petty sabotage. Jersey boy Maurice Green was particularly ambitious:

I used to go out on the cliffs to defuse mines. There was an air-raid shelter from the First World War under Government House's driveway. I had two unfused landmines screwed to the roof of the shelter; I planned to blow up the Kommandant and two of his officers. At the time they were just the enemy, but I'm glad I never managed to do it now. There would have been reprisals.

Another time, four of us – the oldest was sixteen – cut the railway line. The Germans arrested six local citizens and threatened to shoot them. We tried to decide what to do; one of the kids pointed out that the people they were going to shoot were all over forty, while we were young enough to carry on the fight. In the end the hostages were released.

Once I walked into a German billet and took a rifle, a tin helmet and uniform and, dressed up in this, I marched down the road. I was grabbed by some Germans and taken back to their office where I was hung from a coathook by my braces for four hours. They kicked me and smashed all my front teeth in with their rifles.

One regulation they brought in was that everyone had to salute a German officer. So all the kids decided to salute everyone in uniform – the postman, the gasman and the bus driver. Little things like that kept morale up.

Rollo Sherwill and his brother Jolyon were eight and ten years old when they released the hand brake on a vehicle. It rolled downhill and they stole all its toolboxes. Such petty sabotage could cause considerable inconvenience. The boys were found out, but the Germans considered them too young to be arrested.

On Jersey, Oberstleutnant Knackfuss, the Feldkommandant, wrote to the island police in 1943 asking them to stop 'the young people [who] congregate at St Ouen's parish hall, and make disparaging remarks about the German forces'.

As the Occupation went on, the most unruly element of the population were boys in their late teens. Most of the children on Guernsey had been evacuated, but on Jersey the boys aged fifteen to twenty in 1944 had grown up under the Occupation. While their contemporaries in Britain were joining the forces or working in munitions factories, the Jersey teenagers were frustrated and restless, and a steady stream of them ended up in prison. Bernard Hassall was visited in prison by his schoolmaster, who remarked that so many boys were incarcerated that he had no class left.

Hassall was arrested after a woman informed the Germans that he had a cache of weapons, stolen from the German supply store where he worked. He and a few friends had been planning to fight with the Allies when they landed to liberate the islands. Sixteen-year-old Joe Miere was sentenced to two years in Jersey prison after daubing swastikas in tar on houses where Germans were billeted, so that when the British landed they would know where they were. Swastikas were also put on the houses of people who were collaborating: 'Young gangs copied us,' said Joe Miere, 'and were painting any house. They painted a swastika on the house of a girlfriend of a German officer. The Germans searched my house and found some secret leaflets of BBC news digests and some ammunition I had stolen. It was half-patriotism and half-devilment. Today, they'd call me a delinquent.'

Eighteen-year-old Jersey boy Mike Le Cornu also painted swastikas on walls, and was involved in petty sabotage:

> We put chisels in German car radiators when I was working as a mechanic in a garage. There was a little group of us called the Sab squad. Everyone of that age wanted to do something. When I was arrested and questioned, I just acted really stupid and dopey.
>
> One night it was pouring with rain and there was a German car in the garage, so I borrowed it for the night to drive home, and

drove it back early next morning. As I was driving along, I passed a German soldier, and he saluted me because the car had an insignia on the side. Maybe it belonged to some top chap. It was hilarious.

For some of the boys, the mischief turned to tragedy. James Houillebecq was seventeen when he was arrested for sabotage and possessing weapons; he died in Neuengamme concentration camp in 1945. Five other Jerseymen died in camps on the Continent while serving sentences for sabotage. A sixth was shot while trying to escape from the Germans sent to arrest him.

The great challenge for Jersey teenagers after D-Day and the liberation of the Normandy coast was to escape to France and smuggle out information on the German defences of the islands. From Jersey, the French coast is only fourteen miles away at its nearest point, and clearly visible. The little specks of houses across the narrow stretch of water represented freedom, and it was tantalisingly close. Between September 1944 and February 1945 eighty people – sixty-eight islanders, many of them teenagers, and twelve Dutch and French workers – tried to escape by boat. Forty-seven of the islanders were successful, but six were drowned, including a recently married couple, Madelaine and Ronald Bisson. Peter Crill, a future Bailiff of Jersey, was nineteen when he escaped in November 1944 with two other teenagers. Eight young men escaped in September 1944 with maps of the German fortifications. The maps eventually reached England, although three of the young men had to turn back.

Escaping required considerable ingenuity. The use of boats had been strictly regulated ever since eight people escaped in a fishing boat in September 1940. All beaches and cliffs were heavily mined and patrolled. It was difficult to steer at night without any light to see the compass by, and there were always the vagaries of the weather to deal with. An escape required months of patient planning and preparation. Peter Crill and his friends siphoned petrol from German cars until they had enough to power their boat's motor.

Before the liberation of the French coast in the summer of 1944, the only place to escape to was England, which was a good twelve hours' sailing away. An attempt in 1942 to escape from Jersey by Bernard Hassall's younger brother ended in tragedy. Fifteen-year-old Peter Hassall was accompanied by two other boys, Dennis Audrain and Maurice Gould, and they had photographs of German fortifications. Their boat hit a rock and was swamped in a heavy sea not long after setting off; Audrain could not swim, and despite the efforts of his friends he drowned. Hassall and Gould made it back to the Jersey shore, where they were arrested. Bernard Hassall remembers: 'The last time I saw my brother before he was sent to the Continent was in a street in St Helier. A German car roared past and I heard someone shout my name. There were two boys in the back of the car; it was the last time I saw him until 1945. I thought about him constantly, and I was sure he would survive. Maurice Gould died of tuberculosis at Wittlich on the Moselle. He was so emaciated you could have fitted him into a banana box. My brother was with him when he died.'

Peter Hassall was eighteen when he returned home in 1945; he did not speak to his brother about his imprisonment in two concentration camps and seven different prisons for more than forty years. Bernard says that one of the things that haunted him was the drowning of his friend Dennis Audrain.

One of the most extraordinary escape stories is that of a Jerseyman, Dennis Vibert, who in September 1941 ended up rowing to England after the two motors on his boat both failed. This was his second attempt – he had been defeated by a storm in November 1940, but managed to get back ashore without being detected. He was a friend of Bob Le Sueur, who remembers: 'He had been very frustrated. He loathed the Nazis. I felt there was a difference between Germans and Nazis, but Dennis didn't feel that way. He was two miles off Portland when he was at last picked up by a British boat; he hadn't drunk water or eaten for several days. He then joined the RAF. There were a lot of islanders who admired those who had escaped, but more timid people felt there could be reprisals.'

Escaping bitterly divided the communities left behind, as successful escapes often led to punitive restrictions. In the summer of 1940 the Guernsey Controlling Committee, under the guidance of their President, Ambrose Sherwill, had strongly condemned sixty-three islanders who successfully escaped to England from Guernsey between July and September: 'Any further such departures or attempts thereat can only result in further restrictions [on fisher-men]. In other words any person who manages to get away, does so at the expense of those left behind. In these circumstances, to get away or to attempt to get away is a crime against the local population.' The German and island authorities responded vigor-ously, and the island police were ordered to apprehend would-be escapers. Sherwill was scathing about escapers both publicly and in his private memoirs: 'It was a selfish, unthinking act which could only result in retribution.' After an escape from Guernsey in August 1943, all access to the beaches was banned and for a while all fishing was stopped.

Escapers may have been bitterly criticised, but they often had the most patriotic of motives. Many joined the services, and some served their islands by taking vital information to Britain. After D-Day they smuggled out details of the diminishing food supply, which found their way to the British government. British military intelligence questioned escapers closely for information about con-ditions on the islands, and they were fêted as heroes in the British newspapers, earning large headlines and full-length interviews. The periodic appearances of islanders in London brought much-needed attention to the neglected islands' plight.

Much of the information the escapers gave the British govern-ment originated from a group of former British officers on Jersey. Their leader was Major Crawford-Morrison, who as official Air Raids Controller had a perfect screen for his activities. Assisted by Majors Manley and L'Amy and a network of helpers who were working for the Germans, the group managed to put together a map of the military fortifications on Jersey which was filmed by Stanley Green, a cinema projectionist in St Helier. When Crawford-Morrison was deported to Germany in 1942 he smuggled the films with him, and they eventually reached Britain. L'Amy continued to collect information and pass it on to escapers until the end of the war.

The first instance of widespread resistance was the BBC's 'V for Victory' campaign in the summer of 1941. As it did in the rest of Europe, the idea of painting 'V' signs on walls and doors as a gesture of defiance caught the islanders' imagination. The concept originally came from the BBC's Belgian Programme Organiser, Victor de Laveleye, who chose the letter 'V' because it stood for the French word for victory and the Flemish for freedom – *victoire* and *vrijheid*. The campaign was intended purely for the Radio Belgique service and the suggestion was first broadcast in January 1941. Before the end of the month 'V's had been noticed in occupied France. The 'V' campaign was extended to French broadcasts, and within weeks correspondents were reporting its successes to London: there was not a 'single space' without 'V' signs on the walls, pavements and doors of Marseilles; in the Marne department, 'nothing but "V"'s and still more "V"'s everywhere on the walls, on the roads, telegraph posts etc.'.

The BBC, in co-operation with the Political Warfare Executive, had decided it was important to 'give the French a feeling of conspiracy, a feeling that they were part of the show', and the campaign was now extended to the whole of Occupied Europe as an outlet for the first stirrings of resistance. Douglas Ritchie, Assistant News Editor of the European Service, articulated the scheme's aims: to mobilise an 'underground army'. The Germans would be told about the campaign 'in the hope of making their flesh creep'. In May 1941 the BBC set up a committee under Ritchie to develop the 'V' campaign and 'create a frame of mind in which our listeners will feel themselves part of a great army', and to 'give instructions to this army that will be good for its morale and bad for the morale of the German garrisons'. Ritchie began broadcasting under the pseudonym of 'Colonel Britton', exhorting the European resistance movements to defy the Germans. In July the Prime Minister, Winston Churchill, threw his authority behind the campaign: 'The "V" sign is the symbol of the unconquerable will of the people of the occupied territories and a portent of the fate awaiting the Nazi tyranny. So long as the people of Europe continue to refuse all collaboration with the invader, it is sure that his cause will perish and that Europe will be liberated.'

On the Channel Islands, doors, gateposts and walls were chalked with 'V's. Young Maurice Green on Jersey devised Christmas cards which folded into a 'V'. Badges were cut out of old pennies to form a 'V' sign and pinned to the underside of lapels. 'V' signs were chalked on the German soldiers' bicycle seats; after they had sat on them, the seats of their trousers were marked with the 'V'.

In July 1941, when a rash of 'V' signs appeared around Câtel, Guernsey, the island police were asked to investigate. They discovered that the culprits were seven boys aged between six and twelve. The headmaster of Câtel school was told to reprimand them, and a report of the investigation was passed to John Leale, the President of the Controlling Committee, who in turn passed it on to the German authorities. A few days later Inspector Sculpher, the head of the island police, wrote to Leale asking him to pass on to the Germans the name of eleven-year-old Stanley Osborne, who had admitted to having put a 'V' on a signpost. After receiving the report, the Germans asked for the names and criminal records of the parents of the offending children in Câtel. Sculpher duly provided them. Fortunately, there the matter rested.

Children at Guernsey's Intermediate School were also apprehended for putting up 'V' signs. Peter Girard, the headmaster, was asked by Leale to hand the offenders over to the Germans for questioning. He went to some length in his memoirs to explain his compliance with this request: 'Leale insisted no child would come to harm because of his contacts with the Germans. The Germans had demanded hostages if the "V" sign writers were not apprehended. I felt bad but trusted Leale. The children were taken away for questioning and came back, having been fed with chocolates and cakes and covered in smiles.' Leale's promise appeared to have held good; there is no evidence that any of the children or their parents came to harm, but the reference to chocolates and cakes perhaps smacks of an uneasy conscience.

In July 1941, six cardboard sheets were found fastened together with crudely written abuse of Germany on both sides. The German authorities concluded it was the work of children and, unusually, decided it was 'beneath their dignity to investigate'.

Adults also took up the 'V' campaign. Twenty-one-year-old Jersey factory girl Kathleen Whitley (née Norman) was one of those who was caught and served a prison sentence:

We found some 'V' signs cut out of newspaper on the ground down by the beach. I was with my sister and we were defiant. We stuck

them up on the wooden fence right beside some Germans sun-
bathing. They saw us and chased us. We were taken down to Jersey
prison. Four days later, we were court martialled and told that we
had 'insulted the German army'. I thought, how can two little
women like us manage to do that?

We were in Caen prison for seven months; it was nerve-racking.
You never knew whether someone would send you off to Germany,
but the French were good to us and we had more food in prison
than we had at home.

I never regretted putting the sign up; I always felt we'd done our
little bit. There wasn't much you could do here in the war by way
of resistance. We didn't do it out of patriotism, but out of defiance.
We knew the Germans shouldn't have been here, but they were
good and very gentlemanly.

In July 1941 two islanders in Cobo, Guernsey, gave evidence against
Xavier Louis de Guillebon, a French farm labourer, for having
written 'V' signs in blue chalk in a public place, and the Guernsey
police passed his name on to the Germans. He was sentenced
to a year's imprisonment for an 'anti-German demonstration'; he
served eight months in Caen and was released early, in March
1942.

Not all the islanders swung behind the 'V' campaign; the punishments it provoked from the Germans caused some resentment.
When Kathleen Whitley and her sister returned home safely, neighbours did not congratulate them for their defiance, but blamed
them for a brief ban on radios. Some islanders were critical of what
the 'V' signs were supposed to achieve. Guernsey shopgirl Vera
Cochrane thought those who painted them 'rather stupid': 'They
were not in a position to do a great deal, only to make the Germans
annoyed with them, which affected everyone else as well.'

On 9 July 1941, in one of the most controversial actions of the
Guernsey government during the Occupation, Victor Carey, the
Bailiff, offered £25 for information leading to the arrest of anyone
painting 'V' signs. The sum was equivalent to more than three
months' wages, and was an indication of how seriously irritated
the Germans were by the campaign. Islanders were shocked that
Carey, who warned against 'committing these foolish acts which
accomplish nothing, but merely bring grave consequences in

their train', was in effect offering a reward to informers. Alexander Coutanche, the Bailiff of Jersey, urged islanders to avoid such 'foolish actions'.

The 'V' sign campaign was a confusing experience for the islanders. On the one hand they were receiving, via their radios, stirring speeches from the BBC about resistance. On the other hand the island authorities were rounding up civilians – even children – and handing them over to the Germans for having acted on the BBC's instructions. Whitehall was aware of this dilemma in the islands. 'Colonel Britton' was urging every European country to take up the struggle, but references to the Channel Islands were noticeably absent. When the possibility of a special Channel Islands radio service was broached in 1941, it was judged by the Political Warfare Executive that adopting the pro-resistance line of French channels would be suicidal for the islanders, and as they could not advocate no resistance, the idea was abandoned.

The Germans took the 'V for Victory' campaign very seriously, as if it were a nascent resistance movement, rather than merely a bit of persistent graffiti. Whenever they discovered a 'V' sign they issued an urgent demand to the island government to investigate and apprehend the offenders. When no culprits were found for 'V' signs in the vicinity of the Guernsey airport, all radios within a thousand metres of the offending site had to be handed in (they were returned a few months later). What irked the Germans about the 'V' signs on the Channel islands and throughout Europe was that they were tangible evidence of the hold of the BBC over the minds of millions of regular listeners. Goebbels described this as the 'intellectual invasion of the Continent by British radio'. Finally, the Germans decided that the only way to undermine the campaign was to daub 'V' sign graffiti themselves – they claimed it stood for *Viktoria*, 'the old German victory cry'. This proved highly effective, and by 1942 the 'V' campaign had lost its impetus.

In June 1942, the Germans decided that the BBC's flood of anti-German material was not conducive to a peaceful Occupation, and all radios on the islands were confiscated. Possession of a radio would earn a three-month prison sentence. (Radios had been confiscated on Guernsey for three months in 1940 as a punishment for the islanders' involvement in the Nicolle/Symes affair.) This was a violation of the Hague Convention, and was probably the most unpopular measure of the whole Occupation, but the Germans were immune to the islanders' protests.

Julia Tremayne, a Sark housewife, commented that they only heard German news and 'Haw-Haw stuff'.* Rumours were rife, she said, and 'if we believed them we should be in the depths of despair'. She felt cut off without a radio, and talked of the islanders' 'prison life'.

The nine o'clock radio news had become a focal point of the day for islanders; it was their only link with the outside world, the only way they could follow the progress of the war. The radio was also their main source of entertainment, and a tenuous link with relatives in Britain. It was too important in their lives for many islanders to countenance handing it in; many kept a set back, in secret hiding places under the floorboards or in the attic. Others managed to sneak into German quarters to listen to German radios. The greatest favour a German could extend to an islander was to let them listen to his set; the Dame of Sark, for example, was allowed to listen to a German officer's radio. Another alternative was to make a crystal radio, or a 'cat's whisker' set, according to instructions given on the BBC. A wire was attached to a telephone line, another wire was earthed, and a third was attached to headphones or a telephone receiver. The telephone line wire touched a piece of crystal the size of a fingernail. It took a few seconds to find a sensitive spot, but the broadcast would then come very quietly through the telephone receiver. Most islanders listened to the BBC regularly, and this became the most widespread form of resistance in the islands.

Jersey housewife Dorothy Blackwell remembers: 'It was very important to get the news; it was the only means of knowing anything. Churchill's speeches had a wonderful effect on morale. We used to take down in shorthand books how many bombers had

---

* Lord Haw-Haw, the Irish-American William Joyce, broadcast German propaganda to Britain throughout the war. He was tried and executed for treason in 1946.

been lost. But you didn't dare say anything to anyone. We didn't even dare talk to our next-door neighbour – the lady there used to talk a lot. I didn't even dare tell my son.'

There were numerous cases of islanders having to hide radios while their houses were being searched; they found their way into prams, manure heaps, beds, even into a washtub full of soapsuds. On Alderney, Daphne Pope had a near-miss:

> There was a hammering on the door. We had been listening to Churchill on the radio which we kept hidden in the wall. This time the radio was behind the chair. It was the SS, who had come to search the house for a missing prisoner. They stripped back the bedding from the children, but they didn't wake a single child – they were very quiet and very efficient.
>
> I was sitting in the chair in front of the radio. One man had been left behind to guard my mother and me while the others did the search. I was winding up wool, and I had thread round the stool in front. I asked the soldier what insignia he had on his uniform, and he said it was the SS. 'Isn't that the elite troop?' I asked, and he replied yes, and puffed up his chest. They'd done all that marvellous fighting in Poland, I said, and he beamed. Then the officer came back and he stiffened. Had he watched the women? demanded the officer.
>
> Well, he had certainly watched me very closely. I was in my twenties then, and I could bat my eyelids if I had to. The officer asked him if he had searched the room. 'Yes,' he replied.

Not all islanders evaded detection, and many served prison sentences for radio offences. For a few, the punishment became even more serious. Father and son Clarence and Peter Painter were arrested for listening to the BBC news; a house search produced a First World War souvenir pistol they had not handed in to the Germans, and they were sent to Cherche–Midi prison near Paris. From there they were transferred to Natzweiler concentration camp, where they both died in 1944.

Canon Clifford Cohu of St Saviour's, Jersey, used to visit the islands' hospitals and give out the news to cheer the patients up. He was allegedly informed on, and was arrested along with Joseph Tierney, a cemetery worker, Tierney's wife Eileen and two others.

Cohu died at Spergau camp in Germany, Tierney at Celle, and a third man, John Nicolle, in a camp near Dortmund. After the war Premysl Polacek, a Czech prisoner who had been with Cohu in Spergau, wrote a letter in broken English to the Foreign Office in London, describing the canon's arrival at the camp and his death:

> He was a long time on prisoner transport ... he arrived feeble and thin ... The camp had in that time about five hundred prisoners, living in small, round paper tents (five metres in diameter), thirty men in each. In the tents were no beds, but a little straw on bare soil, and some torn and dirty covers.
>
> At work, two days after arriving, the pastor was abused and beaten the whole day. The work was hard and he was already so feeble that he could not lift the shovel. He was abused as '*Du Englische Sau, du wirst uns bombardieron, wir werden dir schon zeigen, du Krüppel*' [You English pig, if you are going to bomb us, we'll bloody show you, you cripple].
>
> I saw him that day in the evening on the return in the camp. Two prisoners must lead him, he could not go alone.
>
> 16 September [1944] he was going to work again, but that was the end of his force ... 17 to 20 September, he could not already go, and so remained in the camp, lying in the tent without help, with some half-dead prisoners.
>
> 20 September I was also ill and so I work in camp. Suddenly we were called, three of us, to undress a dead body. I recognised the pastor ... on the breast, I found a little bible which he probably cashed [hidden] before the SD men [who ran the camp]. It was forbidden to have any book.

Stanley Green, the cinema projectionist, was also arrested for a radio offence. Green was involved in a range of resistance activities. He was a good photographer, and had photographed the maps of the German fortifications for Major Crawford-Morrison. His son Maurice also says his father had built a transmitter. The Germans did not find either the photographs or the transmitter, but they did find a radio hidden in the roof of the cinema. Maurice claims his father was informed on and that the informants were paid, but the two men alleged to have been the informers were themselves imprisoned, and it is possible that they gave information under duress after their arrest. Stanley Green was first sent to Paris, where he was tortured at Gestapo headquarters; his fingernails were ripped out. He was then sent to a French prison at Fresnes, from which he was transferred to Buchenwald. He spent seven and a half months there, and it nearly killed him. He was never to recover from the searing experience of what he saw in Buchenwald, which he later described in detail to his son Maurice:

Dad was put on the job of picking up bodies from the pile of bodies and putting them on a cart and taking the cart to the crematorium and dropping them down a chute. Many of the bodies were still just living, although they were passed as dead because they had typhus and other diseases. Some were being eaten by rats. The piles of bodies stretched for as far as you could see.

Every second week, he was stripped off to the waist and he went down to the boilers with buckets and a shovel and he scraped the fat off the walls and floors. He had to make sure each bucket was levelled off like he was filling it with cement. If he didn't do that, he was beaten by the Ukrainian guard with a club covered with nails. One guard put a bayonet through Dad's foot for no reason; a doctor got some charcoal and cauterised it.

Green managed to smuggle a letter written on cement paper sacking to his other son, who had been deported to Laufen internment camp in southern Germany. The son contacted the Red Cross, who succeeded in getting Green released from Buchenwald. He was taken to Munich, where he was caught in a terrible bombing raid. His SS guards locked him in a shed and retreated to a bomb shelter. Two prisoners with Green were killed when a bomb fell nearby, and everything he was wearing was burnt in the blast. He managed to walk from Munich to Laufen – a distance of over a hundred miles. When he arrived, his son didn't recognise the bowed, skeletal figure as his father; Green's weight had dropped from thirteen stone to five.

Green survived; he was the only inmate of Buchenwald to smuggle photographs out of the camp, and his evidence was used at the Nuremberg trials. He returned to Jersey, where he died at the age of seventy-four, but he never fully recovered from the horrors he had witnessed.

Information from the outside world was highly valued, and one form of resistance that many islanders appreciated was leaflets printed with digests of the BBC news. This required a certain degree of organisation: shorthand writers, typists and printers had to be recruited, and a distribution network had to be set up. Paper, ink and printing machinery were needed when all were in great demand. It was difficult and dangerous work. The Germans recognised the existence of these news leaflets for what it was – organised resistance. There were several underground news services on Jersey and Guernsey; some only lasted a couple of issues, some several years.

The 'Guernsey Underground News Service' (GUNS) was one of the most successful leafleting operations, publishing daily editions from May 1942 to February 1944. It was run by a former journalist, Charles Machon, with the help of Frank Falla and three other men. The members of the team didn't know who else was involved, and worked only with Machon. The leaflet carried a seven hundred-word précis of that day's BBC broadcasts, and it was calculated that it had a circulation of three hundred on all the islands; it was passed secretly from reader to reader. Unfortunately, in February 1944 a copy fell into the hands of an informer, an Irishman called Paddy according to Falla. Machon and another team member were arrested, and under interrogation and threats to ill-treat his mother, Machon cracked. A total of five men were arrested and sentenced to prison on the Continent. Two died, including Machon, but the other three returned alive.

On Jersey, the 'Bulletin of British Patriots' was produced by two brothers, Herbert and George Gallichan. Nineteen-year-old Mike Le Cornu was one of those enlisted to distribute it: 'We tried to expose collaboration. We called on people not to give up their radio sets. I was given these leaflets to distribute by Herbert Gallichan. I never knew who had printed them. I put the leaflets in people's doors and scattered them on the road. I didn't worry at the time, but looking back on it, I don't know how the heck I did it.' In June

1942 the Germans took ten islanders hostage until the leafleteers surrendered, and the brothers gave themselves in. George was sent to Dijon prison for a year, but his brother was in Wolfenbüttel concentration camp until the end of the war.

A less well-known leaflet operation was run by the Jersey Communist Party. Clerk Norman Le Brocq had been a scholarship boy, and became a Communist in his teens. His resistance activities sprang from his political convictions (which have lasted to this day – he is the only Communist ever to have been elected as a Deputy to the Jersey States):

> Prior to the war, I had joined the Transport and General Workers' Union. When the Nazis occupied Jersey, they declared all trade unions illegal, and the T&G went underground. The Communist Party had fallen apart after the evacuation; it only had six members and half of them left for England, but Les Huelin, the secretary, had stayed on. We managed to hide away the CP duplicator – at one time it was in my great-aunt's attic. The first leaflets we made were for the illegal T&G. In 1942 we re-formed the CP, and by the end of 1941 we had set up the Jersey Democratic Movement (JDM), which was a group of left-wing and Labour sympathisers, to campaign for reform after the war. We produced leaflets for all three organisations in print-runs of three to four hundred. We did the T&G leaflets every six months except for the last year when there was a regular monthly review. We published JDM leaflets three or four times a year, and we published a CP news bulletin every month from late 1942 to the end of the war.
>
> We also did news bulletins in French, Spanish and Russian for distribution in the labour camps. We couldn't type the Cyrillic alphabet, so a Russian slave labourer who had escaped wrote it out, and we then duplicated that. We used Spanish medical orderlies to distribute the bulletins in the slave workers' camps.
>
> The leaflets and bulletins were mostly composed of news but the JDM leaflets carried 'atrocity stories' about corruption and mismanagement on the part of the Jersey government. There was a story of two States officials getting two years' rations of coke. I had been seconded to the fuel control department as a junior clerk, and when that issue came out, the blame fell on me and I was dismissed.
>
> We managed to get paper, stencils and ink. At one point we had

more paper than the States; we had friends who passed it on to us from the Town Hall. The duplicator was very slow and laborious, and the ink had run out by 1944. One of our members had a chemistry A level, and he was set to adapt some printing ink to use on the duplicator. What he produced was oil-based, so each leaflet took several minutes to dry. I spent all my evenings doing this work. It took hours, sitting there surrounded by leaflets drying.

We operated on a 'need to know' basis. You only told anyone if they needed to know; you didn't gossip and you didn't ask. Les Huelin just told me what to do, it wasn't very democratic. We were very careful, but we were also very lucky.

In late 1944, after D-Day and the liberation of France had cut links with the Continent, Le Brocq's remarkable duplicator was called into service for the most ambitious resistance scheme on the Channel Islands during the war. The German forces were becoming increasingly demoralised; supplies were running out, there was little fighting for them to do on the islands, while the radio reported heavy bombing of the cities back home and the approach of the Soviet armies on Berlin. A German soldier, Paul Mülbach, managed to make contact with Huelin and Le Brocq, claiming to represent a Soldiers' Committee which was planning a mutiny. After initial suspicion, Huelin and Le Brocq were convinced. Mülbach was a socialist; his father, a socialist trade union official from the Coblenz-Rhein region, had been sent to Dachau, where he died in 1934. Mülbach wanted to organise a mutiny, with the aim of handing over Jersey to the Allies. Le Brocq was made liaison officer:

> Paul's committee decided he would be more effective if he was out of uniform, so he came to me with a list of everything he wanted: a civilian suit, a bicycle, a cottage to live in, a bolt-hole for the first night, and a lorry to collect a hundredweight of quality dripping which he intended to sell on the black market to get money. We thought, what on earth did he think we were? Magicians? Those kind of things were impossible to get hold of then. My wife Rosalie sacrificed her bicycle. We found a suit, and Les took charge of the dripping, and became a black-market king.

Mülbach was disguised; his hair was cut and dyed. The Germans never found him, despite mounting a large search:

The Soldiers' Committee was planning the mutiny. Their idea was to march on the town headquarters wearing white armbands. They were amazingly confident. They had plenty of arms loyal to them, and enough anti-tank weapons; the real enemy was the navy, so they were expecting the fighting to be heaviest around the docks. I thought at the time we were dealing with an isolated bunch of soldiers, but I think they were part of a bigger German resistance network. They used the same slogans and listened to the broadcasts.

The mutiny was planned for 1 May 1945, but a couple of Catholic officers who had gone over to Paul's side insisted it should be postponed two weeks so that it wasn't on Red Labour Day. The island was liberated on 9 May.

I was a nervous wreck by the time of the Liberation – it was only then that I realised what a mental state I'd been through in the last few months of the Occupation.

A few days after Liberation, Mülbach wrote an emotional thank-you letter to the Jersey Communist Party. He said that his committee had initially tried to make contact with 'English patriots', but they 'wished to remain a safe distance from all trouble, sitting on their money and waving the Union Jack behind closed doors'. Then he found the Communist Party: 'I cannot express in words what I owe to these men. We have shown an example of international solidarity only possible among socialists, and as it should exist amongst all socialists and Communist Party members throughout the world.'

Norman Le Brocq: 'After the British had landed, Les made a statement to British military intelligence about Paul. They used him as an interpreter and he was repatriated to Germany.' In 1948, Le Brocq was astonished to hear from Mülbach that he was about to be put on trial for desertion from the German army in 1945. He never heard from him again.

The activities of two well-heeled middle-aged French ladies, Lucille Schwab and Suzanne Malherbe, were not on the same scale as those of Le Brocq and Mülbach, but were to the same end. They tried to incite mutiny on Jersey by typing little notes which poured scorn on Hitler and the German war effort, and encouraged German soldiers to resist. They signed the notes 'The soldier with no name', and slipped them into the Germans' coat pockets, or left them in public places such as cafés where they might be found by German soldiers.

The two women were half-sisters from a wealthy publishing family in Nantes, and made an unusual pair. Lucille Schwab, under the pseudonym of Claude Cahun, was an essayist and photographer, while Suzanne Malherbe, known as Marcel Moore, was a graphic artist. They had become members of 'Centre Attaque', a left-wing group of surrealists closely associated with André Breton, and had dabbled in experimental theatre and the Parisian arts scene of the thirties until, in 1937, they retired to the place of their childhood holidays, Jersey.

They were arrested in July 1944, and held in solitary confinement for six months. A search of their house uncovered a remarkable art collection which included paintings by Picasso and Miró. In his diary, Baron von Aufsess described the pictures as degraded and obscene; they have never been found, and were allegedly burnt by the Germans. The women were sentenced to death early in 1945, but after a plea from the Jersey Bailiff, Alexander Coutanche, that the sentence might provoke the islanders, it was commuted to life imprisonment. Liberation came five months later, but the year on prison rations left the fifty-year-old Lucille infirm.

There is one final aspect of Channel Islands resistance to consider. The Germans had ordered that no islanders should feed or harbour slave workers, but many disregarded these injunctions, and it was quite common for housewives to leave out a few hard-to-spare leftovers, or an old piece of clothing for the foreigners. Very few islanders were prepared to risk dire punishment (and possible exposure to infectious diseases) by taking escaped slave workers into their homes. The story of those islanders who did take that risk warrants only four lines in the official history of the Channel Islands' Occupation, yet it is one of its most moving and poignant episodes.

Guernsey boy Herbert Nichols watched the slave labourers at work day and night building bunkers near his grandmother's house.

The concrete would be poured for thirty-six hours without stopping. Nichols saw the slave labourers marching down in their hundreds from the camp, which was surrounded by barbed wire and watchtowers:

> When they built the bunkers, it was close to Christmas. I was living with my grandmother, and we were huddled around the fire with a little light which was made from diesel in a salad bottle with a shoelace threaded through the cap for a wick. It was early evening and the weather was terrible. We suddenly heard a noise on the porch, and my grandmother went to look. It was a young Frenchman of about my age. He was absolutely frozen and completely exhausted. He had come to the porch for shelter. He was very scared, because you weren't allowed to mix with locals. My grandmother brought him to the fire to get warm and rubbed his hands. She got him some old clothing and gave him a drop of soup, and told him to come back the next day. He came every night for about a week on his way home, and she would keep a little bit of food, and he'd gobble it up. He never said much.
>
> On the last time he came, he gave my grandmother a present. It was wrapped in newspaper. She kissed him on the cheek. When she opened it, it was a piece of soap which wasn't much thicker than the newspaper. It was so thin, it was transparent. He promised to come back after the war. He was the kind that would have done. I think he must have died.

Also on Guernsey, a Salvation Army member, Marie Ozanne, bravely protested to the Germans about their maltreatment of slave labourers. She was arrested by the Germans, and died in 1943, a few months after being released.

On Jersey there was an informal network of families who hid escaped slave workers. By the end of the Occupation there were at least twenty in hiding, some of whom had been concealed by islanders for nearly two years. One of the key figures in this network was Bob Le Sueur. He spoke Spanish and had become friends with several Spanish forced labourers, and he also got to know most of the escaped Russians. His role was largely ferrying people about and finding hideaways; his own home was too dangerous for hiding people because of a large German blockhouse opposite.

One of Le Sueur's closest friends was Feodor Burryiy, who was known as 'Bill'; their friendship has lasted over fifty years, and Le Sueur recently visited Burryiy in Tomsk, Siberia, where he now lives. Burryiy was a Russian prisoner of war who tried to escape within a few weeks of arriving on Jersey in 1942. He was recaptured and was stripped naked, put in a freezing bath, and had to run around the camp with a wheelbarrow full of stones as guards whipped him. Then he was left outside, still naked, for the night. A few days later he escaped again. He was discovered on the road by a baker, who took him to a hut where two other Russians were hiding. Le Sueur remembers:

> I got to know him when a tenant farmer with five children was sheltering him. This farmer had a Russian in the barn, another in the attic, and Bill out in a shed. Then the farmer found him a place with a widow who ran a small shop in the parish of St Ouen's. This woman, Louisa Gould, had just received a Red Cross message that her son had been killed serving in the Navy; he had been very bright and had got a scholarship from the village school to Victoria College [the best school on Jersey] and then another scholarship to Oxford. She took Bill in, she said, because 'I have to do something for another woman's son.'
>
> She was a saintly soul, but not as discreet as she should have been. Word got round. She altered her son's clothing and Bill rode her son's bicycle and they cycled into St Helier together. Everybody asked who she was with, and eventually she was denounced. She got a warning that the Germans were coming to search her house. She and Bill stayed up all night destroying evidence. Bill was moved to my office's lavatory then to another house.
>
> Louisa's sister, Ivy Forster, was also sheltering a Russian, and he had to be hidden above a shop. Bill wanted some drawing materials* which had been left in Louisa's house. We wouldn't let him out of the house, so he irresponsibly gave a message to the milkman. He had to be got out of that house quickly; the owner of the house was a woman with four children. I took him to two conscientious objectors who had come to Jersey in 1940. I had to persuade them to

---

* Bill was a very good artist, and Stella Perkins remembers that he became one of her favourites amongst the escaped Russians because he was very clever with his hands, and made lovely cards out of scraps of silk and bits of paint.

take Bill in, and it wasn't easy. You had to warn them that he had been irresponsible. They took him in, even though in the flat below was a woman with a German boyfriend.

When the Germans searched Louisa Gould's house in June 1944, they found a scrap of paper on which Bill had been practising his English. Louisa Gould was arrested and sent to prison on the Continent; she died in Ravensbruck at the age of fifty-three. The homes of her sister Ivy Forster and her brother Harold Le Druillenec were also searched, and illegal radios were found. The Germans found no trace of Georgio Kozloff, the Russian who had been hiding with Ivy Forster, and she only had to serve a prison sentence on the island. Le Druillenec was sent to the Continent for his prison sentence, and ended up in Belsen, which he was one of the few British inmates to survive. The Germans never found Bill; he assumed the identity of Oscar Le Breuilly, learned English, and stayed on the island until Liberation.

The network helping the escapees was never formalised; contacts were passed on by word of mouth in the camps and in the hideaways. Many of those involved did not know what each other had been doing until after the war. Bob Le Sueur knew of some most unlikely sympathisers who were prepared to help the Russians:

> I knew one hotelier who was married to an Austrian woman. They ran a hotel called the Mayfair which was taken over by the Germans as a Soldatenheim [for recreation], and they kept a flat upstairs. Everyone presumed she was hand-in-glove with the Germans. But in fact her father and brother were Social Democrats and had been arrested and sent to Mauthausen; her father came out a gibbering idiot and her brother died. She hated Nazis. She hid two Russians in the attic during the Occupation. She would go down to the German kitchens and beg for food, and then take the scraps to the Russians. Bill used to eat there; he would never tell us at the time where he had been, but he boasted about the meals. Most of us would have had our nerves in shreds after half an hour, but they lived like that for two years.

The Le Cornu family lived in L'Etacq, Jersey, not far from a slave labour camp. Mike Le Cornu used to sneak into the Spanish camp

and listen to the songs around the campfire; there were several
talented musicians. His family helped several escaped forced labourers; his fifteen-year-old sister Alice became pregnant and married
one of them, Christobal Lopez-Rubio, who remained in hiding
until the end of the war. The Germans published notices in the
press asking for information on the whereabouts of Lopez-Rubio
without success. Mike Le Cornu:

> There was a Russian once who came to our house at dinnertime.
> We scraped up what we had left, and gave it to him to eat. After
> Liberation, he came and thanked us for the food. Then there was
> Peter Botatenko, who came and stayed with us twice. He was a big
> fellow who looked very Ukrainian. At one point, when the house
> was going to be searched, I had to take him in a hurry to a chap in
> St Brelade's. I had my bicycle saddlebags full of food and this Ukrain-
> ian chap on the crossbar, and I went through a German emplace-
> ment. I don't know what I would have done if they'd stopped me.
>
> One night after curfew, there was Botatenko at the door. He was
> supposedly disguised, but he looked more obvious than ever. He'd
> been chased from some farm, and he'd had to roll down a bank of
> brambles and was in a terrible state, so we had to take him in again.

Jerseyman Leonard Perkins used to drop bread at a designated spot
for Russians on the run. Various huts and sheds on remote farms
were known to be relatively safe, and the Russians developed a
system of marking gates or walls to designate a friendly or
unfriendly house. Jerseyman Dr McKinstry was a vital link, supplying false papers, ration cards and medical attention for those
escapees who needed them. Thanks to him, a few Russians such as
'Bill' and Georgio Kozloff were living independent lives by the end
of the Occupation, having been able to find jobs and get food on
their false papers.

One of the hubs of the escapee network was the flat of Stella
Perkins's family in the centre of St Helier. Her mother, Augusta
Metcalfe, and her aunt, Claudia Dimitrieva, were Russian. They
had met Stella's father when he was a member of the ill-fated British
expedition to Archangel in 1919, part of the Allied intervention
intended to defeat the Bolsheviks. He brought them back to England, and eventually moved to Jersey. The arrival of their com-

patriots in 1942 moved them to pity; it was also their first chance of meeting and talking to Russians since they had left their country twenty-three years before. Regardless of the danger to Stella and her three brothers, and despite their poverty, the family's flat became a meeting place for the escaped Russians; some stayed only for a meal, others stayed several months. Stella Perkins recalls:

> These two ladies were known as Russian around the countryside, so the Jersey farmers would send the escaped Russians to us. We shared our food with them as best we could. You could not but help the slave labourers. My mother was a very generous person as well as being very artistic and well educated. There was no discussion about whether to help the escaped labourers or not, they just couldn't help themselves. Besides, it was one in the eye of the Germans.
>
> My mother and aunt talked to them about the Soviet Union; much of the time we all had a jolly good laugh while the Germans would march past in the street just below. Our flat was over the shop and the shop was on one of the main roads to the harbour, so Germans were always coming and going. Neither I nor my younger brothers (the youngest was two and half) ever said a word about the Russians to anyone.
>
> Once there was a very near-miss. We had a Russian staying with us who was learning English, and the Germans suddenly arrived. He had to hide his books quickly and slip into the bedroom while the Germans went into the sitting room and talked to my mother. The Russian crept out of the bedroom when their backs were turned and down the stairs and out of the front door. There was no German at the foot of the stairs, and the floorboards didn't creak. If they had, I wouldn't be here today.
>
> Mikhail Krokhin was with us for six months in 1943 before he moved on. The escapees never said where they had come from or where they were going. Mikhail was very friendly and fun to have around. A lot of the other escaped slave workers used to visit for a chat and a laugh. Georgio Kozloff was a gymnast. I made him a pair of swimming trunks out of a sleeveless pullover.

Kozloff gave his minders several headaches with his daredevilry. He was a great diver, and on one occasion he did a spectacular series of stunts in the open-air swimming pool in St Helier, despite the fact that the headquarters of the Feldpolizei at Silvertide guest house backed onto the pool, and he could be clearly seen from its windows. Stella was with him, and was petrified that the Germans would look out of their windows and see this amazing man: 'Kozloff took too many risks. Most of the others were very careful, except for one occasion, when Norman Le Brocq found two of them on the street having an argument – in *Russian.*'

CHAPTER SEVEN

HAD BRITAIN FORGOTTEN?

> 'Because we are British, we are thoroughly
> neglected.'
>
> *Letter from an anonymous islander in*
> The Times, *December 1944*

Before July 1940, the Channel Islands were a mere 4½-hour boat journey from mainland Britain, across the seventy miles of water from Weymouth. There had been a constant traffic to and fro of passengers, trade and mail. All this had come to a halt. For the five years of Occupation the islands could have been as far away as Warsaw. The only direct contacts with Britain were the Red Cross messages, a few lines long, which came via Switzerland, and in which anything more contentious than 'All fine. Hope you are too' was censored. Thousands of relatives on both sides of the Channel waited anxiously for news. In Britain, newsletters were set up amongst the island refugees to scotch the more baroque rumours and pass on accurate information. On the islands, the people listened secretly to the BBC, hoping that one day there might be a message from friends or relatives who had been evacuated or were serving in the Forces. They also listened for a message of sympathy and concern for their own plight; perhaps a reference to the Crown's oldest possessions in one of the King's Christmas broadcasts, or even a word of encouragement from the great man himself, Prime Minister Winston Churchill. There was nothing.

The BBC broadcast programmes carrying messages to thousands of British families scattered across the Empire by the war. They encouraged the Belgians, Dutch, French and Poles to keep up their morale, easing the sense of isolation with messages of solidarity in the struggle against Nazism. But of the Channel Islands there was not a word. The islanders could be forgiven for thinking they had been forgotten.

The most bitter disappointment came in 1944. The islanders saw the planes flying overhead on D-Day, 6 June, for the invasion and liberation of France. They heard the bombing of St Malo and Cherbourg; from Jersey and Alderney they could see, with the aid of binoculars, the Allied forces moving on the Normandy peninsula. Every day, it seemed that Liberation must be imminent. But it was not. The Allies swept past the fortress islands, leaving their large German garrisons untouched, liberating Paris in August 1944, Brussels a month later, and reaching German territory by Christmas.

Far behind Allied lines, the Reich's British holiday islands were left to starve. From the very beginning of the Occupation, islanders had hoped that an agreement could be reached between the British and German governments, with the Swiss as intermediaries, to allow supplies of fuel, basic foodstuffs and medicines through to the islands. The island governments broached various schemes to the German authorities, and in Westminster suggestions were put to the British government by Lord Portsea and evacuated islanders. Nothing came of either. After D-Day, supplies from France came to a halt, and the islands were under siege from the Allies. The islanders' rations had been drastically reduced by September 1944, yet it took Britain another four months to be persuaded to arrange food parcels through the Red Cross. Why had Britain forgotten them? the starving islanders asked through the months of October, November and December 1944. Just what were the British doing for the islands during the Occupation? What did they know about conditions on the islands? And what, if anything, were they doing to alleviate them?

The fiasco of the 1940 military raids had not dampened Churchill's enthusiasm for such adventures. In his view, the British public needed a morale booster, and nothing would better serve that purpose than the flamboyant, brilliant recapture of one of the Channel Islands to reinstate the integrity of British territory. Churchill's ambitions were not shared by the highest echelons of the military command, but as M.R.D. Foot – himself involved in the planning for a raid on Alderney – points out, there were many relatively untried units in the armed forces eager to win recognition through such an operation. There was also a stock of young Channel Islanders in the forces who were committed and eager to do something for their home islands.

Seven large-scale operations were planned in the course of the war – several of them proposed by the Chief of Combined Operations, Vice-Admiral Lord Louis Mountbatten – but none came to pass. A major attack would have been costly in terms of lives and equipment, and the likely gains were questionable. Mountbatten argued repeatedly in 1942 that Alderney could be captured, and would serve as a useful radar site and base for attacking German convoy routes, as well as providing a springboard for attacks on the Cherbourg peninsula. But he met with stiff opposition: an attack on Alderney could easily be repelled by the Luftwaffe, who had two aerodromes on the French coast within twenty miles of the island. Attacks on Jersey, Sark or Guernsey carried the danger of heavy civilian casualties, because the islands were densely populated. The intended morale booster was far more likely to turn into a bitter embarrassment. Mountbatten was never allowed to launch the operations he had envisaged.

The unhappy compromise was ineffective, pinprick raids, and four minor operations did go ahead. In one of them, 'Operation Dryad', on 2 September 1942, the Casquets lighthouse off Alderney was captured and seven Germans were taken prisoner. The lighthouse was a useful observation post but was indefensible, and was soon back in German hands. The raid strengthened Hitler's conviction that the islands had to be heavily fortified to beat off possible attack. He referred to the operation in the course of a three-hour speech to his military commanders: 'Above all, I am grateful to the English for proving me right by their various landing attempts. It shows up those who think I am always seeing phantoms, who say, "Well, when are the English coming? There is absolutely nothing happening on the coast – we swim every day, and we haven't seen a single Englishman!"'

A raid on Sark in October 1942 had far-reaching consequences. The twelve-man raiding party met an islander who told them that the Germans were polite, and asked them why the King had not mentioned the islands in his last Christmas broadcast. The party went on to kill two Germans, and took a prisoner back to England. When Hitler heard about the raid, and that the prisoner's hands had been tied, he ordered that in retaliation 1400 Allied prisoners in Dieppe should have theirs tied. Most of them were Canadian, and the Canadian government responded by tying the hands of the same number of German prisoners in Canada. Hitler also ordered that in future all commandos should be treated as acting as bandits, and shot. Finally, as a punishment for help given to the commandos by one Sark woman, two hundred islanders were deported from Jersey, Guernsey and Sark to German internment camps in February 1943.

Two small-scale raids in 1943 – one on Sark and one on Jersey – achieved nothing; the members of the former returned to Britain with the disconcerting information that residents on Jersey had not been co-operative; one woman refused to tell them where there were Germans, and told them to ask at another farmhouse. They did so, and found two petrified brothers who told them there was no resistance movement and that people were getting on well with the Germans.

The raids on the islands achieved nothing more than a few scraps of information, but they had very serious consequences for the islanders: Guernsey lost an able President of the Controlling Committee in Sherwill, and the raid on Sark led to more deportations. The raids provoked anxiety on the part of the islands' population, who believed they were futile. No doubt they felt that they could do without this sort of attention from Britain.

The Occupation had become an embarrassment to the British government; it could not even recapture a few islands seventy miles from its own shore. It was decided that reminders of the Channel Islands were bad for the morale of the British public, and the Home Office went to considerable lengths to keep references to the Occupation off the airwaves and out of the newspapers. The islands were rarely mentioned in BBC news bulletins or programmes, and they were omitted from the King's Christmas speech, which was a source of great disappointment to the islanders.

The Home Office also put pressure on Members of Parliament not to raise Channel Island issues at Westminster. But this was only partly successful, as the islands had two stalwart allies in Parliament: Lord Portsea, a stubborn, eccentric old Jerseyman, and Charles Ammon, MP for Camberwell North. Together these two managed to find an opportunity almost every month to press for action over the Channel Islands. The two particular issues over which they harried the government were that the BBC should give the islands some encouragement through a message or programme for them, and that the government should arrange to send food, medicine and fuel supplies to the islands.

Portsea and Ammon first took up the cudgels in the Houses of Parliament in July 1940, a few days after the Germans landed. They were concerned that there were not sufficient food and fuel supplies on the island. In the autumn of 1940 an exasperated Home Office wrote private notes offering to keep the pair informed if they in return would remove questions from the Order Paper, as 'any public discussion on this motion is so undesirable'.

In January 1941 Portsea tabled a motion that leaflets with news of the war's progress should be dropped over the islands (such leaflets, to the effect that Britain was still fighting the good fight, had been dropped once before, in September 1940) and that the BBC should make specific programmes with personal messages for the Channel Island audience. He also wanted a postal link to be set up with the islands via a neutral country, so that the thousands of islanders serving in the Forces could send letters to their families. The Home Secretary himself, Herbert Morrison, wrote an irritable note to Portsea asking him to withdraw the motion. He claimed that it was undesirable to send personal messages via the BBC, and that they should only go through recognised German channels. Raising the matter in the House, he said, could do nothing but harm. But Portsea was not persuaded, and Osbert Peake, the Home Office Minister, was given the task of bringing him round to the official way of thinking. Peake wrote to Lord Moyne, the government's spokesman in the House of Lords: 'I spent about an hour on Saturday morning trying to induce Lord Portsea to withdraw his motion . . . I am afraid I was unsuccessful. He is an obstinate old gentleman, very proud of his Channel Island ancestry, and apparently receives a lot of letters from island refugees . . . he therefore feels that he must make a demonstration of his keenness

to press the government to do more by way of conveying information to the islands.'

Ammon and Portsea continued to raise the matter of the islands
at Westminster without success. In May 1941 Ammon passed on a
memo to the Home Secretary written by a Channel Islands officer
serving in the Forces whose family was trapped on the islands. The
memo accused the Home Office of an 'apparent lack of interest in
the welfare and ultimate fate of the eighty thousand British subjects
who are virtually prisoners in the only portion of the British Empire
that can be correctly described as "enemy-occupied territory"'.
The officer called for a commission to be set up to monitor developments on the islands and to interview escapees systematically about
conditions under the Occupation. He pointed out that rumours
amongst the islands' thirty thousand refugee community were rife
and causing great anxiety; there had been newspaper reports that
all the women had been put in concentration camps and that the
population was near starvation. The Germans had allowed letters
to be sent to British prisoners of war and to occupied France, so
why could not this be arranged for the islands? He also asked why
food supplies were not being sent to the islands when the Germans
had invited the Americans to send supplies to France. The Home
Secretary's reply to Ammon was haughty and brief; he accused the
officer of passing on secret information, and said that the Post
Office was already trying to set up a postal route through Portugal
or Spain. (This never came to fruition, but after March 1941 the
islanders received two-line Red Cross messages at regular intervals.)

The first anniversary of the Occupation, in June 1941, was viewed
as extremely sensitive by Whitehall. No one wanted to remind the
British public of the previous summer's humiliation. It would be
'undesirable' to broadcast any mention of the anniversary as it could
be put to propaganda use by 'ill-disposed' people, said a Home
Office memo. Winston Churchill was sent a letter by the Exeter
Channel Islands Society, a group of sympathisers and evacuees, at
the time of the anniversary, and his proposed reply was subjected
to careful drafting and redrafting by the Home Office before being
forwarded to him for his approval. All references to the anniversary
were deleted, and the final reply was masterfully anodyne: 'No one
who knows anything about the history of the Channel Islands, least

of all Mr Churchill, is unmindful of the services rendered to the
Crown by men from these islands both in the remote and in the
recent past. The most suitable method of making known to all
islanders, the government's appreciation of their loyalty to the
Crown and their services to the Empire, is receiving sympathetic
consideration . . .'

Churchill refused to broadcast a message on the anniversary, and
even the Channel Islands Refugee Committee's request to make a
radio programme on how the island refugees were faring in Britain
was refused.* They had to be satisfied with the Home Office's
suggestion of a message of sympathy broadcast by the Bishop of
Winchester, Cyril Garbett, to island refugees in Britain – which
made no reference to the anniversary or to those left behind on
the islands. The Home Office did admit that 'islanders find Parliamentary answers disappointing after the BBC's references to the
gallantry and suffering of the Allies'.

In the autumn of 1941 Bishop Cyril Garbett spoke to Dennis
Vibert, the Jersey escapee who had virtually rowed across the Channel solo; he was alarmed by Vibert's reports that food and fuel
supplies were running short, and wrote to Churchill asking him to
send Red Cross supplies to the islands. The Home Office drafted
the reply: 'The Prime Minister is sorry if there is a feeling among
the islanders that they have been forgotten and that very little is
said about them . . . he would very much like to make it known
to our fellow countrymen who remained in the islands that the
government has not forgotten them, and to send them a message
of encouragement. There are, however, obvious difficulties in doing
so while the islands are in enemy occupation.'

By November 1941 the Home Office's reluctance to arrange
food supplies for the islands had been complicated by the precedent
of Belgian refugees in Britain, who had organised a system of sending food parcels to occupied Belgium via Portugal. The Home
Office's Charles Markbreiter was worried that Lord Portsea might
get wind of the scheme. He wrote to Lord Moyne that it was

* The Channel Islands Refugee Committee was a group of prominent London-based
islanders who raised money for those islanders evacuated to Britain in 1940, dealt with
all matters relating to their welfare, and lobbied the government on their behalf.

'extremely unlikely' that Portsea would hear of the Belgian food parcels, but in case he did, Moyne should have his defence ready. Markbreiter wrote that 'no one knows whether the Belgians benefit from the scheme, but it is certain the people in the Channel Islands would not. Needless to say, the matter should not be mentioned if it can possibly be avoided.'

The Ministry of Economic Warfare opposed the idea of sending food to the islands; it would only be re-exported to earn money for the Germans, they claimed. They told the Home Office that Belgium was an exception reluctantly allowed for 'propaganda reasons', but that a further exception for 'our own people' would be embarrassing.

At Christmas 1941, the question of a broadcast message of encouragement reared its head again. Markbreiter told the BBC that no reference should be made to the Channel Islands, and that Churchill would not broadcast any message; he explained that it could provoke reprisals against islanders or the confiscation of their radios. The BBC wrote back that they had followed Markbreiter's instructions and had omitted the islands completely from their Christmas Day 'Absent Friends' programme. Lord Portsea was furious, and in January he raised the matter in the House of Lords. Markbreiter drew up a studiedly bland reply for the government, apologising to the islanders if they thought they had been forgotten and concluding that there had been 'several broadcasts of interest to islanders included in the general programmes on the BBC'.

The indomitable Portsea was tired of such bland government statements, and announced in the House of Lords that if the British government would provide a ship, he would collect the food and sail it to the Channel Islands himself. His scheme was greeted with delight by the *Daily Mail*, and offers poured into the newspaper's offices from sailors willing to crew the octogenarian lord's voyage. Neither this plan of Lord Portsea's nor another for him to be parachuted into the islands came to anything, and by this time the Home Office had lost all patience with Portsea.

In October 1942 all the British newspapers carried news of the deportation of more than two thousand islanders to German internment camps. The information had been uncovered by members of the military raid on Sark that month, and the British government had been forced to release it in a statement in response to Hitler's accusations that the raiders had shackled their prisoner. *The Times*, *Daily Sketch* and *Daily Mirror* devoted considerable space to this latest instance of German barbarity. Headlines ran 'Nazis Send Captured Britons as Slaves, Island Raid Reveals' and 'Islanders Starve as Nazis Grab Food'. Under the title 'It Might Have Been Your Fate' the *Sunday Chronicle* declared that Oberst Knackfuss, the Feldkommandant, 'should go down on the black list alongside the murderers of Lidice* and those who stole the food from the Greeks and left them to starve† . . . the real truth has emerged of deportations and forced labour'.

Ammon asked Churchill at Question Time whether he intended to protest at the deportations of the islanders. The Prime Minister's cryptic answer was, 'We do what we can to beat the enemy.' Unsatisfied, a week later Ammon questioned Clement Attlee, the Deputy Prime Minister, about the deported islanders, decrying the lack of intervention over the islands and the little notice taken of their plight in the House. He returned to the deportation issue on several further occasions; the government's silence was deafening, they had no wish to give any more publicity to the issue. But the government was deeply troubled, and within a few months the deportations had been quietly listed as a war crime, for which the Germans could be prosecuted after the war.

The Sark raid had also revealed that the islands were in grave need of food and medicines, and the Channel Islands Refugee Committee wrote to Herbert Morrison in the autumn of 1942 to press on him the urgency of getting supplies through to the islands. They warned that children and invalids were 'now suffering from serious dietetic deficiencies and there is grave fear of permanent injury to their health'. Finally, the UK government gave medical supplies, including insulin, to the International Red Cross to pass on to the islands, but it refused to allow food, dried milk and vitamins through the blockade.

---

* A village in Czechoslovakia, the scene of a terrible reprisal massacre by German troops.
† In 1942 Britain and America organised massive airlifts of food to Greece, after a combination of disrupted harvests due to the war and the Germans' and Italians' failure to import food led to widespread famine.

By November 1942, Portsea's periodic pleas for food supplies to be sent to the islands were reinforced by the news that four thousand tonnes of food per month was reaching Greece from Britain and America. Other parts of occupied Europe were also getting food supplies: Belgium was receiving a thousand tonnes of food per month and four tonnes in food parcels, mainly of nutritionally rich sardines and honey, and food parcels could also be sent to France and Norway. The Ministry of Economic Warfare told the Home Office they no longer had objections to food parcels being sent to the islands from Portugal, 'though it would suit them very much better if nothing was done at the moment'. The Ministry claimed that the islands were better off than France and Belgium (there was no evidence that this was correct), and incomparably better off than Greece and Poland (which was true). A few months later the Ministry suggested that between five and twenty tons of food could now be sent to the islands, but the government did not take up the suggestion.

Six months later, in June 1943, Lord Portsea had hatched another scheme. He pleaded in the Lords that parcels of coffee and tea should be dropped from the air on Jersey and Guernsey, as a way of showing encouragement and sympathy for the islanders. Needless to say, the idea came to nothing.

The Home Office was now the unwilling recipient of letters from concerned members of the public asking why food could not be sent to the islands, which were only twelve hours from Weymouth by boat, when it was being sent to Greece. An ex-Indian Army Colonel wrote to ask if it was true that the islanders were starving; the Home Office minuted on his letter that they did not know what to answer. One of the most persistent and articulate letter-writers was a former Member of Parliament, Edith Picton-Turberville. Markbreiter replied to one of her letters that the government could not be seen to treat its own kind more favourably, and the government was doing all it could, etc. etc.

Before D-Day, in June 1944, the British government actually knew very little about conditions on the islands. They relied on a handful of escaped islanders such as Dennis Vibert, and the returning members of military raids, for a few details. Aerial reconnaissance gave some information about the disposition of labour camps and fortifications, but it could give no insight into the state of food, fuel and medical supplies, or the morale of the population.

The escapees were questioned by the Home Office and MI19, a branch of military intelligence, and reports of the interviews were circulated to several ministries in Whitehall. They did not paint an appealing picture of life under the Occupation. The escapees were highly critical of their fellow islanders, accusing them of collaboration, black marketeering and corruption. But escapees were not representative of the islanders; the very fact that they had embarked on a dangerous escape marked them out as unusually brave and uncompromising, and their judgements derived from their characters. The information they provided was to have a significant impact on the attitude of the government, and in particular of Churchill, towards the islanders' conduct under German rule. In September 1941, for example, Dennis Vibert told the Home Office that the food situation was very serious, and added: 'The Germans have had no need to apply compulsion, as they appear to have received all the assistance that they have asked for. For example, when three hundred labourers were required to work on the airport extensions about nine hundred applied . . . It appears to be the policy of the States to co-operate with the German military authorities, and they have actually been thanked by the German Commandant for their co-operation.' There were too many such tales of behaviour, which Whitehall judged un-British, for it to be favourably disposed towards the islands.

In 1943, a Jersey escapee gave the first information about the brutal treatment of Russian slave labourers on the island. The Home Office suggested to him that he did not mention the matter to the Soviet ambassador; perhaps they feared sensationalist publicity. The government was already aware of the existence of camps on the islands, in particular on Alderney, because of aerial reconnaissance of the fortifications.

Guernsey escapee John Hubert was interviewed by the Home Office in August 1943. He said there had been some cases of malnutrition, but that for the most part islanders were keeping cheerful. It was the collaboration of the island authorities on which he chose to dwell:

Many officials will, I know, blow out their chests and tell great flourishing stories of their difficulties when the war is won, but I really hope that in the midst of their conceit, some reflection will bring to the guilty minds a realisation of their great weakness and cowardice in having failed to resist German orders, even when golden opportunities presented themselves ... as Percy Dorey [President of the Guernsey Glasshouse Utilisation Board] said to me when enforcing a German order, 'I don't want to be sent to Germany.'

I confess to having been proud always of being a Guernseyman, but occupation experiences disclose great weakness. I have always listened to the British broadcasts whilst in Guernsey and cannot describe the confused feelings on hearing Colonel Britton speaking to the occupied countries regarding passive resistance.

There is one willing quisling ... [and] many weaklings ... officials used their position to obtain extra rations themselves and also supply their friends.

In April 1944 the first escapees from Alderney were questioned. Two Guernseymen who had been on Alderney for four months told MI19 that there were about thirty islanders currently working on Alderney, but that there were no longer any Jerseywomen, as they had all been sent home with venereal disease. The escapees also said that there were a thousand Jews wearing the yellow Star of David working on Alderney, and about five thousand 'stripers' – forced labourers so named because they had a stripe of paint down the side of their trouser leg.

After D-Day, the British government received considerably more information. Firstly, the number of escapees increased dramatically as Jerseymen crossed the narrow stretch of sea between the island and the liberated coast of France. The escapees brought news of siege conditions on the fortress islands. In October 1944 five Jerseymen and one Jerseywoman were questioned by MI19. They said that the German soldiers were reduced to eating nothing but horsemeat and mashed potatoes. Their uniforms were disintegrating, and morale was low. MI19 reported: 'The islands have been peculiarly isolated and rumour is correspondingly more rampant. No one ever dared correct a rumour, because if they did, there was grave danger of a "quisling" informer accusing him of having other

sources of information such as a wireless. [The escapees] all think
that leaflets could have stopped rumours and done much to check
the passive attitude of many island government officials.'

Two Guernseymen questioned by MI19 in November 1944 said
a group had emerged which called itself 'The Guernsey Underground Barbers'. Its aim was to punish women who had 'miscon-
ducted themselves with Germans'. The escapees described one
recent case in which a woman informer had had her eyes attacked
with scissors. These islanders were less critical of the authorities
than previous escapees, but they said that the Guernsey Bailiff,
Victor Carey, was too old and 'effete'. His offer of a £25 reward
for information on those painting V-signs was, they said, 'unnecessary and gratuitous'. They added that German discipline was collapsing; there had been a riot over a food complaint in a billet involving
forty-eight men.

Also in November, Guernseyman Fred Noyon arrived in Britain
with a detailed account of the island's food supplies entrusted to him
by a group including members of the government who, exasperated
by the Bailiff's lack of action, had decided to take matters into their
own hands. The gravity of the food crisis was such that on Jersey the
Bailiff set aside his policy of opposing escapes and handed a memo
outlining Jersey's position to a Jerseyman who succeeded in
delivering it to Britain. In mid-November MI19 reported on interviews with escapees: 'Islanders have given up their confidence in the
Home Office of Britain since the fall of Brest [on 18 September 1944]
. . . The islands have been neglected by the UK propaganda and welfare branches . . . there had been no encouragement from the BBC,
no Red Cross help . . . and in the present emergency still no word,
lead or direct intervention by the British government.'

The second source of information on conditions on the islands
was intercepted mail from islanders to deportees in the internment
camps after D-Day and the liberation of France. Reports on the
captured mail's contents were prepared by the Postal and Telegraph
Censorship. In November and December 1944, Whitehall received
extracts from 227 letters before the postal link was cut by the
advance of the Allied front line to the German border. They made
unpleasant reading for the British government.

Ten letter-writers said that they were in such dire material distress that their health was affected, and they felt they could not hold out much longer: 'Life is not worth living, we cannot sleep at nights, we are so worried and distressed ... we are starving here ... I wonder how much longer, it is more than human nature can endure.'

Six other writers expressed strong resentment of the British for not sending Red Cross food parcels, which deportees in the internment camps in Germany had already received:

> I think they have forgotten us entirely in England. They gave it out over the wireless the other day in the House of Commons that the people in the Channel Islands were being well treated by the Germans ... when we heard Churchill say another seven months [until Liberation] the other day, we nearly collapsed ... I don't think there'll be many left to ring Victory bells. The BBC has forgotten us too. How everyone hopes the King will mention us at Xmas or that the BBC will put on a program for us ... but not for us. For France and Belgium and all the rest, oh yes – but not for us. Who are we?

Other writers complained of informers being paid £105 for informing on people with radios, and cases were quoted of brothers and sisters giving each other away out of spite. A few of the letter-writers were pro-German: one girl wrote to say she was engaged to a German soldier, and a man working on the German troops' newspaper felt that 'many of them [Germans] show kinship of race with us'.

One writer complained that there was no fuel for heat or light, and that people were chopping up furniture and shelves to heat a saucepan of potatoes. The Germans were eating ten old horses a week, in the form of sausages. The letter continued: 'Is there going to be some fun here one of these days! British versus Jersey-ites. The locals are rotten and we English are just spoiling to get at them.'

Little of this information leaked through to the general public. The Postal and Telegraph Censorship reports were secret, and the escapees in the latter years of the Occupation were advised not to talk to the press. But rumours flourished amongst the evacuee islanders, who were well-informed about what was happening on the islands. One anonymous islander gave a letter to an escapee to send to *The Times*. It was published on 5 December 1944, and summed up the complaints of islanders at the time: the sense of neglect by the government and the BBC, the disappointment, the growing fear of hunger and the desire for justice.

> It seems so strange and shows a great lack of imagination . . . If we had been French, Polish or any other nationality, we would have been showered with messages and pamphlets . . . because we are British, we are thoroughly neglected . . .
>
> The only people who can get any food now are the collaborators and the jerrybags and there are a few hundred of each kind . . . the States are in a state of complete jitters, and give way to the Germans over everything.
>
> I only hope there will be an inquiry . . . the black marketeers must be dealt with and the informers and quislings . . . the lynching in Rome* will seem a kindergarten game compared with what will happen here when the pent-up wrath and indignation of the masses is let loose.

The Home Office was furious at the letter's publication; a memo commented that 'the tone of the letter is not pleasant and I am surprised *The Times* published it . . . it should not have been given circulation.' Whitehall did not wish rumours of corruption and collaboration to get any wider currency, but MI19's interviews and the censorship reports had clearly indicated that the liberation of the islands would reveal some awkward questions.

Significantly, the one matter relating to the Channel Islands at this time in which Churchill did show great interest was an allegation of treason, which he asked Anthony Eden, then Secretary of State for Foreign Affairs, to look into. Churchill had heard that in 1944 a British soldier, a member of a raiding party, had been betrayed to the Germans by a police constable. His private secretary told Eden, 'there must be other cases than this, and it is important that the guilty parties should be brought to trial'. A few months later, in reply to Eden's enquiries, the Home Office declared that

---

* Presumably the summary executions of fascists after the Allied liberation of Rome.

no evidence had been found to substantiate Churchill's report. However, the incident is revealing of what was uppermost in Churchill's mind in the last months of the war.

Liberation of the islands raised the spectre of the kind of social unrest which had haunted the liberation of Europe. Throughout the late summer and autumn of 1944, Britain had watched in horror as each liberated country had turned in on itself in a frenzy of vengeance against collaborators and fraternisers. The Scourge claimed the lives of thousands of people in France, and women alleged to have fraternised were humiliated in public rituals of head-shaving, tarring and feathering. Churchill found this disgusting. It could not be allowed to happen on the Channel Islands, Whitehall determined. The islands' Liberation, said James Boag Howard, the young Home Office civil servant put in charge of planning it, would be a model one, quite unlike the rough and ready operations in Sicily and Italy.

Preparations for the Liberation began in 1943, as it was expected shortly after D-Day. By April 1944 every detail was ready: every shoe, sheet of toilet paper and tablet of soap which would be needed by the civilian population had been requisitioned and sat waiting in warehouses on the south coast of England. It was decided that the Liberation Force would include as many Channel Islanders as possible; and to ensure that there was no trouble there would be no privates – who were thought likely to be less disciplined than more senior ranks – and no troops from the Allies.

Collaborators and black marketeers were to be given swift but fair justice. Boag Howard had thirteen months in which to fill voluminous files with recommendations on how black marketeers' profits could be taxed and what exactly was the definition of collaboration. He enlisted the help of a handful of prominent Channel Islanders in Britain to help him with these delicate matters, including the former Judge of Alderney, Frederick French, who had become a Brigadier, and Jerseyman Lord Justice du Parcq, a Law Lord.

'Arrangements have already been made for the investigation of collaboration,' said Boag Howard to French in April 1944. But what exactly was collaboration? he wondered. Was it collaboration 'to make the best of a bad situation for oneself and one's fellow citizens by doing one's job as well as possible...?' He was also troubled by the question of black-market profits: 'It seems to us that if anyone in the Islands has been sailing near the wind to obtain financial gain, he will probably have farmed out his gains in such a way that we won't be able to spot him through his bank balances.'

By December 1944, the Home Office had decided that black marketeers should be taxed, and that the opportunity to catch them would be when they changed Reichsmarks into sterling. C.W. Bickmore, the financial advisor to Brigadier Alfred Snow, the Liberation Force Commander, told the Home Office:

> I should like to suggest that it does not lie in our mouths at all to mention collaboration; we have not felt the jackboot and we can form very little idea of what shifts we would have been put to if we had, and when all is said, we must admit that we left the islands in the lurch...
>
> As regards profits, the astute collaborator will not have retained his ill-gotten gains in cash, or even in money in the bank; he will have salted it away in possessions of some sort [but] the witch-hunt for collaboration is likely to be only a passing phase.

Bickmore's final point was the most important. He foresaw exactly the dilemma which was to confront the Home Office in the summer of 1945:

> If at the outset we give any indication of our readiness to lend countenance to accusations of collaboration we shall be undermining the influence of the very instruments upon which we must rely to set the islands on their feet again, for it is only too clear from the information which is coming through to us that there is an element among the population dissatisfied with the conduct of the administrators who stood between them and their oppressors.

While the Whitehall civil servants were putting the finishing touches to their Liberation plans, the islanders were starving. The dwindling supply line with France had finally been cut after D-Day. The German garrison had been strengthened by troops evacuated from France, and now numbered about thirty thousand. Germans and islanders alike were suffering from malnutrition.*

In August 1944 the Jersey government drew up a memo for the German Feldkommandantur; the strictly rationed food and fuel supplies would run out in four months, probably sooner. The following month, the German Foreign Ministry formally asked Switzerland as a neutral intermediary to inform Britain that 'on the former British Channel Islands supplies for the civilian population are exhausted', and suggested that either all civilians should be evacuated, or food supplies should be sent in. The Ministry of Economic Warfare, the Chiefs of Staff and the Home Office saw no objection to sending food, but Churchill did. He wanted the German garrison starved into submission, and scribbled in the margin of a Liberation plan forwarded to him for approval, 'Let 'em starve. No fighting. They can rot at their leisure.'

Churchill would not be budged; responsibility for feeding the islanders lay with the Germans, and if they did not have food, they should surrender. At the end of September he wrote in a minute: 'I am entirely opposed to sending any rations to the Channel Islands ostensibly for the civil population but in fact enabling the German garrison to prolong their resistance.'

An official notice printed in the islands' newspapers two weeks later stated that the occupying power no longer considered itself responsible for feeding the islanders, because it had referred the matter to the British. At the same time the Germans began to requisition food. The islanders became very alarmed – there was a danger that neither the British nor the Germans would take responsibility for the starving civilian population. The Guernsey Bailiff, Victor Carey, wrote a long letter to the Befehlshaber, Oberst von Schmettow, accusing him of ignoring the Hague Convention. Von Schmettow's reply was emotional: 'People in the islands do not know what war is, nor what war means. They can have no idea of what every German town, the whole of France, London and the south of England are experiencing daily in the way of sacrifices and sufferings.' He went on to point out that the islands

---

* By this time, most of the forced labourers had been evacuated from the islands. See Chapter 8.

had had the good fortune barely to have experienced war as the rest of Europe understood it, and warned that 'The German army does not build fortifications of such strength without holding them with the greatest bitterness, and until the exhaustion of its powers of resistance. Even the advent of a calamity for the population after some time, for which the besieger alone will be responsible, will change nothing of the facts.'

After the Allied invasion of Normandy in June 1944, it became increasingly difficult to keep the islands supplied. The German authorities in France suggested that the civilian population be evacuated, as the islands could support the German garrison alone almost indefinitely. But, as von Schmettow pointed out, three-quarters of the islanders were engaged in 'practical service to the troops, so that evacuation without damaging troops' interest could apply only to those who cannot work – sick, children and the aged'. As the pressure on the available shipping mounted, even this much-reduced scheme was abandoned.

Throughout October the British government held to its line that it was the Germans' responsibility to feed the islanders. But, faced with pressure in Parliament, in the newspapers and from the evacuees to send food, the government's resolve was weakening. Herbert Morrison, the Home Secretary, prevaricated in a reply to Charles Ammon, now Lord Ammon, that food could not be sent to the islands until 'the 'time is ripe'. On 2 November Morrison said in reply to a question in Parliament that fuel, food and medical supplies were ready for despatch.

Only Churchill was still holding out; on 6 November he told the Foreign Secretary, Anthony Eden, 'I am entirely opposed to our feeding the German garrison in the Channel Islands and thus prolonging its resistance.' But, the following day, Churchill finally gave way, and agreed that food and medicine parcels should be sent, on the understanding that the Germans continued to be responsible for providing the basic civilian ration.

By November, civilian rations on the islands had shrunk to virtually the minimum necessary to support life: 500 grams of bread, 125 grams of fat, 20 grams of meat and 500 grams of potatoes per week. The Germans' rations were 2100 grams of bread, 500 of meat, 245 of fat and 2800 of potatoes.

The Channel Island refugees in Britain were very worried. Soothing words in Parliament had not translated into action, and on 3 December the Sheffield Channel Islands Society was the first of many local societies to present a petition to Herbert Morrison, the Home Secretary. Nearly nine thousand people had put their name to a statement calling for food to be sent to the islands; Morrison refused even to receive the delegation bearing the boxes containing the petition. There was a steady stream of letters from Members of Parliament enquiring about conditions in the islands, to which Morrison refused to reply. 'Any publicity would prejudice negotiations,' was his only comment. Several Parliamentary questions were deferred or withdrawn. Finally, on 14 December, five weeks after Churchill had agreed to send food parcels, Morrison announced in the Commons that a Red Cross ship would set sail for the islands with food and medicines in the next few days. In fact the voyage from Lisbon was postponed, and it was not until 27 December that the *Vega* docked in St Peter Port with 100,000 food parcels, 4200 invalid diet parcels and supplies of soap, salt, medicines and tobacco.

The food parcels saga had left islanders both in Britain and on the islands extremely angry, as Morrison was only too well aware from the flood of irate letters to the Home Office. The whole business had been so protracted that the government received little credit for sending supplies at all. As the spring of 1945 approached, the collapse of Germany seemed only weeks away, and the Liberation of the islands was at last within sight. Morrison turned his energies to patching up the tattered relationship between Britain and the islands and to preparing the ground for a peaceful Liberation. In March he asked Churchill to mention the suffering of the islands in a speech, writing that it would 'clear [the word was crossed out and replaced with 'improve'] the local atmosphere when our troops go back to the islands'. But Churchill was still unfavourably disposed towards the islands, and his reply was abrupt: 'I doubt if it will be possible for me to introduce the subject into my broadcasts. These have to be conceived as a whole, and not as a catalogue of favourable notices.' Churchill would not relent, and Morrison had to make do with finally getting a programme on the Channel Islands onto the BBC. On 29 March 1945, four and half years after the idea had first been suggested, a fourteen-minute programme on the islands was broadcast. The islanders had to wait until 22 May – nearly two weeks *after* Liberation – before the BBC transmitted a half-hour programme of messages from evacuated islanders in Britain which had been recorded in August 1944.

As the diplomatic exchanges over food went back and forth between Bern, Berlin and London, the British government used psychological warfare in the hope of persuading the island garrisons to surrender. An attempt to recapture the heavily fortified islands by force had been ruled out as too costly in men and equipment. In the early autumn of 1944 thousands of propaganda leaflets were dropped on the islands urging the German troops surrender. A letter was dropped by parachute on Guernsey on 1 September addressed to von Schmettow, asking him to reconnect the Channel Island end of a telephone cable link to France. At the other end of the cable was a captured German general, ready to attempt to persuade him to surrender. Von Schmettow ignored the request, and Berlin announced on the radio that 'the Channel Islands had refused several demands for surrender and were still holding out'.

It was decided to drop a second letter by parachute on the night of 21 September, fixing a rendezvous point for the Allies to meet von Schmettow; this letter probably landed in the sea. A Canadian officer accompanied by another captured German general approached the coast of Guernsey, a request for discussions with von Schmettow was relayed to shore, and half an hour later the reply came that 'Lieutenant General von Schmettow is fully informed as to the military situation and therefore declines any discussion.' As they made for Cherbourg, their boat was fired on by the coastal battery on Alderney.

The German fortresses were left intact. In Churchill's view they tied up a large number of German soldiers and contributed little to the German war effort; he is said to have called them the biggest and cheapest prisoner of war camps behind Allied front lines. Von Schmettow was a German officer of the old school, for whom surrender was incompatible with military honour. It was the German garrison who paid the price for his intransigence. In the last five months of the Occupation, from January to May 1945, they suffered most from the siege conditions. The islanders' position had been eased by the Red Cross parcels, but the Germans' rations became increasingly meagre. Their numbers had been swelled by soldiers fleeing from French ports such as St Malo after its liberation by the Allies in August 1944. Supplies by sea had come to an end, and transport planes became more and more irregular. The German officers did not know how long the situation would last, so stores were strictly rationed; some believed the war could go on for another two years. The soldiers lost weight, and were ordered to take a rest every afternoon to conserve energy. Virtually all exercises and training came to an end because the men were too weak to drill. Their uniforms and boots were disintegrating, and replacement shirts were made from sheets and curtains. There was virtually no gas or electricity on the islands, and the water supply was reduced to two hours in the morning and two in the evening.

Morale collapsed as the news came through that the Russians had reached the eastern German border. Defeat now seemed certain. A handful of soldiers deserted and were hidden by their island girlfriends, but for the majority there was nothing to do but wait for the war to be over and to worry about their families and friends in Germany, now at the mercy of the Russian army as well as Allied bombing raids.

As the weeks wore on, the Germans cut deeper into the islands' food supplies, depriving islanders of staples of the Occupation diet such as milk and potatoes. Milkless days had already been introduced for civilians, and their milk rations were stopped altogether on 23 April; potato rations had been cut and then stopped. German soldiers searched desperately for food and fuel; they resorted to stealing from the fields, and even armed burglary. The officers attempted to keep discipline, imposing severe punishments for stealing, and the list of convictions in early 1945 was long. At least one farmer was murdered trying to defend his property. The Germans collected nettles for soup, and were even reduced to stealing cats and dogs. By May 1945 there were few pet animals left on the islands – most had been eaten.

German soldier Werner Grosskopf said: 'We got so hungry we

collected limpets and minced them and made them up like hamburgers; they were like chewing gum or gristle, but they stopped the hunger pangs for a bit.'

Seaman Hans Glauber arrived on Sark in 1944 after fleeing St Malo:

> We ate cats, dogs, rabbits, limpets, and I even shot and ate two seagulls, which for a German sailor is a terrible thing to do. There is a superstition in the navy that in a seagull is the soul of a drowned sailor. I lost seven and half stone in nine months.
>
> Once we caught a big tom-cat and we put it in a big zinc bucket after skinning it and cutting its head off. We boiled it for about two hours to get rid of all the bugs cats have, and boiled it again with nettles and a few potatoes. Then we put it on a beautiful white tablecloth laid with proper knives and forks and wine glasses, and we washed it down with champagne and coffee. It was a real feast.

Glauber remembered that there were secret stores of tinned food which were held back from the troops: 'We secretly opened them up and ate them, and filled them up with sand and put them back. This was while eight hundred soldiers were lying in hospital malnourished.'

Some islanders, hard-pressed though they were, took pity on these gaunt, depressed Germans and gave them food. Jersey boy Maurice Green remembers: 'For all I dislike the Germans, their discipline was fantastic. When we had Red Cross parcels, they didn't try to grab food off you despite us provoking them. We used to sit on the wall, eating in front of them.'

Guernseywoman Dolly Joanknecht, pregnant with her German sweetheart Willi's child, gave him a cigarette out of her Red Cross food parcel. Willi took one pull, and keeled over in a dead faint; his stomach was empty, and it had been a long time since he had last smoked real tobacco.

CHAPTER EIGHT

LIBERATION

'. . . and our dear Channel Islands are also to be
freed today.'

Winston Churchill, VE Day, 8 May 1945

Every year during the Occupation, Adolf Hitler's birthday on 20
April had been celebrated throughout the Reich with military
parades, bands and speeches. In 1945, the German garrison on the
Channel Islands was among the few corners of Hitler's empire
which still had the time and the inclination to mark the day. Bands
played and choirs sang in the town squares as the Nazi flag was
hoisted.

It was a depressing spectacle for the islanders. More than ten
months had passed since D-Day, and the determination of the
Germans to hold out to the bitter end had not diminished. On 28
February 1945 von Schmettow had been replaced as Befehlshaber
by Vizeadmiral Friedrich Hüffmeier, a loyal Nazi, to ensure that
the will to defend the islands did not falter. On 20 March Hüffmeier
gathered hundreds of soldiers into the Forum cinema in St Helier,
Jersey, to regale them with stirring speeches of loyalty to the Führer
and the Fatherland. He told his troops that all fires were to be
forbidden, in order to conserve fuel for the following winter; there
was no end to the Occupation in sight. It seemed that only a full-
scale Allied assault would dislodge the Germans.

Yet within a few weeks the inconceivable had happened. Late
on 1 May, the islanders heard the news that Hitler was dead.
Immediately, an intense sense of expectancy was aroused; it could
only be a matter of days now before Germany surrendered and the
islands were liberated. The armies of Germany were collapsing, the
Russians were in the streets of Berlin and the Americans were fast

moving to join up with their eastern ally on the Elbe. On 2 May Berlin fell, and on 7 May the general surrender of German forces was signed at General Eisenhower's headquarters at Reims in France.

The first week of May was a strange period of hiatus on the Channel Islands. German soldiers stood awkwardly by as shops openly sold Union Jacks. The demoralised, hungry German soldiers were bewildered, and the islanders took advantage of their crumbling authority by taunting them. Hüffmeier issued a proclamation on 5 May banning all demonstrations and meetings and ordered Alexander Coutanche, the Jersey Bailiff, to reinforce this with a statement of his own the following day. He complied: 'I appeal to you all to maintain your calm and dignity in the days through which we are now passing.'

Jerseyman John Miere wrote a letter to his brother Joe, who was serving his prison sentence in St Helier for daubing swastikas on the walls of German billets, describing the feeling of anticipation on the island:

Dear Joe,
    Great news is circulating around the town. Everyone seems to be going mad – long queues waiting outside of Laurens [a shop in St Helier] trying and fighting to buy UNION JACKS. I reckon that it will be over any minute now and I am sure waiting to see you out again – I am prepared to meet our troops with a super new American flag also a pretty large French and Belgian but I don't seem to be able to get a Union Jack.
    The B-?!!? Huns sure look down in the dumps – damn good job – they wanted this war and they're sure getting it plus a bit extra for which they never bargained for.
    Old Ma Robin the Bitch [a notorious collaborator] is scared to hell with the thought of the Great Führer pegging out – never mind she'll have the runs after we've finished with her.

On 7 May the BBC announced that Victory in Europe Day – VE Day – would be celebrated the following day. Yet many of the islanders were very confused, as Jersey diarist Leslie Sinel noted: 'Everyone got busy after the announcement that Victory-in-Europe Day would be tomorrow, but the position here is not clear as the

Germans are still in occupation; there has been no slackening in warlike preparations on their part, for today new gun emplacements were being made in various parts of the Island ... at night the Germans were at defence posts, guns were manned and searchlights swept the seas.'

VE Day dawned, and while the rest of Europe was celebrating the defeat of Nazism, the islanders were still waiting for Liberation. Coutanche announced – in a message agreed with the Germans – that the islanders could listen to Winston Churchill's BBC broadcast to the nation at 3 p.m., and asked them to refrain from demonstrations and to hoist no flags until after the Prime Minister had spoken. On Guernsey the Bailiff, Victor Carey, and the President of the Controlling Committee, John Leale, were told by the Germans at 10 a.m. that the war was over. The news was published in a one-sheet edition of the *Guernsey Star*.

Crowds gathered in St Helier and St Peter Port to listen to Churchill's speech, relayed on loudspeakers: 'Hostilities will end officially at one minute after midnight tonight, but in the interests of saving lives the "ceasefire" began yesterday to be sounded all along the front, and our dear Channel Islands are also to be freed today,' he declared. There was ecstatic cheering. The islands were to be liberated, and finally, after five long years, Churchill himself had acknowledged them. Flags were hoisted and church bells rung.

The celebrations were a little premature. Two ships, HMS *Bulldog* and HMS *Beagle*, each carrying an advance party of twenty-two men, had left Plymouth at ten o'clock that morning, and were met at noon on the following day by Kapitänleutnant Armin Zimmerman, one of Hüffmeier's aides, on a German minesweeping trawler. Despite the Reich's unconditional surrender, Zimmerman had been instructed by Hüffmeier to seek terms for an armistice. Furthermore, Zimmerman warned that hostilities had not yet officially ceased, and that the British ships could be fired on by German coast guns. Hüffmeier's intransigence only delayed the islands' surrender until the next day, 9 May, when it was finally signed by his chief of staff General Major Heine on the quarterdeck of HMS *Bulldog* at 7.14 a.m., just outside St Peter Port. The same morning, Brigadier Alfred Snow, head of 'Operation Nestegg' to liberate the islands, transferred to HMS *Beagle* and sailed to Jersey, where he received the surrender of the island's garrison at 10 a.m.

Alexander Coutanche immediately sent a radio message to the King assuring him of the loyalty of his Channel Island subjects: 'We rejoice that we can once more take our place and play our part within Your Majesty's Empire.' He sent a second message to Winston Churchill, promising him undying gratitude for his inspired leadership, which had brought victory in Europe and the Liberation of the Channel Islands. The people of Jersey, he said, 'will ever remember your affectionate reference to "our dear Channel Islands"'.

Sark was not liberated until 10 May, when three British officers arrived on the island and asked Sybil Hathaway, the Dame, if she would mind being left in charge of the 275 Germans on Sark until some troops could be spared; she remained in command until 17 May. Alderney was one of the last places in Europe to be liberated: on 16 May its three thousand-strong garrison was taken off to PoW camps in Britain.

After Churchill's speech on 8 May, Jersey factory girl Stella Perkins remembers: 'It was a crazy mood, absolutely crazy. People were suddenly bringing outlandish old radios out of hiding and putting them on their windowsills. There was loud music everywhere. Everybody was shouting and dancing.' Cars and motorcycles hidden from the Germans for five years were unearthed from haystacks and barns. For the first time since the beginning of the Occupation, people could discuss the news openly in the street without fear of eavesdroppers. The curfew and the blackout were ignored as parties went on late into the night with the few bottles saved for this occasion.

In the following days, crowds gathered in St Helier and St Peter Port to greet the British troops as they began to stream off the landing craft with their vehicles and supplies. There was a happiness bordering on hysteria as islanders recognised friends and relations among the soldiers and hugged them in the street, weeping with delight. Leslie Sinel wrote on 12 May: 'More and more men arrived all day, and these received a great welcome – everyone cheered, children clamoured for autographs, and the soldiers and sailors were very generous in showering chocolate, sweets and cigarettes on new-made friends. Many Jerseymen were in the [landing] parties and these received a special welcome, news of relatives on the mainland was sought by all.'

The photographs of the Liberation capture the intensity of emotion. Crowds of people lined the streets in their Sunday clothes, with ear-to-ear grins. The British soldiers had done nothing more than sail across the Channel, and they looked rather abashed as they were treated to a hero's welcome.

Guernsey housewife Daphne Prins got her grandmother's crinoline out of the attic and made a jacket out of a velvet curtain for the Liberation balls with the British officers. Twenty-year-old Jersey nurse Betty Thurban looked up from her work for virtually the first time in her working life and enjoyed herself: 'At the Liberation, there were lots of dances – it was very exciting, meeting all these Englishmen whom you would never have dreamed of meeting. I married an officer in the Liberation Force and went back to England with him.' She was one of many Liberation brides on the islands.

Eighteen-year-old Herbert Nichols was working at a Guernsey newspaper, the *Star*, and on Liberation day he worked round the clock to print the papers with the new orders. It was an exhausting and exhilarating twenty-four hours: 'There were soldiers swarming all over St Peter Port. I brought home tins of food, tea and sugar that day. I traded a German dagger for five hundred Pall Mall cigarettes.'

For the thirty-six thousand German soldiers on the islands, their world had fallen apart. Leutnant Randolf Kugler stood at the window of a house in St Helier and watched the first British ships arrive:

An elderly man was standing next to me and he was crying his eyes out. He had already been through the First World War. I was drunk. The night before we heard about the surrender, we had gathered together all the alcohol we could find and drank it to kill off the pain, anger and frustration. We all got drunk. For a soldier's heart, it was difficult to accept that the British ships were no longer to be shot at. I had shot down thirty planes in my career; it had become a sport, it was either them or us.

Seaman Willi Reiman: 'When the war ended, my whole dream collapsed. Everything was finished; all my plans were over, and I thought we must start again.' Immediately after the surrender, said Reiman, the starving soldiers stormed the army food stores. They could not believe their eyes when they found tins of pork stacked high. They ate so quickly that they became sick, as their stomachs were unused to such rich food.

Within a few days of Liberation, the first consignments of German prisoners of war were being loaded onto ships to be taken to Britain. Islanders gathered to watch them lining up to board the ships; many could not help but feel some sympathy for the soldiers. Even Kathleen Whitley, who had served seven months in Caen prison for painting V-signs, felt pity rather than triumph: 'They looked so dejected and so bowed down, I felt sorry for them.'

Kapitän Willi Hagedorne said: 'Islanders thanked me and said that I must understand that they were glad to have the Tommies back. Everyone was shaking Befehlshaber Admiral Hüffmeier's hand and thanking him for his fair treatment of the islands.'

Many islanders raided deserted German billets for souvenirs such as helmets, rifles, belts and uniforms. The abandoned gun emplacements, tunnels, bunkers and batteries were a child's dream. Having watched the Germans playing with these toys of war for five years, there was nothing now to stop the children from having their turn. Tragically, there were cases of children being badly injured in the days after the Liberation by mines or hand grenades. Herbert Nichols: 'The islands were covered in guns and live ammunition. We had a month firing live rounds out to sea until the British cleared everything up. We used to throw hand grenades around the beach. Several children were badly hurt when they tried to tow a rubber dinghy which had been booby trapped.'

Over the next few months more than twenty thousand Germans were taken to PoW camps all over England, from Cornwall to Northumberland. Most of them had three years of imprisonment ahead of them, working on English farms, before they were allowed to return to Germany. Just over three thousand were kept back to help clear the thousands of mines and dismantle the anti-tank girders on the beaches and the paraphernalia of defence equipment which had accumulated on the islands. The task of clearing the mines on Jersey was immeasurably eased by the refusal of Leutnant Johannes Kegelman to destroy the mines maps prior to the Liberation.

The King and Queen visited Jersey and Guernsey on 7 June, and received a delighted welcome. The roads were lined with islanders waving home-made Union Jacks. For many who had listened to the King's hesitant voice for the last five Christmas broadcasts over their crystal sets, it was a dream come true to glimpse the couple as they swept by in their car.

But the air of festivity struck a sharply discordant note with some islanders. Dolly Joanknecht was eight months pregnant by her German boyfriend, Willi. While everyone was celebrating, her mind was a tumult of anxiety and worries as she and Willi faced the possibility they would be separated for several years, and Dolly would have the burden of bringing up their child alone. Willi managed to stay on Guernsey for a year by volunteering for a clearing-up party, but contact was difficult, and at times impossible. Dolly remembered:

> Immediately after Liberation, Willi came up the road to say goodbye to me, and a couple of people in our street ran out and gave him a food parcel of bread and jam. I said, 'Let me hide you in the wardrobe, stay here.' But he said he had to go, and I remember his footsteps going away.
>
> What hurt me was that everyone was thrilled that the war was over, and they never took my feelings into account. I was lonely; Willi had gone. I was pleased because my mum, brothers and sisters were coming home. But I didn't know what was going to happen. Willi wrote me these lovely letters – he was so romantic.
>
> I had a friend who also had a German boyfriend, Hans, and the two Germans planned to come and visit us for a night. We went down to the town and sat on the steps by the harbour front to wait for them.* We heard Willi and Hans paddling a small boat very quietly. Then we heard the British guard shout, 'Stop! Come here!' A British officer came out of the nearby Crown Hotel, and asked,

---

* Willi and Hans, with other members of the clearing-up party, were being held on a British ship moored off St Peter Port.

'What's going on here?' in a very snooty accent. Willi replied that they were just going for a row, and the officer shouted at them that they must go back to the boat.

A couple of nights later in June 1945, just before I had the baby, I was asleep and I woke to hear footsteps. The door opened and there was Willi. I was so pleased to see him. He stayed the night and we made lots of plans. Hans and Willi had paddled over in a boat, and the plan was for them to meet up to go back before dawn. But when Willi got there, the boat had gone, so he came back to me. Several of the neighbours knew Willi was here, but no one let on. He stayed with me two days and we went down to the town where lots of people saw us and recognised Willi, but they never told on us. The next day I went down with him to the harbour to get him back on his boat. We couldn't decide what to do. I said to Willi, 'Come on,' and I marched up to the British guard with my huge stomach out in front of me and I said, 'Excuse me, guard, my husband is Dutch, and he wants to get on that boat.'

The guard said, 'If he wants to get on that boat, what's stopping him?' When Willi had walked through the barbed wire, the guard said, 'I knew he was German because someone just told me.'

I hadn't seen Willi for several weeks when Aunty spotted him and rushed over to give him a huge kiss. The English officer barked out, 'No fraternising!'

One night Hans went back to visit his girlfriend but Willi wouldn't join him. He was caught and the girl was put in prison for harbouring him.

Dolly had her baby, a boy, whom she named Anthony – after Antonia, the Frenchwoman who had saved her life in prison in France.

I wrote to the British commandant on Guernsey asking if Willi could come and see his baby. I had a letter, I can't remember the exact words, but it was something to do with the Geneva Convention and he just couldn't allow it.

When Willi was moved to a boat for the PoWs in the harbour I used to visit him every day. I would hold Tony up to show Willi. We couldn't talk because he was across a stretch of water. When Tony was just over two months, I took him up to Fort George where Willi was imprisoned then, and he held him for the first time.

Dolly and Willi's relationship was to survive, but Liberation spelt an abrupt end to many a genuine love affair. The departing Germans often had no chance to say goodbye to girlfriends of three or four years' standing, and hearts were left broken.

Willi Reiman remembered that many German soldiers disappeared from their camps to seek shelter with their island girlfriends. The German PoWs called it 'cutting under', an expression normally used of submarines when they disappeared beneath the water. British newspaper reports estimated that up to fifty Germans were being hidden by islanders. In June the *Daily Mirror* reported that a policeman who had noticed two girls carrying parcels every day had followed them and found two members of the Wehrmacht, whom he arrested. In a report to the British government on 30 May, Brigadier Snow cited as his main concern the problem of flushing out escaped Germans: 'There are strong suspicions that ... there are enemy personnel secreted amongst the islanders, and in the near future will arise the task, with the co-operation of the island governments and police forces, of combing the islands in a systematic search.'

Snow voiced his fear that the island governments might not be able to face the unpopularity of organising such a step, and said it would be deeply resented if the army undertook to search the islanders' homes. In the event, either the Germans eventually gave themselves in, or they were found by the British army; there is no evidence that any managed to evade the PoW camps in the end.

If a German boyfriend could not get out of his camp, the alternative was for his girlfriend to go and visit him. Leutnant Randolf Kugler has a vivid memory of the days immediately after Liberation on Jersey:

> We were rounded up and I was appointed as one of the guards for night duty. One night I heard an argument in the dormitory so I went to investigate. It was between the old men who wanted to sleep and the young men who had smuggled their girlfriends in. I settled it by telling all the young men and their girls to go into the next-door stables where there was nothing but straw to sleep on.
>
> All sorts of civilians were coming in and out of the German camps, so the British gave the German guards their pistols back to keep the civilians out and enforce the ban on fraternisation.

Once the Germans were in prisoner of war camps in Britain, the chances of keeping in touch were small. Few island girls knew which camp their boyfriends were in, and any letters they did send were intercepted by Postal Censorship and destroyed.

Randolf Kugler lost contact with his girlfriend, Colette:

I had a serious relationship. We were still together after the surrender when I was a PoW. It eventually faded because it was so hard for us to communicate. No correspondence was allowed between the islands and the camps in Britain. To avoid this we used to send letters via Switzerland and use code words to avoid the censors.

Colette probably met someone else and I became unimportant. At the PoW camps we got Channel Island newspapers and we used to read the section of 'family news' with the birth announcements, which for nine months after we left was very long.

Postal Censorship, which intercepted the letters between the islands and German PoW camps, compiled a report on 133 letters written in the first few months after Liberation. They make poignant reading. The names of the islanders have been heavily obscured with black ink.

In August 1945 a Guernseywoman wrote to Leutnant Hans Taubert: 'I do not know how to start this letter or if it will ever get to you . . . Your son has grown since you last saw him and now weighs sixteen pounds.'

Another island woman wrote of 'little Koni who can walk with the aid of a chair'. Another wrote to a German PoW to ask if his feelings were still the same. A letter addressed to Heinrich Muller was full of gossip, and referred to several German friends:

I am pleased you have seen Hermann. Here we think of you every day and the promises we made which I shall always keep. I have not changed my mind, and never will . . . Please tell Horst to write and that his girl also keeps his promises . . . we send our greetings to you, and all the comrades . . . I hope to hear from Hermann – perhaps I will have a letter from him. Do you know Feldwebel Peter Huppertz? Violet sends her love and best greetings to him and Oberfeldwebel Bruno Amling Sanitaat, his girl sends love and greetings . . . Well, my dear Henry . . . Greetings to Staba Geffoiter

Alfons Krauer from [censored name] with all her love. The ring is now smaller and I wear it now and for ever.

Several letters from islanders were written in German.

The German PoWs' letters far outnumbered those of the islanders. They asked for news, sent best wishes; one wrote that he was 'homesick' for Jersey, another thanked 'dearest' for 'your kindness all the time I spend [sic] in Guernsey', and another wrote of his 'wonderful time' on Jersey. One letter from PoW Dr Walter Lorenz was accompanied by a note, presumably to the censors, from his British camp commandant: 'He appears to be on friendly terms with various prominent residents in the Channel Islands.'

Most of the letters were marked 'condemned', and the War Office noted that they had been destroyed. Only the passages quoted in the censorship reports have survived. The War Office also compiled lists of those islanders who had written to German PoWs in June and July.

Dolly and Willi Joanknecht were lucky. Willi had managed to get hold of some British stamps, which he used to send letters secretly to Dolly from his PoW camp in Devon. In May 1947 twenty-two-year-old Dolly picked up two-year-old Tony and set off, with virtually no money, to join Willi. They were finally married in August of that year; the first Anglo–German marriage after the war, they were told. Willi was still a PoW and was not allowed to wear a shirt and tie; he attended the wedding in his overcoat. The next few years were a struggle. Dolly found a job near Willi, and the toddler Tony spent half his time in the PoW camp. In 1948 the young family tried to return to Guernsey, but Willi was refused a work permit – this policy was subsequently relaxed for other Germans married to islanders. More babies arrived in quick succession and Dolly and Willi did not have the money to go to Germany. It was not until 1967, nearly thirty years after he had left his home, that Willi returned to visit his family. He was the only boy in his street to have survived the war.

Another Jersey girl, Pearl, was as determined as Dolly to be reunited with her German fiancé. It took her two years to find him. He had not had time to say goodbye and she did not know to which PoW camp he had been sent. She applied to all the authorities, but no one would tell her how she could trace him or where to send letters. She did not hear a word from him, but 'there was no question that he would not want a letter from me, no question of that at all. That was one thing I was sure about.' In the end the Quakers helped her find him. After he was released they were married, and Pearl accompanied him back to Germany, where she has lived ever since. In Pearl's view, the Occupation was not a difficult time. Life was quiet, and her relationship with her German boyfriend was no cause for comment. It was only after Liberation, she said, that her whole world was turned upside down.

Dolly and Pearl required remarkable perseverance not only to find their boyfriends, but to stick with them through the difficulties which followed the war. Pearl had chosen to live in Germany, a foreign country which, in the immediate aftermath of the war, was painfully rebuilding its shattered economy. It was a hard struggle to start a life for herself and her husband; now after more than forty years, she has grown so accustomed to her adopted country that she stumbles to remember her English.

After Liberation, women who had fallen in love with Germans had to face open condemnation for the first time. Hatred and resentment against fraternisers, which islanders had hidden for fear of the Germans, now broke out into the open. Even harsher were the judgements of the British press and the islanders who had been evacuated to Britain during the war. Five years of wartime propaganda had maintained that fraternising was un-British behaviour. Islanders returned from having served in the British forces – husbands, brothers and fathers – to find illegitimate children fathered by Germans in their families, and joined the chorus of condemnation and rumours. For the first time girls like Dolly Joanknecht were forced to feel bitterly ashamed of what they had done. Dolly remembers seeing the word 'jerrybag' in a British newspaper:

When I first saw that word I felt dirty, as if I'd done something wrong – and I knew I hadn't. Nobody had ever called me a jerrybag before, nobody.

Willi had written my mother a letter in very broken English saying how much he loved me and that he would never forsake me. She was touched and kept the letter all her life. My brother Georgie, who had been in the forces, never criticised me for having fallen in love with a German. But my brother-in-law was different; he had been in the British Navy. One evening he came to where I was living with my mother after I'd had my baby, and he said to me, 'I've decided you're not having this baby. I'm taking it.' He grabbed Tony. 'You can't do that,' I cried. 'I can. You're not worthy of him.' I grabbed Tony and ran up to my aunt's.

I lost one friend because of Willi. Sylvia had been my best friend. We had been very close from when we were tiny right up to the day of evacuation. We used to sleep together and do everything together. When she came back from Britain, she completely ignored me. I thought, well, if that is the way she wants it . . . but in fact I really wanted to talk to her.

Dolly Joanknecht was fortunate; the few harsh words she experienced were little in comparison with the humiliation and violence that some women on Jersey experienced immediately after Liberation. The Home Office had briefed the Liberation Force that there could be violence against female fraternisers. In 1944 the future Lieutenant Governors of the islands were told: 'The relationship between German soldiers and some island women was of such a nature as to be a potential menace to future public order.'

Military intelligence summaries of interviews with escapee islanders in 1944 had reported that they believed 'feeling in the island [Jersey] is so strong that the girls will find that certain groups of people will probably round them up, shave their heads and treat them as similar girls have been treated in France'. British soldiers had to intervene on a number of occasions to protect women. On one occasion they rescued a girl who had been thrown into the harbour in St Helier by a mob; the Jersey police had failed to intervene. Joe Miere was in a street in St Helier with some of his friends a few days after Liberation:

There was a gang with a flag singing and they grabbed a girl. We told them to pack it in. They called us 'Jerryites' but none of them had done anything during the war to resist the Germans. Then this girl came running past us with blood pouring from her head; she was as naked as the day she was born with blood streaming from where the scissors must have dug in. She was shivering and hysterical so I gave her my old raincoat to cover her up. I never did get it back.

Jersey factory girl Stella Perkins joined other rebellious teenagers daubing swastikas on the houses of women she had seen fraternising with Germans in the last months of the Occupation, but her attitude changed when she watched a horrifying spectacle from the window of her home shortly after Liberation:

> This poor soul had been described as a jerrybag, and I saw her being chased by this mob of people. She was in a terrible state. She was running and crying and falling, getting up, and crying and running, and screaming and falling again. She disappeared out of my view down the hill, and all these people went after her. I never knew what happened to her, but I began to have after-thoughts about what I'd done, putting swastikas on people's homes. I began to think, well, perhaps the woman was just short of money, or needed someone to love her, and she's only a woman after all.

Jersey boy Maurice Green was in hospital when a girl who had had a baby by a German was brought in after having been covered in a tar-like substance and feathered. He claims he knew of another girl who was nailed to a tree by her hands; she survived and later married her German boyfriend. Another girl had a rag doused in petrol stuffed between her legs.

Leutnant Johannes Kegelman was imprisoned in the Pomme d'Or hotel in St Helier, and saw a girl being attacked by a mob: 'I saw someone whom I think was a girl being attacked. There was a crowd around her shouting "Jerrybag, jerrybag." They were hitting her and when the girl ran, the crowd chased her.'

Jersey farmer's daughter Dorothy Blackwell saw how a girl was treated after she had been caught giving cigarettes to some German PoWs. Her hair was cut off and her jumper was hung on the barbed wire fence around the PoW camp. She said of the girl's treatment: 'I don't think it worried us at all.'

On 15 May, a week after VE Day, *The Times* and the *Daily Mirror* reported that eight hundred Jerseywomen had had children by German soldiers. The reports pointed out that under Jersey law, if the mothers were married their husbands had a legal responsibility for the child's maintenance, regardless of whether or not they had fathered it, and there was no divorce law. The papers raised the prospect of returning British servicemen being saddled with the legal responsibility of bringing up German-fathered babies. 'The English papers ... were quite nauseating on the subject and lowered the opinion of the British press held by this small part of the Empire in no uncertain fashion,' commented the Liberation Force's Civil Affairs Unit in a report to the Home Office.

It provoked real antagonism amongst islanders when girls who had been having affairs with Germans effortlessly switched their attentions to British soldiers. Jersey girl Mary McCarthy bumped into a friend who had been closely associated with two of the top German officers. 'A month after the war ended, she was out riding with a British officer. I said to him, "Do you know she's the biggest jerrybag?" He said, "Shut your bloody mouth." I was furious. I nearly pushed him off his horse. Being patriotic doesn't pay.'

It was not only women who were the targets of an upsurge of anger in the months before and after Liberation. All those who had collaborated – or were suspected of collaborating – with the Germans, particularly on Jersey, found themselves the object of violent attacks. Maurice Green remembers that the shop windows of a stamp dealer who had a German wife were smashed. Jersey teenager Joe Miere threw a home-made bomb through the windows of a shop belonging to a family who had entertained 'the worst kind of Germans – rough Organisation Todt types with swastika armbands'.

Many companies dismissed workers who had been employed by the Germans and girls who had fraternised, and the Jersey Attorney-General said that the States could dismiss employees on such grounds if they saw fit. One court case reflected official attitudes; a man who had worked for the Germans had been insulted, but he was told by the magistrate that 'no one was forced to work for the Germans; no true Britisher would work for them'. The island authorities were playing a different tune now.

Questions still hang over the disappearance of many well-known collaborators and informers from Jersey in the month after Liberation. It is rumoured that about fifty of the island's worst collaborators were taken to England in a secret operation organised by

British intelligence in a bid to defuse public unrest. Joe Miere: 'The British took a shipload of collaborators to England. I only discovered last year [1992] what happened to them. They were released in Britain. They were an embarrassment to the British government. The daughter of one of those who had been taken off the island came and told me.'

Islanders remember that passages to England were strictly controlled. Mary McCarthy and her new husband were trying to get a boat to England for their honeymoon at the time and were refused permission, but several of her contemporaries managed to leave for England in those weeks.

There is no surviving documentary evidence to substantiate these stories, but considering how worried the Liberation Force commander, Brigadier Snow, was by the disquiet on Jersey, such an operation is not unlikely.

A number of families on Jersey fled to the local prison for their protection. The case of the infamous 'Mimi the spy', Mme Baudains, was reported in the *Jersey Evening Post*: 'On the day after the Liberation of the Island by the British Forces, Mrs Baudains, generally alleged to be Jersey's No. 1 Collaborator, went to the Police Station with her son and asked to be locked up for her own safety.' She and her son were held in Jersey prison until a convent on the island braved considerable criticism to shelter her. On 23 March 1946 they were put on a boat for England. The *Jersey Evening Post* reported: 'In order to avoid demonstrations of any kind, arrangements for her departure were kept a close secret and there were very few present on the Albert Pier at 6.15 a.m. . . . Mrs Baudains cast anxious looks out of the windows of the van and her relief was evident as she beheld so few present . . . Thus passed from Jersey a character for whose departure the Islanders will have no regrets.'

Those collaborators who remained on the islands astonished islanders with their sang-froid as they queued alongside everyone else at the bank to change their wartime black-market profits from Reichsmarks to sterling. The British government had set a generous exchange rate of 9.36 Reichsmarks to the pound for the islands as a step towards rehabilitating their economies; everywhere else in Europe, the Reichsmark's value had collapsed along with the Reich.

It angered islanders that there seemed to be no attempt to limit the amount of money people were changing, or to make a note of those who had unusually large amounts. Farmers were carrying tomato crates and potato barrels full of Reichsmarks to the banks. One Jersey bank clerk, outraged by the bags stuffed with German money that certain islanders who had traded with the Germans were asking him to change, drew up a list of their names. His sister remembers: 'He was told by one of the Liberation Force officers to tear the list up because Churchill had said that the British Empire was not to know about things like that.'

Collaborators and black marketeers appeared to be escaping the justice which islanders had waited five years to see dealt to them. On Guernsey, the people confined themselves to grumbling, but on Jersey the pent-up anger found an outlet in violence, and fuelled several protest and reform organisations.

One such organisation was the Jersey Loyalists, who were formed to press for a court of inquiry to investigate collaborators and black marketeers and for the public condemnation of fraternisers – the latter were judged 'so affected in health and perverted in mind by enemy propaganda as to render them dangerous to be allowed to mix with male British'. It counted among its members many army veterans and respected members of Jersey society.

The question of what was or was not collaboration had become a source of bitter dispute, and the Jersey Loyalists sought to clarify the matter in a petition to the Bailiff and the States of Jersey on 21 June 1945 which laid down what constituted 'acts of disloyalty or treason.' It included:

a) Engaging in the transportation to and from the island of enemy arms and ammunition, the discharge or embarkation of such, the transportation of the same within the island, and the construction of work of military importance.
b) Assisting the German authorities in their attempts to coerce the inhabitants by acting as informers.
c) Sustaining the morale and the physical well-being of the enemy armed forces by selling to them, by means of 'black market' trading, food and/or other articles which should have been sold to their fellow-islanders who were sorely in need.

d) Consorting, and in certain cases cohabiting, by women with members of the German forces, and some while in receipt of allowances made to them by HM Government on behalf of husbands serving in the British Forces.

e) Engaging voluntarily in work for the enemy, and this particularly when done by men receiving allowances or pensions from HM Government.

f) Entertaining in their own homes, by local residents, of officers and men of the armed forces of a nation with which their own country was at war.

According to these definitions of collaboration, a large proportion of the islanders would have been guilty. Not surprisingly, the Jersey Loyalists' demand for a court of inquiry which would investigate cases and publish its findings was rejected. The Loyalists had envisaged publication of the victims' collaboration, and their resultant social ostracism, as punishment. The States set up its own secret committee of inquiry, but its decision to take no action did not satisfy the Loyalists, who were still trying to get their court of inquiry in March 1946.

Jersey clerk Arthur Kent was one of those who had begun organising to bring the guilty to justice before Liberation:

> We tried to get evidence of people who were collaborating so that in the euphoria of Liberation these people would not be forgotten. When Liberation came, I was given the job of writing to the local newspaper denouncing people. There was one person who threatened a libel action, but it never came to that. One day, I got a letter which contained a revolver bullet and a letter in German. I took the letter to a friend who was in military intelligence; it was a threat against my life unless I stopped denouncing people.

The feeling against collaborators also fuelled the left-leaning Jersey Democratic Movement (JDM), which argued that the maladministration of the Occupation, and the fact that collaborators were not being investigated, was evidence of the need for far-reaching constitutional reform. On 18 June the JDM held an open-air meeting attended by two thousand people, and sent a resolution to the

Bailiff demanding increases in the wages of the working classes. This was followed by another meeting on 1 August at which a resolution was drafted demanding drastic and immediate constitutional changes; a petition was presented criticising the island's electoral law.* Brigadier Snow, Commander of the Liberation Force, was perturbed by the agitation on Jersey, and sent reports to the War Office throughout the summer of 1945 urging that no troops be withdrawn from the island in case they were needed to deal with unrest:

> There is considerable evidence that amongst the population that remained [during the Occupation] ... there is growing discontent with the previous somewhat archaic and undemocratic form of government on the islands. Having experienced a more modern form of government in the UK ... it appears that the returning evacuees may well add to the numbers of those who are not content with the islands' form of government. This unpopularity [could] produce a situation in which the civil government is paralysed, even temporarily, as for instance a general strike.

Feelings were running high. Fantastic rumours, accusations and allegations were being bandied about. For many years, people had not dared to talk. Now their tongues were loosened, and the stored-up resentment against those who had done well out of the Occupation was released. It was particularly embarrassing for the Liberation Force and the Home Office, who could not be seen to treat the islands differently, that there was significantly more unrest on Jersey than on Guernsey, which was curiously calm. Perhaps this was in part attributable to Guernsey's more deferential, traditional culture, which lacked the dissidents needed to provide leadership for protest movements.

Into this maelstrom returned the evacuees from Britain, the deportees from German internment camps and the former servicemen from the British Forces. Many of them were horrified to find their homes stripped of all their belongings – even doors,

* The JDM gathered significant support, and by the end of the 1940s constitutional reforms had been passed as a result of popular pressure on the islands and the influence of the British government. On both Jersey and Guernsey the number of elected Deputies was increased, strengthening the democratic element of the islands' ancient constitutions.

banisters and floorboards had been ripped out for firewood. Their furniture, they were outraged to see, was in the living rooms of their neighbours. James Ryan returned to Guernsey from serving in the forces to find: 'The islanders who stayed behind had got all the best jobs, and they just didn't want to know about us. They'd been on the other side.'

On Alderney, Daphne Pope and her family, who had remained on the islands, were viewed with suspicion by returning islanders: 'They disliked us. They had been told to go to England, or they would lose their lives. So they left their properties, suffered all sorts of misfortunes, and when they got back they found their property in ruins. The only houses which were all right were the ones where the civilians had remained. And there we were, alive and healthy. The ones who went called the ones who stayed collaborators, and the ones who stayed called the ones who went cowards.'

Jersey teenager Bernard Hassall: 'After the war, civilians came back, asking, "Where is my furniture? I left my house locked up." Whatever we had done for them, they weren't thankful. The claws came out: what happened to this or that? they wanted to know. To me, the evacuees were a pack of aliens; they criticised everything. There was a lot of quick condemnation on the islands and it was impossible to clear one's name. The division between those who had been evacuated and those who stayed went on for a while.'

The Sherwill family was reunited: Ambrose Sherwill was repatriated from the German internment camp in June 1945, and the three eldest children came back from England, where they had served in the forces. Rollo, his older brother Jolyon and their mother May had remained on Guernsey throughout the Occupation. Rollo: 'During the war we were always battling for something, for some food which might become available or for some other advantage. When my brothers and sister came back at the end of the war, they thought we were little brats who didn't know anything. There was a gap – a lack of communication. People who came back after the war were totally critical of those who had stayed behind. It was understandable; they had been fighting the enemy we had been fraternising with.'

*   *   *

Reporters from the major British newspapers accompanied the Liberation Force onto the islands. Initially, the press saw the Liberation as an occasion for stirring editorials celebrating the fruits of victory. (On 7 May 1945, without even the grace of an intervening edition, the *Guernsey Evening Press* switched from trumpeting Germany's victories and predicting Britain's inevitable and imminent collapse to celebrating the end of the Occupation and offering elaborate expressions of thanks and loyalty to the Crown and Winston Churchill.) But as the days went by, the reports turned disturbingly sour.

The Times marked the islands' Liberation with an editorial which encompassed every point of contention and took a delicately conciliatory line: 'The islands have suffered greatly, but they have not been turned into battlefields and their freedom has been restored without bloodshed. The police tyranny of the years of occupation has left behind it bitter memories . . . and hunger. Because those who left have taken their full part in the war, because those who remained endured and kept their hope, the liberation of the islands is one of the sweetest fruits of victory.'

The Times and the *Manchester Guardian* carefully avoided any references to collaboration, and emphasised the suffering of the islanders, but they did report on 19 May that an investigation had been set up into the murder of 1000–1200 Russians and Jews on Alderney. They interviewed Daphne Pope's husband George, who showed them 'a secret chronicle which he said recorded over a thousand deaths'.

The popular newspapers reported the growing unrest, and the collaboration and black marketeering which had provoked it, in more detail. On 14 May the *Daily Express* talked of 'an ugly black market which was run by collaborators who are now being rounded up', and quoted black-market prices of £3 for an ounce of home-made tobacco and £50 for a ton of wood. It continued:

Many collaborators need to be found. One called Pierre Laval, a rich farmer, is still being searched for by the police and military. Another is an Englishwoman who stamped on a Union Jack in public. About twelve women on Jersey have been dealt with by the people. One was thrown in the harbour, others were tied to railings. Swastikas were painted on some of the houses with the names of the

women underneath. Yet most of the population of Jersey put up a
tremendous fight against the Nazis even when rations were low.

On 15 May the *Express* reported on Jersey's resistance movement,
which had been planning an insurrection since the beginning of
the month, and which had a secret headquarters stocked with
weapons and canoes. On 11 June the *Express* reported a clampdown
on black marketeers (it was by then too late, since islanders had
been allowed to change Reichsmarks into sterling between 16 and
23 May), with laws restricting the amount of money which could
be sent out of the island and proposals for an Excess Profits Tax
of 80 per cent: 'One man who is said to have made £50,000 out of
the occupation is now having to account for all his income and
expenditure.' The report went on to say that there was considerable
confusion about the tax.

On 24 July the *Express* asked: 'How are we going to prove to the
men and women of the Channel Islands that it is better to live
under loyalty to Britain than under occupation to Hitler and the
Nazis when islanders were paid such good wages by the Germans?'
The paper went on to claim that seven out of ten islanders had
refused to take jobs with the Germans, adding that 'fathers of two
or more children who worked for the Germans are exempt from
criticism, as the choice was too much – a choice of working for the
Germans, or seeing their children die'.

The *Express* also commented that the black market had changed
the islands' social structure: a farm labourer who had a patch of
land to cultivate was wealthier with his half-sack of potatoes than
the richest tax exile millionaire.

On 15 May the *Daily Herald* reported the story of Lucille Schwab
and Suzanne Malherbe, who had been arrested in July 1944 and
sentenced to death for urging German soldiers to mutiny. The
story satisfied British readers' appetites for tales of brave resistance
against the Germans, but thereafter the *Herald*'s coverage changed.
On 7 June it reported: 'In Jersey there is a lack of interest on the
part of the authorities in those islanders who worked with Nazis
who informed against loyal subjects, and who got people sent to
concentration camps, and who have more money in their pockets
due to collaboration. Several underground organisations such as

the Jersey Loyalists and the Jersey Auxiliary Legion have banded together and are planning to petition the States arguing for a special tribunal to be set up without delay.'

By July, the *Herald* was predicting riots: 'Many believe that but for the military, there would already have been open revolt. [There is] grave concern about what will happen when the military go.' The paper ran a sequence of stories on the growing pressure for political reform and justice for informers, commenting: 'In the early days of liberation, many demanded that all collaborators should be punished. Yet now, feeling has crystallised against informers whose activities resulted in people being punished, deported and losing their lives, and black marketeers.'

Under the headline 'Collaborators Get Off Scot-Free' the *Herald* wrote: 'Indignation is as high against collaborators in the Channel Islands as it is in the rest of occupied Europe . . . Some of the cases were as bad as anything brought to my notice in France, Belgium or Holland.'

The most critical reports were in the Communist paper the *Daily Worker*. One headline ran: 'Did or Did Not the Administration Select Men for Deportation to Germany? Did They Not Put Anti-Semitic Laws on the Statute Books of the Islands? We Have a Right to Know'.

On 13 July, the *Daily Worker* revealed that Jersey people had assisted the Germans in deporting Jews, and demanded: 'Is this conduct to go down in the history books unrebuked as a sample of the behaviour that should be observed when British territory is occupied by an enemy?'

'War Office Whitewashes Jersey Authorities', ran the headline of an article reporting that a large number of islanders had worked for the Germans and covering the emergence of the Jersey Democratic Movement. An editorial two months after Liberation said: 'Those whose slogan during the Occupation was, "don't do anything to annoy the Germans" are still holding the same positions in high office, yet these collaborators discouraged resistance such as V-signs.'

Stung by these comments, the Ministry of Information issued a statement on behalf of the War Office on 19 July, saying that collaboration was 'almost impossible to avoid' and dismissing the majority of allegations as mere rumour. It declared: 'The Civil Affairs Unit [of the Liberation Force] is only concerned with those against whom it is possible that a charge of treason or treachery could be brought. Public safety officers of the Civil Affairs Unit are, in close association with local police, sorting out the very few solid facts from the froth of gossip.'

There was another story of Liberation which was very different from the mixture of elation and thirst for justice which characterised the islanders' experience. The freeing of many of the islands' slave labourers proved a far more painful and protracted process.

By D-Day, 6 June 1944, most of the labourers had already been moved from the islands back to France after the bulk of the fortification work had been completed. Shortly after D-Day, SS Baubrigade I and most of the remaining OT workers were evacuated to work on sites in Belgium. A few hundred Russians, Ukrainians, North Africans and Spanish Republicans were left on the islands after all shipping links with the Continent had been severed, and they remained there until they were liberated by the British in May 1945. Most of the Spanish Republicans were sent back to France, although a few stayed on the islands and married local women. The Eastern Europeans were taken to a PoW camp near Guildford, from where they were eventually repatriated either by boat from Liverpool or by train across Europe.

By 1943 Georgi Kondakov, Kirill Nevrov, Ivan Kalganov, Alexei Ikonnikov and Albert Pothugine found themselves in French labour camps, where conditions were significantly better than they had been on Alderney. In the weeks preceding D-Day Allied bombing raids on France intensified, and in the course of the bombing many of the forced labourers were able to escape from their camps.

Escaped Russian slave labourers stayed together in small groups. Understanding neither the language nor the country, the France they describe was a bewildering place. The Vichy government's authority was crumbling and everywhere there was the chaos of war. Bands of outlaws, bandits and resistance fighters lived a hand-to-mouth existence in the burnt-out cellars of half-abandoned bombed towns. The Russians' primary purpose was to find, beg or steal food. They found themselves on the fringes of the French resistance, and were sometimes caught up in sabotage and ambushes in what Kondakov described as 'a mad, stupid war of a revolver and a few hand grenades against tanks'. But, he added, 'we were in high spirits and could have sacrificed anything for victory'. These young Russians had nothing to lose.

Kondakov subsequently joined the Forces Françaises de l'Interieur and fought to liberate the town of Pierrefitte in northern France, while his friend Kirill Nevrov found himself the pampered secret guest of wealthy Parisian Russian émigrés. Nevrov remembers:

> After Alderney I was moved to a camp near Cherbourg. In 1943, a friend stole something and hid it in my suitcase and I was caught. I was tried and sentenced to six months in a concentration camp near Metz, where I spent three months working on the Maginot Line. One day I was at Nancy railway station in a consignment of prisoners on our way to work when two trains came into the station at one platform, and the civilians got mixed up with the prisoners. Suddenly I felt someone throw a coat over my striped clothes and push me under a carriage. The stranger, who was a Frenchman, and I crawled under the train and up onto the other side of the station, where we jumped into the first train. The man hid me under a bench; I had no idea what was going on. When he lit a cigarette, I could see his hands shaking. Eighty kilometres later, a woman got on, and I heard her talk to the man about a '*Russe Sovietique*'. When we arrived in Paris they took me to the boiler-room of the station, and found me one of the boilermen's overalls to wear. The woman then took me to a flat.

After a few weeks, Nevrov was moved to the home of a Russian émigré named Alexander and his French wife Marie José. For about a year, the couple hid Nevrov in their five-storey house in German-occupied Paris. They insisted he learn French and how to use cutlery properly. He drank fine wines, and was told that only horses drink water. As well as their Parisian house, the couple had a country estate. They provided Nevrov with more clothes than he

had ever had in his life – or has had since: 'Marie José treated me
like the son she had never managed to have. She kissed me and
caressed me, and I called her mother. Every weekend she gave me
a one hundred franc note and I travelled all over Paris. You can
imagine how I felt to be living in this house in Paris after the camps;
there were soft pillows, sheets and blankets on my bed.'

The liberation of Paris in August 1944 was a heady experience.
Nevrov remembers the British and American soldiers handing out
whisky in tea mugs, and the streets full of people of every nationality
celebrating.

A Soviet assembly point was set up in Paris for the thousands of
Soviet citizens who wished to be repatriated. Georgi Kondakov
worked there and came into contact with many of the survivors of
Alderney, including Nevrov, whom he hadn't seen for two years.
These were intensely happy days; the taste of freedom was intoxicat-
ing. Kondakov had no money, but he walked all over Paris seeing
the sights, visiting cinemas and museums, his eyes wide with wonder
at his first experience of a capital city.

But the two Russians were homesick, and as soon as the war was
over they made preparations to go home. Nevrov's adopted parents
were heartbroken; they had become deeply attached to this kind boy
with wavy blond hair and full lips, and they had procured for him a
Swiss passport and a new identity, as Robin Pierre. But Nevrov would
not be dissuaded. He and Kondakov were flown by American plane
to Leipzig, then taken by truck to Torgau in eastern Germany, on
the border of the Soviet zone of occupation. Kondakov:

> There was a brass band to greet us at the border. It was comical, its
> members were shabby and poorly dressed. There was an ancient
> castle there and I remember they were throwing the old books out
> of the windows and ripping them up to make beds. I had in my
> hands a book printed in 1578.
> We then had to march to Elsterwerda. It was a long way and the
> whole route was scattered with clothing people had discarded. Kirill
> had three suits and twelve ties, but he threw all of them away because
> we were so tired and we were told we were going to have to walk
> all the way to the Soviet border. A lot of people were being robbed
> by soldiers from the Red Army anyway. We walked for three or four
> days.

At Elstewerda our documents, photos and certificates stating that we had fought in the French resistance were taken away from us by the Soviet authorities. They were kept in the KGB archives until 1986. We walked on to Görlitz on the German–Polish border [about seventy-five miles]. We formed part of a column of 13,500 people, most of whom were women, children and old men. My friends and I were given arms to protect the column from bandits. There was a column ahead of us of about the same size which was attacked by robbers and many people were killed.

We were taken across Poland by lorries and arrived in Ukraine near Lvov. From there we found a train to Bryansk which took us very slowly back to Orel.

Orel had been reduced to rubble. I was walking back to my village when I bumped into two women I knew; they told me my brother had been killed, my home burnt and my father was dying. I sat down and wept.

Kondakov reached his village late at night and fell asleep in a neighbour's shelter. In the morning his mother found him asleep. At the memory, Kondakov's hands trembled and he tried to laugh, but he was crying: 'My family were living in a makeshift shelter – a hole in the ground – and my father was dying. He had fallen ill on the front in the marshes of Belorussia and had been in hospital. A week after my return he died, and I tried to find the wood to make a coffin to bury him in. I had to beg for the nails.'

Both Kondakov and Nevrov had to register with the KGB immediately on their return. As 'repatriates' they were under suspicion of having volunteered to work for the Germans. Kondakov: 'I registered with the KGB the day after my return. The KGB mayor of my district accused me of collaborating with the Germans. I had one certificate left proving I had fought in the French Resistance. I had to go back to this mayor every day for questioning. I didn't go the day my father died, and for this I got into trouble and was refused permission to join the *kolkhoz*. I was given no documents to prove my identity, so it was hard to get work.'

Kondakov moved from place to place looking for a job. Eventually he returned to western Ukraine, tempted to escape to the West. He was accused of stealing and was sentenced to four and half years in a Stalinist concentration camp, building railways in Siberia. 'It was almost as bad as Alderney,' he says. 'There was more food, but I had to deal with the Arctic cold.'

Settling back into Orel was little easier for Kirill Nevrov:

> After the life I had had in Paris, Orel was hell; everything had been destroyed by the war. For eighteen months, I would burst into tears every night and soak my pillow with crying. For the first few months after my return I was questioned by the KGB, and they asked for all the names of the people I had met in France. At first, Kondakov and I were planning to go back to Paris, but then I got a job and I stopped thinking about France. Initially they didn't trust me at the plant where I worked, but I worked hard and proved myself.

Ivan Kalganov was with Kondakov in the French resistance and in Paris. He followed the same route back to Ukraine as Nevrov and Kondakov, marvelling at the shabby military band in Torgau and losing his documents in Elstewerda. But once back on Soviet territory, he was unlucky enough to be chosen for a labour battalion:

> We were taken to the Donbass coal region of the Ukraine to work as miners. I don't remember how long I worked there. I wanted to see my family because I had heard nothing from them for several years, so in 1946 I escaped and found my way home. No one in my family thought I was still alive; I found my mother chopping wood outside our home. I said 'Good morning' to her and she replied 'Good morning,' but carried on working; she didn't recognise me. My sisters travelled from where they were working to see me. Then a policeman came and took me away again, just like the Germans had done. I was sentenced to six years in prison according to Stalin's order of 1941 which forbade anyone to leave mines or plants voluntarily. I ended up serving two years in prisons in Rostov and in the mines in the Donbass. But at least we had enough bread to eat.

Another Alderney survivor, Alexander Rodine, heard in Germany that he was likely to be sent with a consignment to Kirov, Siberia, to cut wood:

> Some of us decided to escape. We managed to get all the way back to Orel from Germany via Kiev in Ukraine. We got into old oil barrels which had been loaded onto cargo trains. It took about three

months and we only had the food and drink which local people
gave us.

What was my family's reaction? I'm going to cry. When I at last
reached my home, I was so tired that I fell asleep in front of my
home – all the villages had been burnt so people were living underground in holes dug with their own hands. My mother found me
and woke me up; she had given up hope that I was still alive. I can't
find the words to describe her reaction.

There was a pause, then he resumed his story:

When I arrived back from Germany, right up until the death of
Stalin I had to go virtually every day to the KGB. Even at night,
people would come to question me. They were looking for an enemy
of the nation in my face.

All the former slave labourers faced the same kind of suspicion on
their return home. At each checkpoint, in Paris, Germany and on
the Soviet border, the Soviet authorities questioned them in order
to establish whether they were prisoners of war, or whether they
had been collaborators and volunteered to work for the Germans.
Both were crimes for which the punishment was severe – death or
labour camps. Stalin had decreed that members of the Red Army
could never surrender, but should use their last bullet on themselves
if necessary; no soldier had any justification for being taken as a
prisoner of war.

The Alderney survivors who are still alive today were too young
to be eligible for conscription in 1941, and could thus prove that
they had not surrendered. But they could never prove that they had
not volunteered to work for the Germans. They were stigmatised as
'repatriates', and their war record has dogged them all their lives.
Official forms such as applications for jobs, flats, benefits, even
consumer goods like telephones and fridges, required information
about the applicant's war service. Being a 'repatriate' ensured that
the Alderney survivors never had access to education or training,
and were not promoted in their work. Cities such as Moscow and
Kiev were 'closed' to repatriates, who were not entitled to the better
pensions, medical care, free transport and immense respect awarded
to 'war participants' in the Soviet system.

Alexei Ikonnikov:

In 1946 I arrived back in Orel. I had been questioned in Paris, and again in Germany at the checking point, and then by the KGB when I got home. They were looking for prisoners of war to put on trial. I had been with Georgi [Kondakov] in the French resistance until the liberation of France, but when I said on the forms that I had been in France during the war, no one believed me. They thought I had been in Germany. There was no chance of advancing in my career. I could only work as an unqualified worker, and I was a cinema projectionist all my life.

The Alderney survivors could not clear their reputations. No one believed their stories, so they stopped telling people what they had experienced. Even their own families were ashamed of them.

Albert Pothugine was fourteen when he was handed over to the Germans by collaborating Russian police in 1942. The injustice of his hard life fills him with anger. He rose to his feet and the tears streamed down his face as he spoke:

You can tell people that we were not volunteers. We have been considered second-rate all our lives for having worked for the Germans. Damn them! Why didn't they protect me? Why did they let me go to Germany? Sometimes I look at fourteen-year-old boys today and I ask myself, how can a boy of that age hold a hammer of thirty-two kilos and work all day with it? When I returned to Russia I was only eighteen years old, and I was already judged a second-class citizen for the rest of my life.

It is through the efforts of Georgi Kondakov during *Glasnost* in the mid-eighties that the Alderney survivors have won some measure of rehabilitation. Kondakov encouraged them to apply to the KGB for the return of the certificates proving that they had fought for the French resistance. Over forty years after Ivan Kalganov was forced to relinquish this precious document, it was returned to him. It entitles him to free transport, but more importantly, it regained him his family's respect. He can now tell his story and be believed, and his son Vladimir listens proudly.

CHAPTER NINE

JUSTICE DONE?

It became clear to disillusioned islanders in the first few weeks after the Liberation of the islands in May 1945 that the long-cherished hopes of finally seeing justice done were not coming to fruition.

For five years islanders had nursed bitter grievances against neighbours, against government officials and against the Germans. They wanted those who had made money out of feeding the German army taxed; they wanted informers put on trial; they wanted to know if island officials had abused their positions to get extra supplies of food and fuel; and they wanted the Germans who had beaten their sons or nephews to get their come-uppance. A mountain of complaints accumulated on the desks of the legal advisors in the Civil Affairs Unit attached to the Liberation Force, who were assigned the delicate task of sifting hearsay and spite from fact. Their job was complicated still further by the intensity of feeling on the islands, and the sensitivity of the British newspaper-reading public to allegations that Britishers had collaborated with Nazism.

Within a few days of the Liberation another complicated dimension had been added to the investigation, as allegations appeared in the British press of atrocities committed in slave labour camps on the islands.

The British investigators had four lines of enquiry to pursue. Firstly, they had to collect evidence of cruelty against slave labourers on the islands, in particular on Alderney, which could be used to try German war criminals. Secondly, there was the delicate question of whether the island governments had at any point behaved improperly. Thirdly, they had to investigate whether there was evidence of collaboration on the part of islanders serious enough to warrant prosecution. Fourthly, there were allegations of war crimes committed against islanders by members of the German military government on the Channel Islands.

The story of these investigations is like a jigsaw puzzle from which a number of pieces are missing. Many of the relevant British government sub-files were destroyed several decades ago. There are no records relating to the post-war period available to the public in the islands' archives, but in the last few years, some of the missing pieces have emerged; most of the surviving British government documents were finally released in December 1992, and Russian documents relating to the islands' slave labour army were declassified in 1993. Adding this new material to what was already known, it has become possible to trace the outlines of the post-war British investigations.

The surviving files, full of statements and detailed correspondence, indicate the commitment with which the British investigators set about their task in 1945. Thousands of people – German prisoners of war, islanders and former slave workers – were questioned, notes were taken and reports drawn up. There was a flurry of correspondence between the islands and London, and then between London and Moscow. But despite all the work of the police, military intelligence, military legal staff and diplomats on the islands, no cases ever came to trial. No German was tried by the British, on the islands or in Germany, for wartime activities on the Channel Islands. No islanders were tried. No criticism was voiced of any of the island governments' actions during the Occupation. Instead, the Bailiffs, Victor Carey and Alexander Coutanche, were knighted, and other senior members of the Occupation governments were also awarded honours.

This was an outcome unique among the countries which had been occupied in Europe. In France, Denmark and Belgium the trials of collaborators dragged on into the late forties; in 1945 fifty thousand people were in prison awaiting trial in Belgium alone.

The ending to the story of Britain's failed investigation on Alderney can be told in the stories of two old men, both German. One was a victim, the other his former tormentor.

Otto Spehr, now in his eighties, lives in an old house in the hills outside Cologne. He spent nine years in Hitler's concentration camps after being arrested as a socialist in 1934, and was on Alderney for eighteen months. He is the last known survivor of SS Baubrigade I, the building brigade run by the SS on Alderney from March to August 1943. He had to give up work in 1955 because of injuries sustained during his imprisonment.

A widower, he prides himself on his hospitality, and proffers strong coffee and sweet cakes. After our long interview, he insisted on treating me to dinner in his local restaurant. As he paid the bill, his fingers fumbled with the clasp of his wallet, and with a gentle smile he apologetically explained that the guards in Sachsenhausen used to stamp on the prisoners' hands, and his have never fully recovered.

Otto Spehr is registered as a victim of Nazism, and over the years he has been interviewed many times by German government agencies responsible for prosecuting war criminals. He has proved a valuable witness in trials against former camp guards from Sachsenhausen and Oranienburg, but no one has ever asked him about what happened on Alderney. He tried to tell the British authorities about the Channel Islands after his dramatic escape to Britain in 1944,* but he says they were not interested. He later worked for the BBC's German service, and remembers being reprimanded for mentioning the Alderney camps on air. 'The British did not want to know that there had been a concentration camp on British soil,' he concludes.

Five hours' train ride away, in Hamburg, another old man is living out his last days in comfort. He is Kurt Klebeck, formerly SS Obersturmführer Klebeck, deputy commandant of SS Baubrigade I on Alderney. He lives in a prosperous, quiet residential area of Hamburg, in a flat which looks onto the local football ground; he became president of the club in the 1960s, a position of influence and respect in the local community. Otto Spehr has known for many years that Klebeck was living in Hamburg. Another former prisoner of SS Baubrigade I told him once that he would bump into Klebeck and a former SS guard, Otto Högelow, in the streets of Hamburg, and that they would laugh at him.

* See page 190.

In the 1960s, Klebeck was the subject of a five-year investigation by the Hamburg prosecutor's office. They questioned Otto Spehr, but the case was eventually closed for lack of evidence. Spehr was told that his evidence was only hearsay; he had not actually witnessed any of the events he described. Spehr protested that prisoners were rarely allowed to witness the deaths of other prisoners, and that he certainly would not have been present when an officer gave an order to kill a prisoner.

He also presented the prosecutor's office with a 'confession' he had found in the course of some enquiries he made in the archives of Neuengamme, the parent camp of SS Baubrigade I. The closely typed two-page document, now mottled with age, claims to be the confession of Otto Högelow, made to the Austrian police on his arrest after Germany's defeat in May 1945. The name of SS Hauptscharführer Högelow also appears in the documents of British postwar investigations on Alderney.

The document is a catalogue of atrocities committed on the island. Prisoners were ordered to put splintered glass in the food of other prisoners; prisoners attempting to escape were shot; prisoners who fell ill were also shot, because there was not enough medicine, or were ordered to 'commit suicide'. Högelow admitted: 'As a sergeant, I gave the following speech: "Men, I remind you once again of the rules laid down in the sentries' orders, and I personally will give any SS man who shoots a prisoner attempting to escape three days' special leave and twenty-five cigarettes." These conditions were condoned by both the heads of division, List and Klebeck, and met with their full approval.'

Otto Spehr was told that the confession did not constitute evidence because it was undated and bore no signature. His quest for justice was in vain. Of Klebeck, he now says:

Let him die in peace. It's not fair that he has never been tried, but that's life. Life is unfair. Some men like the guards get caught, but not the ones who gave the orders. The officers defend themselves, saying, 'We just gave the orders, we didn't actually kill anyone.' If they had prosecuted all the 'big' Nazis there would have been no one left in Germany to govern. He should be left to die in peace now. He is like me, old and crumbling.

The day after the liberation of Alderney on 17 May 1945, two men landed on the island charged with the task of an initial inquiry into allegations of cruelty towards slave labourers. One of them, Major Sidney Cotton, was on secondment from the Sheffield police, and the other, Major F. Haddock, was a member of the legal staff attached to the Liberation Force. No records of their inquiry have yet come to light in the British government archives. Nothing would be known about what they found had someone not secretly kept copies of the statements they collected and the letters they wrote; these copies survived in private hands until 1992, when they were sent anonymously to a national newspaper.

Amongst the papers is a letter from Major Haddock to the Judge Advocate-General's office in London (JAG),* informing a Brigadier Shapcott that charges of maladministration could be made against eleven German prisoners of war being held on Alderney 'who permitted or exercised a policy of systematic cruelty and starvation' during the island's Occupation. This flatly contradicts what British governments have consistently maintained for fifty years – that none of the suspected German war criminals was in British hands after the war.

Alderney in May 1945 must have been an unnerving place. The bleak island was littered with the detritus of war – abandoned vehicles, weapons, bunkers and rolls of barbed wire – and populated by an emaciated, forgotten German garrison and the remnants of a slave labour army, all of whom had horrific stories to tell. Haddock's letters convey a sense of urgency that the officials in London should know the extent of the tragedy which had occurred and recognise the importance of his mission by sending more staff to help him. In one of his earliest letters to the Judge Advocate General's office, written only a few days after arriving, he reported:

> A Pole, formerly of Helgoland Camp, talks of frequently seeing prisoners beaten to death, and other witnesses, mostly Islanders, speak of seeing prisoners beaten and savaged by dogs kept by the SS guards and in some cases shot while working in gangs on the island.

* The army legal department charged with the task of prosecuting war criminals.

Quite apart from brutal treatment there is plenty of evidence that prisoners in these camps, particularly Russians, were systematically starved, and one witness speaks of two or three Russians being brought every day into a hospital and forty-one dying during a period of seven weeks while he was there.

Over the course of the next few weeks, Haddock took dozens of statements from the people on Alderney: islanders from Guernsey and Jersey who had been working there, German prisoners of war, and former slave labourers. There is a chilling repetition in these typed pages of terse statements, on paper now torn and yellowing with age. Again and again interviewees describe how prisoners were beaten and shot, their bodies left to rot beside the roads and about the camps. All but a tiny handful of islanders who had kept their eyes carefully averted had stories to tell of the cruelty and murders they had unwillingly witnessed.

Initially, the German PoWs were reluctant to tell Haddock what they knew. The navy and the Wehrmacht claimed that the camps were nothing to do with them, and had been run by the Organisation Todt and the SS, whose personnel had all been evacuated to the Continent long before Liberation. One German PoW stubbornly lied that although he had been on Alderney since July 1942 he had not seen any Russians, and 'thinks they left before he came'. He said he had briefly seen the SS Sylt prisoners, but that they left a month after he arrived – in fact they arrived eight months after him and stayed seventeen months – and he resolutely stated that he saw no acts of brutality.

But the Germans' wariness soon wore off and the PoWs, particularly those from the navy, became one of Haddock's most detailed sources of information. They may have been motivated by the hope of clemency as prisoners of war, but there is also a discernible sense of horror at the actions of their compatriots. The PoWs were probably telling the truth when they said they had had little to do with the camps, but they saw the slave labourers marching to and from their worksites, and men from the German navy stationed at the harbour had witnessed numerous instances of cruelty when slave labourers arrived or left, and when they were unloading stores. Three naval PoWs witnessed the shipwreck disaster of the *Xaver*

Dorsch and the *Franka* in January 1943 in which about a thousand Russian prisoners, including Albert Pothugine, were trapped.

Naval PoW Josef Welkerling said he saw about eight hundred Russians loaded onto the *Franka*, which then remained in the harbour for two days. The slave labourers were locked up in the hold with no ventilation, light, food or water. When they were unloaded, Welkerling said, 'The SS beat the Russians. Some were too weak to climb the ladder. At least twenty were dead and were taken to the cemetery.'

A second PoW, Werner Hohne, was 'ordered to have nothing to do with Russians, who were not human but only beasts'. Hohne said four to five hundred Russians were packed into the *Xaver Dorsch*. Haddock noted, 'Battened down in hold, no seats, no sanitation. Took soup and bread to ship and brought back fifteen bodies.'

A third PoW, Josef Kaiser, helped Hohne carry the dead off the shipwrecks. Haddock recorded, 'Thinks one of the bodies removed from ships was eaten by rats or Russians.'

Another incident was described by army Obergefreiter (Corporal) Karl Janetzko, who had been used as a Russian interpreter. A seventeen-year-old Russian boy had been accused of stealing food: 'He protested his innocence. The next day his face was badly swollen. They [the German guards] gave him a cigarette to mock him, but he could not put it into his mouth. They made him sit on a stove which they had stoked. Heat unbearable seven feet away. Kept there half an hour – he was crying. Three members of the Feldgendarmerie were there and are still on the island ... the Russian boy disappeared after that.'

According to the German PoWs, the SS were the worst; one PoW saw a Russian prisoner shot by an SS man for wanting to urinate. Another said that 'SS men in canteen spoke of keeping prisoners in Sylt Camp outside their huts all night standing naked'. Otto Högelow is singled out as the man of whose cruelty the SS boasted.

Haddock also took statements from the islanders who had been working on Alderney. Their access to the camps was restricted, but they too saw the brutality around the harbour, and because some worked alongside the slave labourers at the same worksites, they saw the working conditions. Several islanders worked on a farm run by the OT where slave labourers were so hungry that they picked up food left by dogs. One islander saw them digging up the rotten carcass of a calf which had been buried under manure.

On a few occasions, islanders were so moved to anger that they attempted to intervene: one hit an OT man for abusing the slave labourers, another begged a Russian-speaking woman to intervene to stop a beating. For the most part, though, they felt themselves to be helpless observers.

Haddock noted after interviewing islander Frank Bullock that punishments could leave victims incapacitated for days:

> If the prisoners went to relieve themselves without permission they would be beaten with sticks and informed that on return to camp they would be given ten to fifteen strokes with a rubber truncheon. This had to be administered by the prisoners' friends.
>
> In about July 1943, [Bullock] saw two Russians lying on the airport with their heads bashed in and was prevented from helping them by Hubert Rigner, the German OT Frontführer . . . one died, the other went mad. Remembers that OT chauffeur Robert —— used to amuse himself shooting Russians who picked up potatoes on farm. Saw two or three dead removed who were killed in this way.

Haddock wrote of islander William Upson's statement: 'In the summer of 1942 he saw two Russians taking cabbes [cabbages] in the fields. An assistant Lagerführer ran from his office and punched the prisoners until they fell to the ground. Then he kicked them on the head. They died and were left on the ground for a day and a half until some other prisoners carried them off in a wheelbarrow.'

Guernseyman Marshall George Johns was working for the Guernsey States on Alderney and lived at one of the OT camps. He went into hospital in July 1943 for three months, and during that period he kept a tally of the slave labourers who died by notching marks on the side of his bed. He counted the deaths of seventy-three Russians, two Frenchmen and one woman: 'In his opinion most of them died of starvation and cold.'

There were a handful of slave labourers still on Alderney when the British arrived in 1945; they included Poles, Spaniards and Russians, and they gave detailed statements to Haddock. Emile

Sulikowski, a Pole, said that of the thirty men of his brigade in Helgoland Camp in May 1942, only six survived to the end of the year – the rest had died of beatings and hunger. Ivan Amelin, a Russian, saw a man die after being beaten unconscious and put into a truck filled with water. Another Russian saw a compatriot beaten until he bled to death after stealing some potato peelings. A Spaniard, Julio Comin, who worked as a barber at Norderney Camp, saw a German beat a fellow Spaniard nearly blind for giving food to a Russian. Haddock's record of Comin's statement continues: 'An unskilled man called Jakobi conducted the sick parades in a brutal fashion [by] kicking patients in the kidneys. Karl Theiss, Commandant of Norderney, carried out beatings in his office which was next door to Comin's barber's shop. Walls of Theiss's office painted four times to remove bloodstains. Hitler portrait washed clean of blood every day . . . Russians too ill to work being thrown over cliff.'

Haddock's preliminary questioning had substantiated the allegations of appalling atrocities on Alderney. Amongst the PoWs on Alderney, he reported to London, were men who should be tried as well as the witnesses needed for their trials. Channel Islanders and former slave labourers could also stand as witnesses. JAG decided that the matter was serious enough to warrant calling in MI19, and a young captain, Theodore Pantcheff, was charged with the investigation. Pantcheff was a surprising choice because of his lack of experience, but he had a long-standing connection with the island through an uncle who had been a resident before the war, and could therefore be trusted to be conscientious and discreet. As it had been established that a large number of the victims of possible war crimes were Russians, Pantcheff was accompanied by Major Gruzdev, from the London-based Soviet Military Mission.

Anglo–Soviet co-operation did not get off to a successful start. It was not long before Haddock peevishly complained to JAG that Pantcheff was being 'unco-operative with Gruzdev'. Islanders remember Gruzdev as lazy and hard-drinking, and claim that he spent most of his time on the islands either drunk or asleep. But by the time of his departure Gruzdev declared himself 'delighted with the progress already made', and announced that a Russian Military Mission was due to arrive to continue the investigation.

Pantcheff and Gruzdev's task was to investigate the treatment of slave labour on all the islands, but in particular Alderney. Over eleven days in June 1945, Pantcheff 'checked' 1500 PoWs on Guernsey, 1200 on Jersey and 500 on Alderney. Some evidence of ill-treatment was reported to have been found on Jersey, but no documents of this have survived. Robert Le Sueur, who spoke Spanish, was brought in as an interpreter when Spanish prisoners were being interviewed on Jersey by Gruzdev. He remembers: 'Each Spanish worker was questioned about war crimes. It went on for days. We could not get any evidence that would have stood up in court. There were stories of a mass grave, but when it was dug up we found it was a cesspit.'

No copy of Pantcheff's report of his investigation on Alderney has survived in Britain; it was officially stated that it had been destroyed to make 'shelf space'. But a copy was sent to the Soviet government in October 1945, and it is to a poky attic room, full of dusty potted plants, in the Moscow archives that one has to go to find what he discovered. Stamped 'Top Secret', the report was only declassified in May 1993.

'Wicked and merciless crimes were carried out on British soil in the last three years,' Pantcheff wrote in the preface to his report in September 1945. He listed five German officers guilty of war crimes who were being held on the Channel Islands as prisoners of war. Another ten Germans suspected of war crimes had already been evacuated to PoW camps in Britain. Pantcheff listed thirty-one other Germans suspected of war crimes whose whereabouts were unknown. But, he added, they could be easily found in the American, British and French zones of occupied Germany; on this list appeared Maximilian List, Kurt Klebeck and Otto Högelow.

The five guilty men still on the Channel Islands were either in Jersey prison or in a PoW camp on Guernsey, said Pantcheff. They were: Major Carl Hoffmann, whom Pantcheff described as 'a senior HQ officer on Alderney during the time of mass deaths 1942–43'; Lieutenant Colonel Schwalm, alleged to have been responsible for the whole island from November 1943 to 1945; Captain Massmann, whom Pantcheff accused of 'dealing wickedly with prisoners'; a soldier referred to only as Muller (no rank was given), who was responsible for the work conditions of foreign labourers in 1945; and Dr Hodage, who was considered responsible for the unsanitary conditions of the camp and the death of a workman.

When Pantcheff questioned him about the conditions of the slave labourers, Major Hoffmann claimed that 'the meals in the OT camps were tasty and richly prepared', and that Sylt camp was 'from the technical point of view the best of all the working camps I have seen during the war; clean, good blankets, sheets, flowers, military order'. Hoffmann had changed his story since replying to questions from Major Haddock, his first interlocutor, in late May that it was not surprising that so many Russians had died, and 'stated glibly that it was only to be expected when prisoners were underfed and overworked'.

Other German officers claimed that they had complained about the plight of slave labourers. Johann Hoffmann, the OT Lager-führer of Helgoland from January 1943, told Pantcheff that he had complained about the meagre rations: 'Possibly not so many of them would have died if they had been accommodated better. In the first place the huts were set too low in the ground and there were walls of earth almost up to the roof . . . so they were dark and not properly ventilated.'

Leo Ackermann, island Bauleiter from September 1943 until Liberation, claimed he was only allowed to discuss technical matters with the SS. But he added that he had complained about the conditions in the SS camp to more senior authorities: 'A letter was sent to the head of the SS Baubrigade but nothing was done. I only managed to make myself SS enemies and they began to threaten me with a military tribunal because I had stood up for prisoners.' Ackermann said he was told that the prisoners were so thin because they exchanged their food for cigarettes. He admitted that 'several' of the 250 Jews and 150 'criminals' who arrived during his administration in October 1943 had died, but claimed that these deaths were due to 'incurable diseases they had brought with them'.

Pantcheff listed twenty-two Germans who were still on the islands and could act as witnesses against the men suspected of war crimes, and another eighteen who had been moved to British PoW camps. His report gives a detailed summary of the camps' regime:

the food rations had been meagre, the hours of back-breaking work had been long, accommodation was damp and unsanitary, and there was little or no medical care. The report included a summary of statements made by hundreds of Germans, Channel Islanders and former slave labourers.

The British copy of Pantcheff's report may have perished, but the transcripts of the statements he took, and on which his report was based, have survived in British archives. They run to hundreds of pages.

German PoW Franz Doctor worked at Sylt camp from October to December 1943. He told Pantcheff that he knew of ten cases when bloodhounds had driven prisoners over the camp boundary, and the prisoners had then been shot by sentries for 'escaping'. He said that one of the worst SS men was Otto Högelow, who used to give a bonus of fourteen days' leave, and extra food and drink, to SS guards for every five dead prisoners they produced. Guards at Sylt 'competed in getting leave by shooting prisoners for the smallest offences, e.g. they threw away cigarette ends and as soon as inmates bent down to pick them up, they shot them'.

Otto Taubert, a German driver, told Pantcheff that he went to Sylt in May 1943 to buy some cognac. Entry to the camp was usually forbidden, but on this occasion he was allowed in. He recounted the punishment meted out to four Russians for stealing a lamb:

While I was in the outer compound, I saw four men from the inner compound being escorted to the gate between the two compounds. One of them was weeping bitterly and was kicked and pushed around accordingly by the escort who called the sentry . . . the Uscharführer [SS sergeant] called for two SS men from the guardroom and went into the guardroom himself for a moment to get a whip. The handle of this whip was made of woven leather thongs, the whole whip was made of leather . . . From the canteen, I could see the Uscharf indicating to the SS men that they were to fasten the four prisoners to the barbed wire with handcuffs, their hands above their head. Their feet remained unfettered. After the prisoners had been hand-cuffed at the gate, they were whipped by the Uscharf . . . One man was bent double with pain . . . From where I was I could hear their cry of anguish somewhat dulled . . . The prisoner who had cried on his arrival could not walk properly when they were let free. As he staggered, he was pushed after the others towards the middle of the compound.

Another German soldier told Pantcheff:

> As people starved, they became more like criminals, fighting for scraps ... Prisoners appointed as supervisors beat them with sticks and fists. I asked them why they beat their own people, and they told me that if they didn't beat them, they would be beaten themselves in camp. One of them told me that the guards would find out who his friend was and they would beat him up and force him to stand in the camp yard completely naked.

Annie Le Cheminant, a Channel Islander who had been working as a translator for a German officer, told Pantcheff: 'The first time I saw Russians, they were clothed in rags, seemed only half alive, always starving ... the "striped" were even worse. We often gave them bread when they passed our house. Once I had just bought some biscuits and the SS prisoners tore at me and snatched them. The prisoners were beaten so badly, they fell to the ground.'

Several Germans accused a fellow PoW, named Freipond, of beating prisoners. Freipond confessed that the statements were true, and apologised 'to all the people I ill-treated or who were ill-treated in my presence'.

When I relayed the details of Pantcheff's report in the Russian archives to Georgi Kondakov in 1993, he was astounded. Like all the former slave labourers of Alderney, he had believed all his life that the Soviet government had not known of the atrocities committed on the island, and that hundreds of Soviet citizens had died there.

The question which remains unanswered in Pantcheff's report to the British government is how many slave labourers died in the Channel Islands during the Occupation. On Alderney, he concluded that while 337 graves had been found, 'it is impossible to say with any exactitude that the general figure of 337 could represent the full number of deaths on the island'. The final death toll has become one of the most controversial and haunting questions

about Alderney's occupation. When Pantcheff published a book*
on the post-war investigation in 1981, he wrote that there had been
389 burials of slave labourers, but admitted that this was only a
'minimum conclusion'. Survivors say it is a gross underestimate,
and that the true death toll ran into thousands. No one denies that
between 1942 and 1945 Alderney saw the greatest mass murder
which has ever occurred on British soil.

All the survivors agree that the number of burials discovered is
no indication of the number who died on Alderney. Their accounts
may vary in other respects, but their descriptions of the different
ways in which bodies were disposed of bear remarkable similarities.
Kirill Nevrov and Ivan Sholomitsky live hundreds of miles apart,
one in Russia, one in Ukraine, and they have never met; both claim
to have seen bodies regularly being buried on the seashore. The
claim of another Russian survivor, Georgi Kondakov, of seeing
bodies tipped into the harbour is echoed in a pamphlet published
in 1947 and written by a Spanish slave labourer who remained in
the Channel Islands, John Dalmau; Dalmau and Kondakov have
never met. Dalmau was once ordered to dive down to rescue an
entangled anti-submarine boom in Braye Harbour, Alderney. What
he saw gave him nightmares for many years: 'a fantastic picture
presented itself. Among the rocks and seaweed there were skeletons
all over the place. Crabs and lobsters were having a feast on the
bodies which remained intact.'

Dalmau also claimed that 'throwing men over the cliff became
the standard way of getting rid of exhausted workers', and that on
occasions large numbers of slave workers were shot and thrown
over the cliffs. Doubt has been cast on these accounts because it is
claimed that no human bones have ever been washed up on Alderney's shores. The argument cannot be conclusively resolved: all we
have is the word of the survivors.

One of the most controversial claims, which islanders angrily
dismiss as sensationalist, is that slave workers were pushed into the
setting concrete of the fortifications. Survivors have never claimed
that this happened on a systematic basis; clearly, a large number
of decomposing bodies would weaken the fortifications. But the

---

* *Alderney, Fortress Island: The Germans in Alderney.*

accounts of three survivors who have never met each other corre-
late. Otto Spehr in Germany, Kirill Nevrov in Russia, and the
memoirs of a French resistance agent, 'Glaize', published in France
in 1945, all describe how an accident became an atrocity. Glaize:

> One day we were working filling in liquid concrete. Suddenly there
> was a lot of shouting and the SS men came rushing up with their
> dogs; they ordered us to carry on working and said any attempt to
> talk would be very seriously punished. Not until we got back to the
> barracks did we hear that an Italian called Patalacci had slipped and
> fallen inside the wooden planks which were being filled with con-
> crete. He seemed to have fractured his leg and his comrades wanted
> to help him out, but the Germans refused to stop work and the
> liquid concrete was poured on him. He was buried alive in the west
> wall of the casement.

It is hard to believe that survivors who are geographically scattered,
and who have never met since the war, could be fabricating or
exaggerating when their accounts match so closely.

Survivors do, however, differ dramatically in their estimates of
the total number of slave labourers who came to Alderney. This
figure has to be the starting point for the calculation of how many
died. Pantcheff's post-war research, based on surviving German
records, differs from survivors' accounts. He states that three ships
in the summer of 1942 brought a total of 2800 Poles, Ukrainians
and Russians to the island, that in March 1943 a thousand SS
prisoners arrived, and later in the same year 550 French Jews.
Another thousand (mainly German) OT workers and French prostitutes on the island were much better treated than the other labourers, and their death rate would have been minimal. Excluding the
last-named, Pantcheff's figures make a total of 4350 slave labourers.

Georgi Kondakov has calculated from the accounts of more than
sixty Russian survivors that about six thousand Poles, Ukrainians
and Russians came to Alderney: 1100 to Helgoland, two thousand
to Sylt (before it was handed over to the SS) and three thousand
to Norderney. Another survivor, Ted Misiewicz, says this is an
over-estimate, and concurs with Pantcheff that there were about
three thousand slave labourers at any one time in Sylt, Norderney
and Helgoland.

The true total was probably slightly more than Pantcheff's figure; at least five thousand slave labourers were on Alderney between 1941 and 1944. Belgian survivor Norbert Beermart points out that there were already significant numbers of forced labourers on Alderney before the Eastern Europeans arrived in 1942. At the peak, in May 1943, OT records reveal that there were four thousand OT workers on Alderney, and this figure would not have included the SS prisoners. Pantcheff also slightly underestimates the number of French Jews: French historian Serge Klarsfeld said that seven hundred French Jews were sent to Alderney – this figure is based on exhaustive research into the fate of Jewry in Vichy France.

The survival rates varied for different nationalities of workers; only a small number of Dutch and Belgians died, and only a handful of French Jews perished (fewer than ten, according to survivor Albert Eblagon). The nationalities who suffered the worst were the Russians, Poles, Ukrainians and French North Africans. The rough consensus is that between twenty and twenty-five per cent of the OT slave workers and SS prisoners on Alderney died, making a final death toll of between 1000 and 1250 on this one island.

Deaths were at their peak in the last months of 1942. The arrival of winter and the first few months of the Alderney camp regime combined to kill off the most vulnerable, and former slave labourers remember October, November and December as the worst time, with sometimes as many as ten deaths a day. Forty-four death certificates (twenty-seven Russians, eight Poles, one Frenchman, two Belgians, four Dutch and two others) have survived in the Guernsey archives out of a file which originally contained 'several hundred', according to a note scribbled on its cover by the official historian of the Occupation, Charles Cruikshank. Twelve of the Russians who died were teenagers. The worst month was October, when fourteen died, including seven on one day, the twelfth.

Brian O'Hurley, a British man who worked on Alderney for four years, told Haddock that between December 1942 and January 1943 he believed that about seven hundred slave labourers died of starvation. This was the period of the worst management on Alderney, and a commission was sent from Berlin to investigate the large number of deaths. Allegedly, the Bauleiter, Buthmann, was taken

to France and court-martialled, and the change of personnel led
to an improvement in conditions. The death rate remained high,
however, even in the warmer summer weather. Guernseyman
Marshall Johns noted that seventy-three Russian and two
French corpses were brought to the hospital on Alderney in May,
June and July 1943, and there is no reason to believe that all the
dead were taken to the hospital.

Documents have survived relating to the number of deaths in
SS Baubrigade I at SS Sylt camp on Alderney. The SS Neuen-
gamme camp death registers record 126 deaths in Sylt between
April 1943 and July 1944. These registers are highly inaccurate –
only fifteen thousand of the estimated fifty-five thousand deaths at
Neuengamme are recorded. The sick of Baubrigade I were returned
from Alderney to Neuengamme, where they were probably killed.
This is made clear in the SS records of the trial of the Baubrigade
Kommandant Maximilian List and his deputy Kurt Klebeck after
a breakout on a transport of two hundred sick prisoners in 1943.
List had decided to return the prisoners because they 'were too
much of a burden' on the island. At the trial, Klebeck admitted
that 'Alderney was especially bad for Eastern [European] workers.'
Otto Spehr, the only known living survivor of SS Baubrigade I,
claims that at least 350 of the thousand-strong brigade had died
before it was evacuated in July 1944. The rest probably perished
in Buchenwald, where the brigade was sent after working on V2
sites at Kortemark in Belgium.

Added to the death toll on Alderney must be those who died on
the transport ships between the islands and France. The conditions
of the voyage were sufficient to kill a number of those who were
already ill, and the poorly equipped ships were vulnerable to storms,
Allied bombing and torpedo attacks. German PoWs told Pantcheff
that the slave labourers were 'crowded together in holds like her-
rings, without straw, beds, blankets or benches. They were terribly
emaciated . . . When opening the hatches to the holds, a terrible
stench would meet us.' The worst disaster was the wreck of the
Xaver Dorsch and the *Franka* in January 1943, and more lives were
probably lost in October of the same year when the *Dorothea Weber*
sat in Alderney harbour with hundreds of men under the battened
hatches for thirty-six hours without food or water before setting

sail. Another disaster was when the *Minotaure* was torpedoed in July 1944, and about two hundred OT workers and French prostitutes drowned. The total lost at sea travelling to and from Alderney must have run into several hundred.

The number of deaths on Guernsey and Jersey is believed to be considerably lower than on Alderney. The camp staff were not as corrupt on these islands, so the slave labourers received more of their rations. In addition, they were sometimes given – or could steal – food and clothing by islanders. On neither island do accurate German records survive. One list for Guernsey reports that 109 OT workers died in 1942. The bodies were exhumed in 1961 from the Foulon cemetery by the Volksbund Deutscher Kriegsgräberfürsorge, the West German government's organisation dealing with German war graves, and reburied in France. Of those whose nationalities were identified, sixty were French (mostly Algerians), fifteen Belgian, seven Spanish and five Dutch, as well as one Chinese and one Portuguese.

On Jersey, the burial register of the Westmount Strangers' Cemetery from February 1942 to February 1943 records 124 deaths: seventy-six Russians, seventeen French, nine Spaniards, six North Africans, four Poles, two Dutch, two Belgians and eight unknown. This would not have been the total number of deaths for that year; there were numerous accidents at work, such as slave labourers being buried in rock falls. In 1943, when the OT was at its full strength, there were 6700 labourers on Guernsey and 5300 on Jersey, and the death rate would probably have been slightly higher than in 1942. It is impossible to come to a precise figure for the number of slave labourers who died on Jersey and Guernsey, but it must have run into several hundred. The total number who died in the Channel Islands, including travelling to or from them, probably lies between two and three thousand.

Only four men are known to have been prosecuted for war crimes committed on Alderney. Konopelko, a Soviet slave labourer who became a kapo (guard), was tried in Glukow in southern Russia in 1949 and sentenced to twenty-five years' hard labour. A German member of the SS, Lagerführer Puhr, was tried and executed in

East Germany in 1963. Two Organisation Todt staff, OT Haupt-
ruppführer Adam Adler and OT Meister Heinrich Evers, commandant and deputy commandant of Norderney camp, were tried in
France at the Tribunal Militaire Permanent de Paris at Caserne de
Reuilly in September 1949. They were accused of subjecting French
Jews to 'superhuman work' and 'systematic ill-treatment', and of
having deprived them of medical care and parcels sent by their
families. Forty-seven-year-old Adler admitted he had been a
Nazi since 1930 and was a member of the SS; they were both
found guilty and sentenced, Adler to ten years and Evers to seven
years.

The British tried no one.

The British officers – Major Haddock, Major Cotton and Captain Pantcheff – sent to investigate atrocities on the Channel Islands
thought they were collecting information for future war crime trials.
Pantcheff in his report to the Soviet government urged further
work to bring the guilty to trial. But all the evidence they collected
and the interviews they conducted led to nothing. This is one of
the most puzzling aspects of the history of the Channel Islands
Occupation.

It quickly became apparent that there was a confusion about
which country would be responsible for trying Alderney's suspected
war criminals. There were two conflicting principles under the
Moscow Declaration signed on 30 October 1943 by America,
Britain and Russia on the prosecution of war criminals. One principle was that the 'most aggrieved nation' should be the one to
prosecute, but another was that trials should be held in, or as near
as possible to, the place where the crimes occurred, so that local
witnesses could give evidence.

In the case of Alderney these principles clearly clashed; the Soviet
Union was the most aggrieved nation, but a large number of witnesses were either on the Channel Islands or in British PoW camps.

On 14 June 1945, the Office of the Treasury Solicitor wrote to
the Foreign Office, asking for advice on the Alderney case: 'We
suppose that the principle recently decided in dealing with concentration camps in the area of British occupation would apply in the
case of British territory recovered from the enemy. It seems to us,
however, that we could not act in relation to these cases unless we

have some authority for doing so and without presumably some reference to the Russians.'

The Judge Advocate General's office replied: 'the position here [Alderney] is somewhat similar to Belsen,* stronger perhaps because the offences were committed on British territory'. The Foreign Office agreed that the British should try the Alderney cases, but added the caveat that if it was found that all the victims were Russian, 'then under our interpretation of the Moscow Declaration, these Germans should be handed over to the Soviet government ... it would be interesting to see whether the Soviet authorities would take this view of the Moscow Declaration despite its literal text to the effect that they should be sent back to the "scene of their atrocious deeds"'.

On 30 June 1945 the Office of the Treasury Solicitor wrote to the Foreign Office that the large number of statements taken on Alderney 'almost wholly refer to offences against Russians', but went on to cite Belsen as a reason for the British conducting the Alderney trials, and added, 'I suppose we ought either to get the consent of the Russians or to notify them of what we are doing.'

Trials in British Special Military Courts under Royal Warrant on Alderney seemed the best option, agreed the Foreign Office in reply to JAG, adding that there was the further advantage of local witnesses being available. But the Foreign Office had one question: were all the crimes committed against Russians, or had any other nationalities (apart from Germans) suffered?

Brigadier Shapcott from JAG replied five days later that *all* the inmates of the Alderney camps were Russian, and that 'There is no evidence that the concentration camp held other non-German nationals while the Russians were there. When, however, the Russians were removed a number of French Jews took over the duty of completing the fortifications.' The Foreign Office noted that 'for practical purposes Russians may be considered to have been the only occupants of these camps'. To make absolutely sure, the Foreign Office wrote to ask JAG if any atrocities had been committed

---

* At the time, the British were collecting evidence for the trials of the Belsen camp staff, for which they were responsible because the site of the former camp fell within the British occupation zone of Germany.

against French Jews, because 'if there were any serious ones this may make a difference'. JAG assured the Foreign Office that 'no atrocities were committed against the French Jews. On balance they were treated better than others working for the Germans.'

But French Jews *were* mistreated, and there were many nationalities apart from Russians who suffered on Alderney. Why had Brigadier Shapcott misled the Foreign Office? It could have been a genuine error; Pantcheff had not yet completed his report, and the letters of Major Haddock to Brigadier Shapcott had indicated that most of the slave labourers had been Russian. On the other hand, Pantcheff would have been keeping Shapcott informed about the progress of the investigation; a simple enquiry would quickly have established that Belgians, Dutch, Czechs, Poles and others had suffered on Alderney. Neither did JAG make any enquiries to the French authorities, who had compiled considerable evidence of ill-treatment of French citizens on Alderney by 1945.

JAG had the gigantic task of tracing thousands of the Third Reich's personnel and preparing for their trials with a hopelessly inadequate staff. Under the pressure of such a volume of work, civil servants might have decided to simplify the matter of the Channel Islands and disregard the minority of non-Soviet victims. Or Brigadier Shapcott's mistake could have been the result of a decision that trials on Alderney would bring unwelcome attention to the humiliating fact that there had been an SS camp on British soil, and that some islanders had voluntarily worked for the Germans on Alderney.

On receiving JAG's assurance that only Soviets had suffered on Alderney, the Foreign Office decided that the best course of action would be to hand over to the Soviet authorities the Germans suspected of war crimes on Alderney, and all the evidence that had been collected, and leave it to them to try them. 'In this way we might hope to gain a certain kudos for the gesture and we should also be spared the possible embarrassment of the Russians criticising in good or bad faith the leniency of any sentences passed by our Special Military Courts.'

Captain Pantcheff's report sent to the Soviet government in October 1945 was part of the British offer to provide evidence for the Soviet authorities' prosecutions. But what the Soviets needed were the guilty men and the Germans who could act as witnesses, and they were all in British prisoner of war camps in the Channel Islands, Britain and Germany. Without them, there could be no trials. By early 1946 the wartime co-operation between Britain and Russia was breaking down, and any chances of the former allies joining forces to ensure that Alderney's war criminals were put on trial fast receded.

There are only three brief references to Alderney war criminals after 1946 in British archives. A German called Danner was found in a Norwegian prisoner of war camp and accused of war crimes in Alderney. JAG were notified, and their reply was to recommend the man's release because 'the case of Alderney had been handed over to the Russians'. This was a mark of the complete breakdown of relations between Britain and the Soviet Union; the British had washed their hands of the whole matter.

The second reference was in 1947, when JAG wrote to the Officer Commanding British Forces in France with what was to become the standard line for half a century: 'The completed reports were handed over to the Russian authorities for such action as they might think fit. I regret therefore, that no list of the men responsible is in the possession of this office ... the only information that we can give you is ... that the Russians were treated with great cruelty.'

The third reference was to the Kommandant of SS Baubrigade I, Hauptsturmführer Maximilian List, who had been on every list of suspected Alderney war criminals drawn up by MI19. In the late 1940s JAG received a letter saying that List had been found in a PoW camp called Harsseld; pencilled in the margin is a note that List had been handed over to the Russians in 1947, 'so no further action need be taken'. This was not the case; Maximilian List lived in West Germany after the war, appearing in a Hamburg court in 1974 (for a minor offence unrelated to the war), where he admitted to having been the Kommandant of SS Baubrigade I. The former SS prisoner Otto Spehr claims that List lived near Hamburg until his death in the 1980s.

Rumours have flourished about the fate of Alderney war criminals. The man best placed to know what happened to them was Pantcheff. His extremely detailed book *Alderney, Fortress Island* was clearly based on personal copies he had kept of his 1945 investigation. But over the fate of Alderney's suspected war criminals Pantcheff is unreliable. He writes that Maximilian List and Kurt Klebeck did not survive the war, and that the former Alderney Kommandant Major Carl Hoffmann was 'said to have been hung in 1945 in Kiev'. He added, 'It has recently been suggested that he died in West Germany in the mid–1970s, but resolving this apparent discrepancy lies outside the scope of this wartime record.' In 1983 the British government was forced to admit that in 1948 Hoffmann had been released from the London District Prisoner of War cage (to which he had been taken from the Channel Islands), because no request had been received from the Soviet authorities for him to stand trial. Hoffmann returned to Germany and lived in Hamburg until he died of old age in, 1974.

Pantcheff fails to mention in his book what the Russian copy of his report in Moscow makes clear: namely, that fifteen of the suspected German war criminals had been in British PoW camps, along with the witnesses needed to convict them. All of them were probably, like Hoffmann, released in 1948–49 without being tried. Pantcheff's book was checked by the Ministry of Defence and it is probable that parts of it were censored. It is unlikely to be an accident that Pantcheff's report, with its reference to the presence of fifteen Alderney war criminals in British camps, is missing from the British archives. When Pantcheff was interviewed for a television documentary in 1990 he stated that no Germans were prosecuted because 'they had all left before we got here. They were evacuated in the spring of 1944.'

In 1992, it took the Home Office more than three months to collate an answer to my enquiry as to why there had been no trials:

> As the majority of the forced labour victims were Russian prisoners, the case concerning the ill-treatment of the forced labourers was passed with the evidence to the Soviet authorities for their action. In other cases, the individuals considered by the war crimes investigators as possible accused did not fall into Western Allied hands before the cessation of war crimes trials in 1948. Claims that relevant documents were destroyed were unfounded.

This is patently untrue: the accused had been in British PoW camps. Either the officials were lying, or the relevant documents have indeed been destroyed, and the Home Office does not know what the Pantcheff report contained.

The causes of the failure to try the Alderney war criminals must lie in part in the disintegrating relationship between Britain and the Soviet Union in 1946. In addition, neither government was probably enthusiastic to try them. The British did not relish the prospect of the Soviet Union exploiting British trials for its own political advantage, as the Foreign Office documents indicate. Trials on British soil would have been an acutely embarrassing reminder to the British public of several painful facts about the war which the government wanted quickly forgotten: that British territory had been occupied for five years; that British subjects had collaborated and worked for the Germans on Alderney; and that Nazi atrocities, including the establishment of an SS concentration camp, had occurred on British soil. Besides, the British public was already losing interest in war crime trials, and with much bigger fish to fry in Germany, the matter was allowed to drop.

It is conceivable that, as the British government has maintained, the Soviet Union did not request that Hoffmann and the other accused be handed over to them for trial. Such a trial would have revealed that there were innocent 'repatriates', thus muddying the waters of the Stalinist distinction between them and war participants.

The trials had been bungled and neglected. The cover-up began after 1946, when the failure to try the Alderney war criminals became an embarrassment to the British government. It was an omission which would not have put Britain in a good light in the eyes of wartime allies such as France. Whenever the issue has been raised over the past fifty years British governments have been economical with the truth. Pressure on former agents such as Pantcheff, and the disappearance of crucial papers, has meant that piecing together a full story can never be more than intelligent guesswork.

Contrary to Pantcheff's supposition, Kurt Klebeck, the SS deputy commandant, did survive the war, and by an extraordinary stroke of fate he was tried by the British in occupied Germany in 1947. The transcripts of his trial have even survived in British archives. But Klebeck was not tried for crimes he committed on Alderney, but for atrocities perpetrated in camps after his return to Germany in 1944.

After Alderney, Klebeck had been promoted to district commandant of Ahlem-Stoecken, a camp outside Hamburg for Polish Jews who were diverted from the gas chambers to build an underground factory. He was captured by the British in June 1945, and spent two years in a British prisoner of war camp awaiting trial. During his trial he revealed that he had been on Alderney, but the reference was ignored: no one in the British military court asked what this career SS officer had been doing there.

The chief prosecution witness, prisoner-doctor Leon Fajwlowicz, described a regime in which ten to fifteen men died every day from beatings, exhaustion and tuberculosis. On one of Klebeck's visits of inspection, Fajwlowicz complained about the unsanitary condition of the toilets, and overheard Klebeck say to the camp commandant, 'They will die in any case, and if they don't, we'll take good care to see to it that they do.' Fajwlowicz said that Klebeck had used the slang expression 'kick the bucket'. Klebeck denied this, insisting that he would never use such an expression for a human being, only for an animal.

Two other men who were tried alongside him were hanged for their part in the horrific regime of Ahlem, yet Klebeck received only a ten-year prison sentence. The British military judge, P.G.B. Six Smith, pointed out that as district commandant, Klebeck did not have direct responsibility for the running of the camp, and concluded that there was 'no evidence that he himself directly killed or ill-treated a prisoner or that he gave orders to anyone to do so'. Klebeck served a total of seven years, and was released early for good behaviour in 1952.

The British court ignored Klebeck's crimes on Alderney – a camp for which he did have direct responsibility – and they also apparently failed to realise that he had played a key role in one of the most tragic events of the chaotic last days before Germany's defeat. The *Cap Arcona* disaster is well known in Germany; it has struck a chord with the German people because in this atrocity both Britain and Germany were complicit. Documents relating to the British investigation into the disaster in 1945 have survived, and the name of Hauptsturmführer Kurt Klebeck (he had probably been promoted on his return to Germany from Alderney) figures prominently.

At the end of April 1945, Hitler ordered the evacuation of 2353 prisoners from Neuengamme concentration camp outside Hamburg to a ship, the SS *Cap Arcona*, which was anchored in Neustadt Bay off the north German coast. The ship had no defences against Allied submarines or bombers at a time when the German coast was under heavy attack, and its captain refused to board the prisoners. Klebeck himself threatened to arrest him unless he obeyed the order. A total of 6500 prisoners from Neuengamme and other camps were loaded onto the *Cap Arcona* and another ship, the *Thielbeck*. The prisoners were in an appalling condition, and 182 died while waiting to be transferred onto the ships.

On 2 May 1945, the British reached the nearby port of Lübeck, and were told that there were eight thousand prisoners on board three anchored ships in Neustadt Bay. But the following day the RAF bombed the ships. Both the *Cap Arcona* and the *Thielbeck* were sunk, drowning most of the prisoners trapped in the holds. Prisoners struggling in the water or who managed to reach the shore were shot at by SS officers who had escaped in the lifeboats, shocked German residents told the British investigators. The death toll was put at five thousand.

The British investigators concluded that 'primary responsibility must fall on the British RAF personnel' for failing to relay intelligence to the pilots, but added that, at a time when the RAF were constantly bombing that part of the German coast, the Germans must have intended the RAF to kill the prisoners, in an 'act of manslaughter almost akin to murder'. Amongst those listed as guilty was Kurt Klebeck, then in custody at Neuengamme.

In 1992, Kurt Klebeck was a well-preserved elderly man. He closely resembled his younger self: the same clean-shaven, fleshy face and sleeked-back hair. He and his wife had learned to live with the fear that one day his past might catch up with him. When we called, the door was opened a few inches on a chain by his small, worried wife, who relayed questions to Klebeck. He did not deny that he had been on Alderney, but insisted he had only been an ordinary soldier. Then the door slammed shut. Klebeck was nervous, and could not resist stepping onto the balcony of his flat to inspect through binoculars the people who had come asking questions about a history which he had hidden for nearly fifty years. It was a mistake which led to his photograph appearing in newspapers in Britain, Germany, Holland and France.

Klebeck's claims to be an ordinary soldier are belied by the SS records in the Berlin Documentation Centre. His file, although a little burnt around the edges from when it was salvaged from the flames in the fall of Berlin, provides a biography of the man. His background was typical of those who flocked to join the Nazis in the early thirties. He came from an educated middle-class background in Berlin – his father had been an engineer – but had failed to get into a good school. By the age of twenty-seven he had had several jobs, none of which had lasted more than six months. A shotgun marriage had produced a son who died after a month, and a divorce. In May 1933 Klebeck joined the Nazi Party and the SS, cashing in on the party's rise to power. He was married again in 1939, to his present wife; the SS gave permission for the marriage only after her ethnic purity had been verified. Klebeck worked at Sachsenhausen concentration camp as well as Neuengamme, Alderney and Ahlem-Stoecken.

In 1992, after Klebeck's wartime record was first revealed in the press, the German government launched a new investigation, drawing on British wartime records of his SS career for the first time. But as the German Embassy in London admitted eighteen months later, in November 1993, it was very unlikely that Klebeck would ever be put on trial at his age (then eighty-seven), even if witnesses could be found. Like many other Nazi officials, Klebeck will die in his own bed, never having faced full justice.

Meanwhile, in Russia, ageing Alderney survivors pore over recent photos of Klebeck and his SS identity photo, and search in their memories for the faces which terrorised them as boys. Ivan Kalganov and Georgi Kondakov recognise Klebeck's face, although they never knew his name – he was a figure only occasionally glimpsed, giving orders to underlings.

Alexander Kanatnikov, who was in Sylt when Klebeck was deputy commandant, wrote from Gornyak, Ukraine: 'Over the last fifty years, I could never have imagined that somebody might ever take an interest in the sad story of Alderney prisoners. The law which reigned in Alderney during the war was the strict law of the struggle for life. I don't remember the man in the photo, but I look at it very closely every day.'

The second part of the Liberation Force's task was to investigate allegations of collaboration, on the part of individual islanders and of the island governments.

The British government's priorities became clear immediately. Despite stiff opposition from the military, Herbert Morrison, the Home Secretary, insisted on visiting the Channel Islands on 15 May 1945, only a few days after Liberation. He had Churchill's blessing, and his task was to patch up the islands' relationship with Britain. That meant explaining why Britain had abandoned them in 1940 and had not liberated them until the war in Europe was over. At the same time, he wanted to reassure the island governments of Britain's whole-hearted support in the event of questions being raised over their wartime conduct. Forgive and forget, he offered; it was an arrangement which suited both sides. The slate was wiped clean, the islands and Britain could return to where they had left off in 1940. Morrison was reported in the *Jersey Evening Post* as having told the Jersey States: 'I am not sure that everything ... was always within the law ... but if anything has been done that needs white-washing at the other end, I will take care of it.'

Jersey clerk Norman Le Brocq remembered Morrison's visit: 'He made a public statement in the square which horrified me ... he said that he considered that while there had been some minor collaboration and blemishes by people during the German Occupation, he thought the majority of the islanders had shown great loyalty, and certainly any misdemeanours that had happened would not be followed up. When Morrison finished talking, he expected everyone to applaud him but there was just an angry silence.'

On Morrison's return to Britain, he gave a statement to the House of Commons publicly exonerating the islands: 'I am sure the House will join me in expressing our admiration for the fortitude and the loyalty which, with creditably few exceptions, our kinsfolk in the Channel Islands have shown [and] for the courage and devotion to duty with which the Bailiffs and other Crown officers have discharged their arduous and sometimes dangerous responsibilities during every phase of Nazi occupation.'

Norman Le Brocq was not the only one on Jersey to be shocked by the British government's position, amd many letters of protest were written to the Home Office. One Jerseywoman wrote that the Home Secretary was only on the islands for a few hours, and had only talked to States officials. She hoped that the King and Queen would express sympathy but refrain from 'praising or blaming any of us until the commission [of inquiry] had returned its report'. A Colonel West did not mince his words, writing to Churchill that the walls of St Helier were plastered with graffiti saying, 'The States must go'. He added, 'Were you to know the truth Jersey could not be included amongst the "dear Channel Islands" ... a more unworthy Bailiff never held office in Jersey, nor is the Attorney-General any better.' Another Jerseyman wrote to Morrison, 'this civil government was pro-Nazi from the day the Germans came to the day they surrendered'.

On Guernsey, John Leale, President of the Controlling Committee, decided to head off criticism, and gave a long and detailed defence of his government's record during the Occupation to the States on 23 May: 'We were not at liberty to explain many of our actions. Disquieting things kept on happening and it was not perhaps altogether unnatural that a public, tired, fearful and irritated, should at times take a somewhat jaundiced view of some of our activities.' His speech was printed in full in the local papers.

Whitehall was impressed by Leale's speech, and attributed Guernsey's lack of public unrest to his prompt and effective oratory. The Jersey government was slower to defend its island's record. When the States met for the first time after the war, it was declared that 'The great body of real Jersey people, whose families had been associated with this island for centuries, were neither collaborators nor fraternisers ... the great majority of our real people had never had even the slightest association with the enemy and could look back with feelings of pride in their loyalty.'

That did not satisfy everyone; as one passionate letter to the *Jersey Evening Post* put it: 'When a malignant growth takes root in a body the surgeon uses his knife to eliminate it so that the healthy flesh around it may have a chance of survival. In Denmark, Norway and other countries they operated swiftly; only an anaesthetic has so far been administered here.'

In a private memo to the Home Office, Alexander Coutanche, the Bailiff of Jersey, defended his government's role as a 'buffer'. He detailed how the island's authorities had refused to co-operate with the Germans in the recruitment of labour, but admitted that large numbers of islanders had voluntarily worked for the Germans, and that some of this work had been of 'a military character'. He defended the Royal Court's registration of anti-Jewish orders by saying they had 'no option': 'The number of persons affected was extremely small and moderation was shown in the execution of the Order. It could be shown that other oppressive measures against the Jews were entirely avoided by proper intervention of the Insular Authorities.'

The Home Office reassured the governments of both islands that such explanations satisfied them, but pointed out that allegations had to be investigated in case the government was called on to make a statement. It was to be a secret, and extremely tactful, inquiry. The Home Office turned to Lord Justice du Parcq, the most prominent Channel Islander in the British legal establishment, to consider the island governments' record.

Du Parcq drew up a memo in which he listed several causes for concern. The most important was the fact that the island governments had helped the Germans deport 2200 islanders to internment camps in Germany in 1942 and 1943: 'I think that a strong case can be made for the view that the local authorities should have refused to give any assistance in the performance of this violation of international law . . . I should feel happier if I thought a strong line had been taken.'

Du Parcq was also concerned by the behaviour of the Bailiff of Guernsey, Victor Carey, who had referred to Allied soldiers in an order published in the local press as 'enemy forces', and had offered a reward of £25 to anyone who informed on a person writing V-signs. Du Parcq commented acidly: 'I would assume, however, that these orders, with any explanation which Mr Carey has to offer, would be brought to the attention of the Prime Minister, if not of His Majesty before any honour was conferred.'

Du Parcq visited the islands, and then met Sir Frank Newsam at the Home Office on 6 June to discuss the unrest on Jersey. Newsam said the government was reluctant to embark on a 'witch-hunting inquiry' into the island governments' record. Du Parcq agreed, and assured him that the resentment on the islands was mainly directed not against the administration but against individuals who had worked for the Germans, farmers who supplied them with food, and informers.

The Director of Public Prosecutions, Theobald Mathew, visited the islands in July, spending two days each on Guernsey and Jersey, talking mainly to officials. He praised Coutanche, the Bailiff of Jersey, for his 'exceptional ability and skill.' Of Carey, the Bailiff of Guernsey, he was critical: 'It is perhaps unfortunate that the Bailiff, elderly, charming, but not of strong character, who was due to retire when the Occupation started, appears on one or two occasions to have given way to strong German pressure and the three public notices (including one about a reward for information leading to the arrest of anyone doing "V" signs) which resulted were extremely unfortunate.' But Mathew's conclusion was: 'No doubt the administration made mistakes, but ... they are entitled to praise rather than censure.' He warned: 'I sensed the beginnings of some resentment of the critical attitude which it is thought that this country has been adopting towards the administration.'

Mathew's warning was heeded. The discreet inquiry into the conduct of island governments was wrapped up and its findings were relayed to Parliament by James Chuter-Ede, the Home Secretary in Attlee's newly elected Labour Government, on 20 August 1945: 'The islands have every reason to be proud of themselves and we have every reason to be proud of them. That, after a period of great suffering, there should have been a tendency in certain quarters, not fully informed of all the facts, to indulge in recriminations, is not surprising, but I hope, in the interests of the future of the Islands, nothing will be said in this House to encourage any such tendency.'

Chuter-Ede admitted that mistakes had been made by the island governments, but emphasised 'the immense importance of keeping executive functions in the hands of the civil administrations'. He added that the conduct of the islanders towards the Germans 'was generally speaking of a frigid and correct character'.

Both Bailiffs were immediately told about Chuter-Ede's statement in Parliament by phone. 'It is a relief to have that over,' wrote
Alexander Coutanche in handwritten letters to both Newsam and
Charles Markbreiter at the Home Office thanking them warmly
for all their help.

In a further gesture of endorsement, in December 1945 the
Crown showered honours on the prominent members of the
islands' governments. Victor Carey, John Leale and Alexander
Coutanche got their knighthoods, the first-named notwithstanding
Lord Justice du Parcq's misgivings. Ambrose Sherwill was made a
CBE (he became Bailiff of Guernsey in 1946, and was knighted in
1949). A CBE was also given to Edgar Dorey, a member of the
Jersey Superior Council. Three OBEs were awarded, including one
to Richard Johns, the head of Guernsey's Labour Department who
had ensured that the Germans had enough workmen to expand the
island's airport.

The British government had backed off from bringing island
officials to account, but the question of what to do about individual
islanders accused of collaboration was not to be so easily resolved.
At the beginning of June 1945, Home Office official James Boag
Howard warned Herbert Morrison: 'The position in Jersey is rather
acute because certain sections of the population are showing a
determination not to let the matter rest.'

Alexander Coutanche was also concerned that if those islanders
who had been 'unduly friendly' with the Germans were not brought
to book, a precedent would be established throughout the
Commonwealth that such behaviour towards an occupying power
was acceptable. The Bailiff suggested a Committee of Inquiry which
'would allow of some ventilation of public feeling for the time
being'. But Boag Howard was concerned about the impact of such
an inquiry on 'less responsible' newspapers in Britain, which might
'make capital out of the small number of British subjects in Jersey
who had collaborated with the enemy'.

On his visit to the islands in July 1945, Theobald Mathew investigated allegations against individual collaborators, and concluded
stiffly that the worst that could be said about islanders was that
'They may have merited the description of one German officer that
they were "obsequious peasants", but even this in my opinion is

probably unfair having regard to the fact that where opportunity offered, such as the "V" sign incident, hostility to the occupation was shown.'

Mathew made no reference to the fact that the Guernsey police had handed islanders who had written 'V' signs – including children – over to the Germans. Nor that Victor Carey himself had offered rewards to islanders to inform on those writing 'V' signs. Mathew concluded his report: 'There is no *prima facie* case for suggesting the population as a whole behaved in a disloyal manner during this difficult and unprecedented period.'

There was one question with which both the British government and the island governments were wrestling throughout the summer of 1945: what exactly constituted collaboration, and was it a crime under island law?

Jersey's Attorney-General, Duret Aubin, told the States that 'to collaborate with the enemy is to give assistance which the occupying power could not obtain except by the co-operation of the individual concerned'. Under that definition a considerable number of islanders would have been guilty of collaboration. In June the Channel Islands' most senior lawyers flew to London to discuss the matter at a meeting with Sir Alexander Maxwell, Permanent Secretary at the Home Office. Attention focused on two laws which could be used to try islanders for collaboration. Article 2a of the 1939 Defence Regulations Act made 'aiding and abetting the enemy' a crime. That would have covered most forms of collaboration, but there was a fine constitutional issue of whether the law was still in force on the islands during the Occupation. In August 1941 the Defence Regulations Act's application to the Channel Islands had been revoked by an Order in Council.* The question arose as to whether the 1941 Order in Council had been valid on the islands between 1941 and 1945, as Orders normally have to be registered in the islands' Royal Courts before they take effect. The 1941 Order had not been registered because the islands were occupied. So, had the 1939 Defence Regulations Act been

---

* All British laws must be specifically extended to the Channel Islands by an Order in Council. Likewise, if they are to be withdrawn from the islands, another Order in Council is necessary.

revoked, or had it legally held force throughout the Occupation?

In August 1945 Duret Aubin sent a memo on the question to the Home Office. He concluded that the Defence Regulations Act had remained in force, and that islanders could therefore be prosecuted under article 2a for 'aiding and abetting the enemy'. Aubin recommended that Jersey law officers should begin preparing evidence in two or three 'serious cases they know where persons are thought to have been in the pay of Germans as informers'.

There was another law under which collaborators could also be prosecuted, according to Theobald Mathew. They could be tried under the English common law of 'misdemeanours of effecting a public mischief', because collaboration could be counted as 'offences of a public nature ... as tend to the prejudice of the community'. Mathew and the Home Office agreed that any such trials should be held in the islands. Mathew added that it would not be possible to prosecute cases of black marketeering and fraternising, and advised that they be dealt with by 'financial sanctions and by social ostracism'.

During June and July 1945 twenty officers of the Civil Affairs Unit (CAU) of the Liberation Force gathered evidence against alleged collaborators, although 'evidence which has any value is extremely difficult to obtain'. On several occasions Norman Le Brocq was questioned at length on the activities of collaborators by Captain Kent. When Le Brocq asked what was going to happen to the thick dossier of statements, Kent told him that it would all be recorded and forgotten. This prediction was to prove accurate.

On 9 August the CAU sent a report to the Home Office. It concluded:

These statements proved beyond doubt that a number of people behaved in an unseemly, undesirable and even disgraceful way, but none of the statements so far produced makes any allegation which, if true, could prove a charge of treachery or treason and the sooner we face this fact and put an end to the present atmosphere of suspense the better. There might be some violent recriminations from certain elements of the public when this statement is published and it would be advisable for the 'show-down' to take place before the bulk of the Force is withdrawn.

On 2 November 1945 the new Lieutenant Governor of Jersey, Sir Edward Grasset, sent Mathew the names of thirteen people whom the Jersey authorities considered could be successfully prosecuted. But by November an extraordinary decision had been made. It was decided to ignore both Mathew's and Aubin's legal opinions; only cases of treason would now be prosecuted. No documents have survived which explain this *volte-face*, and it appears that, once again, a large number of sub-files have been destroyed. It is clear that when Mathew sent his report to the Home Office on the completion of his investigation in January 1946, he considered only the crime of treason suitable for prosecution. He announced that he had investigated a total of twenty cases, and concluded that while 'a few of those cases disclose some *prima facie* evidence of conduct of a highly reprehensible and even disloyal nature, none amount either to high treason or treachery'.

The only clue as to why the Director of Public Prosecutions changed his position so radically is found in a letter he wrote to Sir Frank Newsam at the Home Office early in 1946, in which he noted happily that the demand for collaboration trials on Jersey was abating. The British government had successfully managed to wriggle out of its difficult position. As soon as it was decided that only cases of treason could be prosecuted, the whole question of trials evaporated. Mathew had established within a few weeks of the islands' Liberation that there were no *prima facie* treason cases. It was not trials for treason that Jersey wanted, but for collaboration. A Home Office briefing memo for James Chuter-Ede claimed that the legal machinery to try collaborators did not exist. This was patently untrue, as both Aubin's and Mathew's legal opinions demonstrated. That did not bother Home Office officials. What did bother them was that such an explanation for the collapse of collaboration trials would not clear the air in Westminster, where there had been persistent interest in the issue, nor on Jersey. So they devised a deft sidestepping of the issue for Chuter-Ede. In reply to a question in the House of Commons on 30 November 1946, the Home Secretary announced that the Director of Public Prosecutions had decided earlier in the year that 'there were not sufficient grounds to warrant the institution of criminal proceedings'. Chuter-Ede was not lying – there were not sufficient grounds to prosecute anyone for treason – but what he omitted to mention was that the Home Office had concluded that there were no laws under which to prosecute crimes for which there *was* sufficient evidence. Even more damaging was the real story, that British and Jersey lawyers had found there were laws under which collaborators could have been prosecuted, but their advice had been ignored. The British government had decided it did not want any such trials.

The truth was that, as the investigations on the islands got under way, three factors became clear which made the prospect of trials a political minefield. Firstly, evidence which would stand up in court was genuinely hard to come by in an atmosphere of extreme tension and resentment – on Jersey in particular. Secondly, it would be a breach of constitutional traditions for an islander to be tried in Britain, but given the strength of popular feeling on Jersey, British officials were concerned that there would be no chance of a fair trial there. Thirdly, there was the embarrassing fact that the demand for trials was far stronger on Jersey than on Guernsey and Sark. Britain had to be even-handed without generating bad feeling between the islands and towards itself, but it could not impose trials on Guernsey. The advantage of trying the twenty cases considered by the Director of Public Prosecutions had to be set against these disadvantages. If the trials collapsed, or the sentences were perceived as too light, it would damage Britain's prestige on the islands and abroad. In addition, the trials might reveal details of collaboration which all the governments concerned were hoping would not come to light for many more years.

Collaborators were left to be punished by social ostracism. Either voluntarily or under duress, a number left the islands for England, New Zealand or South Africa. On 2 November 1945 Sir Edward Grasset, Jersey's Lieutenant Governor, wrote to the Home Office:

Feeling in Jersey against those who collaborated with the Germans ... and were guilty of scandalous conduct shows no sign of abatement and the feeling is in fact increasing. There have been no breaches of the peace caused by unlawful action against those considered to be guilty but this is due to your investigation. I have urged [that] the fullest measures of persuasion that can be exercised without a breach of peace should be exerted on those miserable people [who

had fraternised with the Germans and informed on fellow islanders]
to induce them to leave the island.

A number of islanders did leave in 1945, probably under inducement of some kind. 'Inducing them to leave' was the method used
against the nationals of two countries who came in for considerable
abuse on Jersey at the end of the war. The sudden arrival of the
Germans in 1940 had stranded many Irish seasonal labourers who
had come over for the potato harvest. Ireland was neutral during
the war, and many islanders accused them of collaborating; they
probably had little choice but to work for the Germans after being
stranded without family or financial support. The Civil Affairs Unit
reported that this 'undesirable element' was being closely watched
in the summer of 1945. The other group were Italians on Jersey,
many of whom had run cafés and restaurants before and during the
Occupation. After Liberation, some Italians were told by the Jersey
government to leave the islands, but they had friends amongst the
people. Bernard Hassall was one of those who collected names for
a petition to allow them to stay; he argues that the Italians were used
as scapegoats, and that many of them had been very anti-German.

Financial penalties were devised to deprive islanders of ill-gotten
Occupation gains. As the civil servants had recognised, tracing illegitimate profits was always going to be immensely complex. Both
Jersey and Guernsey enacted steep War Profits Levies of 60–100
per cent, but records of how much this tax raised remain secret.
An Inland Revenue tax inspector seconded to Jersey in 1953 to
assist in the assessment and collection of the levy remembers being
told to leave the financial affairs of certain islanders alone. He is
sceptical as to whether the tax really affected the worst cases of
black marketeering profits:

> Some retail shops stuck out more than others, and it was not difficult
> to start a few cases for investigation. I was well aware of the closely-
> knit political set-up in Jersey, and leaning on the Comptroller of
> Income Tax was not unheard of. The investigators were all on
> secondment [from the UK] for short periods. This had the effect of
> trying to achieve negotiated settlements quickly, with trimming of
> corners as appropriate. I don't think anyone could say that the whole

truth emerged. We did our best in the circumstances. A Jersey resident would possibly have done a better job but taken much longer, and would still have been up against the system which closed ranks at any sign of treading on the ruling class's ground.

One case dragged on until 1949. A Guernsey vegetable grower found that the allegations levelled at him for making huge profits out of growing vegetables for the Germans would not go away. Sir Abraham Lainé had conducted an inquiry into this man immediately after the war. Details reached the British newspaper the *Daily Sketch*, which alleged that he had taken over glasshouses from their owners and grown vegetables and flowers for the Germans while islanders were starving. He denied the charge, claiming that 'what I did was done to save the complete pillage of the islanders' food by the occupiers'. In 1949 he was still trying to clear his name, and sent a petition to the King asking for an investigation. The request was refused. The Home Office noted that in 1947 the man had been investigated by MI5, who found that his bank account had had a debit balance of £340 at the beginning of the war and £70,000 credit at the end.

One final aspect remains to Britain's investigations after Liberation. The Bailiffs of both Guernsey and Jersey were anxious that a small number of German officers in the islands' military governments should be brought to trial for war crimes committed against islanders. They claimed there had been two war crimes: the deportation of islanders to German internment camps and the cutting back of civilian rations during the last year of the Occupation. Evidence was collected, detailed physical descriptions of the alleged culprits were taken, and a list of about half a dozen names, including Baron von Aufsess and Oberst Knackfuss, was drawn up and registered with CROWCASS – the Central Registry of War Criminals and Security Suspects which had been set up by the Allies. All of these men were in PoW camps in Britain, yet once again there were no trials, and the men were returned to Germany. No documents survive as to why the prosecutions were abandoned.

Baron von Aufsess returned in 1948 to the castle in Bavaria where his family have lived since the tenth century. He had always prided himself on his good relations with prominent – and/or attractive – islanders, and as a cultured, educated aristocrat he had made many friends during the Occupation. In due course he was to host a string of distinguished guests from the Channel Islands, including Ambrose and May Sherwill in 1948, and the Dame of Sark, Sybil Hathaway, in 1954.

THE LEGACY

The Second World War has arguably been the dominant influence on the British national identity of the twentieth century, and the second half of that century has been played out in its shadow. Dunkirk, the Battle of Britain and D-Day have been elevated into national myths – not in the sense of being untruths, but because they have come to represent the highest expressions of the resilience and determination against all odds of the British people. The images, the rhetoric and the legends of the war have been recycled, and Britain continues to employ them to interpret the world. The Channel Islands' culture is British; the islanders watch and listen to British television and radio, and they read British newspapers. Inevitably, the British perception of the Second World War has infiltrated their own. It is a history which sits very uncomfortably with the islands' own experience of the war.

The first half of the war had seen countries in Continental Europe fall like ninepins to the German advance; Britain had come perilously close to invasion, and had lost thousands of tons of shipping in the Battle of the North Atlantic. It had required a huge mobilisation of national determination to continue fighting rather than seek peace; what was formed in that crucible was a national perception by the British of themselves as the plucky and defiant David to Hitler's Goliath. They believed that they had shown themselves to be made of sterner stuff than the rest of Europe, which had reached accommodation with the Nazis. At the end of the war, Churchill claimed for Britain 'an unblemished record' in standing up to the Nazis. Only Britain had fought Hitler from the start of the war to its bitter end – at the cost of more than four hundred thousand lives, bombed cities, a lost empire and a near-bankrupted economy.

'We shall defend our island, whatever the cost may be, we shall fight on the beaches, we shall fight on the landing grounds, we shall fight in the fields and in the streets, we shall fight in the hills; we shall never surrender,' Winston Churchill had declared in June 1940. He had his theme ready for the rallying cry should Britain be invaded: 'You can always take one with you.' Leonard Woolf and others among his Bloomsbury friends agreed that they would kill themselves if the Germans invaded, and bought poison in order to be able to do so.

But Channel Islanders did not fight on the beaches, in the fields or in the streets. They did not commit suicide, and they did not kill any Germans. Instead, they settled down, with few overt signs of resistance, to a hard, dull but relatively peaceful five years of occupation, in which more than half the population was working for the Germans.

Despite the British politicians' exoneration of the islands in 1945, the islanders had not lived up to Britain's wartime ideals. Indeed, they had dismally failed them. The first British soldiers to reach the Channel Islands after Liberation were horrified by what they found, and newspaper headlines of the time are evidence of that. In 1945 the idea of Britons co-operating, let alone collaborating, with the Germans was deeply shocking. Nor was it only the British who were shocked, but all the countries of the Empire, towards whom Britain had maintained such a strong sense of superiority. The curious story of Roland le Folet Hoffman, an Australian journalist who committed suicide on Guernsey shortly after Liberation, illustrates this point. A colleague told the coroner inquiring into Hoffman's death: 'He was ashamed and disgusted at the signs of outright collaboration with the Germans that he saw in the Channel Islands.'

The Channel Islands Occupation did not fit into Britain's interpretation of the Second World War. It did not fit into the British collective memory of the war, the collective memory which, as Enoch Powell put it in 1989, 'makes a nation: its memory of what its past was, what it has done, what it has suffered and what it has endured'. The islands' experience flatly contradicted Britain's dearest and most complacent assumptions about the distinctness of the British from the rest of Europe. Under occupation, the British had behaved exactly like the French, the Dutch or the Danish.

In histories of the war, the Occupation has been relegated to a footnote, a curious anomaly. It was left to newspapers to feed the British public's appetite for stories about fraternisation and collaboration, stories whose capacity to shock, grab attention and sell papers is testimony to the endurance of the myth that the British 'do not do that sort of thing'. Rollo Sherwill, son of Ambrose Sherwill, the President of the Guernsey Controlling Committee, says:

> Newspapers write about the Channel Islands' Occupation in the way they do because this was the only bit of the British Isles which was occupied, and we're supposed to have reacted like the British would. But we didn't behave as British people should. We had no alternative, we had to stick to the laws of war. Since the war we have felt like a woman must feel in a rape trial. People accuse her of having led the rapist on. But just as a woman might co-operate for fear of not surviving, so did we. If we hadn't co-operated, we would have been harshly treated.

Sherwill pinpoints the cause of the British people's fascination with the islands' Occupation; they see it as an indicator of how they themselves would have behaved if Germany had invaded, and are horrified by anything that does not match up to how they like to believe they would have acted.

This is what underlay the extraordinary degree of media attention generated by the discovery in the Guernsey archives, when they were first opened to the public in January 1993, of letters proving that island officials had tracked down Jews and handed them over to the Germans. Some of the newspaper headlines were: 'Islanders Aided Nazi Jew Hunters' (*Guardian*); 'Guernsey Leaders Helped Nazis Round up Jews' (*Daily Telegraph*); 'Guernsey Betrayed Jews to the Nazis' (*The Times*); 'Knighthood for Man who Sent the Jews to Die' (*Daily Mirror*).

Guernsey accounted for just three of the millions of Jews who died in the Holocaust, but as the *Guardian*'s editorial said, the revelations 'touched very raw nerves indeed'. They challenged the assumption that British civil servants and police would not have co-operated in sending the British Jewish community to the gas chambers as the French had done. For nearly fifty years the British have believed that there was an element of decency and fairness, integral to being British, that would have prevented a British Holocaust. They believed that, alone in Europe, their consciences were clean. That illusion was shaken by the disclosure that respected servants of the British Crown, some of whom were subsequently knighted (Victor Carey and John Leale), had participated – in however small a measure – in one of the greatest evils of human history.

British interest in the Channel Islands Occupation is largely motivated by the ways in which it reflects on Britain itself, and by the British preoccupation with its own identity. This self-absorption, however, is not apparent to islanders, who feel that Britain has misunderstood, judged and criticised them. As a result, they have reinforced their island mentality to turn inwards and batten down the hatches. They are suspicious of outsiders, and reluctant to give information about their experience of the war to them. Their loyalty to the islands overrides their interest in telling the truth about the Occupation, and they have developed their own version of the war's history in the shadow – and under the scrutiny – of Britain.

In 1945, the Channel Islands were riven by bitter divisions. Neighbour criticised neighbour; farmers who had sold food to the Germans at high prices were loathed; some families could not accept that their neighbours had chatted with soldiers and invited them in for tea, or that women whose husbands were away fighting for the British had slept with the enemy. These divisions were immeasurably exacerbated by the return home of islanders who had spent the war abroad. A demobilised soldier might find his neighbour had been a black marketeer; a man who had worked in a British munitions factory for five years might come home to find his old job had been taken by a man who had stayed behind and worked for the Germans for good wages; there were British servicemen who came home to bring up German-fathered children.

Some of these divisions lasted until the people involved died. In a number of cases, where an islander died at German hands, descendants have inherited a family grievance against other islanders. But, for the majority, the divisions have been buried beneath layers of island loyalty so that a united front could be presented against the criticisms levelled by outsiders. Time dulls passions, and accusations have been tempered by sympathy for the moral dilemmas every islander faced. Islanders now talk of the women who slept with Germans with pity, not condemnation, and they would never dream of passing on the names of such women to an outsider. The divisions have been buried deeper and deeper in the recesses of the popular memory. Books written in the war's immediate aftermath were more honest than those which followed.

What has been lost, and what this book has attempted to illustrate, is the islanders' own experience – of fear, of helplessness, of guilt, of compromise and collaboration. It was an experience they shared with France, Holland, Denmark and the rest of occupied Europe, an experience informed with the moral complexity of war. Unlike the British, those who had been occupied could never view the war in quite the same terms of moral absolutes: of good against evil, the Allies against the Nazis. As American historian and critic Paul Fussell points out in his book *Wartime: Understanding and Behaviour in the Second World War*: 'For the war to be prosecuted at all, the enemy of course had to be severely dehumanised and demeaned ... [Germans were] a perverse type of human being, cold, diagrammatic, pedantic, unimaginative and thoroughly sinister ... their instinct for discipline made them especially dangerous.' The English writer Edward Blishen commented, on seeing the newspaper headline 'Hamburg has been Hamburgered' after a bombing raid: 'The tragic evolution of the war was commented on in the language of a gang fight in a school playground ... such an orgy of brutal over-simplification [would] shape attitudes that would last a lifetime.'

Such simplification was not possible for islanders who had lived as neighbours with the Germans for five years. Michael Ginns, a Jersey schoolboy at Liberation, remembers the difference between the islanders' perception of the enemy and that of the rest of the British people. He had spent nearly three years in an internment camp in southern Germany, and when he showed photographs of the camp to schoolfriends who had been evacuated to England, they refused to accept that the guards were real Germans:

> They had believed British propaganda cartoons literally; they thought all Germans had square heads and brutal faces. When I was in the army after the war, I found it easier to relate to the German and Polish prisoners of war whom I came into contact with than the other British soldiers. For the British, everything on the Continent was alien. In Britain, every German was considered a Nazi, but I never saw one act of cruelty during the five years of the war. Every nation produces its scum, but we saw the man behind the uniform and we saw the human face.

Islanders at the end of the war had a vastly more complex understanding of how good can merge imperceptibly with evil, with every possible muddy, deceptive permutation. This view does not diminish the terrible evils committed by the Nazis, but only reveals how complicity can spread its tentacles into the most unexpected of places. This part of the islanders' experience has not found its way into books: to a British audience it would smack too much of accommodation, precisely the charge against which islanders are most keen to defend themselves.

A collective memory has developed which eschews all controversy and provides a version of the Occupation around which all islanders – whatever their wartime experience, be it evacuation, deportation or occupation – can rally. The Occupation is too traumatic and recent an event for islanders to be able to ignore it. The dominance of British culture ensured that the islands' unique ordeal would be overlaid with the conventions and myths of Britain's wartime experience.

Over the last couple of decades, a large number of islanders who lived through the Occupation have published their memoirs. With one or two notable exceptions, they abide by clearly defined conventions: islanders are cast in the role of plucky and defiant characters who do everything they can to thwart the enemy; most of the Germans appear to be humourless and of subnormal intelligence. Great emphasis is put on the islanders' resourcefulness and ingenuity in maintaining a semblance of normal life amidst hardship and shortages – this was their heroism. It was analogous to the heroism of Londoners and other city-dwellers under the Blitz; ordinary people surviving with cheerfulness and determination. In this version of history, the writers argue that there was no resistance because they had no choice: large numbers of islanders would have been killed in retaliation. But they did attempt to obstruct the Germans in whatever small ways they could. They add that there was no alternative but to abide by the Hague Convention and hope that the Germans did the same. The vast majority of islanders make few references to slave labourers, Jews, fraternisation or the tiny handful who genuinely did resist. There is little hint of how demoralised islanders were, or of how they informed on their neighbours for rewards, or worked for the Germans for high wages.

This sanitised collective memory is buttressed by the few historians who have turned their attention to the subject. Oxford historian Charles Cruikshank was commissioned by Guernsey and Jersey in conjunction with the Imperial War Museum to write the official history of the Occupation. His book, which was published in 1975, devotes only four and half pages out of 314 to the thousands of slave labourers on the islands during the war. References to the island authorities' collaboration, Jews and fraternisation have to be decoded; they bear the marks of compromises hammered out in committees. On the island authorities' injunction to islanders not to offer any resistance, Cruikshank comments: 'This line, which followed logically on the demilitarisation of the islands and the attitude implied by the government's few pronouncements on the subject, was plainly commonsense.' At another point he writes: 'If the island administrations seem occasionally to have leaned too far in the direction of collaboration, it was their judgement that was at fault and not their loyalty.' What Cruikshank focused on was concrete and bullets. Every detail of the British military raids, including those which never got beyond the planning stage, is recounted, taking up nearly a third of the book.

Many of the local historians in the Channel Islands Occupation Society have followed Cruikshank's line. They have researched – in mind-boggling detail – the islands' fortifications and the German war machinery. The 1988 edition of the Society's review is typical, boasting articles entitled 'Alderney's German Jetty', 'German Flamethrowers in Jersey (Part 2)' and 'German Ground Radar'.

The history of the Occupation has become the pursuit of facts relating to a few tightly circumscribed subjects. Islanders would exclaim to me, 'You're not writing *another* book? What more is there to say? We know everything about the Occupation already.' Yet most of the Occupation's history has remained a mystery, the subject of rumours and whispered allegations.

Anyone who breaks the rules of this selective history earns condemnation, such as that meted out to Solomon Steckoll after he published *The Alderney Death Camp* in 1982. Steckoll, a South African Jew, was the first person to bother to find out what had happened to the Jewish women on Guernsey; he uncovered documentary evidence of their deportation and the collaboration of island officials. He also traced and interviewed survivors of the Alderney camps, and discovered details of the British government's failure to prosecute Germans for war crimes committed on Alderney. But Steckoll's sensationalist style, and the manner in which the book won instant media exposure, was seized upon by islanders as a pretext for completely dismissing his findings.

The islanders have virtually succeeded in controlling their history: co-operation is only extended to those writers who agree to abide by their conventions. Fellow islanders are encouraged to leave the histories to those who actually lived through the Occupation. The islanders succeeded in frightening off the last historian to publish a book on the Occupation; he admitted that he had never set foot on the islands for fear of the controversy he may have found.

It was because the wartime archives might challenge the conventions of the history accepted by the islanders, and reveal embarrassing facts about people who were still living, that there has been considerable procrastination about opening them to the public. The Jersey archives were finally opened to the public in 1994, and those on Guernsey in 1993. In fact, the latter occasion revealed that the authorities need not have worried, as the islanders showed a marked lack of interest. While the national British media made much of evidence that Guernsey officials had tracked down Jews for the Germans, the *Guernsey Evening Press* ran the headline 'Archives

Reveal that Island Authorities Resisted German Orders'. The story underneath stated: 'Files reveal that far from complying quietly with German orders, the island authorities protested against many of them and did their best to protect islanders from their worst effects.' One of the examples given to illustrate this point was a dispute over the requisitioning of footballs!

Islanders rallied to Guernsey's defence. Frank Stroobant, a Guernseyman who has written a memoir of the Occupation, was quoted in the *Daily Telegraph*: 'It all happened fifty years ago. People are trying to make up a story about what should have been dead and buried. They should have waited another ten years before opening the files. What would you have done in the same situation? The Germans were cock-a-hoop. To resist them was absolutely impossible.'

Molly Bihet, a Guernseywoman who has written an account of her Occupation childhood, said in the *Daily Express*: 'Maybe there were some things the island could be ashamed of – some of the women fraternised – but you tell me of a war when that never happened. But I do not think we deserve to be blamed for these deaths [of the Jews]. The Committee had to give over those names, but no one knew of the Holocaust then. What were we to do on Guernsey if we had known anyway? There is nowhere to run, nowhere to hide.'

The Guernsey Bailiff, Graham Dorey, also stepped in to defend the island's honour, issuing an unprecedented statement in which he criticised the press coverage, which had 'distorted our war record'. The islanders' version of history survived unchanged; the glare of publicity in those few days of early January 1993 confirmed their belief that Britain was critical and judgemental of issues of which it had no experience and no understanding.

Tangible evidence of the selectivity of the islanders' history is that there are no public memorials to the slave labourers who were on Guernsey. On Alderney a private memorial was erected by the Hammond family, and plaques were presented by each of the nations from which the victims had come. The memorial, which replaced a plaque to the French slave labourers erected in 1951 by the Alderney government, is not well maintained, and it leaves survivors like Otto Spehr baffled. In Germany, Spehr points out, the sites of SS camps have become carefully tended gardens of remembrance, often with well funded museums and archives attached. But the site of the SS Sylt camp on Alderney is a wasteland covered with brambles. Spehr enlisted the help of Chancellor Willi Brandt, and the German government agreed to put up half the funding for a memorial on the site of Sylt, but, Spehr claims, Alderney refused to consider the idea. When I asked a senior member of Alderney's government about the memorial, he said he had never heard of Spehr's request, and referred to the SS prisoners as 'men who had played with little boys'.

There is a memorial to the slave labourers on Jersey thanks to the efforts of the small community of former Spanish prisoners, including Francisco Font, who married a Jerseywoman and stayed on after the war. The crew of a Soviet ship which docked at Jersey in the 1960s contributed some of the funds. On the anniversary of the Liberation, the Russian ambassador comes from London to attend a ceremony of remembrance organised by islanders, and wreaths are laid on behalf of many countries.

On Guernsey there is no memorial to the slave workers.

Another illustration of this selective history is how those islanders who were brave enough to resist have been forgotten. Marie Ozanne died on Guernsey after having been tortured for complaining about the conditions of the slave labourers. She was a member of the Salvation Army, and after the war she was posthumously awarded the organisation's highest honour. But Guernsey forgot her; when a reference to her terrible suffering was discovered in an unpublished diary in 1992, few islanders had heard of her. The island awarded her no recognition for her courage and compassion, and no plaques were erected in her memory. Similarly, Jerseywoman Louisa Gould died in Ravensbrück for sheltering an escaped Russian slave labourer. Charles Machon, a Guernseyman, died in the French prison to which he was sent for setting up the Guernsey Underground News Service, which was so much admired during the war. Yet Machon's bravery has not been recognised. One of his associates on GUNS, Frank Falla, commented in his memoirs, *The Silent War*, that it was hard to understand why the bravery of these people had never been officially recognised either by the island governments or the British government. He quoted Sir John Leale, who suggested in the 1950s that 'It might be difficult for a government which is a signatory to the Hague Convention to recommend honours for those who broke the Convention.' Falla observed, 'My comment on that is, simply, "Rubbish".'

The treatment of Jerseyman John de la Haye is in striking contrast. In January 1945 de la Haye saw an American plane shot down over the sea off St Brelades. He went out on a float through the minefields and got the pilot onto a rock. German soldiers who had followed in a boat helped them both back to shore. For this act of bravery de la Haye received an extraordinary number of honours: the Silver Medal of the Jersey Humane Society; citations on parchment from President Eisenhower, Prime Minister Attlee and the Jersey Bailiff. He also received a gold watch from the parish of St Brelades, was mentioned by the King in the *London Gazette*, and was asked to lunch with the Duchess of Kent on the fortieth anniversary of the Liberation in 1985.

Ironically, it was the Soviet Union which recognised the bravery of the islanders, awarding twenty gold watches in May 1965 to those who had sheltered or fed escaped Russian slave labourers on Jersey.*

Islanders have simplified and moulded their history into one which they can celebrate. The Occupation has become a major tourism asset for the islands, which are dotted with museums commemorating it. Every May, Liberation Day is a bank holiday; there are services of remembrance in the churches, talks by those who lived through the Occupation and local historians, funfairs, knockout contests and bands.

A few islanders are brave and honest enough to challenge this sanitised history. One of them is Joe Miere, the former curator of the Jersey Underground Hospital Museum. Miere has put together an exhibition in the museum which charts every form of resistance in the Occupation – he was himself imprisoned on Jersey for petty resistance. Stung by post-war allegations that islanders had collaborated, he set about collecting photographs of those who had resisted, or had died in prisons on the Continent. He also has

---

* Albert Bedane, Claudia Dimitrieva, François Flamon, Ivy Forster, René Franoux, Royston Garrett, Louisa Gould (posthumously), Leslie Huelin, John Le Breton, Norman Le Brocq, Mike Le Cornu, Harold Le Druillenec, René Le Mottée, Francis Le Sueur, Bob Le Sueur, Dr R. McKinstry (posthumously), Augusta Metcalfe, Oswald Pallot, Leonard Perkins, William Sarre.

photographs of those who did collaborate. His intention was to set the record straight and document both of the forgotten sides of this history. It is this honest desire to recount the richness of the whole Occupation story which had been all but lost. The last wartime generation is now going to the grave with all the stories which never fitted into the straitjacket of accepted wisdom. For that, the censorious British bear the responsibility as much as the defensive islanders.

It is a source of embarrassment to the islanders, and to the British, that there was no resistance in the islands on the scale of the rest of Europe. There were none of the astonishing feats of bravery which characterised the legends of the French, Belgian, Cretan and Greek resistance. While the British were spurring on the European resistance movements through BBC broadcasts, infiltrating agents and dropping arms and equipment, they did nothing to encourage resistance on the islands. After the war, as the leaders of other countries' resistance were being fêted as national heroes, it was uncomfortably obvious that the one bit of British soil occupied by the Germans had produced no resistance movement to immortalise. As the historian M.R.D. Foot wrote in the *Daily Telegraph* in January 1993: 'Twenty-five years ago I had to arrange a set of lectures in Manchester about how resistance had been organised. One of our speakers, Vladimir Dedijer had been a political commissar under Tito. He opened by remarking that every nation had its own resistance heroes, could we tell him who had been the heroes of resistance in the Channel Islands? An awkward silence followed: the question has never had an answer.'

Islanders tell the British that they do not understand what it was like to be occupied; they cannot say the same to the Dutch, Belgians, French and Danish who ask the same question as Vladimir Dedijer: Why did the occupation of the Channel Islands diverge so dramatically from that of the rest of Europe?

In 1940, the string of German victories in western Europe seemed so total and so irreversible that the only option for occupied countries appeared to be to come to some sort of accommodation with the invader. Initially, France, Holland, Denmark, Belgium and

Norway saw the best policy as one of peaceful collaboration with the Germans, in the hope of winning favourable treatment. The Germans claimed to respect 'Germanic' nations such as Holland and Denmark – in the latter they tolerated a considerable measure of Danish sovereignty, and elections continued to be held there until 1943. Denmark's 'model protectorate' was the closest parallel to the Channel Islands' 'Model Occupation'.

Aage Bertelsen, a Danish resistance fighter, admitted that at first, 'we were all in favour, my wife included, of the so-called collaboration policy'. André Gide wrote in his diary on 9 July 1940: 'If German rule were to bring us affluence, nine out of ten Frenchmen would accept it, three or four with a smile.'

The workers of western Europe accepted the new jobs available through German occupation just as the Channel Islanders did. In the first sixteen months after the fall of France, fifty-nine thousand French workers voluntarily took jobs for the Third Reich. By the end of the war, 845,000 French were working either directly or indirectly – in companies contracted to the Germans – for the Reich, representing 42 per cent of the country's economy. By 1944, half of Dutch industry was working for the Germans. In the course of the war, 403,000 Belgians volunteered to work for the Germans. More than 100,000 Danish worked in Germany (a proportion of them were forced to do so). German occupation had dislocated these countries' economies just as it had done in the Channel Islands. They had lost foreign markets and imports of vital raw materials, and working for the Germans seemed the only alternative to economic collapse and starvation.

Indirectly, public services such as electricity, telephone and railway companies were also benefiting the Reich. The railways transported thousands of German soldiers and officials, as well as Jews to the gas chambers. In the same way as local police assisted the Germans on the islands, they assisted them in Europe; the French and Dutch police rounded up Jews and implemented anti-Jewish laws.

At first, resistance in occupied western Europe was confined to symbolic actions. In September 1940, two million Danes – 150,000 of them in Copenhagen – gathered in their local towns to sing folksongs in a gesture of national solidarity. The Dutch took to wearing badges made of coins bearing their exiled Queen's head, and put stamps on the left-hand side of their envelopes because the right belonged to the queen. Norwegians wore a tiny national flag or razor blade in their buttonhole. This was the kind of resistance which became common on the Channel Islands throughout the war.

Accommodation and passive resistance were never possible in Eastern Europe. The Germans wanted to wipe Poland as a nation off the map, and they replaced the country's government with a Nazi administration which ruled with unparalleled brutality. After the invasion of the Soviet Union, captured eastern territories such as the Baltic countries, Belorussia and Ukraine were subjected to the full force of Nazi contempt for 'Bolsheviks', as they called all Soviet citizens.

In mid-1941, the uneasy accommodation and co-operation with the Germans in occupied western Europe began to break down. The countries split between 'quislings' and violent resistance groups, with every nuance of collaboration and resistance in between. A logic of spiralling violence was set in motion, whereby German repression triggered resistance and vice versa – with terrifying consequences. Whole villages were wiped out in savage reprisals for ambushes and assassinations. Occupation came to mean Gestapo raids in the night, arbitrary arrests and torture, and the transportation of thousands of civilians to concentration camps. But not in the Channel Islands. This is where they diverge from the pattern which emerged in the rest of western Europe; they were never caught up in the cycle of violence. It has been calculated that if a German was killed in Norway, ten Norwegians were killed in retaliation; in Yugoslavia, a hundred would be killed; in Poland, a thousand. When two Germans were killed on Sark by a British agent during a raid on the island in 1942, two hundred islanders were deported to German internment camps where they were well fed on Red Cross parcels and survived the war in good health, and no one was killed in retaliation.

Unlike the rest of occupied Europe, the Channel Islands remained in that early mode of accommodation, in part because the Germans adopted a markedly different approach there than elsewhere in Europe. The islands had a German military government which contained few Nazis and no Gestapo; they allowed the island governments a measure of autonomy, which unlike in Denmark continued until the end of the war. The Germans were more tolerant of the islands' own sense of identity, of which loyalty to the British monarchy was a very important part. They allowed the islanders to pray for the King in church every Sunday, and island officials insisted that the population be permitted to retain their allegiance to the King; Ambrose Sherwill did so in his German-sponsored broadcast to Britain in August 1940. Such tolerance was not applied in Holland. The Nederlandsche Unie movement was conceived in the early phase of the Occupation as a rallying point for those Dutch who wanted to co-operate with the Germans while retaining their national identity. Its founding document advocated loyalty to the exiled Dutch Queen in London and collaboration with the Germans. The Germans objected to the former. Within a year the movement had become more openly critical of the Germans, and was banned. It was from such small beginnings that the logic of German repression provoking opposition spawned fully-fledged resistance movements throughout Europe.

There were four significant differences between the policies the Germans adopted on the islands and in western Europe, all of which contributed to lulling potential opposition to the Occupation. Firstly, the Germans did not attempt to change the islands' system of government; they confined themselves to working through the island authorities rather than undermining them. The system worked well from the German point of view, since some of the resentment over food rationing and requisitioning was directed at the island governments, rather than at the occupiers. In Holland, by contrast, the Germans reneged on their promise that their role would only be supervisory of the Dutch government, and in 1941 they abolished local municipal and provincial self-government to restructure the administration in line with the German Reich.

Secondly, in Belgium, Holland, Denmark and Norway the Germans undermined governments by the patronage and promotion of fledgling National Socialist parties. Senior government officials were dislodged in favour of German-sponsored home-grown Nazis, provoking huge resentment and providing the burgeoning resistance movements with an educated middle-class cadre possessing leadership and organisational skills. The installation in Norway of Vidkun Quisling, a Nazi, in February 1942, and his zealous Nazification programme infuriated Norwegians and increased sabotage attacks on the Germans.

Thirdly, the Germans' Nazification programmes forced thousands into open resistance. When Dutch students were forced to take an oath of loyalty to Germany, 85 per cent refused. The rounding-up of Jews in Amsterdam in 1941 triggered a strike which was brutally repressed. The Danish churches led the campaign against Nazification in Denmark, winning huge support; when the Germans shot a resister in August 1943, ten thousand people gathered for his burial. The Germans panicked and fired into the crowd; strikes were triggered and martial law imposed. When the Danish government refused to do the Germans' bidding and round up saboteurs, the Germans finally abandoned their pretence of a 'model protectorate' and took over power in the summer of 1943.

Finally, quotas for forced labour were imposed on other occupied countries, stimulating resistance. In Belgium, workers went on strike when quotas were stepped up. To avoid the labour draft thousands of young men, particularly in France, were forced underground where, without ration or identity cards, they had little choice but to join a resistance group.

In the Channel Islands there were no local Nazis to promote, and the Germans' Nazification programme was a diluted version. On Guernsey German, Polish and Austrian Jews were deported to concentration camps, not those married to British islanders; as a result the measure did not affect islanders, only a few strangers. Otherwise, Nazification consisted of censoring the local newspapers and insisting on German being taught in the island schools. There was no attempt to impose oaths of loyalty to the Reich on professionals such as doctors and teachers, and there were few attempts to force people to work for the Germans.

The Channel Islanders' own behaviour was a crucial contributing factor to the relatively peaceful Occupation. The majority of the islanders were more quiescent than other Europeans. They did what they were told; the German officer's description of Guernsey people as 'obsequious peasants' provides a glimpse of how the Germans regarded the islanders. For the islanders' part, they saw the Germans as they had seen the English tourists and property developers before them – as outsiders to be avoided. Islanders wanted to be left alone to get on with their own lives; the Germans were an annoying irritant, to be circumvented. The islanders' character was to avoid direct confrontation with the Germans if at all possible; they knew they would inevitably lose such confrontations, so they employed other, more wily means to achieve their ends. The result was that the Germans' authority was rarely challenged, and they did not feel the need to resort to violence and terror in order to enforce their authority. As many Germans stationed on the islands remember, the Channel Islands were the one part of occupied Europe where they did not always need to wear a helmet or carry a weapon.

A telling instance of the confidence of the Germans was when thousands of islanders gathered for the funerals of the British sailors from HMS *Charybdis* whose bodies had been washed onto Jersey and Guernsey's shores in November 1943. The islanders were expressing their defiant patriotism, but unlike the funeral in Denmark shortly before, there was no panicky firing of shots to keep control of the crowds. The Germans may have been irritated by the display of passive loyalty to Britain, but they were not frightened; they recognised it as a gesture of defiance, but not the first sign of a mass resistance movement.

One factor which underlay the islanders' quiescence was their knowledge that Britain was still fighting the war. There was no humiliated national honour which required avenging, as in the defeated countries of Europe. In Britain's armies, air force and navy were thousands of islanders, and the achievements of the British forces bolstered islanders' morale and self-respect. It was much easier to put up with irksome German orders when you knew that the previous night the British had shot down a large number of their planes.

In addition, the islands had no tradition of opposing authority. They were rigidly hierarchical, conformist societies. The small elite of inter-connected families who dominated the government of the islands suffered some humiliation at the hands of the Germans, but they quickly recognised that open protest would bring savage repression. Deeply frightened, they focused on the objective of keeping themselves and as many islanders as possible alive. The tentacles of power of this elite stretched into every aspect of island life and economy: getting planning permission, licences, jobs and customers required their patronage. They had the power to stifle those who were disruptive of island–German relations. Any serious resistance movement would have required the participation of some individuals from that elite, with their authority and leadership. It never happened; time has proved that they made an astute appraisal of their best chance of survival. Unlike anywhere else in Europe, the power of the islands' elite survived unscathed; the same families were in power before, during and after the war. The grandson of the wartime Bailiff of Guernsey, Victor Carey, became the Deputy Bailiff on the island (he makes it a principle never to comment on the Occupation). It is a sign of the strength of this system of power that it could withstand the strains of Occupation – the massive expansion of government into every aspect of the islands' economies, and the strict rationing – with no real attempt being made to oppose them.

There were no independent institutions to challenge this elite. In Europe, the Communist Party, the trade unions and the churches played a crucial role in mobilising resistance. The islands' trade unions were banned by the Germans, and only on Jersey did they continue underground, organising resistance activities such as Norman Le Brocq's leafletting operation in conjunction with the minuscule Communist Party and a group of left-wing sympathisers. The churches were central to island life; Guernsey boasts a large number of Methodist congregations, but there is no evidence that they took any stand on the treatment of slave labourers or Jews. Apart from Canon Cohu on Jersey, who died in Spergau concentration camp after having spread BBC news among islanders, no minister or priest is known to have been involved in resistance. Several vicars and pastors of different denominations crop up in letters to the German Feldkommandantur in 1942, pleading to be exempted from deportation to German internment camps; they make a point of stressing their loyalty to the occupiers. If their example is anything to go by, then the islands' churches were anxious to follow the lead of their governments.

There were clear geographical circumstances which militated against any resistance in the Channel Islands. The first was that the islands had no strategic significance. As far as the British were concerned, they were never anything other than a complete irrelevance to the rest of the war. Resistance seemed futile to the islanders. The Channel Islands were not like Sicily, the capture of which was a vital stepping stone to the conquest of Italy. The islands' power to harm the German war effort was strictly limited. Nor were islanders ever called on as the French, Belgian, Dutch, Danish and Norwegian resistances were to assist the Allied liberating armies after D-Day by blowing up bridges and railways, and spying on German troop movements. The British government recognised the pointlessness of resistance on the islands in terms of war strategy, and made no attempt to encourage its development. The raids which the British mounted on the islands never had the objective of contacting resisters. The British dropped no arms or Special Operations Executive agents, and no BBC broadcasts encouraged resistance on the islands. In the view of the British government, all the islanders could do was wait.

Secondly, the islands shared a geographical handicap with Denmark, Holland and Belgium. They were flat, densely populated, and offered no mountainous terrain such as that which sheltered the *maquis* in southern France or the resistance on another island, Crete, or the fjords which provided such excellent secret harbours in Norway. Only at the end of the war, when German authority was breaking down in Holland, Belgium and Denmark, was armed resistance possible in those countries; but on the islands, German authority remained intact to the end. The islands had a huge concentration of German soldiers; a higher number of armed troops per square mile even than Germany. There was nowhere to run to, no means of escape. The shores were mined and patrolled, and the ownership of boats was strictly regulated. On the Continent a resister could slip over the border with forged papers, whereas on the islands the chances of capture were very high. Open resistance such as sabotage would result in almost certain death, for questionable gain.

The result was that the islanders did not succeed in frustrating or resisting any of the Germans' war aims on the islands. On the contrary, they actually helped them achieve those aims, the most important of which was to hold onto the islands. The islanders helped feed, clothe and house the huge garrisons, a role which was acknowledged as crucial by the Befehlshaber, Graf von Schmettow, at a meeting in the German Foreign Ministry in October 1944 when the German government was considering whether the islands' civilians should be evacuated in order to ensure that the garrison had adequate supplies. In addition, the islands supplied thousands of electricians, builders and decorators to help construct defences to make the islands impregnable fortresses. The camouflage they constructed for anti-aircraft guns hid them from British detection; the guns whose concrete emplacements they had helped build were used to fire at British ships.

The Germans' secondary war aim – at least at the beginning of the Occupation – was to establish good relations with the civilian population, for propaganda purposes. They succeeded beyond their wildest dreams; they could never have imagined that within a few weeks German newsreels would be showing soldiers chatting with flirtatious island girls, and that a senior island official would be declaring in a radio broadcast that the conduct of the invading Germans had been exemplary.

It is surprising that islanders did not offer more resistance over some issues. There are three prominent examples. The first occurred within four months of the Occupation on Guernsey, when British secret agents Hubert Nicolle and Jim Symes were handed over to the Germans, along with thirteen of their friends and relatives. By law it was treason to hand over a British agent to the enemy, a point which did not escape the President of the Guernsey Controlling Committee, Ambrose Sherwill, who had urged them to give themselves up. Although the Germans could have shot the agents as spies, and indeed passed the death sentence on them both, they agreed to treat them as prisoners of war, commuting their sentences to imprisonment in a PoW camp. In his private papers, Sherwill anguishes over whether he did the right thing. It was a huge gamble; if more islanders had died than the First World War veteran Louis Symes (the father of Jim), who committed suicide in the Cherche Midi prison in Paris, history's judgement of Sherwill might have been different. Instead of his pragmatism being praised, he might have been tried for treason.

It is surprising that there were no serious protests at the deportation of 2200 islanders in 1942 and 1943. The Germans said that the islanders would be well treated in internment camps, but why should they have been believed? Yet the islanders obediently boarded the ships, and those who remained behind cheerfully waved them goodbye. The only protest was a scuffle caused by a few teenagers on the Jersey quayside. The island governments even helped the Germans in deporting the British-born islanders by drawing up lists and guiding the German soldiers to the appropriate addresses. There were no strikes or demonstrations, and no growth in resistance.

Similarly, there were few overt complaints when radios were confiscated in June 1942; this did not happen in any other occupied country, and confiscation of civilians' radios was against the Hague Convention. The loss of their radios was a real hardship and pro-voked much resentment, but not even that stirred the islanders into open protest.

Readers will have formed their own judgement as to whether the islands' acceptable pragmatism became cowardly subservience. The Occupation is a very human story, in which there is more evidence of weakness than of bravery. There are only a few incidents in this history to admire or to inspire; for the most part it is made up of the kind of shabby muddling through to which most people are prone.

At the start of the Occupation, the islanders' aims were peace and survival, and by and large they were successful in achieving them. There was no violence on the scale of every other occupation in Europe. The islands' governments succeeded in keeping the majority of their civilian populations remarkably healthy and safe: the Channel Islands were probably among the safest places in Europe between 1939 and 1945. Armed resistance would have had little chance of success: it would not have contributed to the defeat of the Nazis, and would have led to the almost certain death of those brave enough to have participated, as well as probably costing the lives of innocent islanders.

The island governments had been told by the British government to rule in the best interests of the islanders, and they defined that duty very narrowly. They did not feel obliged to protect Jews or to speak up for slave labourers, nor to champion the cause of those islanders whom the Germans accused of misdemeanours – including having resisted – and who were sent to Continental prisons, where some of them died. The survival of the large majority of the islanders was at the cost of these unfortunates.

It is in their failure to remember and acknowledge those who were sacrificed to the islands' welfare that the islanders must be judged. How can they belittle the suffering of the slave labourers by denigrating their characters and dismissing them as criminals and paedophiles? How could Therese Steiner, Marianne Grunfeld and Auguste Spitz be forgotten for forty years? Why were the names of people such as Louisa Gould, Harold Le Druillenec, Marie Ozanne and Charles Machon left to fade, unrecognisable to future generations? Only when there are exhibits in all the islands' museums to these people, and well cared-for memorials and plaques in their memory, only when islanders talk as freely about the Jews as they do about how they made tea out of bramble leaves, will they have begun to tell the whole story of the Occupation.

And only then will the British people have begun to accept that the memory of the Second World War does not serve merely to reinforce the separation caused by twenty miles of water which has shaped Britain's destiny. If Britain's national identity is to adjust to the development of European integration in the late twentieth century, so the stock of British wartime legends will have to be expanded to encompass a common European legacy of 1939–45; the history of sixty thousand British citizens under German occupation offers a vital link to the Continental experience of the Second World War.

THE JEWISH QUESTION

The hardback publication of *The Model Occupation* in 1995, the fiftieth anniversary of the Liberation of the Channel Islands, provoked considerable controversy there. Foremost amongst the points that irritated islanders was my handling of the question of what happened to the small number of Jews on the islands. The ensuing controversy in the local newspapers, particularly the *Jersey Evening Post*, usefully served to bring considerably more information to light, and this warrants a new appendix.

Finding out what had happened to the Jews on Jersey was difficult during my original research. In part this was because not much was genuinely known about what happened to them. There were about twenty Jews who remained after Jersey's most prominent Jewish families evacuated to Britain. Those who stayed behind were mostly elderly or recently arrived, relatively isolated refugees with few friends amongst the islanders. Few books on the Occupation have referred to the difficulties these Jews experienced during the war – *A Doctor's Occupation* by John Lewis is one exception – whether because they did not speak of their persecution, or because they did not wish to publicise the fact, is impossible to say.

Some of the Jews who had been on Jersey during the Occupation left after the war, others died of old age. When Jersey's Jewish community reconstituted itself in the decades after the war, it was presumed that there had been no Jews on the island during the Occupation. It has only been in the last few years that this assumption has been challenged and members of the community have discreetly researched the subject.

They were not helped by the fact that on Jersey, unlike Guernsey, few documents on the subject appear to have survived. The few letters referring to the registration of Jews which did exist were amongst those Bailiff's war files stolen in 1991. To date, they do not seem to have been recovered.

Broaching the question in an interview immediately provoked suspicion that I was 'muck-raking'. It was not a subject local historians had chosen to look into. Michael Ginns, immensely knowledgeable on the Occupation, insisted that no harm had come to any British Jews.

But unexpectedly in January 1995, the file on Jersey's Jews belonging to the Chief Aliens Officer, Clifford Orange, came to light in the State Greffier's Office – a form of registry office – in St Helier. It provides the most detailed set of documents on the persecution of the Jews in the Channel Islands to date.

In October 1940 notices were published in the local newspapers ordering all those with grandparents who 'belonged to the Jewish religion' to present themselves for registration at the island's Aliens Office. Twelve people were subsequently registered by Clifford Orange, who questioned them on their Jewish ancestry. A number òf Jews, aware of the danger, did not register, including the stepsisters Suzanne Malherbe and Lucille Schwab, a Mr Harvey and two Azulay sisters who claimed to be Methodists. They all survived the Occupation undetected, although Schwab and Malherbe were imprisoned for resistance activities.

Many of the twelve who registered were very uncertain as to their Jewish origins, and Orange carefully made notes of their conscientious explanations of their ancestry. Several had not lived on Jersey long. Seventy-year-old Victor Emmanuel had come from Hamburg, Germany, twenty-one months before. John Max Finkelstein (sixty-eight) and Nathan Davidson had come from Romania and had lived on Jersey for eight years and five years respectively. Orange annotated Davidson's form: 'Mr Davidson has stated that he has always belonged to the Christian community, and so far as he is aware, his father did also. Believes that one of his grandparents was a Jew, but knows nothing about the others.'

Marianne Blampied (fifty-three), Hedwig Bercu (twenty-one), Margaret Hurban (thirty-one) and Esther Pauline Lloyd (thirty-four) had all arrived in Jersey in the previous three years from Holland and Austria, and the last from Walthamstow, London. There was considerable confusion about whether Bercu was Jewish: 'Miss Hedy Bercu has stated that she is an illegitimate child, and that she has never known who her father was – that her mother subsequently married a Romanian Jew – that her mother was originally Protestant, but adopted her husband's religion,' noted Orange.

Only Samuel Simon and Therese Marks (both seventy-eight) had been born in Jersey. John Jacobs (fifty-eight) had come from London seventeen years before: 'he thinks his father was a Jew – knows nothing about his grand-parents'. Ruby Still (fifty-three), born in Leeds, had lived in Jersey for thirty years, and Hyam Goldman (seventy-one) born in Birmingham, had lived on the island for thirty-two years. Only Mr Goldman, a bee-keeper and gardener, was a practising Jew.

Orange sent the list of registered Jews to the Bailiff, Alexander Coutanche, on 25 October 1940: 'I have the honour . . . to report that twelve persons have duly registered at this Office.' A month later, the Germans instructed the Bailiff that Jews of American citizenship also had to be registered; Coutanche personally annotated the letter, asking Orange to look into the matter.

Mr Orange was also charged with the responsibility of registering all Jewish 'economic undertakings' in October 1940. Jewish businesses, including those belonging to Jews who had evacuated to England, were to be marked as such with a notice, 'Jewish Undertaking'. Those who had been left to administer the property had the responsibility of registering. Orange's notes indicate the confusion and concern the measure prompted: 'Certain legal administrators are not sure whether their clients are Jews or not – what action should they take, their clients being out of the country? Must a Jewess, being a private individual, declare everything she possesses – and must her husband, a Gentile, also declare?' jotted Orange after two telephone calls.

For more than a month, Orange must have been almost completely taken up with the complex problems of registering Jewish property and businesses. Some of the Jewish families who had evacuated to England had left sizeable amounts of property behind, and their solicitors, frightened by the threat of undeclared property being confiscated, hastened to declare the details.

Some bewildered solicitors did not know whether their clients were Jewish or not, and had only a name to go on: 'Mr Podro, Mr Israel and Mrs Hill (née Jacobs) all bear names which we believe are of Jewish origin. We have, however, no knowledge as to whether our clients are of the Jewish faith and it has been impossible for us to ascertain any accurate information on the matter.'

The Feldkommandantur determined that declarations were necessary in case any of them were Jewish, and Coutanche asked Orange to see to the matter. Other cases were equally flimsy, and clearly caused solicitors concern; one company wrote that they knew their clients, when appearing in the Royal Court, had taken the oath under the Christian faith, rather than Jewish, and that they had attended 'social functions' organised by the Church of England.

By 27 November 1940, fourteen Jews' property had been declared, including that of Hyam Goldman and Nathan Davidson, both still resident on the island. Goldman wrote in clear childish writing in thick ink: 'I beg to declare that I have a small grocer shop (Bee Hive Stores) at the above address, a J.U. poster is on the window. Not with-standing the above, by Jersey Judicatory, the above is 5 per cent Jewish and 95 per cent non-Jewish this condition has been stable since 1908. I have no other interests.'

Davidson was only able to sign a dictated letter, a shaky signature with several blotches: 'I am not sure whether I come under the province of the above order, but in case I do, I declare the following: I am running a small grocery shop.'

Amongst the Jews who had evacuated were some extremely wealthy individuals, such as Phineas Cohen, who owned shares and property worth nearly £200,000, and Israel Cohen, owner of seventeen houses and three shops.

As soon as the property was declared, the Germans ordered the next step on 11 December 1940: all Jewish businesses were to be 'Aryanised'. First the nature of the business and its turnover had to be declared, and an Aryan administrator suggested within a week of the order. Ominously, the Germans added in their letter to the Bailiff that 'those businesses whose continuance is not essential for the local economy, no suggestion need be made for an administrator'. By the end of December five businesses had complied, and the Germans wrote to the Bailiff: 'I would like you to examine the question as to whether a closing or a sale to an Aryan is possible . . . I would like the matter to receive prompt attention.' The day the Bailiff received this letter, 31 December 1940, letters were sent to Davidson and Goldman asking them to attend an interview at the office of the Attorney General, Duret Aubin, on 2 January. There is no indication of what took place, but it is likely they were told their businesses had to close. Goldman's repeated efforts to indicate that the business belonged to his wife were ignored.

In March 1941, the Germans ordered that all filing cards for Jews should be marked with a large red 'J' and a diagonal red stripe. Coutanche marked the order for 'necessary action' to Orange.

In May 1941, a further set of measures were enacted against the Jews. They were forbidden from holding a job in a wide range of businesses, from retail and transport to finance. They were not allowed to be employed in any job where they would come into contact with customers. In September 1941, all Jews were banned from owning radios; Goldman, Davidson and John Jacobs duly handed in their radios to the Chief Aliens Officer, Clifford Orange. He added in his submission to the Bailiff that all the Jews on the register had been 'interviewed by me, in person', to ensure they did not have radios. Under another measure, Jews had to request permission if they wanted to move accommodation; the applications of Hedy Bercu, Margaret Hurban and Samuel Simon were successful.

In January 1942, the Assistant Registration Officer wrote to the Feld-kommandantur that he had done as instructed and had told Samuel Simon, Victor Emmanuel, Marianne Blampied and Hedy Bercu to report to the

Feldkommandantur. There is no reference to the purpose of the interview. In March 1942, the Sixth Order against the Jews ordered that they had a special curfew, from 8 p.m. until 6 a.m. In April 1942 Dr Reffler, on behalf of the Feldkommandantur, stepped in to stop the 'forced auctioning of the complete contents of houses or of individual household effects of Jews' until further notice.

In July 1942, the Ninth Order against the Jews was promulgated: it restricted them to entering shops and workshops between 3 and 4 o'clock in the afternoon; Jews were also forbidden to enter any public building or theatre. Infraction of the order would lead to a fine or 'internment in a camp for Jews'. The order was duly registered in Jersey's Royal Court, and Coutanche annotated a note to the Attorney General to take the necessary action. The Attorney General passed the same document on to Orange: 'please notify all Jews of the contents of Order ... I enclose twelve copies of it herewith and I say just that a copy be handed to each person affected.' Orange notes that this was done by 21 August.

There is then a gap in the file until two years later. Esther Lloyd wrote to the Bailiff in September 1944 claiming that she had been wrongfully deported in February 1943. She stated that she had been wrongfully registered as Jewish and that the Aliens Office had failed to explain to her that she was not classified as Jewish under Nazi measures. It was only in Germany that the matter was looked into, and she was returned to Jersey in April 1944 from Biberach internment camp, where she had been sent: 'I went alone and left my two small children here and my husband who was ill most of the winter and is still far from well today also my boy was fretting and under the doctor's care most of the time I was away.'

Mrs Lloyd admitted she went to register at the Aliens Office because she was 'of Jewish origin on my grandfather's side only I thought at the time it concerned me but if all the facts concerning myself had been fully explained to the German Authorities, there would have been no question of my being sent away'.

In reply to a query from the Bailiff about the letter, Orange defended himself: 'in each case of registration, the person concerned was told by me that the responsibility for registering or not registering under the Order rested entirely with the individual concerned ... I wish to state, in conclusion, that I had no knowledge whatever of the intended transportation of Mrs Lloyd and other registered persons in 1943 until after it had taken place.'

There the file ends.

The file offers a fascinating insight into the way the Germans slowly tightened the noose on the tiny Jewish community, with initial requests which appeared relatively innocuous. The Jews were drawn into the trap presumably by a mixture of trust in the island authorities and fear of incurring worse consequences by not complying with the measures. Within two years of the Occupation, every aspect of their lives was severely restricted. It is pitiful to read of the harassment of elderly individuals such as Hyam Goldman.

On one of the most important issues – the deportation of Jews – the file is tantalisingly inconclusive. The letter in the Lloyd case clearly indicates that other Jews remained after the 1943 deportations, but there is no indication of how many of them there were or what happened to them.

An appeal for information from islanders in the *Jersey Evening Post* in 1995 prompted more than a dozen letters with recollections of those registered as Jews, and threw a little more light on what happened to them.

Victor Emmanuel was a retired professor, a German refugee. According to a former pupil, Emmanuel earned his living by teaching German: 'Apart from having to register their names as Jewish people, nothing else was done to them by the occupying authorities except that all were forbidden to undertake any form of business ... Mr Emmanuel hated the Nazis and would always become intensely upset when their forces marched past his house singing their Nazi songs ... By 1945 he had begun to suffer mentally from the strain of occupation and suffered a fatal heart attack shortly before Liberation.'

But a former neighbour has rather different information: 'Mr Emmanuel absolutely hated the Germans ... He was very harassed by the military. I think, being bilingual, they made him do translations for them. He hated them so much that he finally hanged himself under the stairs.'

A sad fate also awaited Samuel Simon. According to his great-granddaughter-in-law, 'the night before his deporatation order was due to take effect in December 1943, he was found dead at home, ostensibly from a heart attack'.

A strange end came to Hyam Goldman, according to an islander: 'He was a rather quiet man who always dressed in white ... At some time in the early 1950s Mr Goldman went missing and after several days of searching the area, his body was found by the police in the large circular water tank (6–7ft high) alongside the cottage where he and his wife lived. He was found to have committed suicide. To the best of my knowledge they were not unduly harassed by the Germans throughout the Occupation.'

Of the remaining registered Jews, Therese Marks died in her bed of old age in late 1940, and both John Jacobs and Marianne Blampied (married to a successful Jersey artist) survived the Occupation.

Like Esther Lloyd, John Max Finkelstein was deported and interned in a camp in Eastern Europe. He was badly treated there, but he survived and returned to Jersey after the war. Ruby Still was also deported; a relative claims this was because she was married to an islander born in England, but local historian Michael Ginns said that she 'had the misfortune to have been selected as a "token" Jew to make it look good in the eyes of Berlin'.

No information was offered on what happened to either Nathan Davidson or Margaret Hurban.

Hedwig Bercu proved to be an intriguing saga. Many islanders had understood that she had been deported to Europe, but fifty years after the end of the war, the truth emerged. An islander who had been a boyfriend of hers told his story.

In 1940 Bercu decided not to go to England for fear that as an Austrian citizen she might be interned, so she stayed in Jersey. When the Germans arrived, they forbade any German or Austrian national from working for a British employer, so Bercu began to work for the Germans, eventually ending up as an interpreter for the German transport staff. Her Jersey boyfriend gave her up because he would not go out with someone who was working for the Germans.

In 1943 the Geheime Feldpolizei raided the lodgings of an Irishman whom they suspected of thieving and found some German petrol vouchers which he should not have had. He said he had been given them by Bercu, who sold them on the black market. Bercu was questioned but then let go. Fearing it was only a matter of time before she was arrested, she elaborately faked her own suicide by leaving her clothes in a pile on the beach with a note saying, 'I am giving myself to the sea.' She then went into hiding in St Helier.

Her former boyfriend saw her after the war, but he never knew who had hidden her. In 1947 she left the island and returned to Germany, where she is understood to be still living.

From these fragments of information, it is difficult to ascertain conclusively how much effect the innumerable anti-Jewish measures had on Jews' lives. At least three were deported, and the sad stories of Simon, Emmanuel and Goldman are disturbing, pointing to harassment and fear. Islanders have claimed to me that Jews whose property was confiscated got it all back after the war, and that Aryanisation was only a matter of shuffling paperwork about. The descendants of Jewish evacuees have mixed reports. But the daughter of Israel Cohen, Rita Sennett, is adamant that the family never recovered a large amount of their property: 'Everything was confiscated because my father was Jewish. From what I heard after the war, there were a few collaborators and they pointed out that we were Jewish. We got three or four houses back and about £400 compensation. Everything my father had worked for all his life had gone.'

Ironically, Mrs Sennett said that one of those who had been the most helpful after the war in trying to secure the return of the family's property was Alexander Coutanche himself.

Jersey took little notice of the discovery of the file on the island's Jews. The *Jersey Evening Post* carried a dense article which emphasised that if the islanders had refused to comply with anti-Jewish measures, retribution would have been severe. In a follow-up article, it claimed that the wartime files 'showed no evidence of collaboration'.

The coverage was in sharp contrast to that the *Post* had given the opening of the Guernsey archives in January 1993, when the degree of co-operation on the part of Guernsey officials was first established. Headlines then ran: 'Guernsey's Leaders "Helped Send Jews to Gas Chambers"'. Local historians were slow to show interest in what is a remarkable set of documents.

The lack of interest on Jersey – and the fury over a report on the file in the *Guardian* – indicate the sensitivity of the islanders on the subject. Why has there been so little interest in the fate of the Jews in the last fifty years? Why do islanders on both Jersey and Guernsey advance the particularly repugnant argument that the Jews registered 'voluntarily', therefore anything that then happened to them was their own fault?

What islanders do not want to acknowledge is that the co-operation of the island authorities must undoubtedly have given the persecution a veneer of respectability. It was not Nazis demanding details of your business or ancestry, but a fellow islander. These vulnerable, poorly-educated Jews trusted the authorities.

Nor do islanders want to acknowledge that there is no evidence that the island authorities protested or dragged their heels at any point in the operation. For Clifford Orange, Alexander Coutanche and Duret Aubin it was a routine matter of administration, which they dealt with efficiently and promptly, with what appears to have been complete indifference to the individuals involved.

Sources

Abbreviations

HO – Home Office
IWM – Imperial War Museum, London
PRO – Public Record Office, Kew
WO – War Office

Sources are cited in order of their first appearance in the chapter. All interviews are with the author unless otherwise stated.

INTRODUCTION
Interview with Rollo Sherwill
John Fowles, introduction to *The Book of Ebenezer Le Page* by G.B. Edwards

CHAPTER ONE DITCHED
Interview with Harry Aubin
The Diary of Reverend Ord, Priaulx Library, Guernsey
IWM interview with Edwin de Ste Croix
Interview with Sandy Whitley
Frank Falla, *The Silent War*
Private papers of Sir Ambrose Sherwill
HO papers in the PRO
Charles Cruikshank, *The German Occupation of the Channel Islands*
Jersey Evening Post
Interview with Dolly Joanknecht
Interview with Herbert Nichols
Interview with Vivyan Mansell
Interview with Bob Le Sueur
Interview with Bernard Hassell
Edward Hamel, *X-Isles*, IWM
Hansard

IWM interview with Reginald Blanchford
IWM interview with Dorothy Blackwell

CHAPTER TWO CORRECT RELATIONS
Interview with Kathleen Whitley (née Norman)
Unpublished memoirs of Albert Lamy
Private papers of Sir Ambrose Sherwill
Television interview with Wemer Grosskopf
Interview with Hans Stumpf
Interview with Willi Reiman
Television interview with Karl-Heinz Kassens
Interview with Johannes Kegelman
Interview with Tom Mansell
Unpublished diary of James Ryan
Charles Cruikshank, *The German Occupation of the Channel Islands*
Private papers of Sir Ambrose Sherwill
Interview with Vivyan Mansell
Interview with Tom Mansell
Guernsey Evening Press

IWM interview with Dorothy Blackwell
Unpublished diary of Fred Woodall,
   IWM
Interview with Herbert Nichols
Interview with Daphne Pope
Interview with Bernard Hassell
Interview with Harry Aubin
Interview with Vivyan Mansell
IWM interview with Maurice Green
Interview with Don Guilbert
Interview with Randolf Kugler
The von Aufsess Occupation Diary, ed.
   Kathleen Nowlan
Interview with Mary McCarthy
Papers in the Guernsey State Archives
Unpublished diary of Cecil Bazeley,
   IWM
Interview with Maurice Green
Interview with Joe Miere
IWM interview with William Brown
Interview with Betty Thurban
Jersey Archives
Interview with Bob Le Sueur
Interview with Dolly and Willi
   Joanknecht

CHAPTER THREE A MODEL
   OCCUPATION

Private papers of Sir Ambrose Sherwill
Guernsey Evening Press
HO/PRO
IWM interview with Maurice Green
Guernsey State Archives
Jersey Archives
Frank Falla, *The Silent War*
H.R.S. Pocock (ed.), *The Memoirs of Lord
   Coutanche: A Jerseyman Looks Back*
Author's correspondence with Wilhelm
   Casper
Interview with Karl Steiner
Interview with Ernst Grunfeld

CHAPTER FOUR SURVIVAL

Interview with Kathleen Whitley
Interview with Edwin de Sainte Croix
Interview with Sandy Whitley

Interview with Daphne Pope
Interview with Ron Hurford
Interview with Bernard Hassell
Interview with Joe Miere
Unpublished diary of James Ryan
Interview with Eugene Le Lievre
IWM interview with William Brown
IWM interview with Frank Le Cocq
Interview with Daphne Prins
Ralph Durand, *Guernsey Under German
   Rule*
IWM interview with Dorothy Blackwell
HO/PRO
Interview with Stella Perkins
'Occupational Observations by One
   Occupied', Guernsey Ancient
   Monuments
Guernsey State Archives
Interview with Dolly Joanknecht
IWM interview with Maurice Green
Interview with Betty Thurban
Interview with Rollo Sherwill
Guernsey Evening Press
Interview with Mary McCarthy
IWM interview with Maurice Green
Unpublished diary of Fred Woodall,
   IWM
Guernsey Evening Press
'Occupational Observations by One
   Occupied', Guernsey Ancient
   Monuments
IWM interview with William Brown
German Administration files, IWM
The von Aufsess Occupation Diary, ed.
   Kathleen Nowlan
Interview with Daphne Pope
Interview with Rollo Sherwill
Interview with Herbert Nichols
Letters in the Mayne Collection,
   St Peter's Bunker Museum, Jersey
Interview with Joe Miere
Interview with Bernard Hassell
Interview with Mary McCarthy
Independent
Guernsey State Archives
Interview with Dolly Joanknecht
Jersey Archives
Jersey Evening Post

CHAPTER FIVE *LES ROCHERS MAUDITS*

IWM interview with Maurice Green
Interview with Mike Le Cornu
Interview with Vasilly Marempolsky
IWM interview with Gasulla Sole
Interview with Georgi Kondakov
Interview with Kirill Nevrov
Interview with Ivan Kalganov
Interview with Alexei Ikonnikov
Interview with Albert Pothugine
Interview with Ted Misiewicz
Interview with Norbert Beermart
Papers in the Centre Juive de Documentation Contemporaine, Paris
IWM interview with Gordon Prigent
Interview with Otto Spehr

CHAPTER SIX RESISTANCE WHAT RESISTANCE

Interview with Joe Miere
Private papers of Sir Ambrose Sherwill
Audrey Anquetil, Wartime Memories
Interview with Dolly Joanknecht
Interview with Betty Thurban
Guernsey Evening Press
Frank Falla, *The Silent War*
Leslie Sinel, *The German Occupation of Jersey*
Interview with Bob Le Sueur
Television interview with Arthur Kent
Interview with Kathleen Whitley
Guernsey State Archives
IWM interview with Maurice Green
Interview with Rollo Sherwill
Jersey Archives
Interview with Mike Le Cornu
Interview with Bernard Hassell
Quoted in Asa Briggs, *The History of Broadcasting in the United Kingdom: Volume III, The War of Words*
Unpublished memoirs of Peter Girard, IWM
IWM interview with Vera Cochrane
Jersey Archives

Xan Franks (ed.), *The War on Sark: The Secret Letters of Julia Tremayne*
IWM interview with Dorothy Blackwell
Interview with Daphne Pope
Interview with Norman Le Brocq
Interview with Stella Perkins

CHAPTER SEVEN HAD BRITAIN FORGOTTEN

The Times
Interview with M.R.D. Foot
HO/PRO
Sunday Chronicle
Television interview with Werner Grosskopf
Interview with Hans Glauber
IWM interview with Maurice Green

CHAPTER EIGHT LIBERATION

Charles Cruikshank, *The German Occupation of the Channel Islands*
Leslie Sinel, *The German Occupation of Jersey*
Interview with Stella Perkins
Interview with Betty Thurban
Interview with Herbert Nichols
Interview with Randolf Kugler
Interview with Willi Reiman
Interview with Kathleen Whitley
Television interview with Willi Hagedorne
Interview with Dolly Joanknecht
HO/PRO
Interview with Joe Miere
Interview with Johannes Kegelman
IWM interview with Dorothy Blackwell
Interview with Mary McCarthy
Jersey Evening Post
Television interview with Arthur Kent
Unpublished diary of James Ryan
Interview with Daphne Pope
Interview with Bernard Hassell
Interview with Rollo Sherwill
The Times
Daily Express
Daily Herald

Daily Worker
HO/PRO
Interview with Kirill Nevrov
Interview with Georgi Kondakov
Interview with Ivan Kalganov
Interview with Alexander Rodine
Interview with Alexei Ikonnikov
Interview with Albert Pothugine

CHAPTER NINE JUSTICE DONE
Interview with Otto Spehr
Papers in possession of Otto Spehr
Author's MI19 documents
WO/PRO
Interview with Bob Le Sueur
The Russian State Archives (formerly the
    Soviet Central Archives)
Quoted in T.X.H. Pantcheff, *Alderney,
    Fortress Island: The Germans in Alderney*
John Dalmau, *Slave Worker*
Yves Delbar, 'The Story of "Glaize"',
    Centre Juive de Documentation
    Contemporaine, Paris
The SS Document Centre, Berlin
Interview with Kirill Nevrov

Solomon Steckoll, *The Alderney Death
    Camp*
Channel Television Documentary,
    Swastika Over British Soil
HO Statement, April 1992
Correspondence with Alexander
    Kanatnikov
Interview with Norman Le Brocq
Hansard
Guernsey Evening Press
Guernsey State Archives
Jersey Evening Post
Private letters

CHAPTER TEN THE LEGACY
Paul Fussell, *Wartime*
Interview with Michael Ginns
Guernsey Evening Post
Interview with Rollo Sherwill
Guardian
Guernsey Evening Post
Daily Telegraph
Daily Express
Frank Falla, *The Silent War*
Interview with John de la Haye

Bibliography

MEMOIRS

Anquetil, Audrey, 'Wartime Memories', privately published, n.d.
Aubin, Harry, The Occupation Bicycle Park, La Haule Books Ltd, 1992
Bihet, Molly, A Child's War, Guernsey Press, 1985
Bonnard, Brian, The Island of Dread in the Channel, Alan Sutton, 1991
Dalmau, John, 'Slave Worker', privately published, 1946
Falla, Frank, The Silent War, New English Library, 1967
Faramus, Anthony, Journey Into Darkness, Grafton, 1990
Franks, Xan (ed.), The War on Sark: The Secret Letters of Julia Tremayne, Webb and Bower, 1981
Hathaway, Sybil, Dame of Sark: An Autobiography, Heinemann, 1961
Lewis, John, A Doctor's Occupation, New English Library, 1983
Nowlan, Kathleen (ed.), The von Aufsess Occupation Diary, Phillimore, 1985
Pocock, H.R.S. (ed.), The Memoirs of Lord Coutanche: A Jerseyman Looks Back, Phillimore, 1975
Sinel, Leslie, The German Occupation of Jersey: A Complete Diary of Events, June 1940–June 1945, Jersey Evening Post, 1945
Stroobant, Frank, One Man's War, Guernsey Press, 1967
Van Grieken, Gilbert, Destination 'Gustav', privately published, 1992

HISTORIES

Cortvriend, V.V., Isolated Island: A History and Personal Reminiscences of the German Occupation of Guernsey June 1940–May 1945, Guernsey Star and Gazette, 1946
Cruikshank, Charles, The German Occupation of the Channel Islands, Oxford University Press, 1975
Durand, Ralph, Guernsey Under German Rule, Guernsey, 1946
Harris, Roger, Islanders Deported, Part I, Channel Islands Specialists' Society, 1980
King, Peter, The Channel Islands War 1940–45, Robert Hale, 1991

Packe, M. St J. and Dreyfus, M., *The Alderney Story 1939–1949*, Alderney, 1971

Pantcheff, T.X.F., *Alderney, Fortress Island: The Germans in Alderney*, Phillimore, 1981

Steckoll, Solomon, *The Alderney Death Camp*, Granada, 1982

Toms, Carel, *Hitler's Fortress Islands*, New English Library, 1967

Woods, Alan and Mary, *Islands in Danger: The Story of the German Occupation of the Channel Islands 1940–45*, Evans Brothers, 1955

GENERAL

Bower, Tom, *Blind Eye to Murder*, Andre Deutsch, 1981

Briggs, Asa, *The History of Broadcasting in the United Kingdom: Volume III, The War of Words*, Oxford University Press, 1970

Calder, Angus, *The People's War*, Jonathan Cape, 1969

Calder, Angus, *The Myth of the Blitz*, Pimlico, 1991

Cesarani, David, *Justice Delayed*, Heinemann, 1992

Edwards, G.B., *The Book of Ebenezer Le Page*, Hamish Hamilton, 1981

Foot, M.R.D., *Resistance: European Resistance to Nazism, 1940–45*, Eyre Methuen, 1976

Fussell, Paul, *Wartime: Understanding and Behaviour in the Second World War*, Oxford University Press, 1989

Grasset, Bernard (trans. Michel, Henri), *The Shadow War: Resistance in Europe 1939–1945*, Andre Deutsch, 1972

Hawes, Stephen and White, Ralph (eds), *Resistance in Europe 1939–45*, Allen Lane, 1975

Hetherington, Thomas and Chalmers, William, *Report of the War Crimes Inquiry*, HMSO, 1989

Hirschfeld, Gerhard, *Nazi Rule and Dutch Collaboration*, Berg, 1988

Lottman, Herbert, *The People's Anger*, Hutchinson, 1986

Mazower, Mark, *Inside Hitler's Greece*, Yale University Press, 1993

Ponting, Clive, *The Myth and the Reality of 1940*, Hamish Hamilton, 1990

Rings, Werner, *Life with the Enemy: Collaboration and Resistance in Hitler's Europe*, Weidenfeld & Nicolson, 1982

Thompson, Paul, *The Voice of the Past*, Oxford University Press, 1978

Index

abortion, 68
Ackermann, Leo, 286
Adler, Adam, 182, 294
Ahlem-Stoecken, 302
air raids: German, 12–14, 20; British, 41, 172
Alderney: British investigation, 277–303; collaboration, 118; deaths, 266, 286, 288–93; escapees, 234; evacuation, 13, 18, 21, 22, 24, 27, 34, 265; foreign workers, 152–3, 158; government, 9, 74; landscape, 7; liberation, 249, 280; life after evacuation, 34, 36; looting, 34, 137–8; memorial, 323–4; raids considered, 224–5; railway construction, 152; slave labour camps, 5, 94–5, 158, 160–90, 233, 234, 266, 269, 278–303, 322, 323, *see also* Helgoland camp, Norderney camp, Sylt camp; survivors, 269–75; war crimes, 293–9, 322; work party, 93
Amelin, Ivan, 284
Ammon, Charles, MP, 31, 32–3, 227–8, 231, 241
Anderson, Sir John, 19, 20, 30
Anquetil, Audrey, 195
Argosy Library, 99
Attlee, Clement, 231, 306, 325
Aubin, Charles Duret, 39, 137, 308–10, 340, 344
Aubin, Harry, 11, 53
Audrain, Dennis, 202
Aufsess, Baron Max von: artistic tastes, 216; on local girls and soldiers, 57; post-war life, 313–14; relationships with Jerseywomen, 57, 67; relationships with local government figures, 80, 105, 136–7, 146; social relationships, 80
Auschwitz, 110, 111
Azulay sisters, 338

Bandelow, Major, 49
Bannach, Kapitän, 61

Barbarossa, Operation, 151
Baudains, Mme, 140, 261
Bazeley, Cecil, 61–5, 104, 196
Bazeley, Lucy, 65
BBC: Channel Islands ignored, 223, 226, 230, 235–7, 333; monitoring, 83; news, 20, 332; radio making instructions, 208; resistance appeals, 136, 326; 'V for Victory' campaign, 204–7; *see also* radios
Beagle, HMS, 248, 249
Bedane, Albert, 325n
Beermart, Norbert, 179–82, 291
Belgium: Alderney camp workers, 153, 179–82, 291; BBC broadcasts, 223; collaboration trials, 277; food supplies, 232; German attack, 15–16; German occupation, 326–7, 329; labour quotas, 330; resistance, 192, 326, 326, 333
Belsen, 146, 219, 295
Bercu, Hedwig, 108, 338, 340, 343
Bertelsen, Aage, 327
Bickmore, C. W., 239
Bihet, Molly, 323
billeting, 39, 41–2, 50, 79, 96, 195, 200
Bisson, Madelaine, 201
Bisson, Ronald, 201
black market: Guernsey, 133–4; Jersey, 132–3; post-war approach, 309; prices, 121, 130–1; profits, 238–9, 261–2, 266–7, 312–13; prosecutions, 131; sources of supply, 130; SS, 188–9; taxation of profits, 238–9, 267, 312–13
Blackwell, Dorothy, 34–5, 51, 60, 125, 133, 208–9, 259
Blampied, Marianne, 338, 340, 343
Blanchford, Reginald, 34
Blishen, Edward, 319
Bloch, J. M., 183, 184
Boag Howard, James, 238–9, 307
Borkum camp, Alderney, 158
Botatenko, Peter, 220
Brandt, Willi, 324

351